TASTE!

How to Choose the Best Deli Ingredients

Dedication

For BKK. For ever.

About the Author

Glynn Christian co-founded the iconic Mr Christian's Provisions on Portobello Rd, London, and is honoured with a Lifetime Achievement Award from the Guild of Fine Food.

Best known in Britain as pioneering TV chef for BBC TV including Breakfast Time and Pebble Mill, he broadcast weekly on LBC Radio with Bob Holness and Douglas Cameron and was a regular guest of Radio 2's Gloria Hunniford and on Woman's Hour. His UK journalistic career includes writing weekly for *The Sunday Telegraph*, during which he was nominated for Glenfiddich Food Writer of the Year, *Elle* (5 years) and for such magazines as *OK*, *Gardens Illustrated* and *House and Gardens*. New Zealand born Glynn is the author of over 25 books on food and cookery as well as works of reference about the 1789 mutiny on HMAV Bounty led by Fletcher Christian, who is Glynn's gt-gt-gt-gt grandfather.

A regular judge for The Great Taste Awards, which he named, and until recently an Official Guide at the Victoria and Albert Museum, Glynn now lives and works in Battersea, London.

Published in 2021 by
Grub Street
4 Rainham Close
London
SW11 6SS

Email: food@grubstreet.co.uk
Web: www.grubstreet.co.uk
Twitter: @grub_street
Instagram: @grubstreet_books

Photographs David Whyte

ISBN: 978-1-911667-23-0

Publisher's note: *TASTE! How to Choose the Best Deli Ingredients* is a revised and updated edition of Glynn Christian's 2005, award-winning, best-selling *REAL FLAVOURS—the Handbook of Gourmet and Deli Ingredients*, which was voted Best Food Guide in the World when it was first published.

Printed and bound by Finidr, Czech Republic

TASTE!

How to Choose the Best Deli Ingredients

Glynn Christian

Grub Street • London

Acknowledgements

More than 45 years in the food business means hundreds, if not thousands, of generous people have contributed to my treasury of food facts. Sometimes they did this unwittingly, when I watched or read. Others did so when I ate with them or they cooked with me.

In each of those years I learned more profoundly that food and cooking is neither science nor art, but is an art that flourishes only if science is present and used. That's a fancy way of saying you can't cook well if you don't understand your ingredients and how they work. Discovering those secrets is what has always driven me to ask that next question, and then to pass on the answer, what Dirk Bogarde taught me was 'the mission to tell'.

My greatest supporters have been those who gave me chances to learn and then to share. First was as the brochure writer for Clarksons Holidays, right at the start of the 1970s package-holiday explosion, when I was tasked with always finding and writing about local ingredients and specialities. That fascinating Europe-wide education gave me an unrivalled platform for Mr Christian's Provisions, where knowledgeable customers and suppliers then filled in the gaps.

The publisher who commissioned *Cheese and Cheesemaking* (MacDonald) led directly to broadcasting in the early days of LBC Radio and then to Pebble Mill at One and to BBC TV Breakfast Time, to TV series made around the world with Richard Patching and with Serendipity Pictures, to *Elle* magazine, *The Sunday Telegraph* and much more.

To all the editors, agents and producers who chose me then, later and now, I say in return: THANK YOU.

Also thank you to Panasonic for supplying a combination microwave, so I could check my recommendations for its use, especially for micro-roasting nuts, spices and for much else including Christmas Pudding, for this new book.

So much of what I learned and want to pass on would be lost without the permanent record of books. My greatest gratitude is to publishers, most particularly to Anne Dolamore of Grub Street for her decades of loyalty, belief and friendship.

Now, what's that delicious discovery you wanted to tell me about?

Contents

Foreword

Onwards and upwards to more delicious eating

Well, what a difference a decade makes. Never has there been a bigger or better choice of gourmet and deli ingredients. Best of all is that so many are made by small artisan producers, some carefully honouring heritage, some creating brilliant new experiences for us.

When I consulted for the Welsh Development Agency thirty years ago, I predicted the best future for the UK would be food with a face, food sold directly to the public by the people who produced it, perhaps only regionally, and that this was also the country's greatest potential for new, sustainable jobs. That's what happened with the evolution of Farmers' Markets and Farm Shops, wonderful springboards for small producers, who from 1994 were then supported by the Great Taste Awards, a powerful influence on artisan food makers that's still growing every year.

Today, some of the most exciting ingredients in the world are British-made charcuterie, recreating traditional hams, salami and saucissons by using tasty heritage breeds and hands-on skills to give unmatched new flavours. Earlier, cheeses were our first tastes of what was possible for keen small dairies, and the choice grows every week, whether you like blue, hard, soft or smelly. In this book you'll discover how to judge a cheese just by looking at it. I also dispel confusion about rice, noodle and pasta types, explain the proper way to enjoy caviar and smoked salmon, the difference between baking soda and baking powder, which sugar is right for what, and tell you the best way to fill bread rolls, brioches and croissants.

Ethnic communities are ever-more generously sharing their best secrets, from exotic spice mixes to different breads or vinegars, including those all-conquering Portuguese egg tarts (*Pastéis de Nata*)— but do you know how to recognise the real thing?

I think of the book as a touchstone of food facts, a necessity today because all that teases is not what it seems. Not everything published in a newspaper, magazine, cookbook or by a blogger is correct. These days, reading labels is ever more important, to detect if something is honest or has 'flavouring' added, usually done for the sake of profit.

These synthetic 'flavourings' are sometimes called 'nature identical' but, although the chemical composition might be matched to the dominant flavour component, they struggle to include the spectrum of micro-flavours in the myriad, complementary components of every ingredient. The use of flavourings is too common and is the antithesis of good food and great eating when there are so many wonderful, pure products available without artificial interference. Regulations do not yet require their use to be included in all product names so, once again, always read the label. Vegans and vegetarians should take special care.

I hope you'll use this guide as factual reference before you even think of going to the internet, where personal interest and profit is commonly put before the full truth. But with care, online shopping is also the source of fabulous ingredients delivered from producers with a face direct to your table, a farmers' market every day of the week, and at your fingertips.

You'll find strong and controversial opinions throughout, like my views on chillies and why spicy shouldn't mean hot. You don't have to agree. What you won't find is much reference to PDOs and AoCs or other once-reliable guarantees of standards. Here's an instance of why: all officially approved Stilton cheeses are made with pasteurised milk, which is not traditional. Stichelton, the ancient name for the village of Stilton, is farm-made with raw milk in the classic Stilton style and geographical region, yet 'regulations' say it cannot be called Stilton. If the idea of a PDO is to protect heritage, then this ruling is the opposite. In France, there is a movement to allow AoC Camembert de Normandie to be made throughout the country, which would nullify the point of the system. Best rely on your taste and on results from the Great Taste Awards, World Cheese Awards and other consumer-led comparisons, as well as reading labels.

So, onwards and upwards to more delicious eating, using fabulous ingredients as a foundation or as exciting accents. There's never been a tastier time.

Enjoy eating my words.

GLYNN CHRISTIAN
London, 2021
www.glynnchristian.mailchimpsites.com

Keeping up to date
Every year hundreds, perhaps thousands, of new products come on to the speciality food market. The best way I know to keep up to date, as well as to garner some idea of which succeed more than others, is regularly to update yourself by checking out these websites, which also list previous winners.
www.greattasteawards.co.uk
https://gff.co.uk/awards/world-cheese-awards/

Beans, Peas and Pulses

NEED TO KNOW

Beans, peas and pulses are known collectively as legumes.

Legumes are important suppliers of protein but don't have all those needed for health.

Soy beans are the only plant food with the protein value of meat, eggs and dairy produce; and you must eat twice the volume for equivalence.

Vegetarians and vegans should eat soy products or combine legumes with grains to equal meat, eggs and dairy.

Except for broad beans, all beans originated in the Americas.

Soaking dried legumes before cooking also starts germination and increases sweetness.

Don't cook legumes in the soaking water as this increases intestinal gas: soak, rinse, cook in fresh water.

Don't cook soaked legumes with salt or bacon as this toughens them: only add when tender and then cook on.

If legumes are introduced slowly in modest amounts daily, the body will adjust, lessening gas problems.

Soy and soy products are likely to cause most intestinal wind.

These most ancient of foods, cheap and nourishing, are looked upon with suspicion, particularly by the hard-up, those who would most benefit from them. A move to legumes and grains rather than red meat would make a mighty contribution to reversing climate change; beans and peas and lentils do not fart methane into the atmosphere.

The greatest argument against legumes is that they cause painful and distressing intestinal wind in humans. Sound knowledge sorts this out. First, concentrate on the thin-skinned varieties of pulses, which cook faster, as they cause fewer side effects. Then, although lentils cook well and fast without the added bother of soaking, you will reduce wind-causing content by soaking, rinsing and parboiling green lentils before cooking in yet more fresh water.

Introduce legumes to your diet slowly, as side dishes rather than main courses. It might take a month or so for the bowel to adjust but if it is treated with respect and not overloaded it is then less likely to wind you.

With that initial patience you are on your way to eating spectacularly well as a vegan or vegetarian, almost thoughtlessly obtaining the high fibre, low fat, low sugar ideals of modern nutritional theory. But remember, legumes do not give all the protein the human body needs, especially not to teenagers and pregnant women.

None of these ingredients has a fat content but it's difficult to find enjoyable recipes that do not add it in some form. You could cook these ingredients a different way every day, but I generally end up cooking them the same way—with tomato, lots of garlic, fresh herbs in a bundle and plenty of fat, bacon, olive oil, duck or goose fat. Butter is good but not as good as the less sweet fats and oils.

Whenever a bean recipe fails to excite you, and you have added enough salt and extra fat and more garlic, then add red wine vinegar teaspoon by teaspoon. Or sherry, or Chinese or balsamic vinegars, of course. The difference will be wondrous, and fast.

Cooked beans in cans are a godsend standby. Heated and drained and dressed with oil and garlic as a salad base, puréed, or drained and reheated with a herb-rich garlic-laden tomato sauce, they make a fast vegetable stew appear to have taken you days to make.

Although good keepers, all peas, beans and lentils will toughen with age and many reach a stage where even the most determined soaking and cooking will never soften them. It is better to buy them in smallish quantities from shops you expect sell enough to have a regular turnover of stock. Do check, if they are in bulk, for excess dirt or insect contamination, but expect some.

Don't bother with produce that is broken. Store in the cool and dark.

Types of legumes

ADUKI/ADZUKI: small, ochrous-red and pillow-shaped, these Oriental beans have long been regarded as the best of them all in Japan, China and Thailand. An important ingredient in Oriental sweet cookery and the basis for the red-bean paste found in dumplings and steamed buns. Commonly shaped and coloured into dull and leaden Chinese desserts and 'cakes' that all seem to taste the same.

BLACK-EYE BEANS/PEAS: essential to Creole cooking, they are a variety of cow pea, hence called black-eye peas in the United States but they are confusingly the seeds of the yard-long bean. A savoury flavour and interesting appearance make them more appealing than most *haricots*. They cook comparatively faster and many people find them lighter on the stomach.

BROAD BEANS: native to the Old World, dried broad beans keep their honoured place in many Mediterranean and Middle Eastern countries. Commonly known as *fava*, they are bigger, flatter and broad than the New World bean family and tend to flouriness and a bit of a chew if you leave on their tough skins; ready skinned ones are more expensive but very time saving.

They have many local names but the shape and the brown colour they develop are unmistakable.

Ancient Romans ate fresh baby broad bans with cheese but as the outer skins of each bean matures they toughen and become bitter. Frozen broad beans have been blanched; once defrosted, those carapaces slip off easily, revealing electric-green shapes that transform a plate or a salad; yes, garlic does help.

BUTTER BEANS/LIMA BEANS: I reckon butter beans and lima beans are the same thing. It doesn't matter if not, for they are interchangeably large, white, flat and aristocratic of flavour.

> *Baby lima beans:* are pale green and mix with sweet corn to make succotash, an ancient Native American dish.

> *Chestnut lima:* is rarely found, has a nutty flavour and mashes like potatoes.

CHICKPEAS/GARBANZOS: an Old-World staple thought to have originated in southern Turkey. Their spicy, peppery flavour, appealing golden colour and hazelnut shape, make these the most attractive and adaptable of all pulses.

They are a standby of Middle Eastern, Greek and Cypriot restaurants, inevitably as hummus, but also found in Spanish and Latin American cooking. They make excellent additions to soups, fascinate in salads and mix well with other vegetables, too. It's very satisfying always to have cans on hand.

FAVA: see *Broad beans.*

KIDNEY BEANS: this is the biggest group of beans and causes much confusion. Simply, all beans that are kidney shaped without being flat are kidney beans.

Don't be confused if you don't find a bean you know here, because throughout the Americas and the Old World there are local names as well as local varieties. When beans first crossed the Atlantic they were given Spanish or Greek or Italian or anything names, and then when they adapted to their new homes they changed both their characteristics and their names again. Only if you are in pursuit of insanity should you consider tracing each bean to its original name. They won't taste any better when or if you do.

Black: very popular in the Caribbean and in the southern United States, these shiny, very black beans are the most like better-known red kidney beans. They cook to purple rather than black and with a firm satisfying texture and meaty-flavour.

Borlotti: also *rose cocoa* beans. Streaked with rose or crimson, they are excellent when tinned and always cook to a sweetish soft texture.

Cannellini: small, white and inter-changeable with *haricots*. Perfect with stews of rugged sausages, garlic and tomato, and make elegant cold salads, too, especially with such firm fish as tuna or hot-smoked salmon.

Flageolets: prematurely podded infantile *haricots* so, green, sweet, tender and expensive. Classic with roasted lamb and perfection with fatty birds.

Great Northern: a small white hari-cot very popular in the US and that could be the navy bean in disguise.

Haricot: the creamy basis for baked beans and another also called navy beans. Very adaptable and sociable as long as there is fat present; think *haricots* stews and cassoulets. French *Haricots Tarbais* are superior, fresh or dried.

Pinto: a shorter, fatter borlotti, speckled and savoury. See next entry.

Rattlesnake: the pinto but so-called in the US South West and Mexico because the pods twist into snake shapes. Thought best for *refritos*, refried beans.

Red kidney: the correct beans for *chili* and *chili con carne* and their big, spicy flavour is good eaten cold in salads. Must be boiled at least 15 minutes if you started with dry beans or they are toxic: canned ones may be eaten immediately.

Sorana: Italy's *fagioli di Sorana* can be flat and white or red and round; both are elegantly flavoured with tender skins.

LENTILS: richer in protein than other pulses, except for soy, and with a high-calorie count, lentils are an important food staple. When eaten with grains, such as dhal with a flat bread, they give the full range of protein at minimal cost to many millions who cannot afford meat.

The point of lentils is rich, comforting smoothness, A pile of lentils served crisp and individual is as pointless as dry toast, no matter how aesthetic the idea seems. They should be simmered until each has a moist creaminess, with some mushed and emulsified. Don't salt or spike with cubed ham, bacon or sausages until tender or they toughen. They make far more sense with game birds than infuriating potato crisps. Soft and lightly puréed lentils make a sensationally good sauce for vegetarian lasagne and lentils are a surprising way to make fish more gratifying for big eaters; rice and lentils make up the Indian dish *kitcheree*, on which the British created kedgeree, without lentils.

There are two types but many names and variations.

Green, brown, continental: these are the lentils most used in European cookbooks, old or new. They have a stronger, earthier taste than red lentils and blend very well with smoked meats, fatty pork, herbs and onions. They do not have to be pre-soaked and take 35–40 minutes to cook, turning mushy after that, which has its appeal. Surprisingly good with fish, especially when spiked with a sea vegetable like black arame.

Lentilles de Puy: a greeney-blue variety from central France with a delicious smokey-sweet tang.

Lentilles vertes du Berry: are very dark green and cook in 30 minutes.

Lenticchia di Castelluccio di Norcia: notably small, with a very fine skin and rich colours in the yellow-brown spectrum. Grown around Perugia and Macerata, and reckoned tastier than Puy lentils.

Red, Indian, Egyptian: these look reddish and cook in 15–30 minutes to a yellow-gold mush with light spicy flavours. The everyday dhal of India, red lentils love such fragrant and pungent spices as cumin, coriander, cloves and every type of curry mix and masala—use asafoetida rather than garlic and onion if you don't have the time to cook onions long enough to sweeten them, which takes at least 45 minutes for 500 g/1 lb.

Vital in the West to winter soups, puréed red lentils can also be served as a sauce, especially for ham and bacon cuts.

MESQUITE BEANS: a naturally sweet flour is made from the high-protein beans in the pods of this desert tree, the one more usually used as aromatic wood for smoking. Creative cooks add it to soups, muffins, breads, tortillas, cakes and biscuits and it seems to help stabilise blood sugar in diabetics.

MUNG BEANS: entrancing dark, frosted-olive green mung beans can be cooked like any pulse and become as soft and sweet as the aduki. Mung beans are commonly used to make bean sprouts, which have no magical nutritional properties but offer about the same as a grain. Sprouts make a nice crunch and are widely used to give Chinese take-aways volume without content or expense.

PEAS, DRIED GREEN OR YELLOW: an excellent, honest and sustaining food hampered by an association with poverty and the past. Available whole or skinned and split, green or yellow; the green is harder to find but I prefer them. Peas rarely hold their shape, which is why they are put into soups or made into soups and their surprising sweetness is why they were always a natural accompaniment to salted meats.

Pease pudding should be brought back to our tables. Made from yellow split peas into a lightly textured purée, perhaps cooked with a ham hock or similar, it is intensely gratifying and when cold and set can then be fried in patties.

> *Pea milk:* milk made from yellow split peas is a vegan option said to be as good as real milk for steaming in cafes for espresso coffees.

SOY/SOYA: soy beans have a protein content equivalent to meat, dairy and eggs and thus are the richest and most sustaining vegetable food on earth. Yet they are terminally boring to the point of being inedible, except when small and green and disguised as *edamame.*

It has been estimated that an acre of soy beans would keep a man alive for 2,200 days, but the same acre of grass-produced beef would sustain him only 75 days. If the huge crops of soy grown to feed cattle were used to feed mankind, it would be a giant forward step in taking back control of Earth's climate.Once they are chopped and cooked and then pressed and drained, the result is soy milk and that opens a new world. But beware. The soy bean harbours the most gas-inducing ingredients of all. Introduce soy bean products like tofu very slowly into your diet, over several months, or your good intentions will be so much hot air.

Soy-based products that are distinctly bean-tasting can be the result of bad production technique, but this is more likely to be the use of inferior bean varieties, which leave a lingering, raw, green bean taste. At least that is how the problem was explained to me in Japan, where I tasted wonderfully creamy tofu, and in Sweden, where an ice cream-type product gives no clue to its soy bean origin. There is no easy solution to this but personal trial and error.

Curd: best known as Japanese tofu, but actually an invention of the Chinese, as most things seem to be. They call it *dau fu.*

Commercially the curd is obtained in many ways. Beans are boiled and then crushed to release a milky liquid that can be curdled with lemon juice or vinegar, giving a welcome slight acidity and flavour. For larger amounts calcium sulphate, gypsum, usefully increases the calcium content but can give a slightly chalky consistency—hardly surprising as it is related to plaster of Paris. Calcium chloride may also be used, often accompanied by emulsifiers that bind in the liquid whey that would normally separate out, thus giving a higher yield and softer, wetter curd; the addition of simple sugars (not sucrose) adds sweetness and a smoother mouth feel. The Japanese use an extract of sea water to obtain soy curd, and there are other ingredients that will do the curdling.

As with dairy cheese making, the exact texture and firmness of the curd will be affected both by the amount of curdling agent and by how much pressing and draining there is of the curd.

Softer curd, commonly called silken tofu, is used for steamed dishes or for adding at the last moment to wet dishes. Firmer curd is chosen for frying, often done to give extra strength to pieces of curd before they are added to a braising or boiling stock.

Although made from a liquid that has been boiled, bean curd must be treated as though it were a fresh milk product and kept submerged under water and refrigerated for safety, where it will be fresh and safe for a few days—up to a week if the water is changed daily. It should be virtually odourless and tasteless, but has the invaluable chameleon virtue of absorbing other flavours, making it a great extender of other foods.

Soy curd/tofu is commonly used as a complementary extender of meat, particularly in South East Asian and Oriental cookery. Apart from its invaluable protein content, bean curd is high in B vitamins and iron, but the latter is in a form difficult for the body to absorb. Vegans and vegetarians are recommended always to eat or drink something containing vitamin C with bean curd, as this helps unlock the iron.

It is important to introduce bean curd gradually into your diet and best to mix it with other food rather than eating in large quantities or on an empty stomach. When you are used to it, treat it as a bland white cheese, and serve it with bright condiments, or add it to highly flavoured foods, giving it time to absorb its surroundings. It may be fried, deep-fried, roasted, toasted, marinated, microwaved, crumbed, stir-fried, chopped, cubed, sliced, whisked into 'cheesecakes', whipped into creamy desserts, frozen into ices. Frozen tofu/bean curd products run the gamut from beany to amazing.

Bean curd skin: also called tofu skins, because this is how they begin and how they can feel in the mouth—like skin. They are made from soy milk rather the way clotted cream is manufactured; the milk is heated until a skin is formed, which is taken away and dried flat. They must be soaked to soften before being used as a wrapper for other foods, and are then deep-fried or fried and poached in a rich stock of some sort, which is when they soften up to the texture of skin.

Milk: can be made instantly at home from dried pre-cooked soy powder or other products of the beans. The end result will look like milk and should have rather less soy taste than the beans. But not always.

How anyone believes the difference in fat content—or anything else—between cows' milk and soy milk justifies ordering soy milk in espresso coffee is stratospheres away from my understanding. If you don't like cows' milk, drink black coffee, the way it is supposed to be.

Miso: a Japanese product that looks like thick, dark, grainy honey but is a paste of soy beans fermented with malted grains. The precise grain added determines the colour and flavour of the result, and some versions are traditionally more salted than most. The most important basic use is for miso soup, miso diluted with dashi or plain water, a highly nutritious and delicious soup with a malty, salty flavour that is basic to the Japanese diet. In my experience, it is much more digestible and causes far fewer problems than other soy bean products; indeed a bowl of miso soup seems to settle everything down.

The basic flavour of miso is warm and sweet with overtones of honeyed fermentation and when diluted there is nuttiness rather than beaniness. Once you discover miso there are thousands of ways to use it to flavour food before, during and after cooking, as well as to enjoy it for itself. Excellent for making marinades.

Chinese (brown/yellow) bean paste is related but not as comfortingly flavoured. Miso should be refrigerated when opened.

Aka: red, rice-based miso, generally highly salted and will last without refrigeration; any mould may be removed and ignored.

Hatcho: made only of soy beans and aged in wood for at least three years. It is rich, dark and complicated in flavour and although it may be mellowed with *shinsu-miso*, q.v., may be used by itself as a tonic drink or in a soup.

Mugi: made with barley to give a pleasant and gratifying flavour, but is said to be more popular in the West than in Japan these days, where it is expensive.

Shinsu: yellowish, young, all purpose and cheapest.

Shiro: made with rice, white and rather sweet.

Soy sauce: see *Sauces.*

TVP: textured vegetable protein is the protein content of soy beans spun into strands, which are like meat fibres and may be shaped this or that way to imitate meats. Like bean curd, TVP is characterless but absorbs any flavours with which it is cooked and thus extends meat dishes, especially chopped or minced ones, to reduce costs or increase profits. That seems reasonable if labelling rules are strictly observed.

Soy protein mixed with meat in sausages is an important advance in nutrition for low income families with children. Vital, accessible protein gets into their bodies without excesses of fat or low-quality meat usually associated with cheap sausages. If soy protein were used as an extender in high-quality sausages, we would all win, eating less animal fat, and supporting an agricultural industry that makes far better use of land than meat production.

What makes me uncomfortable is

the use of TVP as a meat substitute for vegans and vegetarians. Surely it follows that if you are looking for better nutrition, more natural nutrition, you won't want to eat soy masquerading as meat, because it's only able to do that because of perfectly unnatural additives.

Tempeh: another form of fermented soy bean, originally from Java in Indonesia. A special yeast ferments lightly crushed beans and creates a binding white mould. Can also be made with cubed bean curd; giving a creamier texture like ripening cheese. It has a nutty flavour and absorbs other flavours readily. It can be sliced, cubed or crumbled, so is becoming increasingly popular in the West as a meat-like substitute. It should be avoided if ammoniacal.

TEPARY: in the legends of the Tohono O'odham peoples of the US South, the Milky Way is made of white tepary beans scattered across the sky by their coyote deity Ban. These small beans, native to the Arizona desert and thereabouts, are one of the most drought and heat resistant crops in the world and varieties are being introduced into Africa to help ease food shortage problems there.

As well as their capability to flourish in blistering desert conditions, the tepary is particularly high in protein, more so size for size than most larger beans, and was prized as a practical food to carry—less is indeed more. The two most valued varieties marketed throughout the US are the rich, earthy, brown bean and the sweeter, lighter white. Both are prepared like other beans and can be used as the basis for stews and casseroles, for bean salads, for soup or in soups, puréed as dips, in fact, can be used wherever other beans would appear.

There are many other colours and flavours of tepary bean, and my bet is this most ancient food is poised to become one of the saviours of the 21st century.

Bread
and
Baking

NEED TO KNOW

Bread need only be made from wheat flour, water and salt.

Bread made without a raising agent—unleavened bread—is one of our oldest foods.

To leaven means to aerate dough or batter with yeast or a chemical like baking soda.

Gluten in wheat flour stretches to form the bubbles in yeast-raised bread.

Alcohol is also produced, giving the typical yeasty/brewery aroma.

Strong or hard wheat flour means it has a high gluten content.

Best bread flavour comes from slow rising with minimal yeast.

High yeast levels make drier bread that stales faster.

25 g/1 oz fresh yeast is maximum for 1.5 kg/3 lbs white flour: half is better but enriched doughs and pizza doughs can double that.

Do not add salt or sugar directly to fresh yeast as these inhibit it.

A little sugar is used to encourage dried yeast.

Kneading strengthens gluten in white flour and makes a lighter loaf.

Kneading inhibits the rise in 100% wholemeal flour loaves and should be minimal.

There is no need for the sponge technique when using modern yeasts.

Most grains contain no gluten and must be mixed with wheat flour to make a yeasted bread.

Soda breads can be made with soft, low-gluten or gluten-free flours.

Soda breads use baking soda (bicarbonate of soda, sodium bicarbonate) and an acidic liquid, which works from the moment they are mixed.

Baking powder works with sweet/non-acidic liquids and does not work until in the heat of an oven.

Sourdough breads are leavened by yeasts added to dough by a 'starter' from a previous batch.

A sourdough starter using ambient natural yeasts can be made anywhere.

White bread is not 'bad for you' in a varied diet; the flour used is fortified with thiamine, riboflavin, niacin and iron to make it as nutritious as whole grain bread.

Never cut a bread roll, English muffin, or scones, especially when warm, but pull apart, which protects the texture.

If not pulled apart, croissants should be cut only with a serrated knife, using no pressure.

For thousands of years bread has been the staple of life. Because it is grain based, daily bread eaten with such pulses as lentils or beans provides the same protein resource as meat, milk, cheese or eggs. In the West we think of bread as something leavened by yeast or by soda but unleavened breads are both older and still the daily bread of millions.

Discredited theories like the Atkins diet have tarred bread with the feathers of dietary cowardice, so millions brag about eating no bread. When asked if he also went to bed with men, James Dean is supposed to have said he didn't see why he should go through life with one arm tied behind his back. So it is with diet. Variety is the greatest, safest, healthiest most natural diet: living without bread, even modern sliced white bread, is hardly life at all.

Yeast and other leavenings

In ancient Egypt naturally occurring yeasts for beer making were grown in a sweet liquid mixed with starch and the discovery of its leavening action on bread doughs is thought to have been accident rather than design. In Belgium *kreuze* and *kreik* beers are still made spontaneously, with whatever yeasts are in the air yet, as you might expect, EU regulations are changing that.

Once, a brewer's wife used beer-making yeasts to make a bubbly liquid called barm, which she sold to bakers and housewives to leaven their bread but there was no way of knowing what combination of yeasts had been cultivated or how they would perform, so you had initially to 'prove' a small portion of the dough in what was called the sponge, before you used it in the full batch. This sponge technique is still used but is an unnecessary step in modern kitchens. It's better, best in fact, to give bread doughs at least two slow risings, as this is when complicated interactions between yeast and flour give rise to greater flavour. Adding salt or sugar to yeast rather than to the flour is a common reason for amateur bread makers to produce heavy loaves—most of the yeast was slaughtered before it had drawn breath.

Then, in 1850, came German or compressed yeast, made of one yeast only—*saccharomy cescerevisiae*. At last bakers had their own yeast. It worked quickly and consistently on the maltose (sugar) in flour and permanently changed the face of yeast cookery, commercial and domestic.

The new yeast went on the market under three different names: German, compressed or dried. This has confused many people who have tried baking from old recipes: the chances are that 'dried' yeast in a 19th century book means 'compressed' fresh yeast. Best ignore instructions and substitute with an absolute maximum 25 g/1 oz fresh yeast to 1.5 kg/3 lbs white flour but using less and rising slower gives better flavour. A really old recipe calling for barm will also need extra liquid.

BAKING POWDER: a mixture of baking soda and cream of tartar, that is of sodium bicarbonate/bicarbonate of soda and tartaric acid. It works only in contact with heat and so you can be dilatory about getting a cake into bake. There is no point to using both baking powder and baking soda unless you want to darken the mixture, as in Christmas pudding or a colonial banana cake.

BAKING SODA: an ancient alternative to yeast is to combine baking soda (sodium bicarbonate/ bicarbonate of soda) and an acidic liquid, like soured milk or genuine buttermilk and these days yoghurt, sour cream and crème fraîche can also be used. The action starts immediately and so you must get your soda bread or cake into the oven very quickly. A soda bread or soda scones are still one of the fastest and most delicious of treats but too much soda adds an unpleasant flavour. Traditionally made with wholemeal flour but white works excellently.

Cake recipes in Australasia and the USA often include baking powder and baking soda but there is absolutely nothing of sense behind that, except some say the soda might reduce the acidity in any fruit contained in the mixture. Sometimes soda is used when there is nothing acidic present, say in a biscuit mixture but it might add an unwarranted flavour.

DRIED YEAST: these granules are twice as strong, weight for weight, as fresh yeast. Always use less dried yeast even if it looks ludicrously little. American recipes usually indicate a number of packets of yeast; their packets hold 7 g/¼ oz dried yeast, which is the same as 15 g/½ oz fresh yeast. These must be activated according to the pack instructions before mixing into flour. The only type of yeast to which sugar might be added.

EASY-MIX YEAST: this does not have to be proved or treated separately, but is mixed dry into the flour, using the same amount as ordinary dried yeast.

FRESH/MODERN COMPRESSED YEAST: needs only to come into contact with warm liquid to start reproducing and creating gas and alcohol, which it does much more slowly than baking soda, hence why you are able to prove a dough. It performs consistently if it is in good condition and can be kept in the refrigerator for weeks or deep-frozen for up to three months. It is dissolved in warm water and allowed to start working before being added to the flour. Salt and sugar should be added only to the flour, as these inhibit fresh yeast.

A clean smell, light colour and a tendency to crumble rather than collapse are both clear indicators fresh yeast is in good condition.

SOURDOUGH: sourdough bread was once the saviour of the poor, the traveller or any isolated from the mainstream, like gold prospectors. During 21st century pandemic isolations it was again resorted to, not as a stand-by but as a stimulator of vicious online competitiveness. It would be hard to count the number online who believe their method/proportions are best.

To make it naturally, ambient yeasts settle into a flour and water mixture, meaning one made in Battersea will taste quite different in Boston, whether Lincolnshire or Massachusetts. Sourdough starters of different characters and ages are available online for home bakers.

Types of bread and rolls

The first of two absolutely idiosyncratic lists of what I like and that I think you are most likely to find.

BAGELS: a yeasted, white dough bread roll with a hole that originated in Jewish communities in Poland but has been popularised in the US, New York particularly. Bagels are poached in water before baking, which gives the requisite tough, chewy crust. One of the few rolls that may be halved with a knive, ideally serrated. Better eaten warm or split and toasted (on the cut surfaces only some say), and is at its most famous when filled with cream cheese and smoked salmon—lox and bagel. Sometimes sprinkled with caraway seeds, salt, poppy seeds or sesame seeds and chopped raw onion can be spread on top, which bakes to a caramelised brown—not a social breakfast choice.

You find sweet and spiced bagel mixtures, although few are flavoured with much courage and can be mistaken one for the other. Beware the blueberry, for its taste rarely survives the heat of the kitchen but cranberry, cinnamon and raisin, apricot or peanut butter and jelly bagels triumph, as does the non-kosher bacon and pineapple bagel.

BATCH LOAF OR LOAVES: bread baked without tins but so they touch and must be pulled apart, so they will have no side crust.

BATH BUNS: a white bread bun, the dough of which should contain egg and milk and include lemon, chopped peel or sultanas but never currants and must have crushed lump sugar on top.

BLOOMERS: oblong, fat and rounded loaves of white bread, which are slashed diagonally and never baked in tins. Often made with a little milk powder, and then the richer taste stands up extra well to being used in a Summer Pudding or a bread-and-butter pudding, but plastic bread is made into this shape and collapses when you slice.

BOULES: generally, a Frenchification for an ordinary round loaf; see *Cob*. When French, they shout of sweet, floury goodness, offer decent resilience inside and a real crust. Then they make exceedingly good toast or any of the puddings that combine berries and bread. Sometimes they are quite big, called a Campagne or Country loaf and made with a sourdough, well worth seeking and buying.

BRIOCHES: a light, yeasted dough with a high proportion of egg and butter to give a cake-like texture. Sweetness is variable and individual brioches are baked in tapering, fluted moulds, large or small but can baked in a loaf tin, plaited or plain. Most often eaten warm for breakfast but are delicious at tea time or with coffee anytime. A big, cake-sized brioche cut into elegant wedges and toasted lightly is nice for tea; these can also be served with light supper dishes such as chicken or fish with a cream sauce if the brioche is not too sweet.

A loaf-shaped brioche can replace bread in everything from Summer Pudding to Kentish cherry pie or bread-and-butter pudding, perhaps made with apricot compote and orange-flower water rather than raisins.

BROWN: this could and can mean white bread that has been coloured with caramel. Today it more often means bread made with 85% extraction flour, what we used to call wheat meal until that was forbidden. The lesson is not to say brown when you mean wholemeal.

CAMPAGNE, PAIN DE: this is a commonly used catchphrase that means bread with good flavour and texture and a crackling crust; the name is often used in connection with *boules* q.v. but is equally used for cushion or flattened ovals. Generally worth leaving around for a day or two with a view to making

specially good toast or to absorb puddles of decent olive oil on a bruschetta or beneath a really thick and creamy rarebit mix, especially if that conceals a thick slice of real ham.

CANNOLI: familiar to fans of Sicily's Montalbano on TV, these are deep-fried tubes of Marsala-flavoured dough, filled with ricotta and mascarpone and finely chopped candied orange. You must have a cannoli mold to make them.

CHAPATI: the basic unleavened bread of India, Pakistan and Bangladesh. The chapati and its relatives are still regularly hand-shaped and cooked on pans or flat griddles over open fires or in swanky modern kitchens. It should be made with wholemeal flour (Atta) and makes a nice wrap as well as its more traditional role as a scooper and plate-wiper; Roti and Lavash are part of the family of *Flatbreads*.

CHELSEA BUNS: authentic Chelsea buns are lightly sweetened, light, white, yeasted dough in a spiral at least 2.5 cm/1" thick and slightly domed, rather square shaped and with exposed sides where they have been pulled apart from one another after baking. There should be a distinct filling of vine fruits, sugar, lemon zest and mixed spice between the spirals, of which five is the ideal number; they should be glazed with boiled milk and sugar syrup, and then sprinkled with castor sugar. Although made to eat just as they are, very fresh Chelsea buns move to higher estate when pulled apart and thickly buttered. Modern 'twists' with multi layers of very thin dough are tougher to eat and fall apart in a very unsatisfying way.

CHOLLAH: a large loaf of yeasted white flour enriched with milk and a little egg, often slightly sweetened too. The usual shape is a plait, sprinkled with poppy seed. Particularly associated with Jewish food and festivals but not much different from English milk loaves. From better bakers they look and taste like brioche and can be used the same ways.

CIABATTA: the ciabatta was invented by the British baking industry in the 90s as a competitor for the baguette. Ciabatta should be a flattish, long rectangle of white dough with rounded corners, a bit of a waist and is made with an element of olive oil; the shape is said to be reminiscent of the sole of a sloppy sort of casual slipper, but seems equally to be that of a steam-rollered bone. Ciabatta dough is made with water rather than anything milky, which encourages the floury flavour, and when properly made should prove for quite a long time, so there are many large air-pockets, each eager to suck in olive oil or butter. Many imposters have the right shape but wrong texture, like ordinary but bad bread. Can be flavoured with sun-dried tomatoes, herbs, olives or olive pastes, arcane cheeses and the like. Ciabatta is particularly good when a few days old, split and toasted under a grill or over a barbecue. Its holey texture will gulp oceans of melting butter or of olive oil and also help keep toppings from slipping out or off. One of the split sides makes the best open sandwich; an actual sandwich of hot-toasted ciabatta smeared with aioli, with lots of oil-rich salad, sunny tomatoes and a pink, juicy steak is the greatest pleasure imaginable, particularly in the open air and for a sailor home from the sea—even if he's just been paddling in the shallow end.

CINNAMON BUNS: these give over-eating a good name. Particularly American, and specially associated with the coffee carts of Seattle, they are Chelsea Buns that have gone way over the top, survived and gone for it again. Huge, snowy turbans with the moist cinnamon and sugar filling that only Americans ever seem to get right, and even better if there is caramel present. You think you couldn't possibly manage a whole one. You manage.

COB/COBURG LOAF: the name for any round loaf of leavened white, brown or wholemeal bread. They are sometimes slashed or pricked or topped with whole grains but are never baked in a tin. Possibly called a *boule* these days q.v.

CORN BREADS: corn/maize contains no gluten, so cannot make leavened breads. Cornmeal ground from a less-sweet relation of sweet corn, is sometimes used to flavour yeast-leavened breads, much the way gluten-less rye is also fated to do. More commonly cornmeal is made into chemically-raised breads, like soft unsweetened cakes. These are the spoon breads of the USA, because they are served in the baking dish and spooned out as you eat. Pone, Johnny Cakes and a dozen other funny names all mean the same thing. The happy golden colour and inherent sweetness make corn bread particularly good with the robust flavours of barbecued meat and vegetables.

COTTAGE LOAF: bread loaf of any type made of two rounds of unequal size—the smaller sitting on top of the bigger. Not often made commercially now.

CRISP BREAD: unleavened, thin bread particularly associated with Scandinavia. Made domestically only with rye flour but commercial manufacturing often dictates the addition of wheat and other ingredients.

CROISSANTS: several cities claim the invention of these crescents of cholesterol—I plump for the Viennese baker who is said first to have fashioned them on the morning the crescent-emblazoned flags of the invading Turkish army were finally repelled from his city gates.

One of the heights of yeast baking, croissants are made by rolling out rich, yeasted dough with a great deal of butter—so, it's a sweetened, yeasted puff pastry. Mass-produced croissants often have a metallic taste induced by the use of fats other than butter and are not worth the money but you only know this once you have bought and eaten them.   .

Croissants are basic throughout Europe, varying mainly in their sweetness—Polish and Austrian are the sweetest. There is a version stuffed with an almond paste that seems too much of a bad/good thing. Little is quite as restorative as a rich croissant dipped into milky coffee. If you are not a dipper, never cut and squash a croissant but pull it apart, which protects the texture.

If not too sweet, croissants make an enticing change for buffets or in a picnic basket, especially mini croissants. Slice at an angle from the top, using a serrated knife and little pressure. Smear in aioli, mayonnaise or a little sweet chilli sauce and then cold scrambled eggs, smoked salmon with chopped quail or hen eggs, salami with salt cucumber, purées like hummus or excellent ham.

Bake a substantial breakfast croissant by rolling the dough with sliced ham, pancetta, prosciutto or smoked salmon, or with thin sliced hard cheese, and make them bigger than usual; these are good hot or cold with herby or garlic butter or with flavoured cream cheese.

CROWN LOAF: a speciality loaf made by baking a circle of rolls of white dough in a tin—they should only just touch. To make it more crown-like, some bakers use two circles, the top one smaller and joined to the bottom in the same way cottage loaves would be. Great for home bread bakers and feasts, because the rolls are fun to pull apart, for children of all ages.

CRUMPETS: yeast is the raising agent in these round treats, the ones with holes in the top and a nice brown bottom. If you were to cook them at home you'd have turned them over to brown the upper surface and served them quickly afterwards. To serve bought ones with crispness on top and bottom and hot interiors, they should be toasted at least twice, adjusting the time so they do not burn. If using a grill, start off at low heat and only when really warmed through should they get the full treatment. Once the outsides are browned and crisped and the inside piping hot, they will absorb as much butter as you dare. Plus jam. Increasingly used as a savoury base, even for mini-pizzas, when they should be first toasted.

DANISH LOAF: a long, oval, crusty loaf of white bread with a central slash, lightly floured. Not baked in a tin. A reliable bread for all those things where you need bread with muscle, a bread to make croutons, to fry in bacon fat, to slice into puddings or to toast. Some will be mushy and light, so you'll never buy that one again.

DANISH PASTRIES: a rich, yeasted dough similar to that of croissants but the butter is usually incorporated only in one layer and the dough turned and rolled without adding more of it. The pastry is then cut into decorative shapes, filled, iced or flavoured in dozens of ways and the finished products served hot or cold at almost any time of the day. The fascinating but fugitive flavour of the better ones is ground cardamom. Particularly associated with Scandinavia but probably invented in Vienna—the Danes call Danish pastries Wienerbrod. Here and there I find mini-Danish, each just a few mouthsful. They are too girly and bitty for breakfast or brunch, but a wonderfully original thing at tea time or as a dessert with fresh fruit.

DOUGHNUTS: circles or balls of dough fried in fat or oil, sometimes filled with jam or fruit and then smothered in sugar or a thin icing. It is mainly Arabs and Americans who make doughnuts with holes in the middle. Round ones have many names and styles but not as many as modern doughnut chains that find ways to include matcha tea, rose petal jam and every other thing in the cupboard. I'm waiting for savoury ones, cushions of hot bread stuffed with chicken tikka, Bolognese sauce, moussaka or chili con/sin carne.

Loukoumades: are small Greek doughnuts soaked in warm honey.
Ponshki: are Polish or Russian jam-filled doughnut balls.
Olliebollen: are stuffed with grated apple and fruit and spices by the Dutch for New Year's Eve.

FARMHOUSE LOAF: a white bread loaf baked in a tin both wider and shallower than the usual tin loaf. The word farmhouse is imprinted on the side of the loaf, which is sometimes slashed lengthwise and floured; sometimes the *maquillage* of flour is all that distinguishes this from fast-food bread, but more often it indicates a bread at least as good as a Danish or split-tin or Vienna.

FLATBREADS: a catch-all name for the many styles of Indian and Middle Eastern breads now so easily available, some leavened, some unleavened. Some leavened flatbreads, like *pitta* q.v. can be split to make pockets, much appreciated by those who must eat on the go; others like *naan* q.v. are torn and used to hoist food from plate to mouth. Everywhere in the world they are used more as plates, forks and spoons rather than for open or closed sandwiches.

Flatbreads can be just that, a flat round or square of dough, more often than not cooked on a hot flat surface. Some are no bigger than a hand; others could hide a small table top. They are universally delicious, but only when hot and ideally a little charred. When sold as wraps and rolled around sandwich ingredients and then cut at a cheeky angle into segments and kept in a fridge or in a cool pack for lunch, these breads become ordinary and often tough. It's best to choose very wet and highly flavoured fillings, the first to keep the bread chewable, and the second to override the flavour ennui into which wraps can plunge.

Anything flat, leavened or unleavened, lends itself admirably to being lightly flavoured with a sprinkle of something. Oregano and olive oil will give a Greek flavour, so that's also perfect for anything to do with a pizza or pizza-like ingredients. Flavoured salts work well, if used sparingly and so do many seeds. Sumac, the ground smokey-red and acidic berry is very good indeed. Perhaps the best is *za'atar*, a flavouring particularly associated with Jerusalem: it's simply sesame seeds, dried thyme and sumac. *Dukkah*, the mix of toasted and spiced nuts and seeds, is meant to be used with oil as a dip for bread, but is terrific when used as a crust-sprinkle for bread you bake

yourself.

FOCACCIA: a thick, light, flat Italian bread, often slightly sweet, dimpled on the top and drizzled with olive oil. Sometimes it has herbs, tomatoes and the like in the dough or on it. It is thus a thick, semi-naked pizza and can be eaten just as it is, but is better when split and lightly toasted or grilled and then dressed liberally with olive oil and anything that goes with this. The perfectly behaved starting point for fast pizzas or toasted, open-face sandwiches, particularly when there are luscious juices to be soaked up, as with steaks.

FRENCH BREAD: the name too easily given to yeasted bread baked in long rolls, even though French flour or techniques may not have been incorporated. True French sticks, made of a soft flour and with a good holey texture, stale very quickly. Next time you put your hand out to buy a French stick and find it has a sell-by day sometime in the future, pull that hand back, remembering the French buy bread three or more times a day; in France the sell-by date is always today.

The special flavour of true French breads comes from the use of low-gluten soft flour and by proving very much longer than UK or American breads, often overnight. This is shown by large holes in each loaf, which British bakers think is a sign of badly made bread. If baguettes or longuets don't have those holes, they are ordinary bread with an attack of pretension. French breads are also baked in ovens that shoot steam from time to time. The real thing was never made at home. Most are casually called French sticks, but there are correct names:

Baguettes: are the crisp, golden, medium-sized sticks that bulge in the middle because they are baked without confines.

Baton: is the name for short baguettes or longuets.

Boules: are round ones.

Ficelles: are the very long or very thin ones.

Longuets: are sticks baked in roll pans, giving straight, even sides.

Pain de campagne or pain de ménage: are large, hand-shaped, cylindrical or round loaves and sometimes contain rye flour.

GRANARY LOAF: a commercial brown loaf with a measure of malted wheat grains for flavour and texture. Very popular as a make-your-own bread mix.

GRISSINI: thin, well-baked breadsticks beloved of Italian restaurants. There is no secret to making them yourself other than rolling dough evenly and thinly, as they do extremely well on the *Bounty*-descendant islands of Pitcairn and Norfolk.

ITALIAN: usually the sign of dense, floury white loaves with a robust texture and thick crusts that need a strong jaw, that slice wonderfully and hold their shape. They don't usually contain oil, thus dry rather than stale and in a day or two make terrific toast. Crazily, these Italian breads are quite the best for classic British bread puddings, like Summer Pudding, bread-and-butter pudding and so on. It's not surprising Italians invented *bruschetta* and *crostini* and the like—toasted or grilled slices, scraped with garlic or tomato and topped with Mediterranean goodies. Italian loaves marked 'integrale' will contain wholemeal flour but not often: in Italy wholemeal flour, like wholemeal pasta, is reserved for the sick.

KAISER ROLLS: round floury rolls with a chewy rather than crisp crust, the one with a pattern of lumps on top.

LARDY CAKE: bread dough rolled and folded like puff pastry, except that instead of butter, pure lard, brown sugar and sultanas or mixed fruit are incorporated. The final shape should be scored with a sharp knife and the baked lardy cake broken on these marks rather than sliced. It is better warm than cold but either way is wonderful, because so very wicked. If you can get good lard, lardy bread is a wonderful project for two to make and devour on a dark and stormy day. It's not lardy bread if made with butter.

MACARONS: a small round meringue made chewy with ground almonds. Made in a spectacular number of flavours, increased by the type of creamy filling used to sandwich two together, the normal way of serving. Astonishingly expensive in dedicated stores but really affordable and good in many supermarkets. They freeze well, so buy when you see them at a good price even if you don't need them right then.

MADELEINES: elegant, shell-like almond-based sponges that must be served warm. Honey was once the sweetness and arguments continue about whether lemon should be included; I prefer orange and use orange-flower water. When freshly baked with a touch of crispness at the edges they are incomparable, especially when dunked into a superior sweet wine, especially a chilled Beaumes de Rivesaltes or similar.

MELBA TOAST: very thin white bread toast made by splitting a toasted slice and then browning the exposed sides under a grill. But a neighbour makes Melbas in the toaster by splitting the toasted slice, putting the toasted sides together and putting that back into the toaster. Genius. Best when a milk bread is used. Commercial Melba toast is often too crisp and falls to pieces when you bite.

MILK LOAF: a generic term for white bread mixed with milk or milk and water, which gives a sweeter flavour, softer texture and longer life. Often made in small sizes and glazed. Milk powder can be added to a basic loaf to get the same added sweetness and more cake-like texture. The heightened richness makes special sandwiches, particularly with smoked salmon and with blue cheeses.

MUFFIN, ENGLISH: the type muffin men used to hawk through British city streets. Chewy, yeasted and flat, and when split (cutting ruins the texture) they look rather like rag-topped crumpets. Properly, muffins were always toasted whole and then split and buttered on the hot untoasted sides before being put back together again. That

might have been good in the good old days but when I did it recently the muffin's interior collapsed into a disgusting paste that got worse when chewed. Much more popular in the USA than in England and the proper base for Eggs Benedict.

NAAN: neither pronounced nor spelled like one of your grannies but as narn. A light, yeasted, Indian flatbread traditionally cooked on the searingly-hot inside surface of a tandoori oven and thus should be rather tear-shaped, a result of gravity on the soft, spongey dough, and the force with which they must be thrown to stick them to the oven's surface. Available fresh and frozen, and an invaluable way to jazz up any meal, for even from frozen they are crisp outside, chewy and sweet inside, after just a few minutes under the grill; but you must follow the instructions first to sprinkle or quickly rinse them with water.

I use naan breads as a type of pizza base. Hot with fromage frais or soured cream and topped with smoked salmon drizzled with truffle oil and scattered with rocket. Or, more substantially, hot naan topped with yoghurt, chicken tikka, thick blobs of mango chutney and flat-leaf parsley.

PAIN D'ÉPICES: see *Gingerbread*.

PAIN AU RAISINS: a sort of French Danish, a low, pale, swirl of yeasted dough, like an ill Chelsea bun, held together with a little pastry cream or custard, with a few raisins or sultanas, and a glazed top. French bakers tend to put rather too many raisins for my taste, for they fall out as you break and eat; supermarkets skimp on the custard or leave it out. Otherwise, variations are enormous, from a little sweet spicing in the filling, to slatherings of yummy caramel with pecan nuts. And then there are *cinnamon buns* q.v.

PANNETONE: an ultra-high-rise yeasted cake from Italy, traditionally found at Christmas time. The basic one might contain plumped sultanas or raisins; others have candied orange or chocolate pellets or swirls of sweetened sauces. It's a sort of brioche, of course, and when very fresh is so addictive you quickly forget how much it might have cost you, for Italian-made ones do cost a bit. Traditional bakers reckon they hang theirs upside down after baking to ensure the cake does not sink into itself. Lesser versions are just that, but all pannetone are great to dip into sweet dessert wine, port or an Italian *vin santo*.

Fabulous when cut into robust cubes, split, spread *thickly* with apricot jam and then used as the base of a trifle. Or use it to make a superior bread-and-butter pudding with everything self-indulgent—rum-soaked raisins or cherries, candied apricots, elvas plums, chunks of high-cocoa chocolate, toasted walnuts or almonds, all in a wine or liqueur-flavoured custard. Goodness, it's enough to make one buy another. And another. Lightly toasted pannetone is a worthwhile end in itself, and particularly good with fruit or luscious dried-fruit salad: see *Koshraf*.

PANINI: quite ordinary, oval shapes of soft, slightly sweet bread, often flavoured with olives or tomato and the like. Sliced in two and stuffed with good Mediterranean things to eat, salads and mozzarella and roasted vegetables at the very least, they look terrific in a deli's refrigerated display. It then takes 10 or more minutes to get one toasted but squashed flat between two heavy hotplates. Then out it comes, a third or less the size you paid for, and now filled with boiling hot lettuce. Hot squashed lettuce isn't on my must-eat list. Someone must have said they were fashionable.

The idea is based on the toasted Italian sandwiches that are a particular speciality of New York—but there the long crisp rolls are pressed only with the meat, and the salad and mayonnaise are added afterwards. In Italy panini are served only with a slice or two of cheese and ham and the squashing doesn't matter. It rarely pays to do something to a food that is not done in its country of origin.

PETITS PAINS AU CHOCOLAT: the ultimate sin in breakfast fare—or at any other time. Like a sweet sausage roll, they can be made of brioche, white bread dough or croissant dough in which are embedded thick threads of rich dark chocolate. Such is the sweetness and richness of these delights, those made with milk-bread dough are more enjoyable than those made with richer doughs.

PITTA: a flat oval of white or wholemeal bread popularised by the growth of interest in Greek, Turkish and Arabic food. Usually served heated and torn into small squares and used as a scoop. Otherwise, it is opened at the side or cut in half and the space inside encouraged to become a pocket, which is then filled with salad and sliced hot meats or kebabs but it can hold bacon and eggs, curry and yoghurt, grilled vegetables with Parmesan shards, grilled haloumi cheese and spinach, a beef stew, chicken in mayonnaise—or fattened with melting butter and Seville-orange marmalade for an inverted breakfast on the go.

PIZZA: originally a Neapolitan way to fill hungry stomachs cheaply—now an easy way for restaurateurs to fill bank accounts. True Neapolitan pizza (and the better American type) is a thick slab of yeasted white or part-wholemeal flour dough mixed with oil and/or some milk to give lightness and more sustenance. It should be very crisp underneath and around the edges thanks to the generous application of olive oil to the baking tray.

Originally toppings were simple and yet rich, as concentrated as true pasta dressings should be, and were chosen to blend into the dough rather than curl and crisp on top. Cheese has become a common ingredient, especially chewy cows' milk mozzarella or grated Cheddar—but neither is originally authentic. Although now essential, tomato as a topping would also have been unknown. For a long time after they were introduced to Europe, tomatoes cooked to a pulp were merely one of the optional sauces you smeared onto cooked bread in and around Naples.

Elizabeth David says the absolutely original pizza-type dish is from Armenia and the topping was of minced lamb. The French *pissaladière* covers dough (or thick slices of bread fried on one side only) with a mush of onion cooked in olive oil and decorated with black olives and anchovy fillets—a tomato-less pizza, in effect.

Arguments rage that thin, crisp bases are the original, but the Neapolitan woman who taught me to make pizza scoffs, saying bread was all her poor ancestors could afford, not toppings, just as traditionally there was plenty of pasta yet very little sauce on it. But who really cares? If you want thin, bendy, unsatisfying crusts from which toppings slide off, then you have them, mate, and enjoy making those bankers richer.

PUMPERNICKEL: the many packaged varieties of these unleavened German wholegrain breads are essentially the same, with slightly different emphasis given to one or the other whole grain. Thus, pumpernickel and *vollkornbrot* are much the same and versions from Westphalia and Osnabrück differ on purpose, as both these German areas claim to have created the original as far back as 1400. There is just as much controversy over the origin of the word pumpernickel. Some say it is onomatopoeic for the flatulent effect on the eater. Try saying it with a German accent, and you'll hear what I mean.

ROLLS: find a baker who still makes crusty rolls, still makes Kaiser rolls that need strong jaws to chew, and who still produces long rolls that splatter shards of crisp crust when you bite into them, and you have a gem. Other than that, all you need to know is never to cut a bread roll but to pull it apart, particularly if it is hot: if you cut you smear the dough into pap, an insult to the baker, horrid to eat, and it makes you look a klutz.

When filling a roll to eat later, they are less messy to eat if you slice into the top at an acute angle, rather than splitting them on their equator. Don't use any pressure but let the knife do the work, so the roll is not compressed in any way. Their fillings will now sit up proudly, look much nicer on a counter or at a buffet and don't spread and drop as you eat.

RYE BREAD: a generic term for any bread that contains a proportion of rye flour, which itself has a very low gluten content and cannot make leavened bread without wheat flour. The content in rye loaves varies from as low as 15%, which gives a delicious light-coloured, light-textured loaf. The light version, sometimes also a sourdough, is most often baked in a bloomer shape, with or without caraway seeds and is the classic bread for salt beef sandwiches or for its very big brother the Reuben, a tower of salt beef and sauerkraut amongst other goodies.

SALLY LUNN: this light, sweet bread was either originally sold in the streets of Bath by a woman of the same name, or the name is a corruption of *sol et lune*, for these delicacies are supposed to look like the sun and the moon—a rich shining golden top over a pale delicate base. Put more simply, a Sally Lunn loaf is a white flour, yeasted dough bread mixed with full milk or milk and cream, slightly sweetened, perhaps slightly spiced and thus a sort of lesser brioche. It should be glazed with beaten egg yolk and scattered with crushed cube sugar whilst still hot. In Australia and New Zealand bakers use dessicated coconut shreds instead of sugar.

SANDWICH LOAF: white, brown or wholemeal bread baked in an enclosed tin to give a square or rectangular shape. Usually made only with modern fast-rising 'bread' and then sliced and wrapped.

SFOGLIATELLE: the name means little leaves and these look like hollow seashells or lobster tails of very fine leaves of pastry. The most popular filling is based on the light texture of ricotta beaten into a semolina custard, flavoured with vanilla and studded with candied orange, but chocolate and lemon are just as possible. Savoury spinach, potato and salami styles are also found.

SODA BREADS: any breads leavened with baking soda and an acidic liquid like buttermilk. Associated with Ireland, but soda breads were made far more widely. Almost always a free-form cob shape, and deeply slashed with a cross to help faster and more even baking.

Traditionally made with wholemeal flour but this is a bit heavy for many, so feel free to use white or whatever mix suits. Made and baked within an hour, soda bread is wondrous to bring hot to a table, with an invitation to pull it apart. Slicing should wait until it is absolutely cold, when it makes very good toast.

Too much soda gives an unpleasant taste, so go carefully, and if you can't buy buttermilk then yoghurt, soured cream or crème fraîche work beautifully, creating sweeter tastes and milder textures. Soda-bread dough is very companionable and so experimentation is encouraged. A 2020 Great British Bake-off competitor caused a sensation by mixing in smoked salmon, herbs and black pepper. She earned a Paul Hollywood handshake.

SOURDOUGH BREADS: breads leavened by the addition to the flour of some old, soured dough. Souring is another name for fermentation, the action of yeasts on carbohydrates that creates a gas and alcohol. Only part of a mother sourdough, or starter, is used to make a new batch, and then some of that fresh dough is then mixed back into the original mother, which then grows enough to be used once again, and so on. Some people claim their sourdough mother is over 100 years old and it can be but it will be very different from how it began. Having been additionally nourished by the ambient yeast cells in any area for so long, it will have developed a character no other baker or area can emulate. Regional sourdough bread, *terroir* breads, are just as possible as regional cheeses, apples, coffee or chocolate.

A nicely ripened sourdough mother can smell very close to foul, although there will always be enticing sweet notes behind the first gush of sourness. 19th-century gold prospectors in California were christened 'sourdoughs' because they carried sourdough mothers with them, and the smell was difficult to hide. San Francisco is still famous for its sourdough breads.

Invariably the nastiest sourdough 'starters' make the best breads. You don't actually get only a sour taste, but a marvellously rich sweet-acid flavour, varying according to the sourdough itself, the flour or flours used for the bread, how long it took to rise and so on.

Toasted sourdough is one of life's greatest pleasures. Particularly when used as the basis for something special and savoury: a warm goat cheese with a salad including toasted walnuts and a dressing made with walnut oil gets most people's vote for top place. Me? I can't eat goat cheese so bacon and eggs with hot maple syrup and long-grilled, caramelised tomatoes do it for me. Sourdough breads tend to last well, often maturing to a richer and fuller flavour, so a single loaf can give differing pleasures, first as a fresh loaf, and then cruising on to greater heights as toast. see also *Leavening*.

SPLIT-TIN LOAF: a tin loaf with a long slash down the middle. They can also be made by placing two long rolls of dough side by side in the tin. Almost always made with white dough and often the top crust is very browned, perhaps even slightly burned.

STOLLEN: a dense, yeasted German speciality for Christmas and that has a very long life. It's made in a flattish

oblong and the sweet, spiced and liberally fruited dough is wrapped around a central wadge of marzipan, said to represent the Christ Child in swaddling.
SWEET OR SAVOURY BREADS: at home or in a shop, traditional bakers once kept back small amounts of dough to make fruit breads, cheese breads, lardy cake, herb breads and so on. That stopped when bread-making became centralised and commercialised. Now breads with additions are perhaps the fastest growing baking genre. Few independent bakers could survive without offering olive breads, sun-dried tomato breads, olive and sun-dried tomato breads and zillions more, many in increasingly alarming shapes and sizes.

The reflection I make on the trend is to wonder whoever persuaded whom that dried rosemary is a good flavour in bread or that mixed herbs, which I had hoped dead, should be resurrected: it is the resinous, dusty rosemary in the latter that usually makes a nasty taste nastier.

There's a sure way to know what works in a bread dough and what does not. Try a bite of the flavouring on a slice of similar bread. Often you need a third flavour to make the flavouring work as well as it might: that trio structure is the key to almost everything good to eat. Thus, chocolate bread does not work unless there is also a good deal of sugar in the bread, orange bread also needs a sweetened dough, perhaps made with milk and with nutmeg or cardamom, black pepper bread might need tomato purée and garlic: fruit breads really must be sweet and most are all the better for spice—dried fruits and toasted nuts (they must first be toasted, best done evenly in a microwave) are much better than fresh fruits, which work best in cake rather than bread mixtures.

The best-flavoured loaf of all is the traditional French walnut loaf and as usual its simplicity is deceptive. When they are made with fresh walnuts and an honest dough, nothing beats toasted walnut bread with cheese, particularly Cheddars and blue cheeses, or for the best-ever toasted tomato sandwich, particularly if you drizzle on walnut oil.
TIN LOAF: a generic term for all loaves baked in metal tins, but especially applied to loaves that are long, rectangular and have a markedly high rise.
VIENNA LOAF: properly, a style of milk bread baked in a bloomer shape. The shape is so associated with the Vienna loaf that ordinary bloomers or sourdoughs are sold as 'viennas'.
WHOLEMEAL BREAD: the extraordinary difference between domestic and commercial wholemeal loaves is due to ignorance as much as anything else. Dough made with only 100% wholemeal flour should be handled as little as possible or it will not rise well, because of the inhibiting effect of the wheat germ, which is increased with kneading. A good 100% wholemeal loaf should feel heavy for its size but not leaden and when you squeeze it, there should be definite resistance. If it is as soft as sliced bread there seems little point to it. For me the best test of a plain, firm

wholemeal loaf is how it tastes and smells when a few days old: really good ones, with a very high or 100% wholemeal content develop a more complex, sweeter flavour.

ZWIEBACK: this means 'twice-baked' and these are rusks or slices of bread that have been baked dry, but that are usually thicker than commercial Melba toast made the same way.

Proper toast
Those many millions who think bread comes only sliced have never eaten decent bread properly toasted, which Victorian cookery books took seriously enough to give instructions for making. Their advice was to ensure the slices are warmed through before they crisp and brown, which you did by first holding the toasting fork away from the fire and then moving it closer. This is even more important with such as crumpets, which will only char on the outside unless they are properly heated through first. That's the way to toast in front of any fire, even that old gas heater or a barbecue; warm it through first and then brown it. Toasters sometimes approximate this when first used and the element has to heat up and so does toasting frozen slices.

However you make toast it is imperative that it never lies flat when hot but stands on edge to crisp and become absorbent – the point of toast racks. If not it steams to pap, negating the very point of toast. Even worse with commercial pre-sliced

bread. My maternal grandmother Alice Pitman would send back toast put directly onto a plate, saying: 'I asked for toast, not sweaty bread'. Quite.

Types of sweet and savoury baking

BABKE: Polish or Russian, with the dense, satisfying texture of a pound cake, baked in a deep decorative ring mold and leavened with yeast or a chemical agent. Serve plain with coffee when fresh or as an enticing quick dessert with a flavoured cream, doused with syrup or liqueurs, or covered with such cream/fruit mixtures as raspberry fool.

BAKLAVA: little is so moving to the sweet tooth as tiered platters of Middle-Eastern pastries. All baklava, an incorrect but widely used collective name, are variations on a few ingredients. Paper-thin filo pastry or shreddy *konafa/kataifi*, each generously coated with melted butter, are then stuffed, pinched, piled or layered or folded or rolled up with nuts, sometimes spiced. The nuts might be almonds, cashews, pistachios, walnuts or pine nuts, sometimes singly sometimes mixed together. Greek baklava should have/once would have had 33 layers of pastry, one for each year of Christ's life.

Once baked they are drenched in syrup sometimes with honey and commonly scented with rose water or orange-flower water, which prevents staling for weeks, even at room temperature. Each minute variation of square, oblong, triangle or other shape, nut filling or the syrup gives another type and flavour, and each of these will have a different name, even in neighbouring towns.

BROWNIES: a multitude of glorious sinfulness. Brownies can be big, flattish and roundish cookies with a distinct chewiness and studded with nuts or chocolate; peanut brownies are a staple of baking in Australasia. Brownies are also a tray bake cut into squares and should be a little crisp outside, very moist and chewy inside; if not, they are chocolate cakes. Together with muffins, brownies continue to compete with cheesecakes as staple café fare, and are just as easy to make as to buy in, which you might choose to remember when considering the prices charged.

CANELES: a speciality of Bordeaux, the canele is an individual, tall cake grooved with channels, like a miniature gugelhopf but without the hole. Flavoured with vanilla and dark rum, the inside is unique, a sort of egg-custardy, pancake-y, chewy mix with big holes that suggest yeast raising, which is not the case. The outside is caramelised, gently or robustly, during baking, sometimes retaining a crunch here and there when very fresh. A perfect start to all sorts of puddings with fresh fruit, with grilled pears or served with a flood of cold, rum-flavoured custard studded jewel-like with raspberries. But that's just summer. Lightly warmed and then served atop a cushion of stewed fruit surrounded by hot, thin custard, they make winter evenings seem a better thing altogether. A better choice than rum babas.

CHEESECAKES: there is a traditional small English cheesecake containing no cheese at all, but is a sweet sponge on a pat of raspberry jam, baked in puff or short pastry: Some say they should be called Welsh cheesecakes. Home cookery shops in Australia and New Zealand, which have nothing to do with homes and are more often run by Vietnamese or Chinese, are a reliable preserve of these curious treats.

Real curd cakes, cheesecakes and tarts with curd-based fillings, have been a staple ever since men and women began to write down what they cooked or ate. Once flavoured with rose water, nutmeg, orange, lemon, sherry or dried fruits, or all of them, they were an Everest above the uncooked or cooked 'cheesecakes' inflicted today on those not infected with dieting.

To try and to buy the real baked thing you probably need to find a Polish, Russian or Jewish area or a shop run for these people. Austrians and Germans also make them, perhaps the richest versions of all, and most look like a dense-textured cake on a pastry base when cut. If you can bear it, plain baked cheesecakes often mature and sweeten over a few days—the price you pay for this greater flavour is that the usual pastry base is no longer crisp and sweet, particularly if it has been spread with a rose petal or raspberry or apricot jam. The cheesecake world is not fair.

Basque Burnt cheesecake: it's a misnomer for a start but loved by the sycophants who have made this a 'thing', not realizing that if cheesecake is truly blackened it gives a very unbalanced mouth experience. At heart, it is a wickedly rich baked cheesecake, made properly with cream cheese—even mascarpone—and double/heavy cream. The high fat and sugar content means the upper skin is going to brown easily, actually caramellising, and that is delicious even when taken to extremes. Beyond that point it is carbonizing, becoming unpleasantly bitter, a taste that does not blend with the cheesecake, the way caramel does. A dark, golden brown skin is wondrous; truly burned is what you do to meat at barbecues.

New York cheesecakes: cheesecake is close to a religion in the Big Apple. As with any decent religion there are schisms, sects and breakaway movements. The essential New York cheesecake is a baked one, made with cream or curd cheese, usually flavoured with cream and vanilla and sitting high on a pastry base. Its antecedents are the cheesecakes of Poland and Germany and Russia and the like, most usually from the Jewish tradition. Sometimes a little shop will still do things the old way— like putting a layer of rose-petal or apricot jam between the cheesecake and the pastry, but that's not a New York cheesecake. NY cheesecake should be lighter than you expect and have a soothing acidity to balance the sweetness. Except, that's only what *some* people think of as a real New York cheesecake.

Hot on its heels is New York's Italian style, made with ricotta and, so, often a little grainy and regularly not made as high or thick. Here the cheese is more a subtle background, in fact proper ricotta is not truly a cheese as it is made from whey and has little casein in it. Its bland sweetness tells you it retains the sugar of milk and none of the fat, and ricotta cheesecake hurtles up many realms closer to God when mixed with cream and/or with ground almonds; it's just as rich as cream-cheese style NY cheesecake, but is subtler in flavour. This sublime mixture of ricotta, cream and almonds can be served and eaten fresh pretty much as it is, but for a cheesecake is baked with eggs to make a firmer set. The best I ever ate was in Naples, their particular Easter special, studded with cooked wheat grains and candied orange, perfumed with orange-flower water and baked in seriously rich pastry. Second best is one I make with a spectrum of orange; candied orange, orange zest, orange juice and orange-flower water. The New York connection with cheesecake works well for the rest of the USA. When Junior's Brooklyn restaurant offered their cheesecake on QVC shopping channel, they sold 70,000 in 24 hours.

A third type of cheesecake is often

found in small delicatessens where food is made on the premises. This is the unbaked cheese, often set with gelatine, and they are no bad thing as long as they also contain a measure of whipped cream or rich yoghurt to give a fluffy, light texture. Those without gelatine often use only flavoured cream cheese, sometimes just whisked up Philadelphia, and are thus thin and miserable and claggy, scarcely thicker than the biscuit base, a swizz and a disappointment. They leave your teeth sticky.

Whatever your delicatessen does, you should always store a wet or a gelatine-based cheesecake in a refrigerator, for even if made with the finest ingredients it will go sour in warmth, or it will dry out, or both.

Quite plain New-York style baked cheesecake can be made special with the accompaniment of a purée of sharp fruit—blackcurrants, gooseberries, red currants with orange, or rhubarb with orange and a touch of green root ginger would all be good. Very special jams or preserves do just as well: think black or red cherry, rose petal, lime marmalade with plenty of peel in it, or apricot, but everything must be well chilled. Spunkily flavoured ice cream is even better, for everything but your cholesterol count.

CHURROS: a sweet Mexican and South American snack taken up by Spain and gaining popularity. It is a choux pastry extruded in grooved strips, deep fried and then coated in cinnamon sugar, best eaten warm and often dipped into chocolate. Lesser versions use chemical doughs.

ECCLES CAKES: gorgeous when made correctly, which is more and more difficult to find. They should be a round but flattish mound of crisp and flaky pastry, about the size of a small hand's palm, in which there is a generous filling of lightly spiced currants with a good measure of candied peel. The top should be sticky and with a crunch of sugar crystals and syrup, ideally of demerara sugar. It is thought criminal for there to be more than or fewer than three slashes on top. Wonderful served warm and specially recommended with fine Farmhouse Lancashire but a superior Cheshire or Cheddar do very nicely.

ENSAIMADAS: an ancient breakfast speciality of the Balearic Islands. Traditionally coils of thin pastry flavoured with lard and served with lots of icing sugar. Not the same made with other fats and variations, as are now found in South America and SE Asia.

FRIANDS: these funny little ovals of almond-enriched sponge cake are *financiers* reinvented in Australia by being baked in that shape. When very fresh and warm, and when the high butter content has caramelised a little of the mixture around the bottom edge, they mate well with coffee. At room temperature or less they seem heavy and greasy and to cost rather a lot for what they are. They commonly have a fresh raspberry baked into the top, and just as well.

GINGERBREAD: you'll find this both

hard and chewy or cake like. The chewy original was often not much more than honey, flour and ground ginger. It kept for ages and ages, hence why you could have gingerbread cookies on the Christmas-tree and eat them after Twelfth Night. Ditto a gingerbread house. It was once common to gild gingerbread men with gold leaf, making them superior gifts for good luck.

Lebkuchen: are a softer German style that include ground almonds and are seen as iced and decorated stars, hearts and more at Christmas.

Panforte: from Sienna is a survivor of the original gingerbreads.

GUGELHOPF: this egg-rich, yeasted cake, also called *kugelhopf* and related to babke and brioche, and to pannetone, contains chopped peel and other dried fruit. It may be eaten plain but the very high yeast content means it stales too quickly for the taste of those not from Central Europe. Butter, jam or syrup will put that right particularly when it has been warmed. Like babke, gugelhopf may also be found covered with chocolate and nuts.

MUFFIN, AMERICAN: like a large cup cake and when first popularised they were made with bran and touted as a health food. Next popular type was studded with blueberries, but we eventually latched on—cooked blueberries have virtually no flavour. Now we have cranberry muffins (excellent), banana muffins, courgette (zucchini), chocolate, double chocolate, white chocolate, poached rhubarb and raspberry muffins, and cream-cheese-coconut-pine-apple-white-chocolate and macadamia nut muffins—and everything else, including bitter chocolate with a couple of rum-soaked cherries in syrup hidden under the top crust.

Some argue there is a special muffin mixture, and there probably is, but frankly you can bake any cake mixture in suitable tins and call them muffins. I have always relied on the comfort of Betty Crocker muffin mixes. If you make muffins at home, put only one dump of batter into each muffin tin—topping up with a second spoonful somehow inhibits the rising.

PANFORTE: classically a speciality of Sienna, this 'strong bread' is a brave survivor of what would be recognised by medieval folks as a gingerbread. Panforte is honey and sugar mixed with nuts and candied fruit, with plenty of sweet spices and flour. It comes in a flat disc, big or small and is usually topped and tailed with edible rice paper, which also helps stop the surfaces becoming sticky.

It keeps for ages if kept cool and should be served in thin wedges with coffee or tea or with a fortified wine: it's too gutsy and too sweet to eat with wine or champagne. Panforte makes a terrific ingredient to serve with or to chunk into or over ice cream, to chop over grilled peaches or nectarines or to bake into big meringues; serve these with fresh fruit and whipped cream for an outrageous end to an otherwise sedate meal.

Pies, traditional

Cottage and Shepherd's Pie: Cottage pie is made with minced beef, Shepherd's pie with minced lamb. Both were what you did with leftovers from roasts and versions made with fresh mince never taste the same as the traditional versions.

Fidget Pie: an old pork and apple pie in a lard pastry.

Fruit mincemeat pies: the best include suet and that is a nod to the times these included minced lamb, as their origin is almost certainly the Middle East, underpinning their relevance to Christmas.

Pasty: famously associated with Cornwall, these crimped half-moon pastry cases were carried into mines for sustenance. Beef chuck or skirt steak was sliced very thin (not chopped or cubed) and layered with equally thin onion and potato flakes plus swede. The type of pastry had to be rugged and closed with 18–20 crimps. No other vegetables should be included. Anything called a Cornish Pasty must be made in that county, so a pasty made elsewhere may contain other ingredients.

Squab pie: traditionally made in Devon and Cornwall, it is based on lamb or mutton plus apple and prunes plus spices, very medieval and rarely seen these days.

QUICHE: whatever happened to the classic British savoury flan? Nothing, except the name. They are now called quiche and the true quiche is forgotten.

The quiche Lorraine is a wibbly-wobbly savoury custard tart in an open pastry case, a down-home yet noble celebration of honest backyard fare of fresh cream and eggs, made savoury with a little white of leek and of pre-cooked green bacon. No onion. No cheese. So, if it's a quiche, no spinach, salmon or ham or tomato or anything else. Those are savoury flans. They and quiche must have a blind-baked pastry case, because the low temperature to set an egg custard is not enough to cook pastry properly.

RAISED PIES: once the cases of cooked meat were called coffins and not eaten. As foreign ideas refined British bakers' expectations with shortcrust, flaky, puff and hot-water pastries, pies became essential to every walk of life, from the pasties carried in the pockets of Cornish miners to the raised pies of many game birds that graced royal tables.

Raised pies are peculiarly British and so called because while still warm the unique hot-water crust must be raised—shaped—by hand, over a cylindrical shape. The pastry is flour, lard and hot water and holds an uneasy position between edible new-style crusts and inedible old-style, largely because beneath the crisp golden outer crust there is too often a distressing greeny-creamy uncooked layer. This might be commercial fudging because it's possible to cook a crust through without imperilling the filling.

Game pies: a famed and showily decorated must on the side board of stately houses. Layers of different game and ham held together with a rich aspic, so it could be sliced. Small ones, a game version of pork pies, are wondrous when eaten outside.

Mutton pies: also known as Scotch pies, these are spiced mutton or lamb, sometimes with potato in the pastry and often served with mashed potato on the top.

Pork pie: pork and fat minced together to make individual to large slicing pies held together with a firm, rich aspic. The protected Melton Mowbray pies must be made with chopped rather than minced fresh pork that is uncured and so cooks to a grey rather than pink. Lesser pies often have little or no aspic and find difficulty baking the pastry enough, but such superior counters as Harrods and Fortnum & Mason rarely disappoint.

RUM BABAS: part of the classic French repertoire I have never understood. They are made of savarin dough, a sweet, very highly-yeasted dough, and are baked in small ring shapes. They should be saturated with rum-flavoured syrup, which dissuades the growth of mould but that does not always disguise the taste of staleness, precipitated by the high yeast content. If they are nice and fresh they can be decorated with chilled fresh fruit and whipped cream to end a meal.

Bottled rum babas in syrup are usually only slightly acquainted with any rum I know, so there can be no blending of flavours to create something fresh and original. Rum do, altogether.

SCONES: scones are the sleeping giants of baking, and if produced and marketed properly would soon see off the upstart muffin and greasy friand. For a start, scones are simpler more honest things. Because they are simple, they are easy to glorify with any of the sweet or savoury additions you might add to muffins. They are good hot or cold and virtually demand simply to be split (*never* cut) and slathered with butter, a very good thing.

Originally made to use up soured milk with baking soda, they became more generally popular when the introduction of baking powder meant you could use fresh milk, giving a nicer, lighter version. That's the way they should be but baking powder's replacement also of yeast meant eggs were added to the mix in emulation of rich whigs, a top treat of the rich. Whether you say scone or scown, the inclusion of egg is wrong; call them something else if you insist on doing this, even saying rich scones is enough to show you know the difference.

And what about scones and clotted cream or whipped cream? Devon says cream on first but the Cornish say jam on first, which means you might also have buttered the scone half, making the cream more a decorative dab. Or not. I care less about this than if you put eggs into scones. Oh, almost forgot. A small amount of sugar in scone mixtures gives a smoother texture, just as it does so satisfyingly to all baking.

TARTS: these are closer to patisserie

than baking, I know, but some seem to have established firm footholds in deli and café food around the world.

Bakewell tart/Bakewell pudding: the tart has an almond filling (frangipane) over raspberry jam in pastry and is usually topped with flaked almond. Bakewell pudding is also baked on pastry but adds egg to the filling, making it more sponge-like.

Fruit tarts: individual or big enough to slice, the most popular offer raspberries or strawberries over a *crème pâtissier*/custard base, sometimes held with a jelly. Raspberry is by far the better. Never buy when you see the strawberries have a white centre as these are the least melting and succulent varieties.

Portuguese egg tarts, Pastéis de Nata: Oh, that pastry! The outside should be flaky and crackle when you bite into it, perhaps with an ephemeral back-taste of scorching because of the high heat needed to get the effect of fine open petals cradling a silken, golden, condensed custard that has to be very sweet to avoid splitting. The flower effect is achieved by rolling and then slicing the layered pastry, as you would Chelsea Buns. Each slice is put into individual moulds with a twist of the thumb, which turns up the cut edges; you must see a swirl in the pastry underneath each authentic tart.

Tarte au citron: extraordinary when made with butter in the pastry and flavoured only with lemon juice and lemon zest. Well worth experimenting with other flavours, especially lime or Japanese yuzu. When you make one, brush melted chocolate onto the inside of the blind baked crust before adding a pre-cooked and cooled filling. Soggy bottoms happen quickly: look carefully at any sell-by date.

Charcuterie

NEED TO KNOW

Pigs are the animal world's most efficient converters of carbohydrates into protein and fat.

45 kg/100 lb of feed produces 10 kg/20 lb of pig flesh; cattle convert the same amount to 3 kg/7 lb.

Curing means to salt flesh to exude moisture and then further dry by hanging.

Saltpetre added to salt helps keep cured meat free of dangerous pathogens and produces an attractive pink colour.

Salami and saucissons sec are salted, low-moisture flesh chopped or minced, forced into cleaned intestines, and stored cool in low humidity to develop flavours unique to the ambiance and pig breed.

Hams are separated rear legs dry salted and air dried, perhaps smoked.

Gammon is sides of pork cured in one piece.

Dry-cured products are produced using salt only and when cooked do not exhude liquid or white matter.

Commercial wet (brine) salting by injection, gives a greater weight return but lesser flavour and softer texture; liquid and preservatives are added for extra weight and these can be expressed, seen especially when frying bacon.

Brine baths are used to cure cuts for salt pork.

Traditional charcuterie aimed to use every part of the pig.

Pâtés and terrines are minced flesh and lesser organs, flavoured, cooked and stored under protective coatings of the pig's fat.

Bacon and pancetta are made by dry salting the belly (streaky bacon) and loin (back bacon). These were called green but were then sometimes smoked.

The cheeks of long-jawed pigs made chaps in the UK, guanciale in Italy.

The head is made into brawn or head cheese.

The small intestines are chopped and used as stuffing for sausages, chitterlings or andouilletes, or they were dried for later use as sausage casings.

Black puddings are blood, thickened with barley or oatmeal and textured with glistening blobs of back fat.

Faggots and pâtés could include liver, and the trotters could be boiled and stuffed and then stored in their own jelly or under fat.

Charcuterie originally meant a French shop where you could buy cooked or cured meats from the pig. From being peasant and farmyard based, charcuterie in the 20th century also became big business and factory-led, ensuring every product with the same name tasted the same. Those cut traditional corners and their products are far less salty or smoked than the originals for, once given the chance, modern palates chose to avoid the old, high-salt flavour of well-preserved meats.

Commercial processing methods so changed the flavour of today's pig and its products the general public tends neither to recognise nor like, say, a genuine ham, which is relatively dry and dense. Instead, many prefer the moistness and bright colour of products with artificially high-water content, and that have been battered and re-shaped into a false and often slimy tenderness.

Cue the millennials. There is a renaissance of heritage in every aspect of cured meats and world leaders in this are Britain's 20-and 30-something charcutiers. Once, our climate was too damp and unreliable to produce anything like the air-dried Italian salami and French saucissons sec. Today, small systems using controlled temperature and humidity reproduce artisan curing ambiance from Penzance to Aberdeen, and the results are quite astonishing. Whilst following traditional styles and names, but adding new variety and flavours by careful choice of pig breed, modern British charcuterie is perhaps the most exciting aspect of 21st-century gourmet and deli foods.

Types of pig

All around the world, heritage breeds are again being bred to produce their old specialities and tastes. Enthusiasts move breeds back to their geographical origins, so charcutiers can more accurately reflect by-gone tastes as those breeds once more eat and live as they did.

The advantages of free-range heritage pigs over the modern factory pig are a more savoury flavour and a thicker layer of fat. Then the fun begins, because the same variety of pig fattened on acorns will taste different from a brother or sister fed corn or peaches or that has rootled, the way pigs should.

A few special breeds are unchanged,

like the pigs for genuine Parma ham and the Spanish *pata negra* pigs, and those on Corsica and Sardinia, believed to be a breed Ancient Romans would recognise. Throughout the world old breeds and wild pigs are being rediscovered. New Zealand, for instance, has two sorts of wild pig, neither of which descends from species introduced by the Maori after they began settling there in the 13th century. The big Captain Cookers are probably descended from such old British breeds as Tamworth and Berkshire. Smaller kune-kune are also European in origin and some characteristics suggest they originated in Poland.

Popular breeds in the UK include:

BERKSHIRE: a particularly light and delicate meat from an early maturing pig, originally from around Wantage, Berks.

BRITISH LOP: these attractive pigs with the large floppy ears that give them their name are one of the biggest rare breeds. They originated in Devon and Cornwall, and can be used for both meat and bacon.

BRITISH SADDLEBACK: a black pig with a white saddle across its shoulders that is a cross between the old Essex and Wessex breeds, from the Dorset/Hampshire borders and Essex. The mostly black skin means it is protected from sunburn and so happily lives outdoors. The top-quality flesh is full-flavoured.

ESSEX: another pig we almost lost. Direct descendants of the Saxon and Norman pigs that foraged in ancient Epping Forest and that were improved by mating with Neapolitan boars. It produces a marbled meat that's particularly sweet and delicious.

GLOUCESTERSHIRE OLD SPOT: from the Vale of Severn, these delightful pigs were traditionally kept in orchards and fattened on windfalls. Another well-marbled meat, sweet, delicious and tasting the way pork should.

LANDRACE: this large white pig is thought of as British but was only imported from Scandinavia in 1949 as part of the post-war need to increase food production. Its success was largely at the expense of smaller traditional breeds. Crossbreeding makes the British Landrace different from other Landrace types.

LARGE BLACK: a West Country breed much admired for hardiness and mothering skills and that makes very succulent pork and bacon. Because its black skin protects it from sunburn, it's happy to live outdoors with minimal attention.

MANGALITSA: a recently introduced Hungarian breed, and until recently almost extinct, the mangalitsa's woolly coat immediately sets it apart but its greatest appeal to the gourmet is that it creates by far the thickest fat, and also marbles it through its flesh, like wagyu beef. This keeps the flesh tender and exceptionally well favoured even after curing into hams and sausages; as fresh meat it has no porcine equal. Still uncommon in Britain but worth pursuing for something memorable although cross breeding is already diluting its singular virtues.

MIDDLE WHITE: an early maturing breed, this time from Yorkshire. Its meat is particularly sweet and the Japanese, who know a good thing when they taste it, have even built a shrine in this breed's honour. Middle White piglets are the preferred choice as suckling pigs.

SADDLEBACK: a relatively new breed that combines the ancient Essex and Wessex pigs. Known for deep flavour and for making great crackling on a roasted joint.

TAMWORTH: from the Midlands, it's a ginger-coloured pig particularly prized as a bacon producer, but you'll find the rest of the flesh is deliciously full flavoured.

Storing air-dried produce

Whole, air-dried products are better kept out of the refrigerator and hung in a cool, well-ventilated place. But once they have been cut they must be treated with care. They may not go mouldy, but will easily go rancid, particularly if sliced. Even the flavours of the more robust salamis are delicate and likely to be swamped by something powerful in a refrigerator, so always wrap these products well in cling film, but let them warm a little before eating, otherwise their essential sweetness will be hidden from your palate.

An unfluctuating room temperature is generally thought more conducive for whole air-dried hams than bringing them in and out of a refrigerator once cut. The tradition is for them to be loosely covered with a light, open-textured cloth, which allows 'breathing'. Refrigerate bought sliced ham of any kind.

How hams are made

A ham is made from the detached hind leg of a pig. If a leg is cured while joined to the side of the animal it should be called a gammon, but this is how Wiltshire hams are cured. Rules are made to be broken.

SHOULDER (US — BOSTON BUTT) HAMS: commonly called Picnic Hams, use the top of a front leg (*palatilla* in Spain). They are fattier, have more muscles, have a looser texture and are invariably smoked.

TRADITIONAL PRODUCTION: the original way to preserve a ham is with dry-salting. The raw meat is rubbed with dry salt at regular intervals, which draws the fluids from the flesh that in turn dissolve the salt, which is then absorbed back thus preserving the flesh. There is a risk the brine will not penetrate right to the bone, which causes bone taint, a very nasty taste signalling potential danger if eaten.

Each leg requires more or less salt according to shape and age and this requires great knowledge to get right. Adding sugar and spices to the salt encourages differing flavours and both the breed of pig and the food it has eaten will be an influence. Once the brine has been drained, the hams must be dried further.

Green ham means it matures unsmoked; smoked ham has enhanced flavour.

Ireland uses peat smoke.

Virginia uses apple and hickory wood.

Oak is common in the UK.

Manuka or ti-tree is commonly used in New Zealand.

Hams have always been made from other animals. Some, like turkey ham, are commercially produced to be kosher and halal conforming. You might find other hams to add to the list of:

Bear, beef, emu, goat, goose, horse, kangaroo, lamb, mutton, ostrich, turkey, venison including moose/elk, caribou and reindeer wild boar.

With or without smoking, further drying allows the final development of flavours. This can take as much as 24 months and is why traditional hams can be so expensive.

Sometimes air-dried hams are boned before curing, some are boned after curing. If you want a traditional ham that is also boneless, it is better to choose a ham cured whole and then de-boned. Beware of boned hams too obviously pressed into an even shape. This is often done after curing but before drying and so liquor is expressed too soon and too quickly, which is not conducive to the development of flavour.

MODERN PRODUCTION: a faster method of salting and draining soaks the meat in a brine bath, but this broad-stroke curing leads to a tougher end product. The newest technology automatically weighs each raw ham and then injects it with a predetermined proportion of brine, ideally using a major artery as the main point of entry. By using the animal's natural channels of communication, the brine travels quickly and evenly throughout the flesh. Results seem better than the brine bath, but experts say they can still detect a certain toughness. Today, more and more, faster and faster curing techniques are being invented, but none so far has been able to identify the subtle differences recognised by a man rubbing in salt with his hands.

Any smoke or other flavour addition is likely to be artificial or a 'nature-identical flavouring' which is another way of saying the same thing.

Cooked pressed hams, hams for slicing and those sold sliced will have been brine cured but not matured and dried, indeed they often have extra water added to them. Many have been artificially created from anything but leg meat. What seem separate muscles are individual pieces pressed from a slurry; if you see little bubbles in 'ham' flesh, this is the absolute clue it is not the real thing, for all that it might taste of pig and make nice sandwiches.

Types of air-dried ham

It would be pointless to estimate the different types of air-dried hams produced, even in Britain, for those who make them on a farm will do it differently each time, and even the well-known ones vary a little. Some few of these may be found in delis and supermarkets, sliced and pre-packed or cut to order. Capreolus, a leader in British charcuterie, makes air-dried Pannage Ham from British Lops, who rootle and stuff themselves in ancient tradition on New Forest acorns and that is reckoned to equal Spain's *bellota* hams.

(B) Britain (F) France (G) Germany (I) Italy (S) Spain

BELLOTA (S): a number of ham styles in different parts of Spain use *bellota* to indicate their prime quality and meaning their pigs have fattened on acorns; a finely tuned palate will taste them in the fat.

BLACK FOREST (G): more highly smoked than Westphalian, and a tasty foil in sandwiches or salads when a subtle product might be overwhelmed.

BRADENHAM (B): originating in Chippenham over two centuries ago, the Bradenham cure includes molasses, and is smaller and more expensive than most. Its black skin and highly individual flavour draws on the molasses and such spices as juniper. Now made by one of the big conglomerate companies.

COBURGER: a Dutch ham made only from the top of the leg.

CORSICAN: hams and most types of charcuterie are made from pigs fattened in the wild on chestnuts and acorns until their haunches give the correct hollow response (like a baked loaf) when thumped. Found readily in South of France markets, they're a true taste of the past, because the pigs have changed little for millennia.

GERMAN: there are many regional smoked hams (*landschinken*), often simply called country hams—if just air-dried the flesh is translucent but not if cooked.

GUELDER HAM: a Dutch smoked ham.

JAMBON D'ARDENNES: an excellent Belgian ham.

JAMBON DE BAYONNE (F): the best-known French ham, eaten without further cooking, it differs from air-dried hams of Spain and Italy by being lightly smoked.

JAMBONS DE CAMPAGNES (F): local variations of the Bayonne and depending on their excellence will be recommended for use as is, or for cooking.

JAMON SERRANO (S): the basic Spanish air-dried ham, guaranteed up to very high standards when stamped with the elaborate 'S' of its consortium. It has taken at least nine months to produce, including the *calado*, when it is poked in three places by a sharpened horse bone to test for maturity and sweetness by smell.

LACHSSHINKEN: a great but increasingly rare treat. This is the lightly-salted, slightly-dried, lightly-smoked loin of pork, wrapped in fine fat. It is soft, meltingly so, and its name means 'salmon ham' for the cure, the texture and the flavour are not a million miles from a lightly smoked salmon. It should be served just below room temperature in quite thin but not too thin slices, and should never be cooked, although it would be sublime.

LANDSCHINKEN: a catch-all name for Germany's many smoked country hams.

MUTTON/LAMB HAM: rare but worth

pursuing, these are prepared exactly the same way as pork ham and are thought specially good if made from the Lake District's ancient Herdwick breed.

Mutton hams can be too strongly flavoured for many but Capreolus cures theirs with rosemary, juniper, garlic, pepper and sweet port and then smokes over beechwood, giving a 'scented, fruity and smoky' appeal.

Lamb ham is less challenging and might include sugar in the cure and it's a target for domestic enthusiasts to make. Cold smoking is good if you can arrange it. Macon ham is a relatively new name for these.

PATA NEGRA (S): Spanish hams produced exclusively from small black-footed Iberian pigs fattened on acorns. Like cockatoos, they have a riveting ability to take whole acorns into one side of their mouth and to spit out the shells from the other, whilst chewing without cease. A welcome sign of the real thing is to see the cured flesh streaked with fat, giving an altogether bigger and more gratifying flavour: see *Bellota*. Some to look for:

Jamon de Guijuelo: small hams with pink to purple flesh likely to be a little salty and made only from the black-footed Iberian pig or agreed others with 50% of that blood. Class 1 is fattened only on acorns, class 2 starts with acorns and finishes with fodder, class 3 is fed on fodder only. These hams are guaranteed under Spain's Denominacion de Origen system and are not the real thing if they do not show the DOC symbol.

Jamon de Teruel: also protected by a Spanish DOC, the meat is sweeter and more delicate, and made from Landrace and related breeds.

PALETA: the Spanish name for air-dried shoulder from the front leg, so will have more of the tasty fat if from an acorn fed *bellota* pig. Described as 'madness in the mouth'.

PARMA (I): Parma is not a collective for Italian air-dried hams, but a specific product protected by DOP status. It is breaking the law to sell or to call anything but a genuine Parma ham by this name. See below.

PRAGUE: named for the capital of what is now the Czech Republic, Prague ham has long been thought the best air-dried ham to be cooked and served hot.

PROSCIUTTO: is Italian for ham; if you want one of her excellent air-dried hams you must ask for *prosciutto crudo*. These all have protected status.

Culatello di Zibello (I): the rarest prosciutto of all, made only from the pear-shaped top muscle of the rear leg; the name meals 'little bum'. Cured uniquely in a district with noted humidity, culatello and the lesser *fiocco* hams need constant care and rotation of ambiance to keep them sweet, for 20 up to 36 months. The texture is notably velvety on the palate and the flavours are described as sweet with a distinctive, scented woodiness, often called muskiness. Best eaten unaccompanied by fruits or salads. Bread and butter do nicely, largely because that's all you will be able to afford after buying culatello.

Prosciutto di Modena (I): you should

taste nothing of salt in the notably intense sweetness of this ham. The pigs can be grown in a number of regions but the hams must be made and matured at an altitude of around 900 metres in the province of Modena, particularly in the hills and valleys close to the Panaro river.

Prosciutto di Norcia (I): perhaps the least well-known Italian ham. Made in the districts of Valnerini at about 500 m above sea level, it has a rather light flavour, and salt should be barely present.

Prosciutto di Parma (I): around eight million hams are produced from pigs bred and grown all over Italy, but to the same standards. The notably sweet moistness and light skin colour are a result of their two-step curing: during the second stage the skin is covered in peppered fat, slowing moisture loss and preventing discolouration. Look for the branded ducal crown and the word PARMA: without these they could be made almost anywhere from any sort of pig.

Prosciutto di San Daniele (I): considered an elegant aristocrat, the hams are flattened and always keep the trotter. The small production area is in the far north east. They are branded with an SD.

Prosciutto Toscano (I): uses herbs in the curing and aging in Tuscany.

Prosciutto Veneto Berico-Euganeo (I): only 400,000 are made in the hills between the provinces of Padova and Vicenza. They are branded VENETO and display the winged lion of Venice.

ROHSCHINKEN: a Swiss ham whose name tells you what it is, raw ham.

SMITHFIELD (USA): Smithfield, Virginia, hams are from pigs who dined on acorns and wild nuts before fattening on corn and peanuts.

SPECK: you will find this rather like German air-dried hams, for it comes from the alpine valleys of Bolzano, in other words the South Tyrol. The smoking gives away the connection. Although speck is the German word for bacon, this isn't bacon.

SUFFOLK (B): this is quite sweet and is smoked before being allowed to develop its 'blue bloom': a rich colour and good full flavour.

VIRGINIA (USA): Virginia hams should be made from pigs fed on peanuts and peaches.

YORK (B): well-known even in Europe where many an anonymous ham is sold as *Jambon d'York (F)* some would say the anonymity is a blessing, for otherwise those who know the real thing would do awful things to the manufacturers. A real York ham is blessedly mild and pink and might have been smoked to varying degrees; originally this was said to smoke from oak left over from building the cathedral. A dry salt cure is used rather than brine and sweetness is due to careful tending during the maturation, which takes three months and should be accompanied by the growth of a green mould. A York needs to be soaked 12–24 hours before cooking. Most sold under this name are made by very untraditional methods.

Types of cooked hams

Cooked hams, boneless and meant for slicing, are the charcuterie counter's equivalent of sliced white bread. There are some exceptions, but it's a journey best begun with suspicion in mind.

First, most cooked ham is not ham, that is it is not from the detached leg, not even when in a ham shape, because everything about most hams is artificial. Pork for such products can come from all parts of the animal, and is always cured in a salt brine that plumps rather than dries out the flesh; those sold as Virginia hams probably have sweeteners added to the cure. Once curing is completed the meat is shredded and tumbled to make it even in texture. Then it is pressed into closed moulds, either square, 'D' or ham shaped, and steamed to prevent weight or moisture loss. These reconstituted hams are quickly recognizable from small bubbles and air pockets in the meat, where none should be.

Other cooked hams are not reconstituted, as above, but are natural muscle meat joined in an unnatural way. They might even be formed from muscles from different pigs—even from different pigs from different countries.

The objective is to bring a cheaper product to the market and there is merit in that. But how sad to see people preferring this literal dilution of one of our oldest foods, thinking real ham too dry or too strongly flavoured. You do get what you pay for with ham, and the bottom end of the scale in cooked hams is tasteless, and barely worth eating nutritionally.

Slicing and serving a whole air-dried or cooked ham

The technique is sensibly based on what will desiccate soonest. Thus, you should begin with the flesh of the narrow shank and then move on to the shank half, that is the narrower of the two portions on either side of the bone, essentially the upper front when the leg was alive. Only then should you move on to the thicker juicier butt half, as it is the longest lasting portion. Do it the other way round and by the time you get to the shank it will have dried so much it will be inedible.

A serrated knife should never be used and the fat must only be cut away as you go, for it helps protect the uneaten flesh and keep it moist. Each slice should be cut towards the shank. Once sliced, or if you have bought slices, refrigeration is recommended, but let them warm slightly, still covered, before serving or you will not enjoy the natural sweetness.

I grant great melon is a good accompaniment, but better by far are fresh figs or a juicy pear, or some seriously fragrant mango: fresh lychee or mangosteen or rambutan are more 'creative' accompaniments, and why not?

The end-of-knuckle pieces are delicious diced and thrown into a sauce or pasta dish, or when finely minced as the basis of a stuffing or worked into a Bolognese-style pasta sauce; but do check for rancidity.

Salami and Saucissons Secs

NEED TO KNOW

A salame or saucisson sec is uncooked pig meat, raw pork, that is then cured with salt and air-dried; no heat is used.

Intestines are the traditional casings.

Salami are usually minced with firm back fat and, sometimes, with a little beef.

An Italian salame made only of pork has a metal tag stamped 'S'; with beef it says SB.

Venison, wild boar, donkey, goose or game birds might also be used or included, particularly in Italy. Look for cinghiale wild boar, salame d'oca for goose and a beef salame made from the enormous white toros de Chiannina.

In France, spices and herbs may be added and saucissons secs have a broader range of sizes and shapes than Italian or other air-dried sausages.

Italians use few spices and herbs and rarely use garlic as this would go rancid; they might add truffles, which works because they are not cooked.

The flavour of salami is determined by the proportion of meat to fat and by the texture that each ingredient is minced.

The larger the pieces of meat and fat, the sweeter the salami; look for the plump Jesus de Lyon if you like this style.

Go for fine texture and/or high fat content if you prefer brighter, higher flavours; Italian Milano and Hungarian salami are popular examples.

Each part of an intestine harbours or attracts different types of bacteria and accompanying enzymes, so each part used as a casing donates a different flavour to a salame. The large saucisson sec called Rose de Lyon, uses the last few feet of the pig's large intestine, including the puckered sphincter: the saucisson's name has nothing to do with its colour.

The encased mixture is either tied overall with string or tied both ends, so it may be suspended.

Each product should lose about 35% of its weight through evaporation, the time varying from weeks to months according to traditional preference.

Some Italian salami are pressed between boards, which absorb the liquid expressed, and these cure faster than those left to evaporate in the air.

During the air-curing process some salami will be wiped free of exudate, some will not; some may be dusted with talcum to seal any holes in the casings. In France they might be dipped into herbs or black pepper.

In Hungary and Italy, a fine white bacterial growth is encouraged on the skins; the enzymic action of its by-products further tenderises and flavours the meat.

Salami and saucissons secs are made to be eaten simply, with bread, and perhaps some cheese and a few unobtrusive pickles. The Scandinavians, Dutch and Germans tend to serve them for breakfast, with bland sweet cheeses, too.

Salamis should not be cooked, even those that have been heat-treated rather than air-dried, but a leftover end-piece of salame might be cut into cubes to finish a spaghetti sauce or for inclusion in a salad. Or you can roll slices around a flavoured cream cheese as a snack. They should *always* be skinned, unless coated with herbs or peppers. If you have a piece that you are to slice yourself, peel it first.

Never eat a salame or saucisson sec that is soft or spongy in the centre or that smells sharp; it may be too young meaning it could harbour evil pathogens or it could be somehow infected by bad storage. It's generally a bad idea to eat any charcuterie that has been exposed and warm for any time, especially if sliced.

Salami and saucissons may be stored uncut for a long time in a cool airy place without refrigeration and will still be safe to eat; even if they dessicate they'll still be safe to eat. Once cut, they should be treated like a fresh product , with the exposed end sealed from air-borne contaminants with paper or film, and also refrigerated.

(B) Britain (F) France (G) Germany (I) Italy (S) Spain

CHORIZO (S): beware, Spanish chorizos are almost the only sausages that do not use a clear casing for cooked or air-dried versions. The chilli content can be excoriating so take good advice. Chorizos that require cooking are designated *à la parilla* or for the grill, and should have an opaque skin.

COPPA CRUDA (I): between a ham and salame, this is not chopped but is a piece of airdried pork usually from the neck, pressed into a skin and often has noticeable runs of fat. Sweet and satisfying, it's commonly enjoyed by those who do not like salami. Very good coppa cruda is made on Sardinia.

COPPA PIACENTINA (I): a coppa made throughout the Italian province of Piacenza, but no higher than 900 m above sea level.

DESULO (I): made high in the Sardinian mountains from the local Desulo pig, these salami have big sweet flavours that linger long on the palate.

FELINO (I): made with white wine and notably slim, lean and delicate.

FINOCCHIO (I): indicates fennel seed and particularly good to eat.

HUNGARIAN: fine textured, high

flavour, sometimes flavoured with paprika, hot, sweet and/or smoked.

JESUS DE LYON (F): shortish, fat and in netting, so-called because thought reminiscent of a swaddled Jesus.

LARDO (I): cured slabs of back fat, usually with rosemary, sometimes with other herbs. Eaten sliced thinly or can be used in cooking ideally only half melted. Lardo di Colonatta, a suburb of Cararra, is highly rated; the curing is done in tubs of the famed local marble.

MILANO (I): finely textured and contains garlic.

NAPOLI (I): coarse but aromatic and lightly smoked.

ROSETTE DE LYON (F): Lyon's most famous big saucisson sec, made only with leg meat and coated with coarse black pepper.

SALAMI DI VARZI (I): made between the Po and the Appenines, are coarse meat with fine fat, garlic and red wine; soft texture and sweet taste.

SALAME BRIANZA, SALAME PIACENTINO AND SALAMINI DI CALABRIA: are relatively coarse, mild tasting and of reliable quality.

SWISS: likely to include a style of paprika.

Soft options

A few cured sausages break the rules and are soft and spreadable.

N'DUJA: excoriatingly hot because of the high proportion of roasted red Calabrian chilli peppers. The meat content includes parts of the head and the high fat content contributes to its longevity, as does a degree of smoking. The spreadability lends itself to wide use as a garnish or coating, even as a pizza topping, but the heat easily blitzes other ingredients.

SALAMA DA SUGO: made with finely chopped pork including tongue and liver, spices and red wine since the 14th century, it is put into a skin, and tied with eight lengths of string into a pointy Christmas pudding and then aged 6 to 24 months. Once then boiled for hours it is savoury and slightly acidic, perhaps why the makers suggest it be served with New World mashed potatoes or pumpkin.

SOBRASADA: a spreadable cured sausage from the Balearics but variations like the French *soubressade* are found elsewhere. The texture relies on a high fat content and it is flavoured with paprika. Inevitably a hot version developed, identified by being wrapped in red or red and white string. Eaten like a pâté or spread on local flat breads, it also melts in to stews and sauces.

Smoked dried sausages

CERVELAT: this finely minced salame-like sausage, usually a mixture of beef and pork, is packed into a long gut casing and then smoked a golden brown. The texture and mild flavour are popular with those who are not normally keen on charcuterie.

LANDJAEGER: popular snacks with skiers, these robustly flavoured small sausages usually have a flattened look, as they are pressed between boards for smoking. They should be quite hard and dry and consist mainly of spiced beef. Red wine is incorporated into the mixture too. Excellent with hot wine and with cold beer.

METT(WURST): this can be many things and each area of Germany will have its own, i.e *Braunschweiger Mettwurst, Berliner Mettwurst*, etc. Made from pork and beef, it is air dried then cold-smoked. A very smoky flavour and all can be heated to eat with, say, cabbage. Sometimes made as a spread, too.

SCHINKEN(WURST) OR HAM SAUSAGE: a Westphalian speciality of coarsely chopped or flaked ham, mild and tender. *Schinkenplockwurst* has large pieces of fat but is easy to cut. If the colour is dark this indicates a high beef content, otherwise the meat used for this one is pickled pork.

TEE(WURST): spicy and salmon pink and smooth but available in many variations. *Ruegenwalder Teewurst:* is considered the best and is made only of pork and spare rib bacon. Usually sold in small sizes and is also available as a spread.

Other air-dried meat

BILTONG: created in the early days of European settlement of South Africa by *voortrekkers*, biltong can be made from domestic and game animals, as well as fish, chicken and ostrich. It is first lightly picked in vinegar and spices, especially coriander seed, and then air dried. See *Jerky*.

BRESAOLA (I): *Bresaola della Valtellina* can be made with beef or veal. They should be notably sweet, very hard, very lean and a solid piece. Serve sliced very thinly indeed, often moistened with olive oil and lemon juice. I always thought these translucent, scarlet slithers tasted of meaty soap.

BUNDNERFLEISCH: from the Grisons in Switzerland are made from dry-salted beef.

JERKY: there seems to be no flesh that is not somewhere being turned into jerky, including alligator and earthworms. It originated as *ch'arki* in the ancient civilisations west of the Andes and was simply prepared with only salt or was naturally freeze-dried in high altitudes. Commercial jerky is flavoured and/or smoked in hundreds of ways and commonly has very high sugar and salt content.

Fresh sausages

These are sausages made for immediate use and made from fresh rather than cured meat. Sometimes they are pink when cooked, a result of the addition of saltpetre, a scourging bactericide of ancient use and that adds a characteristic flavour. Many rail against it, but I would rather a bright pink sausage safe to eat than a doubtful grey one. All the sausages in this section must be cooked before eating and so should be sold in transparent casings, the world-wide convention of the trade.

In Britain the fresh sausage is lovingly known as the 'banger', perhaps because badly-filled ones or ones cooked over too high a heat tend to explode. British bangers of all kinds have included bread or cereal as part of their fillings for centuries, for their absorbency kept the fat where it should be, making the sausages juicier, tastier and a greater giver of energy, important for low-income workers. It is thought the Industrial Revolution increased the cereal content to today's high level. The need for cheap filling food for the thousands of labourers who left the country for the city meant traditional sausages were extended with all kinds of farinaceae, but although the contents changed the traditional names did not.

Don't be persuaded by 'all-pork' or 'beef' sausages. The claims might be true at an artisan butcher shop or in some Farmers' Markets, but generally the rules about names refer to that proportion that must be meat, i.e. if a type of sausage is allowed to have 30% filling and only 70% pork meat, and if that 70% is indeed all pork it will legitimately be sold as a 100% pork sausage. Naughty, but not nice.

For a premium and with some effort it is increasingly easier to buy chunky, chewy sausages, and ones with real herbs and spices rather than an infuriating parade of 'flavours' or 'nature-identical' oils that are never natural and rarely identical. It is vital to read the names and labels of sausages more and more carefully and always to think twice about anything called something 'flavour': beef flavour sausages, for instance.

As with ice cream this means they are not the real thing, but have had those dratted flavourings added. The contents are then likely to be a chemical formula rather than recognizable food. However, there is one ingredient you should not denigrate: soy.

Soy protein has the same protein as meat, but is without any fat/cholesterol content and is also very much cheaper. For low-income families sausages extended with soy protein are a thrifty way to get protein into themselves and their children—and the children need the extra calories that any added fat might bring. It's just a shame the good qualities of soy protein are so often sold in mixtures with chemical additives with questionable long-term effects.

That takes me to the question of pricking. Sausages should never be pricked before being cooked 'to let the fat out and stop them bursting'. Instead you should cook them gently so the melting fat is absorbed by the other sausage contents and everything stays tasty and juicy.

The best way by far to cook sausages is at a medium to low heat in an oven: say 170-180°C/325-350°C/gas 3-4 for around 45 minutes. It's the only way they brown evenly and they never ever burst. Best of all is the gorgeous rich smells they make as they bake, and anticipation has always been the greatest spur to culinary enjoyment. If you don't like fat in your sausages, please go away and eat something else.

When you are buying fresh sausages there are a few things to watch for, indicators of better or worse quality. First, the filling should look consistent from one end to the other, so even if it is a very coarse mixture it must be pretty much the same where ever you look, with no unusual clumps of meat or fat. Second, the filling should be evenly packed with no visible air-bubbles and thicker or thinner parts. Colour should also be even, with no patches or smears and the skins should be rather shiny: a dull skin or stickiness could mean it's old and getting dangerous. Last of all, trust your nose: if it smells sour and funny, it is.

Fresh sausages should be cooked within a couple of days of purchasing. If you don't think you can do this, it is best to freeze them. Defrost them fully, using the automatic defrost programme on your microwave before thoroughly cooking them. And last but certainly not least, cooking fresh sausages from raw on a barbecue is asking for trouble, particularly if they have come directly from a refrigerator. The outside might be burned but the inside will be raw or worse, be lukewarm, just right for rapid growth of bacteria.

Sausages for barbecues should always be pre-cooked, by putting them into cold water, bringing them to the boil and simmering until cooked through. Don't do this much in advance but take them directly from the pot to the barbecue. The point of starting them in cold water is the sausages heat up at the same rate as the water does, and so heat and cook through evenly, without bursting or splitting.

Fresh sausages with casings

This class of sausage is called *Rohwurst* in Germany.

AMERICAN BREAKFAST SAUSAGES: smaller and slimmer than British sausages, they also contain much less cereal filler, are more coarsely cut and rather peppery with a distinct herbiness. Some are smoked and these are my favourite, particularly with buckwheat pancakes and maple syrup.

You are just as likely to find this mixture sold as skinless patties, which give much more fat in the pan, the basis for a delicious milk gravy made by stirring in flour to create a simple brown roux and then milk.

BRATWURST: the name means a frying sausage, so a bratwurst can and does contain almost anything and be shaped like a long thin frankfurter or a thick British pork sausage. They should be sold uncooked and thus have a transparent skin. Generally the fillings will be chunky and have nothing but pork, fat and flavourings inside the casing.

Bratwurst are used in many ways: apart from gently frying or oven-baking they can be boiled in water and served with sauerkraut or slapped into bread rolls or bread. I like them better when having been boiled for five minutes or so they are taken from the water, dried and then fried a rich golden brown in butter or bacon fat.

Sometimes bratwurst are sold 'scalded' to give them a longer life in shops and cafés: you can eat them as they are but they are much better if heated through thoroughly, as above.

CHIPOLATA: a small English sausage very popular with children and those with barbecues. The name is derived from *cibolla*, Italian for chives, for they should contain some of this member of the onion family, but I'd be amazed if you found any that did. Cook as you would the basic English sausage.

COTECHINO: an Italian sausage of about 500 g/1 lb. It should be pricked slightly and then cooked in simmering water for several hours. I also like to finish it off by browning it in a little butter or fat. Part of the special flavour of a cotechino is that it will—or should—have been air-cured for up to a month before being sold. It is best served with masses of soft, cheesy polenta or buttery mashed potatoes.

CUMBERLAND: one of the few traditional British sausages that remains and tastes something like it should. Essentially a pork sausage turned into a large coil, it should have a minimum of bread or cereal, be coarsely cut and rather peppery. A Cumberland coil which feeds two or more, should be baked slowly in the oven until golden brown and wallowing wickedly in a pool of excess fat. Its pepperiness and the fat combine marvellously with excellently mashed potatoes and a simple green vegetable like cabbage, which has an affinity with virtually every hot sausage of merit. If herbs are added in it is not a genuine Cumberland, for all it might be delicious.

ENGLISH BEEF: generally a paste of beef and pork with permitted fillers and perhaps a little herby and peppery, sometimes also tomato flavoured. In countries with lax or indifferent food rules they might contain nothing but mutton, fillers, additives and beef 'flavour'.

ENGLISH PORK: there are as many of these as there are manufacturers. Generally made from pork into a paste of varying consistency plus other ingredients to enhance flavour, extend and preserve life. Here and there you do find a butcher who will go to some trouble to achieve a degree of authenticity, i.e., to include detectable amounts of sage and a few pieces of meat to chew upon, even if they are gristly.

I'm afraid we put up with bland sausages simply because we put up with them and that's that. The cost of increasing the texture and enhancing the flavour by including some decent herbs is negligible. Indeed sausages, with taste and texture seem to be a touchstone for better foods everywhere. Farmers' Markets are great hunting grounds for good sausages but many use traditional names with no respect and peddle their incorrect 'twists' instead.

MERGUEZ: thin, very hot pork sausages brought to us from Algeria via France. Nice barbecued or cut up into casseroles, and sometimes sold scalded.

SALSICCIA: the generic Italian term for all sausages, fresh and cured. The best in Italy are thought to be the *salsiccia di Calabria*. Amongst the many variations on a simple theme the best and best-selling (often judged Australia's best sausage) by far, is the fennel sausage, a chunky pork sausage (made with a little white wine I suspect) and a scatter of fennel seeds—*finocchio* will be somewhere in its name. It's a great sausage but even better eaten outside, where the palate always appreciates bigger flavours: the sudden burst of savour when you bite into a fennel seed when chewing already delicious sweet pork enlivens eating no end. As fennel also aids digestion there seems never to be a reason not to have another.

SAUCISSES: French fresh sausages. Saucissons or saucissons secs are air-dried salami.

TOULOUSE: the most famous French fresh sausage. It should have a high meat content and be flavoured with quatre-epices and perhaps white wine. All round the world its contents, size and extra flavourings vary enormously.

ZAMPONE: this Italian sausage is stuffed into the skin of a pig's trotter. If you find it at all it has probably been scalded to lengthen its life, although modern vacuum packing means that pre-cooking is less important. Cook in the same way as cotechino, perhaps slightly longer, to ensure the skin is deliciously gelatinous. It is especially good with hot pulses and potatoes. *Zampone di Modena* is one of the best.

Fresh sausages without casings

Some sausage mixtures are sold without the usual skins. In Britain this is simply called sausage meat and is much used as the base for stuffings or for sausage rolls, good or bad.

Much better is to mix sausage meat with fresh herbs, breadcrumbs, grated lemon rind, some mace, nutmeg and black pepper, and a good slosh of well-flavoured white wine or vermouth, and then bake it in pastry. It makes delicious picnic fare.

CREPINETTES: usually minced pork, but sometimes other meats, seasoned and spiced and wrapped up in a piece of caul fat; thus, they are similar to English faggots, which include offal, pig's liver particularly. Whilst researching my book *Edible France* (Grub Street) I discovered parts of northern Provence make the same thing, but call their faggots ... *gayettes*. Honest.

KEFTETHES: these Greek uncased sausages are more meat patties. Beef or veal is the usual basis and there are always breadcrumbs, onion and the obligatory oregano and mint. They are not the same if they are not cooked in very hot olive oil.

Scalded sausages, smoked and unsmoked

Usually finely minced and sometimes smoked, but always lightly cooked to prolong their life and preserve their texture. This is by far the largest group of sausages, and many are for slicing. They are always in a coloured opaque casing, indicating they do not need cooking before being eaten.

This an area where many traditional

names and style have been ambushed and bastardised without reason, yet awarded. It's increasingly hard to know what is what but this list might help.

BIERWURST: a large, German slicing sausage that does not contain beer, but which is excellent with it. It is always eaten cold and has a peppery flavour.

BIERSCHINKENWURST: is the same thing with small chunks of ham included.

BOCKWURST: a name used generically for most German sausages that are extremely finely ground, like frankfurters and *wieners* and *knackwurst*.

BOILING RING: this Polish sausage, which is usually tied into a horseshoe shape and weighs about 500 g/1 lb is chunky, garlicky pork, sometimes lightly smoked. Reheated in boiling water like the frankfurter, it is invaluable for adding to things in slices, especially cassoulet, bean casseroles, and rugged poultry dishes—see *Kielbasa*.

BOLOGNA: many things to many people. Known in America as *baloney*, and in Australasia as *Devon or luncheon sausage*. It is finely minced pork with a peppery taste, sometimes smoked and usually made in a fattish shape. Quite good sliced and fried but usually eaten in bread rolls or as part of a mixed hors d'ouevre.

CERVELAS: not to be confused with *cervelat*, which is German and a type of salame, this French saucisse is not unlike a shorter, thicker frankfurter, but might contain garlic and is often slightly dried. Reheated like the frankfurter and its family. In Switzerland it is called a *Chlopfer* and served grilled.

CHEERIOS: always referred to as 'little boys' by my mother. These are 'cocktail-length' saveloys or frankfurters, useful for parties. Usually red-skinned, they are sometimes called 'weenies', which also takes us back to mother, I suppose.

CHORIZO: although Spanish by name, this paprika-flavoured sausage is made by a number of countries and is not always scalded, and can also be air-dried. Chorizo can be hard and stubby, or a metre long. Opaque skins mean they are cooked or air-dried and can be eaten as is: chorizo that should be cooked should have a transparent skin. They may be cooked whole or in slices and make an excellent addition either way to dishes of beans, cassoulets and that sort of thing. Some are sweet, some are very hot.

FLEISCHWURST/EXTRAWURST: one of the nicest of the finely ground styles, it is pale, firm but moist, and variations contain garlic, pistachio nuts or pieces of red pepper. Their decorative appearance makes them perfect for *aufchnitz*, a selection of sliced meats—what Americans call cold cuts. The Swiss make excellent sausages of this type.

FRANKFURTERS: these should be made from a paste of fine pork and salted bacon fat and be cold-smoked, which gives a yellowish colour to the skin. The best have a distinct but subtle presence of spice, especially coriander. Often they are made with whatever is to hand and even in Germany such sausages can have lots of fat or none at all.

Frankfurter is now a name for any long thin sausages and in the United States you can buy chicken, turkey, ham or beef frankfurters. Once they get around to making one with fish, that really *will* be a fish finger.

To heat these and other similar sausages, put into cold water and bring slowly to the boil—they will burst if you plunge them into hot water. Sliced frankfurter is delicious in hot or cold potato salad or a salad of cold French beans. A frankfurter is what you should find in a hot dog—except when you find a weiner.

GARLIC SAUSAGE: one of the best-known slicing sausages and made by most European countries. The French ones are usually fairly fat and in an artificial casing; sometimes they include chunks of ham and thus are simply a ham sausage containing garlic.

GYULAI: a Hungarian paprika sausage, that's quite dry and of high quality.

HAM SAUSAGE: the other half, with garlic sausage, of the big two of the slicing sausage world. Chunks of ham in a paste of ground up ham, stablisers etc. If you can find one, the genuine Polish variety is usually a better choice.

JAGERWURST: finely minced veal and pork with a very peppery taste, sometimes with green peppercorns.

KABANOS/KABANOSSI: piquant, smoked, chewy pork sausages that are very thin and very long, 50 cm/20" perhaps. There are two types, the soft and the dried—one is simply older than the other. The soft one makes an excellent snack or, cut into long thick diagonal slices, a good addition to salads. The hard one is popular for chewing but better sliced and cooked, especially in a dish with lots of garlic, tomatoes or beans, or all three: great for meat interest in a tomato-based pasta sauce, or for adding to cooked green lentils. Much better than frankfurters in a potato salad or mixed into a tumble of roasted root vegetables, hot or cold.

KEILBASA: Polish for sausage, and thus for Polish sausage, which usually means a boiling ring. American food writers tend always to use such foreign terms and names as keilbasa, rather than saying Polish sausage.

KNACKWURST: short fat frankfurters, really, usually tied together in strings.

KRAJANA: another Polish one of roasted ham and pork, but without garlic.

KRAKOWSKA: an excellent Polish mixture of ham, pork, beef and garlic with a flavouring of nutmeg—you should be able to see big pieces of flesh. The darker, wrinkled, older and drier version is quite different from the fresher one, but both may be enjoyed sliced and cold or cooked in any way you can conceive.

MAZURSKA: not a dance but music to anyone who is a Polish sausage lover. Like a slightly larger 'banger' in size but filled with chewy pork, garlic and pepper, and smoked. Simply heat in water and serve with buttered cabbage or spiced red cabbage and some good relishes. Perfectly indispensable for cooking in winter dishes but equally wonderful sliced and served cold in summer.

MORTADELLA: the big fat one for slicing. There are many, many, many types and some horrid stories—this really was once made with donkey meat, I believe. The best types should include green pistachios but all have cubes of fat, thus it can be disagreeable if warm. Chilled enough to keep the fat solid, it is nice on fresh crusty bread or in mixed platters, but not memorable.

Strangely, true mortadella is considered a cooked salame, for cured meats are used; bologna is said to have been invented as a simpler and, to American eyes, safer substitute. The best will be *Mortadella Bologna* which will have a minimum of 15% fat.

MYSLIEWSKA: a dry short sausage of pork that is heated in water like a frankfurter. Coarse and chewy and quite peppery, but I prefer the mazurska.

SAUCISSON: confusingly, the Swiss name for a delicious smoked sausage containing ham, brandy, leeks and paprika. Served hot.

SAVELOYS: a corruption of the French *cervelas* as far as etymology goes, and a corruption of most other things as far as the product generally goes. They should be made from finely minced pork and, like a fat frankfurter, should also be cold-smoked, but often the smoke is an artificial added flavour and modern red food colourings will be too fluorescent. Rarely made with any quality these days, but keep asking and they might be.

SCHUBLIG: a lightly smoked, fine Swiss sausage with a thick skin. Served hot.

TUCHOWSKA: a slender Polish sausage of pork plus beef and a little garlic, coarse but solid and smoked. Excellent cold but can be sliced into casseroles. Slightly wetter and fatter than wieska.

WEINERWURST: first cousin, if not brother, to the frankfurter, but often shorter in length. The *real* 'little boys' and hence weenies, etc.

WEISSWURST: varying in size but always *very* white and firm and sometimes sold as white bratwurst. They should be made of young, pallid-fleshed veal, perhaps with some chicken, and often include parsley. Like bratwurst they are especially good if they are first heated in water and then browned in fat or butter. They should be light, delicate and taste of veal rather than any additives, a common failing. A little gentle French mustard is all they need as an accompaniment. The Wolseley on London's Piccadilly serves them with mashed potatoes and butter-fried apple segments, and there are said to be people who have two servings, instead of one serve and a pudding.

WIESKA: one of the basic Polish sausages, and which can be eaten sliced and cold, boiled, grilled or stewed or as an ingredient in stews and casseroles. It has a full flavour and coarse-textured mix of pork and beef with a touch of garlic.

Cooked or boiled sausages

These nearly always include offal or blood and so these, the German

Kochwurst, are steam-cooked in their casings. There is considerable crossover with the previous category.

BLACK PUDDING/BLUTWURST/BOUDIN NOIR: based on blood thickened with cereals like barley or oatmeal and often with cubes of back fat and onion flavouring. Made in many qualities and sizes, black pudding is usually sliced and fried to serve hot, especially for breakfast. Some skin it, some don't. *Blutwurst* is very firm and comes in natural casings.

French *boudins noirs* are often more delicate, containing cream and spices. Taken from their skin and mixed with grated apple, perhaps some good sausage meat and a lively dash of Calvados, *boudins noirs* makes an imaginative stuffing for a chicken or turkey, slid between the skin and the breast.

BRAWN: made properly, with lots of pepper and *big* pieces of meat, brawn can be the most delicious of charcuterie treats. It should be made from the many contrasting meats of a well-boiled pig's head set in aspic from its own cooking. English brawn stops there but continentals tend to put the whole lot into a gut, or even a stomach—the Poles do this. Brawn is much better if served slightly chilled with a sharpish accompaniment, like a vinaigrette sauce, pickled cucumber, gherkins and olives.

FLEISCH KAISE: a Swiss meatloaf with a small proportion of liver.

FROMAGE DE TETE: French for brawn.

HASLET: this is particularly English, a sort of meat loaf made only from offal and which should be cooked in a lace of caul fat, not often available and not often worth eating. But it could be. Eaten cold or hot in slices.

HEAD CHEESE: another name for brawn.

KASHANKA: a firm Polish blood sausage usually in a natural casing.

KALBSLEBERWURST: smooth rich calves' liver sausage, usually the best tasting of any liver sausages.

LEBERKAS: a speciality of Bavaria, but not often special, for it is a baked meat loaf with a high liver content—and meat loaf is nearly always awful unless you make it yourself. Thinly sliced and grilled or fried it can be fine in Bavaria, but those found elsewhere are often crammed with filler and preservative.

LIVER SAUSAGE/LEBERWURST: the price and quality depend both on the amount of liver included and the type of liver used. Generally, such sausages are made with pork liver and pork meat. Some are firm enough to slice and are wrapped in fine fat, others are meant to be spread and these are often gratifyingly rich in flavour. There are variations also in the texture of the mixture and the inclusion of spices, onion and so on. None is usually heated before use, but if they are rich and full flavoured some of the slicing liver sausages could be fried or grilled or heated on toast as an accompaniment to game. See *Kalbsleberwurst*.

ROTWURST: a spicy coarse German blood pudding.

SULZWURST: German for brawn.

TONGUE SAUSAGE: one of the best-looking sausages for making arrangements of *aufschnitz* or cold cuts, because it features big pink cubes of tongue.

WHITE PUDDING: much the same as black pudding but without the blood, so largely fat and oatmeal or barley and sometimes with pork too.

ZUNGENWURST: a superior blood sausage in which whole pieces of tongue are suspended. It looks better than it tastes but no-one seems to mind.

Types of bacon

BACON, DRY CURED: dry-cured bacon is the name for traditionally cured bacons made by rubbing salt into the raw flesh of belly or loin of pork, rather than soaking it in a brine bath. The results are noticeably more tender, sweeter and tastier, and this is getting better as we reintroduce heritage and free-range pigs. When cooked there is no white curd or exhudate in the pan, and the rind goes a golden crispness rather than a brown toughness. The cooking smell is cleaner and clearer and richer, the real smell of real bacon: be sure you keep the extra fat for frying eggs or potatoes or tomatoes or bread—or anything.

In some areas, bacon is almost always sold smoked, yet unsmoked bacon, known in the UK as green bacon, is a far more useful and delicious and direct flavour altogether. If you are starting a journey of discovering better foods, there can be no better place to start than with green, dry-cured bacon.

BOZCEK: is Polish and is lean belly of pork, salted, smoked or unsmoked, cooked or uncooked. The cooked, smoked bozcek is delicious sliced and eaten with mustard and can also be fried or grilled. The raw bozceks are my favourite way to get a smoky bacon flavour into any dish, from pâté to casseroles.

KASSLER: the eye of the loin, salted, very lightly smoked and cooked. Cut thin or thick it is succulent and delicious in sandwiches, salads or *aufschnitz*. It can be sliced and grilled or fried, and makes the most superior and attractive ham for ham and eggs. My friend Nicholas Scott in Melbourne, who has cooked for three duchesses, ('only two of them were royal') roasts kassler whole, to slice at table, a wondrous way to enjoy a pork roast quickly without the fuss, the fat and the leftovers. Take the trouble to serve something especially fruity: lightly spiced cherry compote, de-seeded kumquats poached in orange juice, crab apples in cider or very good *mostarda di frutta* q.v., and the best possible baby potatoes boiled whole.

PANCETTA: the same pork-belly cut that gives us streaky bacon but the Italian brine is flavoured with such herbs and spices as nutmeg, fennel seeds, pepper and garlic and the result air-dried for up to four months. I've even known one that included dark rum in the cure and that was exceptionally good.

Pancetta is regularly specified instead of bacon in American recipes; but it is only worth paying the extra money if you are using enough to appreciate the flavour. A few slices or chunks in a large stew are pretentious: quite a lot in a simple pasta dish is ambrosial. However, once I discovered you can and should also eat pancetta in its uncooked state, this opened a spectacular new world, for here you really appreciate its subtle extra flavouring. I know the idea of raw bacon sounds worrying but it's more than bacon because of the air-drying: bacon is never air-dried.

Pancetta was traditionally cured between boards, *pancetta tesa*, which gives an old-time shape to the slices: as markets for traditional cured products ever expand the flattened version is seen more and more. One version is rather heavily covered with dried rosemary and another made in Sardinia from the Desulo pig is coated in black pepper. There are cheaper pancetti, made by faster, less traditional methods and in my experience these are also very good, and here and there you will find them made with wild pig—usually called wild boar, incorrectly.

Arrotolata: a whole rolled side for slicing.

de Calabria: easily spotted because the skin is red with chilli pepper, and made only in Calabria from piglets four months old.

Magretta: almost totally fat free, seemingly a contradiction in terms for bacon.

Piacentina: is rolled into a cylinder weighing between 5 and 8 kg. It is noted for a characteristic sweet spiciness and a good aftertaste.

Serve pancetta in see-through slices instead of more expensive air-dried Italian prosciutti—with fresh figs or melon, with dark-red plums or perfumed white peaches. When pancetta is wrapped around a chilled lychee or rambutan, the world seems to stand still.

PASTRAMI: salted, spiced and smoked brisket of beef. Firm of texture and covered with black pepper and other spices, it should be sliced extremely thinly and served cold or hot, especially in sandwiches—who hasn't heard of pastrami on rye? When you are planning a cold buffet, the bite of pastrami can be welcome relief amidst the sweetness of ham, chicken and turkey.

PORCHETTA: properly, this is a whole, boned suckling pig, rolled with a stuffing of pork mince, herbs, fruit, nuts and sweet wine. Probably originating around Rome, it is commonly found in markets, major delicatessens and festivals throughout Italy, where it is served cold in thin slices between bread. Domestically it can be made from pork loin with the belly attached. At that size it can be served hot as a centrepiece—there will be plenty of left overs for sandwiches.

SOPOCKA: a smaller Polish version of kassler that gives elegant oval slices.

SPECK: German bacon, of which there are many varieties. The most unusual is simply salted back fat: sometimes this is smoked, or as *Ziguener Speck*, it is coated in paprika. Thinly sliced or cubed, it can be used to add richness to cooking, for rendering or to make crisp lardons. The paprika speck is eaten as is, very thinly sliced, an interesting experience. Two very superior Italian versions are *Speck dell'Alto Adige* and *Valle d'Aosta Lard d'Arnad*.

Chocolate

NEED TO KNOW

Chocolate is native to Central and South America and was brought to Europe by Columbus and Cortes.

Only English speakers say cocoa instead of the correct cacao.

Cacao/cocoa butter is the only fat that melts immediately at body temperature, thus its instant mouth appeal.

Chocolate that melts slowly in the mouth contains little cacao butter or uses substitutes.

Reduce over indulgence by freezing small portions that then melt slowly in the mouth, extending the pleasure.

Per cent numbers on packaging mean the content by weight of cocoa solids.

The higher the cocoa solid content, the deeper, richer and more bitter the taste and flavours.

High cocoa-solid content does not automatically mean low sugar or low sweetness.

Chocolate's theobromine does elicit feelings of being in love.

Too much theobromine causes chocolate poisoning, especially in the elderly, and is very dangerous for dogs but less so for cats.

100 g/4 oz bar of high-cocoa solids is about 95 mgs of caffeine: a double-shot espresso is about 80 mgs but cafetière-brewed coffee might have 50% more.

Quality chocolate is a profound brown; redness is a good sign.

Quality chocolate should be very shiny and make a distinct cracking sound when snapped and first bitten; the broken surface should look like bark.

Dull-looking chocolate means low-quality fat content, poor manufacturing or poor storage/old age.

Carob is a chocolate substitute made from locust beans and is always sweet and like milk chocolate.

White chocolate is not true chocolate as it contains no cocoa solids but is solely cocoa butter/fat with milk and sugar; it is always sweet.

Chocolate was a drink until the mid-1800s and gritty, greasy and floury.

Love-rat Casanova thought it more invigorating than champagne.

In 1569 Pope Pius V refused to ban chocolate as a Lenten drink because he thought it too disgusting to drink at any time.

Dutchman Van Houten first separated cocoa solids and butter in 1828.

In 1848, Joseph Fry of Bristol invented smooth eating chocolate by mixing a lesser amount of cocoa butter into cocoa solids.

When short of chocolate in baking, replace each 25 g/1 oz with at least 3 tablespoons cocoa powder to 1 tablespoon butter.

Line pre-baked, tart cases with melted chocolate to stop moisture problems.

Dust tins for chocolate cakes, muffins or brownies with cocoa rather than flour; no more white patches.

C hocolate's origin is the seeds of multi-coloured pods that grow direct from the trunk of cacao trees. The ridged pods grow up to 25 cm/10 inch long and turn from green to yellow through purples and reds to a russet brown. Two pods are rarely the same colour on a tree, giving a surreal nursery-rhyme look to cacao plantations.

Inside the pod is a mass of sticky white beans and the precise flavour a bean gives is a combination of its essential characteristics, plus *terroir*, the effects of soil and climate, and whether harvested early or late and the method of fermentation and drying.

Use these to identify affinities to use in eating or baking: rose, lime, passionfruit, coffee, black pepper, mango, coconut, orange, chillies. Almost nothing that's a treat can't be made more so with chocolate. Chocolate cakes, muffins, fairy cakes, butterfly cakes, lamingtons, chocolate sauces, chocolate ice creams, mousses—but why leave it there? Opportunities to combine chocolate with other flavours should never be avoided.

And with wine or spirits? Absolutely, matching the weight of the wine with that of the chocolate, thus, fortified wines like Pedro Ximenez sherry or Madeiras, Muscatels including Australia's Liqueur Muscatel, or a rich Tokay. Try the red-berry flavours of trinitario-based chocolates with Beaujolais and young fruity Burgundies, a Shiraz or Hermitage with pronounced fruit and black pepper on the palate with high cocoa solids, a gutsy tropical-fruit tasting gewürztraminer with milk chocolate.

As you go, you might also find over-roasting, inferior or artificial ingredients, super-sweetness and poor manufacturing.

Who makes the best chocolate? Which variety is best? What's the ideal cocoa-solids content or sugar level? The answers are thrilling. You will know only by eating as much as possible.

Types of chocolate pods

Although there are very few varieties of cacao tree, and most flavour variations are the result of *terroir* and processing, trees can also produce rare local sports and variations, such as Venezuela's *chuao* and *porcelana*, both considered to produce exceptional chocolate.

CRIOLLO: this is the aristocrat, appropriately compared to the chardonnay grape, which gives us Champagne and Chablis. It now grows particularly well around the Indian Ocean, giving spicy, floral notes, welcome acidity and a long-lasting aftertaste, the criollo's particular contribution to fine chocolate.

FORASTERO: 95% of the world's cacao trees. It is high yielding, with beans giving immediate mouth flavour and sensation, but that are generally coarse and un-distinguished. Like poor quality coffee, forastero tends to be roasted very high to disguise its shortcomings.

African grown forastero beans tend to be spicy and acidic; Indian-Ocean beans are fruitier yet notably bitter; Ecuadorian beans give a soft, floral and clear chocolate, with overtones of orange blossom. And so on. There are rare forastero-based chocolates of elegance, usually from South America, evidence of singular *terroir* characteristics, high-quality decisions and superior processing.

TRINITARIO: combines the best of the forastero and the criollo, yielding a concentrated essence of the syrupy pleasures of dried fruit balanced by floral woodiness and good acidity, often reminiscent of fresh tobacco. Importantly, it gives a lingering after taste, multiplying the most attractive skill of the criollo.

NACIONAL: considered the oldest pure variety, those in Peru and Ecuador produced the finest chocolates in the 18th century. Thought to be extinct because of introduced disease and hybridisation, a very few pure trees have been discovered and are being multiplied.

How chocolate is made

FERMENTING: the pods are split and the sticky white beans, or seeds, are left two to nine days to ferment, which diminishes bitterness, develops the fat content and turns them brown.

ROASTING: the beans are roasted, which dries their outer skin and develops flavour. Like coffee, the higher the quality, the lower the roasting level.

PROCESSING: the beans are coarsely crushed to form cocoa nibs or they are ground into a paste with some heat, allowing the cocoa butter (fat) to be removed under pressure, leaving a paste called chocolate liquor, which sets on cooling, and is basic, unsweetened chocolate.

REFINING: milling continues the reduction of cacao particles by grinding, so they are each less than 2 micrograms, too small to be detected by the human tongue.

PRESSING: the liquor might be further pressed, which results in cocoa powder. Or it can be reblended with cocoa butter, sugar and flavouring, including dried milk powder for milk chocolate. CONCHING: slow whipping further ensures the natural gritty texture of chocolate is slowly transformed into velvet smoothness but this will still be rather matte in appearance and white blotches can appear. This 'raw' chocolate is what you might buy in a Mexican or other market. To make modern chocolate, tempering is required. TEMPERING: this complicated procedure first warms the liquor to 45–50°C, then reduces it to 28°C and then takes it up to 31°C, all with constant stirring.

Eventually, the feral crystalline structure of chocolate is tamed and forms only the tiniest of crystals. These give the fabulous shine and crisp crack when you snap it, the fake-proof sign of great chocolate.

Types of chocolate

BAKER'S CHOCOLATE: Baker's is a trade name in the United States and thus is not a standard or type of chocolate. BAKING 'CHOCOLATE': the general term for chocolate substitutes, made from vegetable fats and simulated chocolate flavourings, and thus should not really use the word chocolate. CACAO/COCOA BEANS: an A1 gourmet ingredient to have in your cupboard. When sold ready crushed they are called nibs. Roasted cacao beans have a thrilling taste with undisguised feral, jungle notes that take the palate and mind to places they don't expect and there is always natural bitterness. Their spiciness tells you that cinnamon would enhance the flavour enormously, as do other sweet spices. Vanilla is *de rigueur*.

Coarsely grated or chopped they transform chili-style dishes and Bolognese-type sauces and can also be grated and scraped into puddings, desserts, ice creams etc. or over them as a garnish. Good to find in brownies, they transport tiramisu and chocolate icings.

The high fat-content means they are likely to rancidify, so keep them refrigerated or frozen. Also sold unroasted as raw cacao beans, but these are much less useful. CHOCOLATE NIBS: chopped, roasted cacao beans, used as above. COCOA POWDER: the solid content of the cacao bean separated from its fat or butter. It is still about 20% fat by weight, negligible in the amounts used. There are two types, straight forward cocoa powder which is the most common in Britain, and 'dutch' or 'dutched' cocoa, favoured in the US and by the bakers of both.

Standard cocoa: a truer more natural flavour and with characteristic astringency. It is harder to mix into liquids and mixtures but gives unquestionably richer flavours to baking, darker colour and bigger, broader flavour in drinks.
Dutched cocoa: looks darker but smells and tastes earthier and often starts with a bean that is high quality. It has more fat content and tastes marginally less of chocolate. It is especially good for baking and for milk-based cooking or drinks, as it dissolves rapidly in milk and quickly

blends with cake or biscuit mixes. Dutch or dutched might not be used on the label but 'alkali' or 'alkalised' means the same thing. A quick web search will show you which brands are available where you live.

COOKING CHOCOLATE: this is any chocolate with which you decide to cook, because all can be used according to your palate's preferences. In older cookery books, and to unsophisticated palates, cooking chocolate means a bitter, high-cocoa solid chocolate now seen as a gourmet ideal. Some, like the classic Chocolate Menier were also quite sweet, a combination seen less often.

COUVERTURE: a type of chocolate with a very high cocoa-fat content, especially suited to professional and catering use because it melts and covers easily. Couverture varies in cocoa-solid content but this is generally high and so, with its high cocoa-fat also, it is expensive and usually available only in big catering-style weights. Couverture has been conched, but to give professional sparkle and snap it must be tempered, another reason why it is usually sold only to the trade.

Chocolate-'flavour' couvertures based on vegetable-fat *attempt* to do the same thing cheaply for the consumer market, but shouldn't.

DRINKING CHOCOLATE: originally made in Europe by pouring hot water onto compressed chocolate pastilles—see *Mexican chocolate*. The result had a sandy texture and cocoa-fat continuously separated and rose, so had continuously to be stirred to keep it emulsified, which is why chocolate cups had holes for spoons in the lid. Once eating chocolate had been perfected, mixing this with hot water or milk gave a smooth and infinitely more voluptuous and exciting drink. See *Hot chocolate*.

'Drinking chocolate' made of cocoa powder, milk powder and mountains of sugar, should be called something else.

EATING CHOCOLATE: all chocolate can be eaten. This description is a hangover from the days when only sweetened chocolate bars and elaborately filled chocolates were considered the thing, and high cocoa-solids chocolate was 'cooking' chocolate. Like cooking chocolate, it is a term that should be dropped.

GANACHE: chocolate is melted together with cream, in varying proportions according to its end use. More cream keeps it mellifluous on the tongue, less cream gives it more body, for use as a superior icing for instance, that will harden on the outside, stay luxuriant inside, as when used for chocolate truffles.

Ganache may be flavoured with anything *concentrated*, from vanilla extract to any spirit or liqueur, crystallised fruit, toasted nuts, alcohol plumped vine fruit or infusions of herbs and spices. It is ideal for piping or spreading into or onto meringues, cakes and biscuits, stuffing with nuts, stuffing into prunes or dried figs.

Watch out for water-based ganache perfected by Aneesh Popat of The Chocolatier, a big step up for those who want to reduce calories; I find it difficult to tell the difference.

GIANDUJA: the classic, combination of hazelnuts and chocolate. Once made only with dark chocolate but now more commonly with milk chocolate; much improved if the new style of high cocoa-solids milk chocolate is used.

Check the sell-by-date because hazelnuts get bored with perfection, and go rancid after a few months.

HOT CHOCOLATE: add water or milk to good plain, flavoured or milk chocolate and make a delicious hot drink without the fattiness, grittiness and flouriness our ancestors would recognise. There are good chocolate powders too, but these are often very sweet, too sweet, and it's a matter of perseverance and cost to find your ideal.

Some South American drinking chocolate has no added ingredients but high-quality European styles can include pistachios, cardamom, saffron and 23-carat gold in one variety, marshmallows or salted caramel in others.

The texture of drinking chocolate should always be improved by whisking vigorously just before serving. In Mexico they use a special wooden whisk, the *molinillo*, but a wire whisk or an old-fashioned rotary egg beater does as well.

Beware of 'flavoured' hot chocolate drinks: the chocolate will be genuine but very little else will be, unless you add in genuine vanilla, ground cinnamon, rum, Cointreau and such.

MEXICAN CHOCOLATE: Mexicans make this by rolling roasted cacao beans, crushing them and melting the cacao butter simultaneously. Something non-porous is used because wood or marble soak up the fat.

The sacred trinity of cinnamon, vanilla and sugar—and sometimes ground almonds, too—is added and the mixture is shaped and cooled and set. The result is like the pastilles of chocolate sold in Europe for centuries as the base of hot chocolate drinks. It is fatty and slightly gritty because the crystals of chocolate have not been pressed, conched and tempered. Better for eating than for making hot drinks.

MILK CHOCOLATE: chocolate to which has been added concentrated or dried milk, which give an unavoidable caramelised flavour, mainly in the UK and USA.

Milk chocolate made by European or South American companies seems cleaner and smoother even though it has fewer cocoa solids and less milk; perhaps the effect is because it also contains higher amounts of sugar.

Milk chocolate is difficult to use successfully in cookery because its flavour is already diluted and sweetened, but this doesn't stop the serving of pallid, sticky, sickly and bland objects in cafés and sweet shops around the world. It's also common for some or much of the cocoa butter to be replaced by fats made from hydrogenated or part-hydrogenated palm kernel or coconut oil.

The great news is that artisan producers are increasingly offering milk chocolate with high cocoa-solids content, and this will change the mind of many milk-chocolate haters. These are delicious and open up new fields of flavour in cooking and patisserie.

RUBY CHOCOLATE: introduced only in 2017, ruby chocolate is grown and made by a patented system for Barry Callebaut. Broad opinion is that it sits between milk chocolate and white chocolate and so is aimed at those who prefer blander, sweeter flavours.

TRUFFLES: chocolate truffles are shaped ganache and should look like free-form, rough, real truffles straight from the ground but are inevitably moulded into balls and other non-truffle shapes.

WHITE CHOCOLATE: white chocolate is cocoa butter, plus sugar and milk. It can be elegant and clean to eat but mass-market white chocolate is usually claggy in texture and overly sweet. It's likely that some of the expensive cocoa butter has been replaced by substitutes, based on hydrogenated or part hydrogenated oils. Read the label.

What else is in chocolate?

COCOA BUTTER SUBSTITUTES: cocoa butter is solid at 33°C but molten at 34°C and thus should melt in just a few seconds if held in the mouth or palm. Substitutes melt more slowly and are commonly hydrogenated or part hydrogenated oils. These are commonly used in milk chocolates.

FLAVOURING/'NATURAL FLAVOURS': these should never be seen in expensive chocolate products, unless the flavour is so arcane or too expensive to use naturally. These platforms of the food industry are brilliant chemical constructions, often calling themselves 'nature identical' but they are at best approximations and rarely include the many minor flavourings that occur naturally in Nature.

LECITHIN: this natural emulsifier is widely used to enhance shelf life but is rarely found in products at the top end of the market. You will be surprised to discover how many brands of self-annointed grandeur and expense contain it, as well as indefensible added 'flavours/flavors'.

SUGAR: cheaper chocolates are always sweeter chocolates, because sugar is so much cheaper weight for weight. The higher the quality of the cacao/cocoa-solid content, the richer the flavour and the less sugar will have been used, or should have been used. The less sugar there is, the more the quality of the basic beans is revealed.

VANILLA EXTRACT: this is the most expensive addition to chocolate, generally four times costlier than cocoa solids. Its origins as an orchid in South American jungles gives it a natural, *terroir*-based affinity with the cacao bean.

VANILLIN: an artificial, synthetic approximation of vanilla for flavouring: the use of vanillin and high sugar content are usually indicators of low-grade cocoa solids, both used to reduce cost at the expense of quality. These days, many palates prefer vanillin in blind-tastings.

SUGAR AND MILK PRODUCTS: these are the cheapest ingredients in chocolate and, as contents must be listed in descending order of volume, you never want to see these preceding the cocoa-solids count.

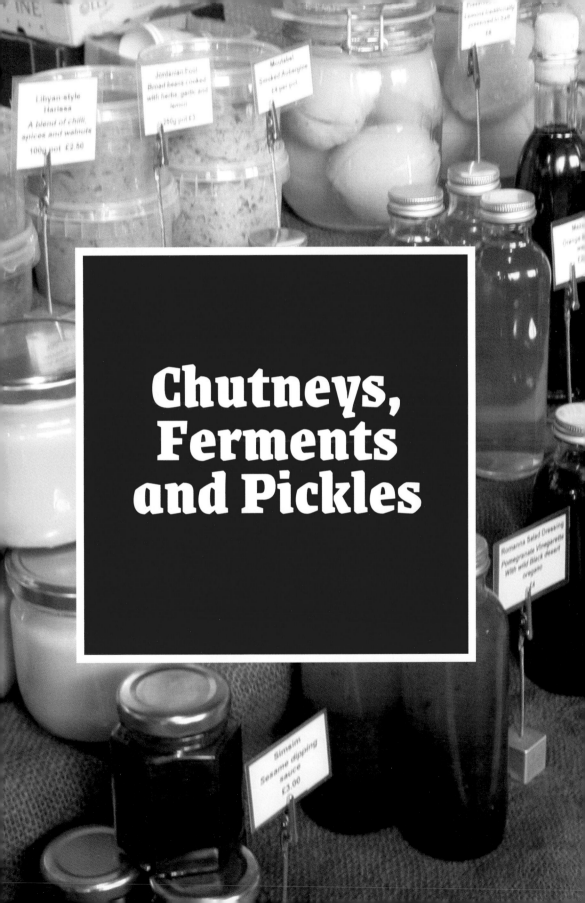

Chutneys, Ferments and Pickles

NEED TO KNOW

*A pickle can mean any vegetable pre-
served in acid or salt with little or no
sugar.*

*A chutney is usually based on fruit and
contains sugar.*

*Indian chutneys are often herb based and
can be fresh and uncooked.*

*The US particularly enjoys sweet pickles, a
compound style, i.e. strawberries in sweet
vinegar.*

*Modern culinary-style pickles fresh fruit
or vegetables by soaking in vinegar only a
short while.*

*Ferments mean vegetables preserved by
lactic acid.*

*Vegetables can be pickled without lactic
fermentation in a 15% brine solution.*

*Some vegetables need both salt and
vinegar to control their unique micro-organisms.*

*Onions are pickled in hot vinegar; add
vegetables and you get spreadable pickles;
add fruit and sugar and you have chutneys.*

*Make chutneys smooth and you have
sauces, and ketchups.*

Chutneys

Chutneys are condiments but Indians
would not recognise most Western
chutneys, even though the word came
from there. There they are usually
freshly made and the best I tasted was
in Mauritius, a whizzed-up mix of coriander leaf, garlic and coconut with a
tiny amount of chilli and fresh ginger.

Western chutneys are spiced and
often hot, too. Based on fruits, they
always contain both vinegar and sugar
and are often quite coarse in texture.
Sometimes the major fruit has been
brined separately, and then added to
the base sauce at the end of the cooking process. Mango chutney is the best
known, but peach is very good, too.

Chutneys mix well with mayonnaise,
and a whole bottle makes an instant

reliably aromatic and intriguing base
for braising.

Ferments

This is an ancient preservative method
that uses interaction with naturally
occurring sugars on vegetable skin.
Lactic fermentation works when very
fresh vegetables are put into 8–11%
brine: putrefying bacteria are inhibited
but sugars ferment to make lactic acid,
a mild preservative. After or during fermentation a replacement 15% brine
stops fermentation or putrefaction.

Other fermented foods include milk
as in kefir and kombucha, and a sweetened tea, but they use a mixture of
yeast and bacterial cultures.

Pickles

A broad term because olives, onion, piccalilli, beetroot and cucumber can all be called pickles. Mixed pickles vary from the delicious Italian examples of crisp mixed vegetables in a light, vinegary brine, which are excellent as hors d'oeuvres, to the Oriental bottles of lime pickle, mango pickle, and so on.

Fruit pickles sound wrong but are especially good when right, particularly cherries, strawberries, peaches, apples or plums, all of which might have plenty of sugar, too.

Types of pickle and ferments

BEETROOT: bottles or cans of small pickled beetroots are very useful, cold as a salad garnish or hot as a vegetable. Drained and heated in orange juice and butter, with a little lemon for accent, they become quite special. Excellent in sour cream spiked with horseradish, with garlic, with parsley, with paprika or in any combination of those.

CAT-TAILS: when bigger they are bullrushes, which can be boiled and eaten with butter. When young tops are barely 14 cm/5″ long and no thicker than a small finger they can also be eaten, or pickled. Their flavour is rather green and feral, somewhat like asparagus and artichoke. Find pickled cat-tails in speciality food shops in Montreal.

GHERKINS: what the French call cornichons. A very determined flavour, commonly made from baby cucumbers but real gherkins are different, a relation that's native to the Caribbean. Must be kept covered with liquid or they discolour and soften. Integral to hamburgers, for some.

CAPERS: the un-opened flowers of a Mediterranean creeper. They are not lactic fermented but put into jars of vinegar brine, which preserves by the joint action of acetic acid and salt. Capers should be the dominating ingredient in *tapenade* q.v.

Two things to be certain about—you should never buy cheap capers, and they must be covered with liquid, sauces or a dressing until the moment you eat them, for they quickly develop a taste that makes goats positively fragrant. Then, there's great enjoyment when the mini-balloons explode in sauces, sandwiches or with fish and smoked foods, especially ham, fish and hot-smoked salmon.

Caper berries: with their slender shape and curved stems they look like olives that have done well for themselves. They offer a challenging culinary experience with their tough skin and seeds that have a raw woody flavour. Aimed, I suspect, at those who buy anything new.

Salted capers: considered to have better flavour than vinegar-brined ones. Rinse and then soak for a short time, some say in milk. Soak too long and you dilute the caper flavour.

CUCUMBERS: cucumbers are easily

lactic-fermented because their fresh skins have plenty of *lactobacillus* bacteria on them, so they quickly ferment and become sharper and more acidic.

All types are first fermented slowly in a cool temperature, except for New Green cucumbers, which ferment quickly in a warm temperature. Then they are put into another brine, which might be flavoured.

With no vinegar in the brine a white film or crust can form on the top but this is harmless and can be removed as it forms, otherwise slices of lemon control it.

Traditionally, pickled cucumbers are sliced diagonally or lengthwise and eaten as a relish. Very good with salt beef, as you know, but any hot or cold smoked meat or sausage is transported into a better part of heaven by the addition of crisp slices of pickled cucumber. I particularly like dill cucumber with smoked fish, especially hot-smoked salmon.

Bread and Butter pickles: these are sold sliced and have sugar added.
Dill cucumbers: taking up to three months for the initial curing, these rely heavily for flavour on fresh fronds of dill, but the brines can also contain peppercorns, red pepper/ capsicum and garlic, bay, parsley or horseradish. Grape, blackcurrant, oak and cherry leaves can also be found in the bottle.
Kosher pickles: a particularly New York name for dill cucumbers, where they might be fully cured or half cured, when they will be crisper and greener.
New Green cucumbers: not lactic-fermented but lightly salted and ready to eat in a few days. They should be eaten quickly as well as being stored in a very cool or refrigerated environment; if they are not kept cool they soften and then lose colour flavour and texture.
Salt cucumbers: the simplest, and after fermentation are put into a plain brine.
Sweet and sour cucumbers: have extra flavour added to them by mixing vinegar or acetic acid into the second brine. A variety of other herbs and spices might also be included.

KIMCHI: a Korean family of over 100 different fermented vegetable pickles eaten as a side dish, a wrap and as a condiment. The most popular in the West is cabbage kimchi and the Korean version is identified by inclusion of fish sauce or dried shrimps, giving a characteristic smell and taste. Since the 16th century kimchi has included chillies, sometimes in fiery amounts, but this is not essential. Ginger root, daikon radish, carrot, garlic, herbs and spices might also be added.

Kimchi is one of the few fermented foods to have proven to have nutritional benefits. The high content of the umami taste is associated with an enhanced feeling of well-being but is really caused by high chilli content that creates serotonins to compensate for the burning of the palate, an opiate-like effect which is truly addictive. These two effects explain verifiable stories of Korean soldiers refusing to serve unless guaranteed supplies of kimchi.

MOSTARDA DI FRUTTA: an extraordinary Italian condiment that puts sugar-preserved/candied fruits into a syrup brightened with nose-attacking mustard oil. That from Cremona uses mixed fruit and is the best known, but elsewhere only green apples and quince are used. Typically served with boiled fatty meats like *bollito misto* or trotters, but goes with anything fatty, especially cheeses and much charcuterie.

MUSTARD PICKLE: what the Americans call piccalilli.

ONIONS: to me onions in every form represent the worst of British cooking, onions with everything, often raw. Next is vinegar on chips.

Not every sauce or stew or soup needs onion as a base. Cheddar cheese, caviar and tomatoes, among other things, are far nicer if they are not massacred by the acidic sharpness of raw onion, which then stays on the palate to disfigure the taste of your wine or pudding.

Pickled onions are worse. Eat them if you like, but don't mix them with fine food or wine—and keep your distance.

PICCALILLI: a law unto itself. First the vegetable content should be crisp, and so are lactic-fermented or brined rather than being boiled in the sauce. The sauce is made from onions, garlic, spices, vinegar and, of course, mustard, according to each manufacturer's specific recipe, and then thickened with cornflour. The usual vegetables added to the sauce are silverskin onions, gherkins and cauliflower florets. The yellow colour is turmeric but commercial manufacturers might use colouring, because turmeric fades in sunlight.

RED CABBAGE: with or without apple, this is a very cheap canned vegetable that goes a magically long way. Always cured on the day it is gathered, pickled red cabbage can stand a lot of cooking—allowing you to improve it at home so it tastes homemade.

Sliced or chopped apple, bacon and spiced vinegar make the best improving combination. Garlic and orange juice with both hot and sweet paprika is another wonderful combination; so is garlic and juniper berries and gin, but only stir in the latter as you are serving for it is distressingly fugitive when heated. A touch of molasses gives colour and body.

Red cabbage is first choice with any hearty meal, especially for game or fatty continental sausages.

SAMPHIRE/SALICORNE: see under *Herbs.*

SAUERKRAUT: the truth about sauerkraut is no less astonishing than that about soft roe (sperm) or salami (uncooked meat). It is made the same way a farmer makes silage for his cattle; indeed the smell can be distressingly similar.

Sauerkraut is white cabbage that has been subjected to lactic fermentation but it is rarely drained and re-brined. The sauerkraut you buy in tins is very good but has been cooked. If you buy sauerkraut uncooked you can eat it as it is, but it's more usual to drain and rinse it and then to flavour it with bacon, onion, garlic, apple, caraway or wine—even champagne. You then cook it for up to an hour; it should not be mushy but have absorbed the cooking liquid you have used, which should have equalled half the original volume of the sauerkraut.

Cooked together or separately, sauerkraut and rugged pork sausages, bacon or starchy vegetables all belong to one another.

Choucroute: is the name in France and the dish that cooks it with other ingredients has the same name. They are more filling and richer than expected and in Cognac I ate a version into which champagne really was poured. I had a conscience about doing that to champagne but no conscience about serving sauerkraut with a mix of smoked fish, especially hot-smoked salmon, for a major birthday. It was so good and colourful my guests forgot to ask my age.

WALNUTS: picking the young green walnuts for pickling is dangerous work as walnut trees have extremely brittle branches and each nut must be picked individually, unlike ripe walnuts, which are shaken from the tree. The green walnuts are trimmed before being pickled, typically in malt vinegar, but around Christmas time you may find them packed in such luxuries as port. To me these are the savoury equivalent of glacé fruit: you rarely taste anything of the original.

Coffee

NEED TO KNOW

Arabica is the finest of three varieties of coffee bean.

Robusta coffee beans give harsher flavours and up to 2½ times more caffeine.

Liberica beans are coffee, but not as most of us know it.

Coffee strengths on packs are not caffeine levels but degrees of roasting.

Instant coffee is usually robusta and thus high in caffeine.

Boiling water should not touch ground or instant coffee: 92 °C is the ideal.

Pour off-the-boil water from a height to reduce its temperature.

Frozen coffee grounds cool water that is too hot.

Sealed refrigeration or deep freezing prolong the life of ground coffee and beans.

The higher the roast, the lesser quality the bean—you taste the burn not the bean.

Don't mix different roasts; it's like mixing fine claret with plonk.

Skimmed milk gives better cappuccino foam than full-fat milk because it is protein not fat that foams.

The ideal coffee per cup is a dessertspoon to a tablespoon of ground coffee: the US uses less, Sweden uses more.

It is eSpresso, not eXpresso.

Caffeine and bitterness come in the second half of the average espresso extraction of 20 seconds.

The short ristretto is not the strongest espresso but has the least caffeine and bitterness.

First coffee house opened in Mecca in 1511.

Floriano's on St Mark's Square, Venice, opened in 1645.

First in England was in Oxford, 1650.

London's first was on Cornhill in 1652.

London's coffee houses morphed into the Commercial Union, Baltic Exchange and Lloyds.

T he instant beverage millions enjoy has the same name and origin as a drink once considered a gift from God, and which, properly made, smells and tastes as though touched indeed by the Divine hand. National drink of the Americas and of the Middle East, coffee had its origins in north-east Africa, possibly first recognised by a shepherd in Ethiopia, who noticed a distinct spriteliness in his sheep—or was it goats?—after they had eaten a certain red berry. The shepherd/goatherd Rhaldi also felt invigorated after trying some, but local Sufi mystics decided such pleasure must be associated with the Devil and threw the berries onto a fire. The heavenly aroma changed their minds, they raked out the charred seeds, threw them into water—and on the story goes.

Many who have persevered for years have still to taste a good cupful. Getting value and flavour is never easy and cannot be cheap. Yet little else can be so rewarding.

What is coffee?

The coffee bean is the seed of the berry of an evergreen shrub with glossy, green, lance-like leaves and a jasmine-scented white flower that grows in volcanic soil between the Tropics of Cancer and Capricorn; the finest quality is produced higher than 1,600 m above sea level. The best trees produce only 3 kg of coffee beans in a year and Brazilian bushes produce 500 g/1 lb annually, explaining much of the expense.

The berries are known as cherries and because blossoms, green, ripe and over-ripe cherries may be on the same branch, harvesting should be done berry by berry, as green or overripe berries give inferior flavours. It is now rare for coffee to be picked by hand. Instead, whole branches are pulled away with a mixture of beans, hoping that processing will separate the good from the bad.

Each cherry has a skin, a pulp, a tough parchment, a thin silver skin and the seeds or beans, in that order. Normally there are two seeds, facing each other with their flatter sides together. On some stunted or old trees only one bean develops, and this rounder seed is sold as peaberry coffee. The flavour from them is no different, but Kenyan Peaberries are an exception and have a notably greater fragrance.

Types of coffee bean

COFFEA ARABICA: indisputably the finest coffee variety. Originally from Ethiopia, or somewhere close, it will grow high above sea level. The higher the garden the slower the growth, and this produces beans with greater integral sugar and more refined flavour. The bean shape is an elongated oval and quite flat.

COFFEA ROBUSTA: native to Zaire but can grow more easily and prolifically over a wider geographical area than arabicas and is far more disease resistant. The faster-grown flavour is muddier and less refined than arabicas but when well-produced adds attractive and useful up-front boldness to blends. It gives up to two and a half times more caffeine than arabicas and because it is cheaper, is usually the dominant content of inexpensive bean mixtures.

The green robusta bean is smaller, irregular, convex, and browner than arabicas, but not even experts guarantee to tell arabicas from robustas once roasted.

COFFEA LIBERICA: is mostly grown and drunk in South East Asia. It is noticeably rank in smell and taste.

Types of coffee bean processing

The pulp and skins can be removed from beans in two ways, wet or dry. The wet method is preferable but requires great amounts of water, not necessarily available where coffee is grown. Both styles of processed green coffee beans last well. Some, such as the Java, are said to improve for up to 20 years but the flavour we appreciate comes only when the bean is roasted, which releases the oils and aromas present and adds others.

WASHED: a pulper removes most of the outside skin and flesh. Next the beans are fermented, softening the remaining mucilage, which can then be washed off. This fermentation must be carefully timed for it affects appearance and flavour. The special advantage of washed coffee is that under-ripe berries that give a distinct peanut flavour float to the top and can be removed. Over-ripe berries known as 'stinkers' give a flavour rather like silage, a disastrous effect—except many in the Middle East pursue and value this eccentric flavour. Some French fancy the flavour too,

calling such coffee *le nectaire*.

The beans are now known as parchment beans, and a machine like a roller mill removes the parchment and silver skin. Washed beans are often given a polish in another machine, which makes both colour and quality more durable.

UNWASHED: the coffee cherries are dried in the sun until crisp but need constant attention to stop mould developing. When dry, often with mechanical help today, the pulp and parchment can be removed. The drawback is that there is no guarantee of consistency of colour or quality, because unripe and overripe beans and other debris are included even after careful grading.

Types of coffee roast

It is a sin to highly roast the best beans and a blessing that the cheaper ones should be. Roasted coffee beans are grossly swollen by gasses equal to an internal pressure of five to seven atmospheres, the same as in a champagne bottle or a London bus tyre, but revert to their original volume once processed, so a spoonful of beans gives half that volume once ground. You should also see evenness of colour bean to bean and in each bean. Only when the coffee beans are broken, crushed or ground will the full aroma be released.

The smell of a roasted coffee bean is tantalizing nasal shorthand for what might be possible; the promises can be broken easily. Once ground, its treasures can be plundered by how long you store it and how, by the way you make it, by the mineral content of the water used, the condition and heat of any milk or cream. On the occasions when all is perfect, and you brew coffee that would interest the impotent dead, every battle on the way is forgotten and forgiven. Remember roasting levels are not a guide to the caffeine content and should reflect the quality of the bean; the higher the quality, the less the roast level.

LIGHT ROAST: an elegant lift to the aristocrats, best made by jug/cafetière style and drunk black.

MEDIUM ROAST: an excellent choice for breakfast, with or without hot milk. When made strong it should not be bitter.

AFTER-DINNER ROAST: in spite of the name, good for all day drinking, made more or less strong, it's roasted from medium to a little more than that. This is the highest a quality bean should be roasted or you risk tasting the roast rather than the roasted bean.

DARK/ESPRESSO ROAST: a dark roast is a very fine balance and too many fall off the tightrope. Black-roasted beans are *not a requirement* for espresso coffee but a conscious over-caramellisation to give colour and high but bitter taste to low-quality beans. Medium roasts make the best espresso coffee, commercially or domestically.

Choosing your coffee

A reliable way to establish the style and weight of coffee you prefer, is to begin with Kenyan or Central and South American styles, for these fragrant well-bodied coffees are the perfect middle of the road standard. A medium-roasted Colombian bean gratifies most tastes and then you face further coffee adventures with a firm footing. And there are adventures, as more specialist traders offer more coffees from single estates, which like chocolate, unpasteurised cheese and fine wines vary year to year according to *terroir*, weather and production qualities. You can even order roasted beans direct from Pitcairn Island, the *Bounty* mutineers' refuge.

Much coffee is blended to avoid variations year to year, and top-priced blends should have a regular appearance of size and colour. Blended or unblended, the best beans commonly retain a sliver of silver skin in the seam down the middle of their flat side. If a blend mixes arabica and robusta beans, you'll generally see a range of sizes but no broken or misshapen beans if the price is toward the high end.

Knowing your way around coffee is a lifetime study, and exciting because of that. Just when you think you know it all, something changes. Here are broad outlines of the constantly changing sources.

Africa

West Africa is the home of robusta coffee, East Africa is the origin of arabicas and produces some of the finest available in bulk, and most African countries produce a quantity of both.

WEST AFRICA: largely from Angola, Cameroon and Zaire, these are mainly robusta; strongly flavoured, reliable croppers but lacking character, subtlety or variety.

EAST AFRICA

ETHIOPIA: at up to 2,600 m above sea level, the Highlands produce some of the world's highest grown coffees, exceptionally fragrant, almost perfumed and described as winey or gamey. They are usually unwashed/dry processed:

> *Harar Longberry:* a heritage coffee with superior mocha and fruit flavours.
> *Limu:* light to medium weight, floral with a distinct spiciness.
> *Mocha Djimma:* earthy but fruity and with hints of chocolate, this was perhaps the original coffee.
> *Sidamoo:* floral and bright with a citrus edge.

KENYA: together with Colombian coffee a benchmark starting point for exploration of coffee. High-grown Kenyan coffee has superb natural sweetness and gives full flavour when only lightly roasted; a medium (after dinner) roast develops extra acidity that balances the accompanying increase in flavour. Kenya Peaberry is small whole beans considered to have enhanced fragrance and flavour.

TANZANIA: similar to Kenyan but perhaps a thinner body.

UGANDA: outstanding arabicas, with the quality of Kenya.

The Americas

BRAZIL: this country produces an awful lot of coffee and a lot of it is awful. After major crop failures Brazil has been working hard to change both growing areas and to develop new hybrids but most are aimed at mass markets and average taste. Any with the following in their DNA are likely to be special.

> *Bourbon:* acknowledged as an aristocrat, with outstanding fullness and aroma.
> *Santos:* wonderful body, elegant acidity and excellent colour and flavour.

COLOMBIA: the best is truly great coffee and like Kenyan an excellent starting point to learn about quality coffee. Colombian beans produce more liquor per bean than most and have a full sweet flavour rarely marred by excess acidity and typically fill the mouth with the velvety smoothness of a well-matured red wine. It is thus depressing to hear Colombian coffee described as bland, but that is mainly in the United States. There is a reason.

Americans drink coffee much weaker than Europeans, sometimes only a quarter the strength; they have been fooled into using fewer beans by Colombian coffee's apparent strength through the fast, full colour of its high liquor yield. It's worse if it is made in the unspeakable percolator or kept hot for longer than 30 minutes.

Colombians you might find and enjoy are Medellins, Excelso, Manizales,

Armenicas, Libanos, Bogatoas and Buccaramangos—and doesn't the last one even sound great?

COSTA RICA: the connoisseur's secret. Well-perfumed, mild and like noble clarets has delicious full sweetness supported on an elegant tangy acidity, giving an unusually balanced cup.

ECUADOR: thin, sharp coffees that appear anonymously but usefully in blends.

GUATEMALA: high-grown Guatemalans are mild and mellow with a particularly fragrant bouquet and aromatic flavour. Look especially for Coban and Antiquas.

HAWAII: stretching a geographical point, I know, but worth it. Most Hawaiian coffee is grown on the volcanic soil of Kona on Hawaii, the Big Island. It is sweet and mellow with a unique extra nuttiness. Even if it not from that district, Hawaiian coffee is sold as Kona, except in Portugal where that is a fearfully rude word. Must be in Brazil, too.

MEXICO: essentially good quality, but Mexicans like it roasted with a sugar coating giving a strong caramel flavour that easily slips into horrid bitterness.

NICARAGUA: rich coffees with a complex array of flavour notes, sometimes of spice.

PERU: tangy, perhaps spicy and with well-bred body.

VENEZUELA: as elegant and delicious as Colombian coffees but more delicate and lighter and thus too easily misunderstood or dismissed. The most delicate, aromatic and balanced are the Meridas. Caracas coffees are equally distinctive but lighter, and popular in France and Spain.

Arabia

The Yemen is the home of what is thought to be the original Mocha, which can be so full-flavoured it is sometimes said to taste as though mixed with chocolate, an effect also described as gamey. Most Mocha sold is a blend if you look carefully. It is the proper high-roasted coffee/blend to be pulverised for making Turkish/Greek/Arabic coffee. But beware Mocha, or any other variety from this part of the world, may include over-ripe beans or stinkers, and then gamey becomes farmyard.

Caribbean

Caribbean coffees will have mellow, sweet and mild characteristics.

Blue Mountain beans cost over £100 for 500 g/1 lb in 2020 London but does that make this limited high-grown coffee the world's best? It is certainly rich, sweet and mellow but the cost is more properly a market-led reflection of the small quantity produced, and proof the quality-intoxicated Japanese pay almost anything to buy almost all of it each year. Blue Mountain coffee trees are grown in Kenya, but unless in the same soil and at the same extreme height, cannot taste as though Jamaican. Like Mocha, any Blue Mountain coffee at a reasonable price will be a blend and most of us can only guess at its accuracy.

Cuban coffee growing is government controlled and if you find Turquino or

Serrano Cubans, these are 'dark, thick and strong' and specially suited to the stove-top coffee maker. Coffees from Haiti and from the Dominican Republic are thought very good.

India

Mysore is best known and is mellow and quite light but to me can be muddy. It is commonly used in Mocha blends or blended with Mochas.

Monsooned Malabar: is recognisable in green form because the beans have turned yellow, if you follow me. When roasted they give a dark chocolate flavour with a bitterness that in this case is attractive. The effect was originally the result of the humidity and time involved in sailing-ship deliveries to Europe. Now the beans are exposed to monsoon season temperatures and weather changes.

Indonesia

JAVA: rich, heavy and almost spiced, these are amongst the hallowed names of coffee.

Celebes: Bali and Timor produce good coffee, mainly based on robusta. Sulawesi produces arabica coffees.

Kopi Luwak: coffee cherries that have passed through the digestive tract of a civet cat; when extracted, the beans taste as though roasted. The smooth, mellow and caramelly flavours are phenomenally expensive per cup but the cruelty with which civets are commonly caged and kept means Kopi Luwak should be avoided until there are guarantees civet

cats have not been ill-treated.

Old Colonial: is a common name for types known as Old Java or Old Government Java, once guaranteed to have had a minimum ten years tropical storage but the slightly musty flavour and dark brown colour were a greater effect of the slow humid shipping that created Monsoon Malabars. Any you find are likely to be delicious, but younger and paler than they used to be.

Sumatra: when good these are considered amongst the world's best. Like Javanese coffees they are notably heavy and full in the mouth, but syrupy and flavoury and thus refreshing and stimulating. Madheling and Lingtong are worth pursuing.

Papua New Guinea

Coffee's home here is in the Highlands and now produces coffee quite as good as Kenya's, whence came the original stock. A constantly rising star, and a definite talking point at a sticky dinner party, which can then legitimately go on to such related PNG subjects as birds of paradise, uncontacted tribes, nose-piercing and the niceties of selecting penis sheaths; woven shapes or hollowed gourds is a good starter subject.

Making coffee

Of all coffee-making methods only the percolator should be avoided as this is likely to use boiling water and will also boil the brewed coffee. Electrically controlled percolators should avoid these pitfalls but then you have to clean them.

Union Hand-Roasted Coffee of London once invited me to a comparative coffee tasting, of the same coffee made different ways, jug/plunger, filter and Italian stove top. It was startling. I discovered the way you make coffee is more important than what you have spent on it.

The general opinion was that jug, cafetière, plunger or French press coffee all give a fuller, racier coffee plus a fine suspension of coffee solids that add a zillion micro-flavours. This means more flavour than filter/drip coffee and more body than Italian stove-top coffee.

DRIP COFFEE: another name for filter coffee.

FILTER COFFEE: also called drip coffee, this is usually elegant with nice acidity and mellowness. It can be made automatically in a coffee maker which then keeps the coffee hot and this is especially common in the USA.

Or you can manually pour hot water through coffee grounds in a paper filter. The paper filter absorbs oils, the source of coffee's most refined flavours and natural sweetness and a metal filter in a coffee maker also collects oil and fine particles. Thus, filter coffee is emasculated coffee, no matter how strong you make it. The oils and the fine elements suspended in coffee made other ways are very important contributors to the flavour spectrum.

The coffee should be ground medium fine because water is in contact for a short time. It's an advantage to wet the coffee with just some of the water and then to let it swell evenly before you add the remainder.

CAFÉ AU LAIT: is a coffee made with filter coffee and hot milk; coffee made with cold milk is a *white coffee.*

JUG COFFEE: use coarse-ground coffee and put a level tablespoon or more of this per cup into a warmed jug. Pour in water that has boiled but been allowed to subside for 15 seconds or more, stir a couple of times and leave for three to five minutes. Pouring the water in from a height will ensure it is not too hot. Bringing the ground coffee directly from the refrigerator or freezer also helps prevent this. Strain as you serve. This method lets you taste as it brews.

If jug coffee seems too strong or too bitter you have used grounds that are too fine, have brewed too long, or you should change to a lighter roast or higher quality. If it is too light flavoured you have under-brewed, possibly because the grounds are too coarse, or you should choose a darker roast. The medical view is that coffee made this way can cause cholesterol to rise, but you need to be drinking more than five big cups a day.

PLUNGER/CAFETIÈRE/FRENCH PRESS: add the coffee and all the water as above, and then give an immediate plunge and withdraw, which wets all the grains and gives even brewing. Then a brew of three to four minutes is recommended before the final full plunge. A coarse to medium grind is best.

ITALIAN STOVE-TOP COFFEE: also called the stove-top espresso, this is best domestically if you like a more concentrated brew. Because stove-top makers come in several sizes you can do it right every time, but you mustn't even consider making two cups of coffee in a machine designed to make four or six or more. Fine to medium-fine ground coffee. The short time the water is in contact with the coffee can give a lack of mouthfeel or body.

ESPRESSO COFFEE: espresso coffee was invented as a commercial process. The hissing machines not only filter the water but also deliver it at a precise pressure and temperature. Modern electronics make it easier for domestic machines to get close to these if you spend enough money, but I suspect espresso works best when left to the professionals. See Espresso entry on page 96.

POD ESPRESSO COFFEE: immensely useful for a quick domestic coffee fix—or are they? The very finely ground coffee in each pod is six-seven grams, whereas the recommendation for a single-shot espresso is about nine grams. The quick passage of water extracts very little caffeine and nowhere near full flavour but there is a trick to get more taste and kick. Wait 10–15 seconds after the first brew and then press the short-brew button again; you get a strong stream of very good colour and flavour, which is best if you stop half way through. This does not work if you use the longer brew button.

Cold coffee

COLD BREWED: this gives satin-smooth coffee with acidity and bitterness reduced by about two-thirds. It is usually made very strong, creating a coffee cordial that can then be diluted when needed.

A good general proportion to make it is to add three or four times the volume of water, so add two cups of cold water to half a cup of coarse coffee grounds and then leave 12 hours or more but it can over brew and start to extract bitterness, so taste to be sure. Refrigerating reduces the extraction greatly so room temperature is best. Strain and then refrigerate, when it will last for days. A finer quality gives better results and a medium roast Colombian is a great start.

Reheat in the microwave without boiling, diluted or not, with water or milk. Or serve over ice cubes, which will dilute it as you drink.

ICED COFFEE: leftover brewed coffee is rarely strong enough then to be diluted by ice cubes. Brew a double strength batch or make a cold-brewed cordial, as above, or very strong instant coffee, or make your own essence with lots of instant coffee and a little water, or to use a liquid coffee essence.

You may serve iced black coffee but most people seem to prefer it with some dairy addition. Mix it with chilled milk, cream or half-melted ice cream, in which case be creative, using, say, chocolate ice cream to make a mocha iced coffee. Whipped cream is a welcome topping and so I suppose you might as well add nuts, grated orange zest, crushed coffee beans.

Strong instant coffee seems peculiarly suited to being served iced: ideally make a very strong essence of instant coffee and very little water and then top up each glass with sparkling water or soda. Half sparkling water and half milk plus a scoop of ice cream gives a sparkling black coffee ice-cream soda, and if it's made with a robusta-based coffee, this will keep anyone awake. Very grown up if you ignore the children present and also add brandy or rum.

The Greeks and Koreans use instant coffee to make startling drinks—see below.

Tasting coffee

Like wine, coffee gives different flavours according to soil, climate and altitude and that's before you make it your way. Wine-tasting language is relevant to assessing coffee and the three criteria are body, acidity and fragrance. BODY: the overall effect in the mouth. Full-bodied coffee fills the mouth with a velvety softness, stimulating taste buds over the entire palate to give a 'long' finish, flavour and sensation that lingers in the mouth and down the back of the throat. Lesser coffees and badly made ones are flatter and less sensual and 'short' or 'middle' finishers, that is they affect taste buds only towards the front of the tongue and mouth and do not do that for long.

ACIDITY: called dryness in wine. This makes coffee feel clean in the mouth, giving satisfying balance to the initial sweetness. It is sensed more towards the edges of the tongue and must not be confused with the bitterness of over-roasted or over-brewed coffee. Bitterness is more usually detected across the back of the tongue, a last-chance warning by Mother Nature, because bitter foods are often poisonous.
FRAGRANCE: as with wine, coffee tells you most of what there is to say by its nose. Like wine, it should not be sniffed in namby-pamby whiffs but with a big, single breath, then held so it can permeate, stimulate and inform.

For more on how to taste see my book *How to Cook without Recipes* (Portico).

Decaffeinated coffee

There are three decaffeinating methods, all applied to the green coffee bean. Each removes 97–98% of the caffeine. CARBON DIOXIDE: under pressure this removes caffeine and then evaporates, leaving no residue.
ORGANIC SOLVENTS: these chemicals are specific to caffeine and have been criticised but the trace deposits are around one in a million and not measurable in subsequently brewed coffee.
WATER METHOD: green beans are brewed in water, from which the caffeine is removed. When this water is used to brew more beans, it extracts the caffeine from them.

Instant coffee

The range of instant coffees is fast approaching the complication of fresh coffee and the best instants are better than inferior real coffee. Improved techniques mean more arabica beans are now used, making instant coffees less stimulating.

Beans for instant coffees are brewed, usually by a percolating system for maximum extraction, and then the brew is concentrated. This prolonged exposure to heat is a major cause of the difference between instant and fresh coffees.

A reminder: pour on the water from a height to reduce the temperature and aerate the mixture. If you like milky coffee, you get much better flavour by putting the milk directly onto the coffee and then adding the water: you don't spoil the coffee with water too hot and the milk and water emulsify better.

FREEZE-DRIED: coffee is frozen then ground and when passed through a vacuum tunnel the solid water content turns into vapour, which is exhausted without changing back to liquid. The dried particles contain much of the original coffee content—but those are damaged if you pour on boiling water.

Instant espresso coffees are an innovation that has been particularly successful and they are very good for cooking, too. The internet has alerted the world to two different ways of using instant coffee, one to drink, one to eat.

GREEK FRAPPÉ: a whipped instant-coffee-based pick-me-up even found made to order in bars. In Corfu, three versions differ according to sweetness:

Straight (sketos): 1–2 teaspoons of instant coffee and no sugar.
Medium (metrios): 1–2 teaspoons of instant coffee with two teaspoons of sugar.
Sweet (glykos): 1–2 teaspoons of instant coffee with four teaspoons of sugar.

Combine your choice with 2–3 tablespoons of water and shake to create a stable foam. You can also use a milk frother or a milkshake maker. Pour over ice cubes in a tall glass, adding water, sparkling water or milk to taste—perhaps a mixture. De-caffeinated works as well.

KOREAN OR DELGADO: whipped instant coffee with very high caffeine content. Use one or two tablespoons each of instant coffee, white sugar and water. Beat for three or more minutes to form a thick foam that peaks like meringue.

Dollop onto hot or cold milk and over hot cocoa or chocolate to make celestial mocha flavours, which it also does on chocolate cake, brownies, tray bakes, cup-cakes and muffins. An adult topping for ice cream and when heaped onto a tall glass of sparkling water this makes a memorable coffee soda.

POWDER: the concentrated coffee is sprayed onto a hot drum, losing more of the valuable aromas and oils, so you always knew you weren't drinking the real thing, even though it was 100% coffee.

Coffee plus

ALCOHOL: a legendary companionship and very few alcoholic drinks are awful with coffee, except beers and lagers. Don't do it by half measures in small cups or you can't pour a useful slug of alcohol without making the coffee cold. Far better to serve them separately.

Irish coffee, popularised by the Buena Vista café in the Fisherman's Wharf area of San Francisco, should be made with hot strong coffee, Irish whiskey (note the spelling), sugar (some say brown, some say cube) and cream, originally liquid double or heavy cream but now commonly whipped.

CHICORY: toasted, ground, and added for the sake of its bitterness and for economy. Understandable in times of war or famine, chicory has always had its adherents and its enemies. Its popularity is slightly on the decline in the UK, where it has never had a really large following, but it is still popular in parts of France. Camp Coffee Essence contains chicory and is essential when making a classic English Coffee and Walnut cake.

DRIED FIGS: ground and added to a Viennese coffee, a unique experience.

FLAVOURED BEANS: for some time now, it's been thought cute to serve coffee made from beans impregnated with such flavourings as amaretto, raspberry, royal mint and almost everything else. Sure, with one stroke they remove the hassle of serving liqueurs and keep insobriety at bay, but is this any way to treat coffee, to treat yourself? You can be assured the beans so flavoured weren't much cop to start with—and anyway, how many of the 'flavourings' are real?

MILK: hot milk rather than cold adds silkiness to coffee and warm cups keep coffee hotter longer.

SPICES: classic additions to coffee, cardamom, cloves or cinnamon being the most usual. The first two might be added in a pinch, ground, or as a whole spice or two put into the coffee pot. Cardamom is the most exotic and commonly found throughout the Middle East, sometimes anchored in the spout. Otherwise, stir coffee with a cinnamon stick or sprinkle ground cinnamon onto a topping of whipped cream.

SUGAR: raw and brown sugars or honey sound like good ideas for sweetening but their distinct flavours disguise the fragrance and tastes of high-quality coffee. Anyway, sweetness does not balance bitterness, only the acidity of lemon or lime juice does that. Better drink a higher quality with natural sweetness and fragrance.

The espresso story

Espresso coffee was invented to make a cup at a time in cafés. It was first developed in 1822 by Louis Rabaut, a Frenchman, but it was Italians who perfected the technique and made it work faster, thus their term for the invention, espresso, not you will note, expresso. It took until 1902 for the Italian company Bezzera to patent the world's first successful commercial machine.

Essentially what happens is this; hot water builds up a head of steam in a tank and when a valve is opened beneath the water level, the steam pressure forces a measured amount of hot water out, through the compacted coffee.

Arabica coffees are thought best for producing the correct honey-like dribble of flavour, but some robusta in the blend adds a brightness of acidity and extra effervescence to ensure a good crema, the lid of froth that should cover an espresso as a sign of quality coffee and a spotlessly clean machine.

If ever you are uncertain which café of several you should patronise, look at the pipe through which milk is steamed: if this is shining and clean you are safe, if it is caked in old milk, perhaps even caramelised, take your patronage elsewhere.

Types of espresso coffee

These are the coffee styles a modern barista should *prepare to order*.

AMERICANO: a large cup of coffee made by diluting a single or double espresso with hot water, which destroys the crema, so the result looks like instant or filter coffee. The added water should not come from a second tug on the espresso handle but from a separate source. Filter coffee is often served as an Americano. See *Long Black*, which is different.

CAFFE LATTE: an espresso shot with three times its volume of steam-heated, frothy milk, but little or no actual froth. The correct form is to pour concurrently into the cup from opposite sides, but this is rare. See *Flat White*.

CAPPUCCINO: one third espresso, one third hot milk and one third foam. Italians consider it a breakfast drink and smirk at anyone who orders one after 11am. Ordering a cappuccino with lunch or dinner appears very gauche in Western Europe but Middle Europeans turn to it with a sweet or savoury snack in the afternoon. It's perfectly proper without a sprinkle of cinnamon, cocoa or grated chocolate.

CON PANNA: an espresso with whipped cream, also known as Vienna coffee.

DOUBLE SHOT/DOPPIA: two measures of ground coffee but might not come with twice the amount of water, as this depends on the style of the barista.

ESPRESSO: three to four Imperial tablespoons, about 60 mls of liquid which takes 20 seconds or so to be expressed, but less is welcomed. Caffeine and bitterness arrive in the cup after the first 10 seconds, so shorter extraction gives a sweeter result with less caffeine: Italian baristas are more likely to serve a *ristretto* q.v., explaining why Italians drink endless coffee without seeming wired.

The Italian custom is to down espresso in one or two gulps, usually while standing. The cup won't be returned to the saucer until empty.

FLAT WHITE: invented in Australasia, this is a double espresso topped with hot milk but little or no foam and in a cup rather than a tumbler or mug, giving a shorter, stronger-tasting, less milky coffee than a latte. The style is woefully abused.

LATTE MACCHIATO: a tumbler of foamed milk, about half filled, with a single espresso shot poured into it, so it 'marks' the milk with ever-changing marbling: see *Macchiato*.

LONG BLACK: much misunderstood, this is another Australasian invention made by putting hot water into a cup and topping that with a single or double espresso, done in that order so crema will be apparent on top. Do it the other way round and it is an Americano.

MACCHIATO: espresso marked with a dash of hot milk: see *Latte macchiato*.

MOCHA: a mug of vaguely equal portions of espresso, unsweetened hot chocolate and frothed milk. A chunk of fine chocolate melted in a double espresso, with or without cream is wicked and addictive and choosing a high-cocoa-solids milk chocolate is particularly recommended.

RISTRETTO: the ultimate for coffee lovers. The barista should take 12–15 seconds maximum—giving a couple of tablespoons of coffee, and less is better. This short brew delivers the fragile oils, natural sugars and flavours, but few of the caffeine or bitter contents, which appear only in the second half of an espresso extraction. With fine beans and light roasts it will taste as though sugar has been added and the lingering aromatic oils coat the palate for an hour or more. The over-roasted beans of most chains mean even a ristretto tastes bitter. In many the ristretto is unknown and instead you get a 'short black'.

ROMANO: an espresso served with a curl of lemon peel or a thin slice of lemon, both of which will reduce bitterness.

SHORT BLACK: a full-pour single espresso and this is not a ristretto.

VIENNA: see *Con panna*.

Dairy including Cheese

Butter is one of our purest products, just churned cream, pasteurised or not.

Cream is aged or ripened to increase flavour before churning.

Salted butter adds only salt as a preservative.

European and Scandinavian butters introduce a bacterial culture instead of salt; this is known as cultured or lactic butter.

Lactic cultures improve keeping quality but add flavours that differ country to country.

European and Scandinavian cultured butters can give unfamiliar results in British and American baking; sometimes labelling says only that they are unsalted.

UK and US unsalted butter is not cultured.

Sweet cream butter is US unsalted butter.

Butter heated with oil reaches a higher temperature before burning.

Cook in melted butter only after it has fallen silent, meaning residual water has evaporated.

M ilk was the great sustainer of the Old World. Ever since its men and women husbanded animals bigger than wolves, their milk gave more reliable sustenance than their meat.

Thick or thin, golden or white, milk magically offers the complete spectrum of proteins the human body needs without having to kill. According to geography, it might stream from cows, yaks, sheep and goats, from camels, reindeer and horses and more.

Not everyone enjoyed the benefits. Much of Asia and the Orient, Polynesia and the New World had no milking animals or avoided them, because drinking animals' milk is not natural for weaned humans. Malabsorption of lactose, the milk sugar, is the problem but most digestions will adjust and so milk and milk products eventually entered diets everywhere.

Guaranteeing nutrition safely and for longer than fresh milk lasts, gave us butter, fermented milks and creams, cheeses and, once we could, ice cream. The 20th century added pasteurisation to make wholesome milk available to millions, while also destroying *terroir*, its ability to reflect seasons and pastures.

Now we manipulate this natural product, by adding and subtracting, extract its rich cream, powder it, condense and freeze it. Plant-based milks pretend to replace it; none does except soy-milk.

So, still milk sustains us. Here are some of the better ways milk does this.

Provided there has been a preliminary 'holding' of the cream to ensure uniform hardness of the fat globules, you can make butter from sweet cream to which you have done nothing else. If you leave cream longer to ripen, naturally occurring bacteria multiply and their enzymic actions and side effects increase the flavour, by raising the acid content in particular. Such flavour enhancement or change can be aided by the addition of a bacterial culture or 'starter'.

The cultures introduced into the cream used to make Danish, Dutch, German, French and other European butters are what give the distinctive and consistent but differing flavours of these countries' products. To many, these cultures give a cheesy flavour, which is why they do not always suit Anglo or US baking and cooking. These cultures were used to preserve butter before pasteurisation, but salt was the choice of UK butter and of that from the USA, Canada, Australia and New Zealand, because it keeps butter without affecting its flavour.

Most butters are made with cows' milk, and both the breed and their feed affect the colour. Jersey and Guernsey cows produce the brightest natural colour and 100% grass feeding encourages this in other breeds.

Types of butter

CLARIFIED BUTTER: melting butter means the solid matter can be removed leaving only butter oil, which then cooks smoke-free and safely at a far higher temperature than whole butter.

To make your own, melt a good quantity over gentle heat and simmer quietly until white particles of milk solids have stopped forming, which might take as long as 45 minutes. Scoop away the deposits or strain through muslin.

Clarified butter including Indian *ghee* q.v., gives better results when frying pancakes or eggs and when browning onions because it won't burn before the job is done. Mixing with a vegetable oil enables even higher frying temperatures and crisper results.

Niter kibbeh: is Ethiopian clarified butter heightened with spices.

Smen: in Morocco clarified butter laced with salt, and sometimes with herbs and spices, is aged and fermented, often for months, sometimes for years. It is rancid, over-ripe-blue-cheese pungent but is claimed to mellow with long ageing. Used in small amounts, especially to add unique flavour to couscous and dabbed into coffee.

CULTURED OR LACTIC BUTTER: Europeans once aged their cream highly, so the increased acidity then preserved the butter, although for shorter periods than salt might. This encouraged the growth of flavouring compounds, which differed region from region, country from country. When pasteurization became mandatory there was no chance for those to develop and so lactic cultures were added, developing unique flavours in European butters. Thus unsalted European and Scandinavian butters are not sweet butter as is widely thought, even by professionals, and they are not a better ingredient in UK and US baking. There is a snobbish belief that cultured butter is more suited to fine cooking and baking, especially if from France, this is not true; shortbread made with cultured butter can taste vomit-like.

FARMHOUSE: artisan-made butter in small quantities. Those from western English counties are less salty than most, which contributes to their notoriously short life. Check these are sweet and wholesome and not streaky, indicating the combination of different batches and/or possible problems with rancidity. Salted Welsh butter is possibly the saltiest regional butter of all, especially when cut from great blocks by farmers' wives in Swansea market.

FLAVOURED BUTTERS: an increasing trend with artisan makers, flavoured butters add surprise and extra dimension even to a sandwich. Easy to make yourself with almost anything, from grated orange zest to roasted peppercorns, cumin and nuts, or with fresh herbs and garlic, of course. Dulse, chilli/paprika and black garlic butters are made by Irish Abernethy Butter, the favourite of top food journalist and critic Jay Rayner; their Smoked Butter won three Great Taste stars. Make your own with Liquid Smoke in tiny amounts. Contrary to expectation it is not synthetic, but any truffle butter is likely to be so 'flavoured'.

GOAT MILK BUTTER: it takes several days for the very fine globules of goat cream to rise naturally and there's not that much of it to then churn, so this very white butter is expensive. Low lactose is a benefit.

GHEE: is the clarified butter basic to the cookery of the Indian continent.

HIGH-FAT BUTTER: the flavour contribution of this uncommon butter is notably good in cake and biscuit cookery. It is less useful in pastry making unless you add more liquid than normal, because steam from ordinary butter's water content is important to lightening pastry, particularly layered styles.

LIGHTLY SALTED BUTTER: not always basic UK or US butter with less salt and a blander flavour: sneakily, a major Danish brand is cultured butter and thus has added flavours.

SALTED BUTTER: made by adding salt to butter made from cream that has ripened before being pasteurised and churned.

SPREADABLE BUTTERS: made by emulsifying butter with vegetable oils. Once the oils might have been hydrogenated to make them solid but these were a health threat and should not be seen nowadays. The calorie level is the same as full-cream butter but there is a lessening of cholesterol content. When my family ran a home cookery in the 1950s, we made butter spreadable by whipping it with warm water.

STAKA BUTTER: a Cretan speciality made by thickening the residue of clarified butter with flour.

SWEET CREAM BUTTER: a US other name for butter that is not cultured; it can be salted or unsalted.

UNSALTED BUTTER: unsalted butter should be butter without salt but the term can also be used for cultured butters, which have added flavours. Read the label. Classic unsalted butter should taste like clotted cream and give unctuous richness to everything from scrambled eggs to Victoria sponges— and everything in between. Salt is usually added to any cooking or baking.

WHEY BUTTER: an ancient way to get maximum return from milk, made by cheesemakers. Rennet, starters and other ingredients flavour milk for cheese before it is separated into curds and whey. Thus the whey is uniquely flavoured by them, too. Cream left in the whey is separated and then churned, giving a butter that includes cultures but those of cheese making and giving butters with flavours unique to each cheese maker.

Recommended European butters

Beurre d'Ardenne, Belgium.
Beurre d'Isigny, France, from pasteurised cream. *Beurre d'Isigny* of raw cream does not have PDO status.
Beurre Charentes-Poitou, France, including *Beurre des Charentes* and *Beurre des Deux-Sèvres*.
Beurre Rose, Luxembourg.
Mantequilla de Soria, Spain.
Mantega de l'Alt Urgelli la Cerdanya, Spain.
Rucava white butter, Latvia.

Cheese

NEED TO KNOW

All casein-based cheeses start by changing milk into solid curds and liquid whey.

Curds and whey form naturally as milk ages and develops acidity.

Curds and whey form in fresh, sweet or mildly aged milk only if a curdling agent is added, either animal rennet or something plant based.

Cheese can be made from the albumen found in whey; ricotta is an example.

Cheese is made from cows, goats, sheep, buffalo, camels, reindeer, yaks, horses and more.

Vegetarian cheeses differ only by using a plant-based rennet alternative.

Vegan nut-milk cheeses should be called something other than cheese.

Every nuance of curd handling gives a different cheese; these include cutting, milling, salting, pressing, temperature, size, surface treatment and ageing.

Unpasteurised milk reflects the season and feed of the milking animal, the terroir.

Pasteurisation dulls or dismisses seasonal and terroir influences and kills integral organisms that naturally acidify and flavour milk for butter and cheese.

Pasteurised milks are manipulated to replace lost terroir by adding 'starter' cultures of selected bacteria to sterile milk.

Starter cultures can add tastes, flavours and sweetness different from traditional cheese styles and origins.

Fat content is not a proportion of the cheese but of its solid content—see below.

Air and heat are the worst enemies of cut cheese.

Air-tight wrapping and cool or refrigerated ambiance preserve cut cheese best.

Bring cheese to room temperature still wrapped before serving.

Fat content explained

Understanding the fat content of cheese is important for those who wish to control energy intake yet include cheese in their diet. It's not what it seems, and is good news for those who thought they should not eat rich-tasting cheeses with high fat content.

A cheese's fat content is not a percentage of the cheese you get in the hand, but is a percentage of only its solid matter and a cheese's fat content is not related to the richness of the original milk. Milk fat is concentrated the more the curds are pressed.

A 25 g/1 oz portion of hard-pressed Parmesan made with semi-skimmed milk may have 10% or more fat than the same weight of a full-milk Cheddar and be almost 20% higher than the same weight of Camembert, which is not pressed.

A buttery Brie of up to 60% fat, or a Camembert with up to 50% fat are both very wet, so there is less solid matter and thus less fat content with each bite than in drier cheeses. Great news.

Types of cheese

If cheese didn't exist, you probably couldn't imagine it. Who would believe it possible? Thousands of different foods spanning every imaginable taste from savoury to sweet, most made by forming solid curds from the casein in milk. If only it were that simple. The slightest difference in temperature, of fat content, of pressure on the curds—even the time of year—will give you an utterly different result. And that's only cows' milk. However, there are basic threads of commonality that, once understood, will guide you to greater cheese pleasures.

Once you know how each of these cheese types looks, you can assess its condition and probable flavour just by looking, a boon at a cheese counter.

Fresh cheeses

Fresh soft cheeses deteriorate and sour exceptionally easily and must be kept chilled at all times. They are the exception to the rule that cheese tastes better when at room temperature—these taste better when below room temperature, but lightly chilled rather than deeply refrigerated.

All fresh soft cheese is basically curd, but the term curd cheese is usually used for those not made with full-fat milk. Even the lowest fat versions should smell clean, fresh and milky with no sourness, but they may have a chalky graininess, something diminished by the use of stabilisers and emulsifiers or of homogenisation, which do for curds what the Fairy Godmother did for Cinderella.

Type 1a, acid-curd

The original and simplest way, allowing milk naturally to sour, also called ripening, during which the lactic acid formed will solidify the milk and then split it into curds and whey. Soft curds can be lightly drained to make a softer curd cheese but further draining produces a firmer curd that can be shaped.

PANEER: is an Indian acid-curd cheese made with fresh milk by adding vinegar or lemon juice. Citric acid and tartaric acid can also be used. Such cheeses will always have a light acidic bite, refreshing when balanced and new, but quickly turning harsh and unpleasantly sour.

MASCARPONE: is an ancient Italian

indulgence originating south of Milan during the Renaissance. It is high-fat cream thickened with an acid, heated a little and drained lightly with no pressure, making a texture like a thick velvety custard. It is the draining that makes it a cheese rather than merely a soured cream. It has the lactic sharpness of crème fraîche and is more like clotted cream without the lumps, a molten cream cheese. It is for slathering on almost anything savoury or sweet. It can be used to enrich risotto, sauces, cheesecakes or ice creams. Now specially encountered in tiramisu, the meal-ending that masquerades as a traditional pick-me-up, which is what tiramisu means. It was only created in the late 20th century and layers mascarpone with sponge fingers, coffee, chocolate and alcohol.

Type 1b, sweet-curd

Obtained from fresh milk with a curding agent like rennet. Rennet is made from the stomachs of young ruminants and when added to fresh milk makes curds and whey without adding acidity to the milk's natural flavour. Vegetarian rennets use thistle, nettle and other plants and you'll find instructions on how to make your own on the Web. Non-animal curdling agents called vegetable rennets are made commercially from a specialised fungus.

Absolutely fresh milk or cream is rarely used for cheese making, for as it sits and ripens it develops a fuller flavour with more acidity. Getting a balance of sweet and sharp in the milk is the secret of many great cheeses;

traditional Lancashire cheese was always made from a mixture of morning milk which had ripened, plus fresh sweeter evening milk.

You can make cheese by curdling only cream, but it is very rich, and you would have to buy or make it. A commercial cream cheese is so called because it is rich and creamy tasting but is made with full milk, not cream. Homogenization of curds and whey means lower fat cheeses can now ape their betters, so cream cheese may simply taste that way but be quite low fat. Read the labels, ask the questions.

Unctuous triple-cream cheeses have extra cream added to the curd: Brillat-Savarin is a famed French example.

Type 1c, cottage cheese/farmers or pot cheese

Curd cheese that has been drained and washed so no whey remains, the part of milk that contains sugars. The richness and calorie count will depend only on the fat content of the milk used. It is usually made with skimmed or semi-skimmed milk, hence its blandness and thin flavour, which easily sours. Needs to be disguised.

Type 1d, fromage frais/fromage blanc

These French fresh cheeses are soft curd cheeses with a deceptively rich texture and velvety mouth feel, even those that are fat free. This is because once made, the curds and whey are forced through fine nozzles to homogenise the mixture, and that gets rid of any grittiness.

Ripened cheeses

The differences between ripened cheeses depend on what is done to the curds of the cheese by way of heating, cutting, draining, milling, molding or moulding, pressing, flavouring and so on, including treatment of the surface. These are identifiable from the appearance of the cheese, your starting point for assessment.

Type 2, bloomy unwashed rinds, soft-paste

Bloom is a furry white mould on the rind. These are mild, buttery cheeses with a balanced acidity and the rinds should have a mushroomy smell. Bloomy cheeses made with unpasteurised milk have much more flavour, a distinctive lactic farminess, and only Camembert de Normandie or Brie *fermier* should have any small brown or red markings on the rind.

The curds are sliced into molds and drain naturally with no pressing. They mature in about a month, developing a characteristic white furry mould on the outside—*penicillium candidum*. They ripen from the outside, so perfection is a satiny firm body with the same texture top to bottom, like soft butter. Freelance artisan cheesemakers can buy an array of cultures that vary the appearance and taste of the mould.

Fermier examples can be difficult to ripen evenly and so accepting a degree of central chalkiness is better than risking an over-ripe cheese. The rinds may be eaten, but it is eccentric and dangerous to eat any of these cheeses when runny and ammoniacal for they are overripe and such flavours were never the target of the makers.

These cheeses are specially good with fresh fruit; it's hard to beat perfect Brie with a perfect pear or Neufchâtel with red-fleshed strawberries. Camemberts are sometimes baked but this is not a French custom. Fougerus from Rouzaire are aged with fern fronds. Brie de Meaux was voted King of Cheeses at the 1815 Vienna Congress and when perfect is still life-changing.

Benchmarks: Brie de Meaux, Camembert de Normandie, Chaorce, Fourgerus, Neufchâtel (France); St Killian (Ireland).

Type 3, washed or brushed rind, soft-paste

The 'smelly feet'/'town drain running into the sea' cheeses, recognised visually by straw or red-coloured bacterial growth on the rind. They universally have a sweeter, gentler and more appealing savoury flavour than the nose advertises; the stinky, cooked-brassica skins are rarely eaten.

A soft curd is broken up as it is put into molds but rarely pressed. During ripening the rinds are washed with brine, wine, beer or other liquids that encourage the surface growth, which should not be overly sticky. The body is unctuous even waxen in texture, sometimes a little rubbery, so often bulges provocatively. Beware of any hint of ammonia, sliminess on the rind, or runniness, all signs the cheese should be retired.

Most unusual types are French

Vacherin and Swiss Mont d'Or, made only in winter, matured in spruce and very soft; they are often baked with wine and herbs.

Pair washed-rind cheeses with strong flavours, dark breads, pickles, big beers, smoked meats and charcuterie. Some Canadians are said to dip such cheese into their beer—and eat the rind, too?

Benchmarks: Pont L'Évêque, Maroilles, St Paulin, Munster, Reblochon (France); Limburger, Tilsiter (Germany); Stinking Bishop (England); Durrus (Ireland); Oka (Canada); Fontal, Bel Paese, Taleggio (Italy); Ridder (Norway); Limburger (USA); Havarti (Denmark).

Type 4, scalded cheeses

Also called pressed, uncooked cheeses.

Type 4a, lightly pressed

Expect a clean, light lactic flavour, sometimes salty but always with an underlying creaminess. The curd is obtained from hotter milk than for bloomy or washed rind cheeses and the curd is cut and drained at a higher temperature, the scalding, and is then lightly pressed in molds. The light pressing means they crumble easily when mature but have no appreciable rind. Retained whey shortens the cheese's life because this sours easily but there should be no moulds on the outside or discolouring on cut surfaces.

It's an eye-opener to taste a fresh farmhouse-made cheese cut from a full block, which explains their traditional popularity eaten with rich fruit cake. Commercial versions must be drier and blander and only approximate the pleasure. Great melters and toasters, Cheshire is judged the very best for a Rarebit, Welsh or not. Lancashire is traditionally baked with onions in a pie and updates very well crumbled over roasted vegetables or vegetarian pasta dishes.

Benchmarks: Farmhouse Caerphilly, Cheshire, Lancashire (England).

Type 4b, hard pressed

The curds are pressed harder and longer, giving a firmer cheese, which takes longer to mature. Curds for Farmhouse Cheddar are milled to evenness and then traditionally turned by hand to achieve the desired acidity, the proper cheddaring process, but which is now done mechanically for other Cheddars. These cheeses usually have a noticeable rind; Gouda is brined, commercial Cheddar is sprayed with hot water, and cheese cloth is used to bind handmade Farmhouse Cheddar.

Avoid any such cheeses that are cracked, mouldy or 'oiling' on the cut surface. Acidity on the palate is a good thing but bitterness indicates something has gone wrong, often with the starter culture. Modern starters can add a sweetness that is not traditional although now widely accepted.

Hard-pressed cheeses are universally as good for cooking as for eating but using a sharper, bigger-flavoured cheese means you use less and get better results; using bland 'cooking' Cheddar is pointless and very wasteful. Although harder to find, older versions are revelatory. Vintage Cheddar can be over two years old and comes with delightful crystals (*calcium lactate*) in the body, as might rich golden Old Gouda.

> *Benchmarks:* Balderson Heritage (Canada); Cantal (France); Derby, Sage Derby, Dunlop, Farmhouse Cheddar, Lincolnshire Poacher (UK); Coolea (Ireland); Edam, Gouda (Holland); Morbier, Salers, Tommes (France); Monterey Jack, Dry Jack (USA).

Type 5, cooked, hard pressed

The drained curd is cooked at even higher temperatures (43°C for Gruyère, 55°C for Parmesan) to give dry and tough curds that are then pressed very hard indeed. These cheeses take a long time to ripen, during which they soften and sweeten and then also last well.

Swiss Appenzeller and Gruyère also have a washed rind, so expect a rich nose. Le Gruyère Premier Cru is the only cheese that has won the title of Best Cheese in the World at the World Cheese Awards in London four times: in 1992, 2002, 2005 and 2006. Swiss Emmental has the big holes and is more likely to go stringy when heated. GRANA PADANO: is made south of the Po in Lombardy where cows feed on grass and hay. They are lighter in colour and faster to mature than Parmesans, flakier and cheaper.
PARMIGIANO REGGIANO: is made north of the Po in Mantua, where cows eat clover and lucerne. Yes, you can call it Parmesan but never the awful 'parm-uh-zhaan', neither Italian nor English. It is underrated as a table cheese when

young and in Italy you'll find them as *giovane*, *tipico*, *stravecchio* and *vecchio*, progressively older and more expensive.

Instead of forever grating Padano or Parmigiano for use like salt and pepper, cut them into very small cubes and enjoy explosions of their flavours as you eat. It is said these cheeses should not be served with fish or seafood pasta or risottos but I have had super success breaking that rule. Just saying ...

> *Benchmarks:* Allgauer Bergkase (Germany); Appenzeller, Emmental, Gruyère, Sbrinz, Raclette du Valais, Tête de Moine (Switzerland); Beaufort, Comte (France); Grana Padano, Parmigiana (Italy); Jarlsberg (Norway); Twineham Grange (UK); Gran Canaria (USA).

Type 6, plastic-curd cheese

Made mostly in Italy, where it is known as pasta filata, except for mozzarella, which is made everywhere there are cows and factories and pizza ovens. 'Plastic' refers to the texture of the cheese at the curd stage, rather than any reflection on eating texture and taste. The curd is soaked in hot whey, which makes it putty-like, thence it is kneaded and stretched to develop its particular textures before being teased or rolled into shapes from little balls (bocconcini) to huge Provolone.
HALLOUMI: originates in Cyprus and from its simple origins has become a vegetarian star—it's almost like meat but isn't. The rubbery slabs once developed their texture in brine baths but now the texture is created mechanically. Halloumi is less eaten fresh than

sliced and then grilled, fried or barbe-cued. Olive oil and dried Greek oregano make it a worthwhile choice rather than an anaemic substitute for meat.

MOZZARELLA: made with buffalo milk, the most common milking animal of southern Italy, mozzarella di bufala should be porcelain white, very soft and was meant to be eaten very fresh, as it is especially in sandwiches in New York's Italian quarters. If stored in whey or light brine the sniff test will tell if it is souring or soured. Add it in clouds to a pizza at the last moment, or bury it beneath other ingredients. The rubbery yellow mozzarella you are sold as moz-zarella or pizza mozzarella should be renamed.

Burrata: a mozzarella ball stuffed with stracciatelli, shredded mozza-rella, and single cream; one of the cheese world's most wicked and thrilling indulgences. Pull it by hand into ragged, dribbly clouds to top a perfect tomato and basil salad, slath-er some onto prosciutto with oozy ripe peaches and Parmigiano shards, layer chunks with prawns and crushed grilled tomatoes over ice-berg lettuce or plonk it onto any ripe fruit or fruit salad.

Fiore di latte: mozzarella made with cows' milk.

Mozzarella di bufala: fresh buffa-lo mozzarella is like eating milky clouds of a newborn's breath and if there is any skin if must be very thin; thick means older and this sometimes separates from the body. There is more than one type of moz-zarella di bufala made in Campana

in the south-west of Italy.

Mozzarella di Ciliegine: made in the shape of cherries.

Treccione di mozzarella: braided into a plait, up to 3 kg/6 lb in weight.

Mozzarella straciatelli: shredded and sold bathed in light cream and is also the luxurious centre of burrata.

Benchmarks: Burrata, Mozzarella di Bufala, Mozzarella Fiore de Latte, Provolone, Scamorza, Straciatella di Bufala (Italy); Halloumi (Cyprus).

Type 7, whey cheeses

Not strictly cheeses because they are not casein. Heating whey makes the available albumen collect in cloudy flakes, a process known rather won-derfully as flocculating: these contain many of the vitamins and virtually all the sugars of the original milk but are fat free. Today milk is usually added to the hot whey to increase the yield. They are moist and still relatively low-fat cheeses but the sweetness indicates the presence of lactose, milk sugar. There's no escaping calories.

True ricotta is one of the most useful of all cooking cheeses, lighter and more biddable than curd or cream cheese for everything from stuffings to cheesecakes, cooked or otherwise. It has all the clean fresh flavour of milk and when bought from a wicker-im-pressed cake that is still drooling with excess moisture makes the best cook-ing cheese of all, perfect for everything from savoury stuffings to sweet cheese-cakes. Try lightening ricotta with cream and then firming it to cutting texture with ground almonds and flavouring that with orange-flower water and orange zest; serve as is or in pastry and sprinkled with micro-roasted pine nuts as a 21st century fast-food version of the *Torta Pasquelina* of Naples.

A small loaf shape of ricotta can be baked with a slick of olive oil and topped with fresh herbs, becoming a light sliceable treat. Add eggs and it is rich enough to be a main. The mixture of ricotta, almonds and cream or milk can be made savoury too, say with chicken flakes, fresh tarragon and toasted almonds.

In Scandinavia boiling whey is continued until the lactose (sugar) caramelises and turns the cheese golden brown: *brunost* and *gjetost*, but when made with goats' milk whey the flavour is very challenging.

Benchmarks: Brocciu (Corsica); Brunost (Sweden); Gjetosts (Norway); Ricotta (Italy); Mizithra (Greece); Gjetost (Scandinavia).

Type 8, Blue cheeses

Traditional blue cheeses start with a scalded, lightly pressed curd that has fissures in which moulds will grow. Once a maker had to rely on ambient conditions, especially in caves, for the blue veins to develop but now when in a mold, the moist curds are injected with *penicillium roquefortii* or something similar; the softer body of Italian Gorgonzola uses *penicillium glaucum*. Spain's Cabrales blue still relies on natural invasion of spores while ageing in caves in Asturias.

Blue cheeses are the absolute ground-zero reason to release your very best sweet pudding wines, including Madeira, sherry and port. Present a gang of friends with a perfect blue cheese and a choice of pudding wines, varying from the lissome German, including an ice wine, through unctuous Bordeaux to the heady muscats of Southern France and then to the chewy masterpieces of Australian and New Zealand vineyards, perhaps even including a liqueur muscat—oh and a sweetish champagne, sec or riche. You can also do this the other way around, offer one wine but a choice of blue cheeses. Fewer might accept the invitation. Not always a bad thing.

Crumbled blue cheese makes accents in chilled salads or hot pasta and finely chopped Roquefort makes a gratifying last-minute addition to a creamy sauce for fish dishes. Blue cheeses all make excellent sandwich spreads when mixed into softened butter.

The warning signs of a blue cheese past its best are browning in the body, an unpleasant sourness on the nose rather than a rich acidity, obvious oiliness or weeping, or an excessively moist crust, which will also smell foul. Whatever their condition, the crusts should never be eaten, especially not used for soup, the equivalent of expecting shoe leather to make a good beef bouillon.

ROGUE RIVER BLUE: from Oregon USA won the overall best cheese at the World Cheese Awards in 2019. A seasonal, matured, autumn-made cows' milk cheese wrapped in vine leaves soaked in pear brandy, giving sherry and port aromas over powerful blue characteristics with unexpected caramel sweetness included. Also smoked.

ROQUEFORT: is a sheep-milk cheese but included here because it is such an icon of blue cheeses. Each of the caves of the Combalou mountain in which it matures harbours a slightly different strain of *penicillium roquefortii*, giving variations of flavour indicated on the label such as Caves de l'Abeille, Cave Baragnaudes, Cave Arnals, Cave Le Saul, Cave Rodat. The first is a light style suited for everyday eating, the second is considered an exceptional cheese and for great occasions, the third is—no, you eat your way to your own conclusions.

STICHELTON: is made the traditional Stilton way and in the same region, but with unpasteurised milk, so it cannot use the Stilton name or get PDO status. Comparing the two is like having the light turned on and off, with Stilton a faded memory of past glory but Stichelton a tangy, creamier blast from the past, the Stilton almost three-centuries of our ancestors would recognise. Sparkenhoe Blue is another raw-milk equivalent.

STILTON: cheese has PDO status and although traditionally made with unpasteurised milk current regulations require pasteurisation, with all the reservations this means.

New, gentler styles of soft blue cheeses that also have a bloomy rind are a good way to introduce blue cheeses to doubters.

Benchmarks: Bleubry (Canada); Blue Cheshire, Cornish Blue, Dorset Blue Vinney, Oxford Blue, Sparkenhoe, Stilton, Stichelton, Shropshire Blue, Blue Wensleydale (UK); Cashel Blue (Ireland); Bleu d'Auvergne, Fourme d'Ambert, Roquefort (France); Dolcelatte, Gorgonzola Naturale/Piccante, Gorgonzola Dolce (Italy); La Peral semi-blue, Cabrales mixed milks, Picon-Bejes-Tresviso (Spain); Rogue River Blue, Smoked Oregon Blue (USA); Mycella (Denmark).

Type 9, smoked and coated cheeses

Smoking commonly overpowers a cheese unless it is intrinsically brightly flavoured and savoury, ideally ewe or goat milk; some washed rind cheeses smoke well too, for they have an acidity which balances out any bitterness in smoke residue.

The use of ash as a coating will help dry a cheese and encourage the controlled growth of moulds that will in turn affect the texture and flavour of the body, commonly done with goat cheeses and on the few cheeses made in Champagne, all rather dry and chewy. We should be grateful for some advances away from tradition. Once the *Champenoise* used to mature the same cheeses under the bed, in the wife's urine in a chamber pot—it was called *fromage de cul* or bum cheese. Served as a nice wee cheese, I suppose.

Type 10, Goats' and sheep milk cheeses

Many traditional cheeses would once have been made with ewe or goat milk.

In Britain, cows were much more expensive to feed and their cheeses went to the boss. Anyway, sheep milk gives the greatest return of curd. The fat globules of both milks are so small they are naturally homogenised milks, making them so much easier to digest especially for infants unable to tolerate cows' milk.

All around the world, goat and sheep farmers are spearheading a huge increase in the interest and enjoyment of cheese made from these milks. To farmers, the advantages are enormous: they are not obliged or disobliged by milk-quota systems and because goats and sheep are free of diseases harmful to humans, the milk does not need to be pasteurised.

Whereas goat milk cheeses can be so white they seem blue, sheep milk cheeses have a warmer colour, which becomes benignly golden in pressed ones, like Sardinian Pecorinos or Spanish Manchegos, both cheeses that deserve great approbation. *Quesecos de Liebana* is a Spanish cheese made from a variety of milks.

Type 10a, Goat
Whether soft or pressed, goat milk cheeses can be light, lemony and herbal but all increase to become powerful and savoury as they age. Small truncated cones and logs are common shapes, some with an ash or charcoal coating that protects the surface from insects and encourages flavour-enhancing moulds. However, and it is a big however, goats' milk invariably has

undertones of what some call nuttiness, others recognise as musky.

If you have never eaten goat cheese before, take the merest smear or thinnest flake as a first taste. Some palates dramatically heighten the flavour of the oil that gives the goaty tang. The minutest amount blows up to fill the mouth with what you might imagine is the taste of licking between the rear leg and testicles of an aged male goat on a particularly hot day. The taste is so horrific victims can go into shock and severe panic. You must quickly get something fatty into their mouth, butter, milk, or cows' milk cheese. As with chillies, water, beer, wine or anything non-fatty won't wash away the oil but make the effect last longer.

Benchmarks: Banon, Chavignol/crottins de Chavignol, Pelardon, Picodon, Pouligny-Saint-Pierre en blanc and bleu, Selles-sur-Cher, Sainte-Maure de Touraine, Valencay (France); Beacons Blue, Harbourne Blue, Ribblesdale Blue, Ticklemore, Elrick Log, Highfields (UK); Queso Majorero (Fuertaventura, Spain).

Type 10b, Sheep
Sheep milk has the highest butterfat fat content of milks and gives the greatest yield of curd per volume of milk, hence its age-old appeal to peasants of yore and to smallholders today. Sheep cheese is often sold as Pecorino, the Italian name. They should have none of the farmy/nutty taste of goat milk cheeses, and as well as always being rich, they usually have a generous

salt content and can develop a robust sharpness. Thus Pecorino cheeses are as good as a condiment, a sheepish Parmigiano. They should be made from sheep milk but are commonly made from that of cows with a special starter culture added to give the acidity and punch needed. Read the label.

Feta should also be made from sheep milk but is much more likely to be made from bleached cows' milk.

Most of Spain's great cheeses are made with sheep milk. The most famous is Manchego, a cheese that should be as famous and popular as beaches and flamenco. A fascinating eating cheese and a great savoury grater instead of Italian granas. Just coming into view are cheeses from the Canary Islands.

Benchmarks: Feta (Greece); Ossau-Iraty-Brebis, Rocadmadour (France); Pecorino Romano (Italy); Pecorino Sardo (Sardinia); Beenleigh Blue (UK); Kasseri, Kefalotiri (Greece); Cratloe Hills (Ireland); Torta del Casar, Queso Zamorano, Queso Roncal, Queso Manchego, Idiazabal (Spain).

Roquefort: see under *Blue*.

Buying and tasting cheese

The huge number of cheeses fall into a surprisingly small number of categories. Each of the categories above is based on a technique that results in a recognizable family of cheeses, with broadly related flavours and appearances. Know the characteristics of each cheese type and you can judge the flavour-family to expect just by looking.

Cracking, greyness, unexpected colours or moulds, pronounced bitterness or sourness, oiliness, and unexpected textures are simple ways to know if an unfamiliar cheese is in good condition or not, even if it is a style typically smelly, runny or sharp tasting.

Once you decide a cheese is good to taste, fast judgements are not the thing. The fat content of a cheese coats the taste buds, slowing your assessment. So chew slowly, hold the cheese in your mouth a while until you can taste it all over your palate, and once you have swallowed think about the palate again.

The taste buds should be presenting you with ever-changing flavours. If the flavours stop half way along your tongue, the cheese has a short finish and so is incomplete and unsatisfying to eat. If it leaves flavours all the way to the back of the tongue and that linger for some time, it has true quality, offering the complete spectrum of tastes as well as many flavours.

Cheese with a short finish is never good value, no matter how cheap, and a cheese that fills the mouth and leaves flavour after you have swallowed is always good value, no matter how cheap. Either way, you'll need less to feel satisfied, for it has fed many senses and not just answered hunger pangs. That's value for money.

How to serve cheese

There are a few rules once you have brought to cool room temperature while still wrapped. That step is important to ensure you taste the full flavour spectrum, because flavour changes from the exterior to the centre. The differences are why diners should never cut across a wedge but should cut parallel to or at an acute angle to the cut side.

This is important for such as Brie and is especially so for a wedge of blue cheese and this is why it is posturing ignorance to scoop Stilton, Stichelton or other blue cheese—even if you are going to eat it all at one go. Scoops originally gathered the mites and weevils on a Stilton's crust, which were eaten with the cheese; they had nothing to do with serving the cheese itself. The flavours of a Stilton and every other blue cheese concentrate as you get to the centre but it is not riper there, it is bluer, because this is where the needles that injected the blue mould met. The true pleasure is enjoying the differences of flavour from inside the crust as you go towards the centre, achievable only from a perfect wedge. OK, once you have a wedge on your plate and you are going to eat it all, start and finish where you like. Just don't cut off the point of a wedge that is being shared.

Enjoy port or any other red or white sweet wine with blue cheeses, not in them. The addition of port to a Stilton can only to have been to disguise inferior cheese that had veered off on unwise adventures.

How to store cheese

Most fine cheese is ruined by adherence to old and new wives' tales and a misunderstanding of cheese-making. To get maximum pleasure from cut cheese, it must be protected from the air and kept wrapped when coming back to eating temperature. Let no one tell you otherwise. Think how much trouble cheese makers have gone to in creating nuances and pleasures for your palate by excluding air. It's only fair you take as much care.

The body of cheese ripens largely anaerobically, that is without direct contact with air, or with very little. Once cheeses have been cut they start to rot rather than ripen because of oxidisation and air-borne contamination. They should be stored at a cool temperature with the exposed edges protected from the air until the last minute before eating, and yes that can mean cling film and a refrigerator.

For the best flavour, cheese should be eaten at cool room temperature, so letting cheese 'breathe' unwrapped or storing it in a cheese bell at room temperature—or both—are the worst and most dangerous things imaginable. Cheese is the most perfect medium for bacterial culture but makes no distinction between good and bad, especially threatening to the very young and the very old.

Why should a refrigerator destroy cheese? An old-fashioned larder and safe would have been very much colder in winter than a domestic refrigerator;

cling film and the warmest part of a refrigerator are possibly the best friends cheese has ever had.

You do not see cheese 'sweating' in cling film or any other wrapping, but might see condensation on a cold cheese brought into a warmer ambiance and if the wrapping is loose. Cheese only sweats from its body if it is too hot and then it is fat content that has melted and migrated to the surface. Greaseproof paper does cheese badly for two reasons: it slowly absorbs the fat content and, being porous, lets air in and out, whilst also keeping a layer of slow moving air trapped against the surface, exactly right for the growth of unwanted moulds. A waxed paper is better and knowledgeable cheese mongers use specialist wrapping materials that are best pressed tightly to cut surfaces.

The cheeseboard

The classic cheese board goes for contrast. A savoury blue cheese (Stichelton), a full-flavoured pressed cheese (Farmhouse Cheddar) and a bloomy rinded example (Camembert de Normandie) make the ideal foundation. Within each of those flavour styles there is much opportunity for originality, vertically and horizontally.

The vertical cheese board offers a choice of flavours from top to bottom of the spectrum of cheese types. The savoury cheese might be a Majorero sheep cheese from Fuertaventura rather than a blue, the pressed cheese a lighter sweeter Wensleydale and the soft cheese some majestic Brie de Meaux.

A horizontal board works best when you also want to present a single special wine. It offers cheeses of the same category but of different ages, styles or piquancy. So, soft fresh and aged goat cheeses with an edgy dry Provençale rosé, a choice of flowery Swiss Gruyère and other washed rind cheeses with a deep Meursault; English farmhouse cheeses with elegant Australian Cabernet Shiraz; or a trio of blue cheeses with a chilled sweet, late-picked Riesling from New Zealand.

Good bread and plain crackers are all you need plus excellent butter for those who must.

For travellers, here are recommendations from the other side of Earth.

Australian cheeses

A selection of a few favourites by Russell Smith, Chief Judge, Australian Grand Dairy Awards.
ASH BRIE (COW). QUEENSLAND: A smooth creamy paste combined with delicate earthy, floral notes, an exceptionally good example from grass-fed cows. Woombye Cheese Company.

FURNEAUX (COW). KING ISLAND, TASMANIA: The most flavoursome of Australian Brie-styles. The initial sweet milky flavour persists even as the cheese develops more earthy, pungent flavours.

HEIDI FARM RACLETTE (COW). BURNIE, TASMANIA: A consistently superb cheese with the typical pliable texture. Big flavour with pleasant sulphur notes and extended mid palate nutty flavours and lingering umami savoury characters. A great melter at three months and an outstanding table cheese when older. From Saputo Dairy.

HERITAGE RESERVE CHEDDAR (COW). BEGA, NEW SOUTH WALES: Only available from the Bega Cheese factory shop at 18-24 months, with big bold flavours, calcium crystals and a slightly crumbly texture as the proteins begin to break.

KING RIVER GOLD WASHED RIND (COW). NORTH EAST VICTORIA: Yeasty aromas and flavour reminiscent of Taleggio with a soft, luscious paste, a slightly gritty rind with a smoky, nutty flavour. Milawa Cheese Company.

LA LUNA (ORGANIC GOAT) CENTRAL VICTORIA: The Loire Valley-style gives this soft ripened cheese a silky-smooth texture becoming creamy with citrus notes and hints of fresh hay, which develop as the cheese ages. Uses a mould exclusive to Holy Goat Cheese.

MARINATED GOAT CHEESE (GOAT). VICTORIA: Meredith Dairy makes the finest quality goat cheese available in Australia and internationally. This soft cheese marinated in garlic and herbs has a refreshing citrus tang and a soft, spreadable texture. A favourite for many Australian cheese lovers. Another plus for this producer is their total dedication to regenerative farming.

MONFORTE (RAW COW). ADELAIDE HILLS SOUTH AUSTRALIA: The producer's flagship, this is a raw milk, semi-hard cheese with a complexity that is initially sweet, milky and fruity with emerging brothy and toasted nut flavours and a subtle earthy undertone. Section 28 Artisan Cheeses.

OAK BLUE (COW) SOUTH GIPPSLAND, VICTORIA: The most complex of blues made at Berry's Creek, a cross between a Gorgonzola picante and Stilton, exhibiting the best flavours of the world's great blues.

RIVERINE BLUE (BUFFALO). SOUTH GIPPSLAND, VICTORIA: The complex savoury flavours and the creamy texture develop due to careful selection of cultures by Berry's Creek and high-quality milk from nearby Sunrise Plains.

VENUS BLUE (SHEEP). SOUTH EAST VICTORIA: Good balance of blue aromas and subtle flavours with a slightly firm but smooth texture. The starter cultures are developed from Prom Country Cheese's own flock's milk. Best from five months on.

WARATAH WASHED RIND (SHEEP). EAST VICTORIA: Produced in spring and summer months using a complex mix of starters and a Geotrichum mould: a mild cheese at four weeks, then developing pungent and funky brassica notes. Prom Country Cheese.

New Zealand cheeses

A very short list of recommended and best-selling cheeses curated by uber-caterer Grant Allen and Jacqui Dixon of Sabato in Auckland, one of the best gourmet and deli ingredient shops in the world.

CLEVEDON BUFFALO WALNUT GOUDA: an unexpected affinity between the richness of buffalo milk and green-sweet fresh walnuts made this an instant hit.

EVANSDALE TANIA SMOKED: a farmhouse Brie-style that is hot-smoked by manuka (ti-tree) chips to make a unique offering.

GRINNING GECKO KAU PIRO: a washed rind cheese with typical pungent smell, hence the name that means stinky cow in Te Reo Maori.

KAIKOURA TENARA: soft ash-coated goat cheese with a fudgy interior and subtle flavours of walnut and cinnamon. Can been aged for up to 150 days.

KINGSMEAD ROBIOLINO: an Italian-style very creamy soft cheese.

MAHOE VERY OLD EDAM: mild, fruity in flavour, smooth to cut, with crunchy crystals and a full nutty aftertaste. Won NZ Champions of Cheese four years in a row.

MEYER GOAT GOUDA: sweet, creamy and recommended for melting; also available aged or smoked.

MT ELIZA BLUE MONKEY: rich and buttery, marbled with intense blue flavours that melt in your mouth. Single farm origin from half-Jersey cows.

NIEUWENHUIS POUKAWA FOG: ashed soft white goat cheese log with a Geotrichum rind that slowly engulfs the fudgy centre.

OVER THE MOON: a goat Camembert-style that's delicate when young and becomes tangy and very complex as it quickly ripens.

Cream

NEED TO KNOW

Cream is the lighter but fattier portion of full milk.

Cream is largely water but also contains most of the butterfat.

Single/light cream can be whipped if you incorporate egg white.

Double/heavy cream is churned to make butter.

Whipping cream gives greater volume than double/heavy cream but has less texture.

Soured cream and equivalents are thickened by the action of lactic acid.

Homogenisation make low-fat creams seem richer and thicker.

Different types of cream are obtained by different degrees of separation, so that single cream has more of the original milk in it and double cream has less. To make single/light cream from double/heavy cream or to make double/heavy cream go further when you are whipping it, dilute with full or skimmed milk.

Types of cream

CLOTTED CREAM: the richest and most heavenly cream of all and still mainly produced in Devon and Cornwall, where it has DOP status. It has a minimum fat content of 55% and is traditionally made by putting full milk in shallow pans that are left until the cream has risen. Then you slowly heat this to a temperature of 82°C and allow it to cool overnight. By morning the cream has coagulated into thick lumpy clots that are then skimmed off. Commercially, the same effect is obtained by scalding separated cream in shallow pans and then transferring it into tins or bottles. I don't think it tastes as good, but this may be because it is subsequently sterilised.

Ashta: is Middle Eastern and includes many things claiming to be clotted cream; traditionally it was made by scraping away the fine curd from the top of boiling milk but can now be made with cream and with cornflour or bread as a thickener.

Kaimak: is Near Eastern, made like clotted cream and incorrectly claimed to be a cheese. This could be what Phoenicians introduced to Cornwall and Devon when they came to trade for tin and copper.

Staka: unique to Cyprus and often incorrectly called cheese but it is not curded. Traditionally it was made from goat or sheep milk left to itself for a day or two, when the tiny fat globules would eventually rise and be collected. There are other methods using heat and related products including a type of butter.

CRÈME FRAÎCHE: once peculiarly

French but now a British table mainstay, it is a cultured soured cream, originally sweeter and creamier than UK soured creams, which were based on lesser single cream. Lower fat versions are now common because homogenisation gives these the bigger mouth feel of richer creams. Crème fraîche is good for finishing or making savoury sauces, anywhere you would have chosen whipped or clotted cream, particularly with a rich, sweet chocolate cake.

> *Crème fraîche d'Isigny AOC:* like eating smooth clotted cream with a touch of acidity. If you want fresh cream in France without a lactic acid content, it is *crème fleurette.*

DOUBLE/HEAVY CREAM: minimum butterfat content of 48% and gives the best texture for whipped cream. Reduced to half its volume by gentle simmering and then flavoured with herbs or a vegetable purée, double cream gives the simplest rich sauce of all. It does not curdle if boiled, unless you also include something very acidic. When combining with another liquid, add the thicker to the thinner, or curd is what you'll get.

Double cream freezes very well, better if lightly sweetened. Stir well or whip after defrosting.

EXTRA-THICK CREAM: double/heavy cream that has been homogenised in the same way as many *fromages blancs* q.v., so it spoons from the carton as thickly as whipped cream.

FROZEN CREAM: double cream is frozen in single portions and sold in free-flow packs, so you never need go without cream or have to throw away any that has gone off. Thoroughly recommended.

HALF CREAM: not widely available, this has a butterfat content of no less than 12%. It's what is called coffee cream in Europe and Half and Half in America. A sort of super-rich homogenised milk, it is perhaps too rich for day-to-day drinking but excellent for cooking, for the higher fat content helps cakes and biscuits to keep longer.

SINGLE/LIGHT CREAM: this must have at least 18% butterfat but can have more. It is used as a pouring cream and can be used in coffee. It is always homogenised to prevent separation of the cream and milk; even so it does not freeze well because it tends to separate.

SMETANA: a Central European style of soured cream available in low and high-fat versions.

SOURED/SOUR CREAM: this is single cream that has had a culture of bacteria added to it after homogenisation and pasteurisation. The culture forms acid as a by-product, giving the subsequent thickening and light acidic flavour. It keeps very well under refrigeration and is perfectly indispensable once you know about it, used to accompany everything from baked potatoes to fudgy chocolate cake.

WHIPPING CREAM: has a minimum butterfat content of 35%, which is the ideal for getting the maximum volume of whipped cream. You have to whip it longer than double cream and that incorporates more air, giving greater ultimate bulk but lacking the richness of the real thing.

Fermented Milks

NEED TO KNOW

Developed to make raw milk safer to drink.

Most are like thinner yoghurt.

All use an added bacterial culture, which produces acid.

Kefir is cultured with bacteria plus yeast, and greatly reduces lactose content.

Sour pasteurised milk is dangerous to drink as there is no control over what is causing acidity or thickening.

Fermented milk drinks are made by the addition of a specialised culture that gives a pleasant acidic tang and thickens it slightly but does not form a curd unless left a very long time. In general they are less sour than yoghurt because they are less concentrated and thus are used in chilled summer soups and in cooking.

Traditionally these drinks were developed because the acidity defeated toxins in raw milk and so made them safer to drink, but some have other advantages, like the much lower lactose content of kefir.

CULTURED BUTTERMILK: it's difficult to buy true buttermilk, the liquid left over after cream has been churned to make butter. Instead, skimmed milk is fermented with bacteria obedient enough to give the acidity and approximate flavour of the real thing. It works like buttermilk in such as soda breads but how it can be called buttermilk escapes me.

KEFIR: made with a 'mother' or starter culture of grains that is a mixture of bacteria and yeasts, kefir is sharp with lactic acid, slightly effervescent and has a very low alcohol content. Kefir has a distinct health claim because it reduces milk's lactose considerably. Made with every type of milk, the mother can also ferment in fruit or vegetable juices, dependent on their nutritional content.

KUMISS, ALSO KOUMIS: an ancient feature of Kazakh life, this is mare's milk with an introduced ferment. The increased acidity will make it safer to drink and it is credited with many health benefits. If it is not mare's milk it is not kumiss.

LASSI: yoghurt whisked up with water to make an acidic refresher that's better with sparkling water and should have a touch of rose water.

LEBEN: fermented milk associated with the Middle East that's thinner than most yoghurt and used as both drink and as food. In North Africa it means buttermilk.

SOURED MILK: all manner of bacteria make milk sour and thicken and many of those that settle and grow in pasteurised milk are downright dangerous. Dissuade friends and children from drinking soured pasteurised milk.

Other Milks

BUTTERMILK: rarely available today, this is what is left after you churn cream to make butter. If made from unripened cream it is quite sweet; ripened cream gives buttermilk a slight sourness and this acidity works with baking soda to raise soda bread. See *Cultured buttermilk.*

CONDENSED MILK: reduced by two thirds and then sweetened. Generations of the inhabitants of hot countries are hooked, and every beverage, including tea, is served with condensed milk. When microwaved with care in a large covered bowl it makes a wondrous caramel sauce. Chilled, and then whipped with an equivalent volume of double/heavy cream, it makes a superb ice-cream base that never goes icy; see *Plum ice-cream recipe* on page 162. Indian ice cream or *kulfi* is traditionally made by reducing milk over heat but condensed milk can be used to make it much faster.

DULCE DE LECHE: a South American caramelised reduction of sweetened milk widely used in baking and desserts. An excellent equivalent is quickly made by microwaving condensed milk. A vegan version is made with coconut cream and milk plus brown sugar.

EVAPORATED MILK: unsweetened condensed full milk.

Ice Cream

NEED TO KNOW

Dairy ice cream: guarantees the fats included are all dairy fats; nothing else is guaranteed—see below.

Ice cream: if the label says only this, the contents will be made from milk and other fats and the label must also say 'contains non-milk fat' or 'contains vegetable fat'.

Low-calorie ice creams: a contradiction in terms because ice cream needs cream and sugar. Substitutes will be seen on the label. Up to you.

Pareve: kosher and dairy-free, thus stuffed with substitutes. Baffling.

Premium ice creams: can contain dairy or 'superior' non-dairy fats. Contain less air, cost a little more; never in bulk packs.

Standard ice creams: basic standards, competitively priced, containing milk plus non-dairy or vegetable fat and the maximum amount of air permitted. Bulk packs.

Super-premium or luxury: dairy ice creams with high fat content and low air additions. Likely to be in smaller packs. Egg and egg yolks sometimes also included.

I ce cream is the greatest example of a small portion of something totally natural, inescapably voluptuous and honestly flavoured being more enjoyable than a greater portion of something merely cold, smooth and approximate.

True dairy ice cream is expensive and so the market is crammed with approximations designed to be cheap or to have lower calorie content. Read the labels. Some try valiantly by using coconut milk, which is at least natural, as is stevia, a herb with sensational sweetening power but no calories.

For anyone who cares what they put into their bodies, ice cream, gelatos, sherberts and sorbets are amongst the most challenging choices. If you buy in cones or tubs from an ice-cream parlour, you won't know what you are eating. Here are some of the ingredients you will not be told about.

What else is in ice cream?

EMULSIFIERS: a chemical way to mix water and fats, to make the product feel richer in the mouth than it would without them.

FLAVOUR/FLAVOURING: a manufactured 'equivalent' is used instead of the real thing. Chocolate 'flavouring' is not the real thing; 'strawberries with strawberry flavour' would mean a mixture of strawberries and a flavouring to make the 'flavour' go further.

STABILISERS: soak up excess water, stop ice crystals forming in fluctuations of temperature; dramatically increase amount of air that can be trapped. Premium products should not use stabilisers.

SWEETENERS: sugar is essential to the bulk and satiny texture of real ice cream and much of that is replicated artificially by emulsifiers and stabilisers. Artificial sweeteners are not allowed in standard or dairy ice cream; but the demand for lower calorie ice cream products means that sugar-reduced, calorie-reduced products are increasingly seen. Provided they are labelled as such, they may include fructose (fruit sugar) or alternative sweeteners.

The herb stevia gives natural calorie-free sweetness but does not give the mouth-feel and texture of sugar. Check the label to see which of the above has been added as compensation.

Other Frozen Sweeties

GELATO: more milk than cream and slow churning takes in less air than in ice cream, making gelato feel richer than it is. Gelato is stored and served at a higher temperature than ice cream, so the mouth enjoys its tastes and flavours faster than ice cream, because the taste-buds get to work sooner.

SHERBERT: a sorbet (see below) that has some dairy content, often milk or ice cream, and is always frozen with air content.

SORBETS: sugar and fruit juice or pulp, frozen with the addition of air; without air they are an iced lolly. Sorbets have no fat content but are not a low-calorie alternative to ice cream.

Yoghurt

NEED TO KNOW

Yoghurt is pre-digested milk and absorbed three times faster than fresh milk.

Yoghurt is not a natural product as bacteria must be added to milk.

The bacteria create acid that thickens milk and kills many micro-organisms.

Low-fat yoghurt can be higher in calories because of added sugar for 'mouth feel'.

All yoghurt is live but commercial brands are very diluted or inhibited.

Traditional added bacteria are thought not to survive in the gut.

Acidophilus strains are believed to survive and have measurable benefits.

Note all claims for yoghurt and gut health are preceded by 'may help ...'

Pro-biotics is another name for the cultures in yoghurt.

Strained yoghurt is higher in calories but lower in lactose.

There's no such thing as 'natural' yoghurt. Pre-digestion of milk has traditionally been by two bacilli, *lactobacillus bulgaricus* and *streptococcus thermophilis*. Neither is found in milk but must always be introduced, usually by adding ready-cultured yoghurt to that milk. As the bacilli digest the milk to fuel their lives, they create acidity that thickens the milk and kills potentially dangerous bacteria and, so, even if not pasteurised or boiled, the milk becomes safer and longer lasting, imbuing yoghurt with seemingly magical health-giving properties.

In essence, yoghurt is a safe way for the body to eat the full range of protein that humans need without killing and eating animals, important in poor subsistence lifestyles.

In the West we gave yoghurt a reputation it did not deserve. Yoghurt's proselytisers reasoned Bulgarians lived a long time because they ate a lot of goat, sheep and buffalo-milk yoghurt, ignoring genetic contributions and that Bulgarians lived a basically healthier life on a more balanced diet than most in the West. The same theorists concluded yoghurt's acid-producing bacilli were the key, that they were the same as those in our digestive system, and if we ate more of them they would purify our bowels, making us healthier and less mortal. It's not true, for although the two classic yoghurt bacilli are similar to some in our guts, they are quite different and do not survive there.

An echo of this belief is still heard in mistaken claims that yoghurt will replace digestive flora lost by taking antibiotics. For many sick people, eating milk products quickly makes them worse if their digestive system is upset, for milk is simply a ready supply of food upon which bad as well as good risk organisms thrive. Anyone who suggests milk or milk products will settle an upset stomach is living in the Dark Ages.

There is better news. The much rarer yoghurt bacillus, *lactobacillus acidophilus* might have some part to play internally. Even if it doesn't, it gives yoghurts a sweeter, smoother flavour that is very attractive, and as it is now widely available an acidophilus yoghurt seems a good choice. Note as you check this out, that all reliable books and websites claim only that yoghurt, even with acidophilus, '*may* help'.

Connections with good health mean yoghurt is also thought good for dieters, and it can be, provided you think clearly and read the labels.

Unlike cream, yoghurt will infallibly curdle if added to liquid that is boiling hot or that will subsequently boil. Let the yoghurt come to room temperature then whisk it into the hot liquid just before serving. Otherwise, you can stabilise plain yoghurt by heating gently and thickening with cornflour.

Strained yoghurt can be used in Indian marinades as an alternative to authentic freshly made and drained milk curd.

Types of yoghurt

FRUIT AND FLAVOURED YOGHURTS: may be made from any kind of milk, but are generally sweetened with sugar and thus offer far more calories than you imagined. Some of course are made from skimmed milk and some are artificially sweetened. A fruity yoghurt that is genuinely lower in fat and contains no sugar is hard to find. Read the label, remembering ingredients are listed in order of volume.

GOAT-MILK YOGHURTS: goats' milk is difficult and thus expensive to separate, so is always full-fat. The fat globules are very small and so are more easily digested, even by those who have problems with cows' milk, a contribution to the legend that yoghurt is what gave Bulgarians longer lives. The greater availability of powdered or frozen goats' milk means making your own is easy.

Beware when serving it that some people simply cannot abide goats' milk anywhere near them, as it turns into a sweaty, musky nightmare on their palate.

HOME-MADE YOGHURTS: UHT or long-life milk are widely thought to give the best and creamiest result, and that's because it is homogenised. You can use any milk, including that made from powder. In fact, many add milk powder to milk to make thicker, richer yoghurts.

LOW-FAT/DIET YOGHURTS: will have been made from skimmed or part skimmed milk and can be usefully sweetened with artificial substances. But not always. Look carefully at the label because many low-fat yoghurts contain more sugar than a full-fat yoghurt, to compensate for the lesser mouth feel of the reduced fat content and thus low-fat yoghurts might be higher in calories than a full-fat milk version. Remember that any substance ending in *ose* is a sugar; *sucrose, glucose, fructose, galactose, lactose* and more. Honey is a mixture of some of these simpler sugars.

SHEEP-MILK YOGHURTS: the original Greek yoghurts were made with sheep milk, always high in calories as its fine fat globules cannot be separated from the rich milk. Strained sheep-milk yoghurt is a nightmare for dieters, absolute bliss for others and never has farmy or musky flavours.

STRAINED YOGHURTS: often called Greek-style yoghurts, for these were the types first marketed. By compacting the solids through straining off the whey, the fat/calorie content is concentrated but the lactose content is greatly reduced. Low-fat versions are made with homogenised fat-reduced milk.

Fish Eggs, Fish and Seafood

Caviar

NEED TO KNOW

Caviar is a broad term for the salted, fresh eggs of many large fish.

Caviar from fish other than sturgeon must be prefixed with the fish's name.

This is the most complicated of gourmet & deli ingredients, because of both wild and farmed sources and the impossibility of sampling before buying.

The best caviar is from sturgeons, found in every ocean and such fresh water as the Gironde, the Great Lakes, the Mississippi and China's Amur River.

Like the crocodile, the sturgeon is unchanged since prehistory.

All wild sturgeons are endangered and protected.

Malassol is the most lightly salted and highly prized standard of sturgeon caviar.

Caviar is sometimes pasteurised for longer-life.

CITES imposes strict limits on export of 'wild' caviar, to protect the fish and local food sources, which has led to the expansion of farmed caviar.

Caviar is now farmed worldwide, from Exmoor in the UK's West Country to Germany, France, USA, Uruguay, Russia and China.

Crossbreeding of sturgeon species produces types more suited to farming.

No-kill caviar is produced by milking the eggs prematurely; these must be hardened with a calcium solution and have a firmer texture.

Wild species are being multiplied by introduction of fry into natural habitats.

Caviar was best known from the Russian and Iranian shores of the Caspian Sea; the traditional species were the beluga, oscietra and sevruga.

Each sturgeon species produces caviar of different sizes and flavour distinctions.

Caviar has twice the nutriment of most meat and is equal to the finest pork.

Caviar has always been eaten as a local standby: US caviar was once given away in New York bars to increase drinkers' thirst.

China now produces more than half of the world's sturgeon caviar.

Caviar should not be touched with any metal other than gold; use bone, shell, semi-precious stone, wood or plastic.

Air and heat diminish caviar quickly.

Onion and egg as accompaniments were introduced post-WWI to disguise the taste and smell of suspect caviar stored too long during war; it is incorrect and pretentious to use them today.

Caviar should not be cooked but added to a sauce just before serving or used as a last-minute garnish on hot or cold foods.

Tasting and serving

What's the fuss about? Rarity and expense contribute to expectations of unique experiences and these are justified when served perfect caviar. There's the colour, black or grey, often with dark green or gold flashes, or rare albino eggs that shimmer like miniature pearls. On the nose and the palate there's a whisper of the sea but not of fish, often notes of hazelnut, maybe the earthy richness of derelict seaweed, and then constant bursts against the palate and tongue that dissolve into briny oyster-like complications silkened with oil, bringing butteriness and creaminess. The next mouthful will be different with new nuances and profundities. That's what caviar should be and that's why there should be nothing acidic present, save only soured cream and its friends. Or vodka.

I know it's repetition, but please remember that onion was introduced after WWI to prevent the nose from detecting the fishiness of old-aged caviar and egg was to coat the palate so it could not taste it. They negate every nuance of what you pay so much to experience but have become popular because it's perceived the ceremony enhances the experience, which probably means others are likely to notice how much money you are spending.

The traditional test for freshness and flavour is to smear a small helping onto the ball of your thumb, sniff deeply and then to lick it off. The slightest whiff or taste of fishiness means something is wrong. You do not employ such technique if you have washed in something scented, or have not washed for some time.

Caviar deteriorates rapidly when exposed to the air and the finer the caviar the faster the deterioration. It might last for an hour but if it has not been treated properly before opening it will oxidise and sour sooner— much sooner. Ideally, you should open caviar to the air for no more than the moments it takes to transport it to the table.

Just before serving, open the chilled container and turn the caviar into a delicate dish of the finest, whitest porcelain, never onto silver or directly on to ice. That vessel should be cosseted in ice and taken to the table with small spoons of gold or gold-plated silver or of bone, shell, horn, wood, even plastic. Or such semi-preciousness as amber, malachite or lapis lazuli. Whatever is to hand.

The late, great Robert Carrier taught me to eat caviar on thin toast with thickly smeared unsalted Isigny butter, and he was absolutely right. My favourite Christmas treat, ideally for two, is warm, saffron-fragranced brioches, a bowl of chilled soured cream and as much caviar as the budget permits. The colour, temperature and texture contrasts forbid anything but festivity.

If not toast, then small blinis, pancakes of wheat flour or buckwheat. And lemon juice? Well, only if you use the absolute minimum, and even then ... I wouldn't, you shouldn't.

Those who truly enjoy caviar eat it directly from the spoon, or spoon it onto the top of the fleshy cushion between the thumb and forefinger and lick it off.

Because there is so much caviar about, its salty zing is increasingly used to heighten and brighten unexpectedly, in creamy sauces for fish or veal, on such earthy vegetables as artichoke, indulgently on foie gras, diabolically wicked on a salad caprese—even on a deconstructed sticky toffee pudding, taking salted caramel to startling places.

Buying caviar

Read the label. Fabulous packaging and prices plus the dizzying modern choice because of farming should not blind you. Whatever it sounds like, look to see the origin of the caviar, which has to be on the tin somewhere; is it wild or farmed? In a restaurant they should tell you on the menu. It is always worth doing on-line research before you buy or order. Huge restaurant mark ups, like those for wine, are not justified for caviar, when a modest percentage will still be a good profit.

Optimum storage temperature for malassol caviar is -2°C/30°F but this does not mean deep-freezing, which is fatal to caviar, reducing it to a sorry sort of soup, but unopened tins and jars keep well for several weeks in a domestic or retail refrigerator. It is important the container is turned upside down every day or so, to keep the oil evenly distributed. Anyone who does not know this and do this should not be allowed to sell caviar.

Types of caviar

Just a reminder, the classic Caspian sturgeons are the Beluga, Oscietra and Sevruga.

Albino: exceptionally rare but the Sterlet sturgeon produces it.

Amur: see *Kaluga.*

Aquitaine: the Gironde in south-west France is a traditional home to sturgeon but where they are now also farmed in great abundance.

Avruga: see *Herring.*

Beluga: from the monstrous white Caspian sturgeon, these are the largest and most fragile eggs, which do not keep well. The most expensive by far, beluga is not generally thought the best flavoured but enjoyed more for its rarity and the obvious swagger of its size.

Californian: the native Californian white sturgeon is successfully farmed inland by Tsar Nicoulai to produce a variety of superior caviars.

Danish: see *Lumpfish.*

Flying Fish: exceptionally viridescent roe, a favourite of the Japanese, but with a determined crunch not a million miles away from having sand kicked into your mouth.

Golden: many farmed sturgeons and their hybrids produce golden versions in small enough quantity to justify high prices but when I tasted one it reminded me of boiled eggs. Historically golden caviar was obtained three ways:

In Russia Cossacks hacked holes through late winter/early spring ice, to spear sturgeons for immature, golden yellow roe said to make the senses reel.

Golden caviar for the Shahs of Persia came from the rare albino oscietra.

Or it was from young oscietra.

Hackleback: this small sturgeon native to the US Mississippi and Missouri regions still supplies a 'wild' caviar of jet-black, small eggs with a notably creamy taste.

Herring: smoked, small-grained herring roe mixed with flavourings and colouring is sold under such names as Avruga and Anuga. Nowhere near the real thing but useful when no-one will know better.

Kaluga: from the biggest freshwater sturgeon, which can be 1,000 kg and 5.6 m long; native to the Amur River on the north-western Russian/China border, it produces much admired caviar, judged mild and creamier than many.

Lojrom: truly delicious small-grained, luminously golden roe made by the Swedes. Often sold as Caviar of Kalix (the variety of salmonid that produces it), it is well worth seeking if you fancy recreating royal Swedish banquets, where it always features.

Lumpfish: from Denmark, lumpfish roe is black or red, with an uncomplicated flavour with few nuances. Used to accompany smoked salmon or on canapés of thin, buttered toast, it is pretty and expensive looking. Once, desperate for a new idea for a dip for crudités, I mixed the black

version with a little mayonnaise, lemon juice and cream cheese. It was an absolute sensation. Not for the flavour, but for the colour. It turned a bright blue and both children and adults ate it with mixed gusto, and horror. Blue food does that.

Oscietra: spelled many ways, a Caspian sturgeon that provides masses of eggs varying from grey to black and are medium in size. Commonly chosen as the best flavoured and for the most satisfying mouth-pop. The oscietra produces so many sizes and colours of caviar it is not unknown for wicked packers to pass off the larger ones as beluga. There is an infallible test. If you crush a beluga egg, the resultant smear will be grey-black; oscietra will always leave a brown-yellow smear.

Paddle fish: a freshwater sturgeon found in Mississippi, Tennessee and Kentucky that gives a small grey bead, very like sevruga, and with a 'fresh sea-breeze finish'.

Pressed caviar: called caviar jam by many, this is late-season, lower-quality or broken caviar salted and pressed and quite inexpensive. Pretty canapés and lots of decorative possibilities.

Russian varieties: Russia eats and exports an astonishing array of fish eggs, all called caviar. There's pike, pollock and herring, perch, carp, cod and hake, various grades of salmon caviar, zander, crucian and capelin caviar, which is particularly recommended and sometimes found in sushi and sashimi.

Salmon: usually from Canada or Russia, sometimes sold as Ketovia/Keta, this is usually the roe of the Canadian chum (dog salmon) or something similar in Russia. This 'lesser-caviar' is pink-orange and large and cheaper. In candlelight and with overawed friends I have known it presented as legendary golden caviar with total success. The trouble is those eggs can be as big as tapioca—would you eat fishy tapioca?

Sevruga: a small-grained Caspian roe that many hold gives a better flavour than beluga.

Shad: American shad are related to herrings and said to provide a roe comparable to caviar.

Trout: smaller eggs than salmon caviar but just as orange, bright and shiny.

Whitefish: native to the Great Lakes, the roe is a gorgeous pale golden colour, with a mild flavour and clean pop.

Further reading: Caviar—A Global History by Nichola Fletcher (Reaction Books).

Fish and Seafood

ABALONE: meat from a number of univalve molluscs, sold frozen or in cans. The best kind is from Japan or the Shandong province of China. Can be eaten directly from the can, and if cooked again is best done quickly to avoid toughening.

In New Zealand there is an equally admired equivalent, the *paua*; as well as curiously rich but subtle flesh that tastes the way I imagine a pearl might, it has an irridescent shell that makes spectacular jewellery, often confused with butterfly wing.

ANCHOVY: native to the Mediterranean and the English Channel, anchovy are caught as far away as the Black Sea and Scandinavia. The best are said to come from the area between Nice and the Spanish province of Catalonia, as do many of the best recipes for their use; in Spanish they are *boquerones.*

Anchovies are sold in many forms, whole or filleted, in salt or in brine, in oil or in vinegar, but the older way of salting anchovies whole is difficult to buy these days. Dry salted anchovies are thought superior but must be thoroughly rinsed or soaked in water or milk.

Russians preserve them in spiced vinegar, the Norwegians in a spiced brine, Italians do anchovies in a chillied oil, *alici en salsa piccante,* reckoned to be amongst the very best way of eating them. In Freemantle, Western Australia, anchovies are canned as Ozchovies.

Anchovies packed in brine or oil are interchangeable, although the former should be rinsed with water or milk and the latter are less highly flavoured. The most common uses for flat fillet or curls of anchovy are on pizza, or in such salads as Salade Niçoise, and for assertive canapés.

The unexpected ability of anchovy fillets to dissolve into an unctuous paste when heated with olive oil, or merely to disappear into other liquids, is what makes them a standby of those who take to them. Merely stirring a couple into the oil or butter, or both, to go onto pasta opens new vistas of flavour. Naturally, you would add lots of sliced garlic from the start (chopped would be too mimsy here), and chunky fresh herbs. Parsley excels with anchovies.

Look for *anchoiade*, an anchovy paste of salted whole ones, parsley, oil and garlic, spread on oil-soaked bread and baked until brown, a peasant version of the anchovy toast served as a savoury in London's men's clubs. The Piedmontese of Northern Italy make *bagna cauda*, used as a pasta sauce or a hot dip for bread or raw vegetables, and is regarded as reliably indigestible unless brought up to it from birth; it uses equal weights of anchovies, garlic, butter and oil.

I prefer the French caper-olive-and-anchovy paste *tapenade*, or the civility of Patum Pepperium, the Gentleman's Relish, that is blissful spread thinly on hot buttery toast with decent tea in front of a drawing-room fire.

CAVIAR: see above.

CLAMS: canned clams or baby clams are essential in any store cupboard, and are usually Japanese or Spanish. All are good as long as they are in brine or a light soup of their own juices. They are cooked, of course, and can be used straight from the tin with the least preparation, just some lemon juice, perhaps some oil and garlic or a special mayonnaise. They help all other seafood dishes too.

Mix them with prawns to make the usual boring cocktail more interesting, or use them instead of prawns in fish sauces, stuffings and so on. Chop them roughly into batter and make fritters for lunch or serve as an extraordinary accompaniment to roast chicken or turkey, which were once regularly stuffed with oysters. Put them at the bottom of fish soufflés in lots of garlicky butter or stir them into pilaffs of saffron rice. Like all shellfish they toughen if cooked too long, so don't.

Clam juice: the liquor left after clams have been steamed open and is an outstanding stock for fish sauces or fishy flavouring for pies and soups. It is popular in Bloody Marys and when ready mixed with tomato it is called Clamato, of course.

CRAB: whether the excellent crab products are from Cornwall or imported, the problem in the deli is working out exactly what is inside the pack, frozen or canned.

Crabmeat: frozen or canned, this description is usually indicative of better value for money with white meat and little adulteration by brown meat.

Russian and Alaskan crabmeat is

considered superlatively good and interchangeable as they come from the same geographical area. Russian crab from the Kamchatka Peninsula and sold under that name signifies that the crab was processed within hours of being caught and the can will contain only the leg and claw meat of male crabs, plus natural juices. Alaskan King Crab is the US equivalent.

Dressed crab: this usually means that inferior brown meat plus other impertinences have been mixed with a small proportion of white meat, often into a khaki-coloured paste. Full details are exposed by the order of ingredients on the pack.

Even where both white and brown meat are included but kept apart in products sold as dressed crab, the proportion of white may be distressingly low in the interest of marketability. Buy warily, or do your own dressing.

Crab is excellent to dress other fish or in fish sauces but also with avocado, pineapple, mango and other tropical fruit; a small amount added to a stir-fried mixture of vegetables or of vegetables and chicken will be a triumph. Singapore's famed chilli crab relies on masses of tomato ketchup to be authentic.

EEL: smoked eel is like richer kipper, and is perhaps the least esteemed but one of the best tasting of all fish products, one that always leaves the mouth refreshed and the palate stimulated. Available hot or cold smoked.

Baby eel, elvers, anguillas: white, matchstick-like, and available in small cans from Spain. Soft and delicate, with a nutty rather than fishy taste. Drain gently and serve with a little oil, lemon juice and garlic. Or mix them with egg yolk and a splash of white wine or dry sherry to make fritters, which is how I like them best. See Whitebait.

Eel fillets, smoked: go well with other smoked fish as a starter and particularly enjoy being served with hot or cold scrambled eggs; they make terrific additions to seafood salads or pasta.

Smoked eel: when you can get a chunk of whole smoked eel, those from New Zealand are thicker, fattier and more succulent than European eels. Usually found frozen, it is wondrous cold and unctuous enough to survive grilling or other heat. It makes a sensational spread mashed and seasoned with lemon or lime juice and cognac. Fingers of toast or of dark rye bread spread with this and topped with chopped smoked salmon and capers convert the sturdiest disbelievers.

Herrings

Herrings are one of man's oldest foods from the sea.

North Atlantic natives, herrings migrate from Arctic seas to the Irish Sea and Eng- lish Channel from spring onwards.

Peak season for herrings is late summer.

As herrings mature and swim south they become pilchards.

A female herring lays about 50 million eggs a year.

Most herrings are eaten preserved in some way.

Herring flesh is equal in nutrition to salmon.

Fine bones deter many—but see below.

F resh, salted and smoked, you eat all whole herrings the same way. Start at the tail end and pull the flesh towards it, the way the bones point. Anyway, you can eat the bones.

British salted and smoked herrings

The British traditionally relied on smoke to preserve salted herrings.
BLOATERS: whole herrings salted for a very short time, in brine rather than dry salt, and then cold smoked. Despite chilled transport systems, these have virtually disappeared because they don't 'keep'. Yarmouth produced the best during October and November and were eaten almost as soon as they had come from the smokehouse. 'The epi- cure will eat them before he goes to bed rather than wait for breakfast,' said the Wine and Food Society in 1944, when you could still get them. If you find them, perhaps in Norfolk, grill or lightly fry them.

BUCKLING: lightly brined after behead- ing and gutting, they remain unsplit and any roe or milt is left in place. They are hot-smoked and so keep well and may be eaten cold or lightly grilled and make an excellent fish paste with just a little butter and perhaps cream, plus mustard.
KIPPERS: split, gutted, salted and then cold-smoked, genuine kippers have a glorious pale golden glow rather than a dark, treacle-like coating. Most you buy have been par-cooked to prolong their apparent edibility, and the colour and flavour of the smoke will have been painted on.

A few centres like Craster in

Northumberland and the Isle of Man still cold-smoke authentic kipper over oak chips; the best time for kippers from the Isle of Man is July and August.

The powerful smell made when heating kippers is especially pungent and hangs around for many hours. Here are some solutions. Forget grilling or frying, as they cause most pong and also intensify the saltiness and risk drying. Better is to bake under cover with a little water, to poach in a frying pan or best of all to jug, which is to put them head down in a tall jug, pour on boiling water to just under the tail, cover and leave at least five minutes: this gives the juiciest, least salty results.

Nothing is better with kippers than the runny yolk of fried or poached eggs and a more substantial lunch is to offer both on a bed of spinach. Otherwise, extend the pleasure of a few kippers by making a pâté, mixing the cooked or uncooked flesh with puréed kidney beans, mashed potato or rice with heaps of unsalted butter, lemon juice, a touch of Tabasco or other chilli sauce and as much garlic or parsley as can be imagined. Soured cream is a great addition, as is any amount of coarsely chopped, soft-boiled egg. More toast, anyone?

RED HERRINGS: the most important larder standby before refrigeration. Red herrings were highly salted and highly smoked and thus almost indestructible. If you find some, soak them for many hours in milk or water before grilling or poaching. A soft-poached egg, cooked without salt, is a perfect foil, as with so many smoked fish.

Continental & Scandinavian salted and smoked herrings

European processing styles are based on salt or vinegar rather than smoking. Before processing ashore, most herrings are made into basic salt herrings at sea, keeping them safe but inedible.

BISMARK: fresh, unsalted herring fillets marinated in vinegar with onion, so fairly rugged.

BOKKING: a cold-smoked entire fish that must be cleaned before eating.

FILLETS: in bulk or in jars, this is the way tons of herring are eaten. The fillets have been salted, then soaked and treated in a number of ways. Some go into a red wine sauce, some into a tomato sauce, some are in oil. There are dozens of varieties commercially available and hundreds more are made in the home. Use the fillets as part of an hors d'oeuvre, or slice them small for use in potato salads. They can be mashed into a paste with stewed, or chopped, raw apple and with egg yolk as a simple pâté. Most fillets are called *matjesfillet* but they may not be, so see below.

MATJESHERRING: this properly means herring gathered in early summer when the roe is still developing but it is used loosely. They are either lightly brined with some sugar content or heavily brined in the usual way of salt herring. It's likely *matjesfillets* have been lightly salted and whole *matjesherrings* are more heavily treated. In either case, soak them in water or milk to remove the salt you do not want. If preserved other than in brine, you will not need to soak them.

They may be eaten just like that, especially the fillets, or perhaps with onion—and in Holland green beans are usual. Or you can make a marinade, warm or cold, and flavour them according to personal taste.

ROLLMOPS: eviscerated fresh herrings, the two fillets joined together only by skin. No bone or fins should remain. The double fillets are rolled around pickled cucumber, sometimes with carrot and onion, and kept in an acidic-brine liquid, usually made with a white vinegar. It is easy to play with this idea at home, using spices and apple with cider vinegar for instance. Soured cream, dill and more pickled cucumbers are by far the best accompaniments plus frozen vodka or aquavit. Rollmops are touted as a great cure for hangovers but any accompanying alcohol is more useful.

SALT HERRING: the basic preserved herring, inedible as is and that must be soaked for at least 24 hours before it can be used. Fillet and serve it with soured cream, pickled beetroot and cucumber, onion rings, potatoes, hard-boiled eggs, gherkins and decent wholemeal or rye bread. Once soaked the whole or filleted herrings can also be vinegar-pickled or put into any number of mustard, tomato, onion or sour cream sauces.

STROMMING: the Baltic herring, smaller and leaner than the Atlantic variety and is usually served in less aggressive and fierce ways. Once soaked it is usually put into mild pickles, with mustard and dill sauces or in soured cream and dill—using small amounts of raw onion rather than vinegar to provide any acidity. The Swedes use diluted Attika, a white vinegar otherwise too powerful to eat.

SURSTROMMING: beware. Baltic herrings are packed with half the expected level of salt, and then sealed in barrels left in the sun. Alan Davidson's *North Atlantic Seafood* says birds drop dead from the sky when the barrels are opened. It is acceptable to find canned *surstromming* bulging, a sign of proper fermentation. Barrels or cans should be opened in the open air, with the wind behind you and with chopped red onion held close to your face, which allows you to get the fillets to your mouth before your nose realises the imminent assault. Then quickly reach for water or beer or anything, so you can rinse out your mouth. Why?

MACKEREL: mackerel is quite one of the most fascinating—and delicious—fish there is. Even the reason for its name is bizarre. Mackerel is the English version of its French nickname, *maquereau*, which means 'pimp' or 'procurer', because adult female mackerel escort inexperienced female shad to ripe males, for which gourmets Eartha Kitt and Noel Coward are grateful.

Mackerel has the highest proportion of fatty matter of any fish and this deteriorates very quickly. They spawn in August and September and fresh or smoked mackerel should be avoided then. In October they start putting on condition, and by December are quite perfect.

I tend not to rate tinned mackerel of

any kind or provenance, especially the ghastly smoked mackerel pâtés, which are overburdened with farinaceae (as, in my opinion, are most English-produced seafood soups, but perhaps you have better luck). Many mackerel products come from abroad and are thus a slightly different and always inferior species, by common consent.

Smoked fillets: boned, flat, torpedo-shaped, inevitably artificially coloured and smoke-flavoured and with flesh that's a gummy paste.

Whole smoked: find whole, naturally smoked mackerel with only the head and gut missing, their skins a pale, iridescent gold rather than lurid copper and then you've found the real thing—almost certainly from Cornwall and quite superb. Avoid a slimy or sticky skin, which will actually be poisonous, and go for something firm but not rigid. Those with wavy lines on their bodies are females, those with straight lines are male, and much tastier.

They are best slightly chilled, served with lemon wedges and a good, creamy horseradish sauce, indispensable with smoked mackerel. Or, lightly grill them and serve with something quite sharp, like spiced red cabbage and a purée of celeriac, into which you have stirred a lot of finely chopped parsley and garlic.

MUSSELS: although available packed with flavours ranging from tomato to onion and pickles, or with vinegar, mussels packed only with brine and their own juices are by far the best.

Go for those from Scandinavia, ideally Norway's Limfjord.

In pasta dishes or added to seafood salads you'd hardly know they are not freshly cooked and dressed with good oils and vinegar, perhaps a little chopped preserved lemon and heaps of parsley, they can come to table as a salad all by themselves.

Frozen: ideal for anything, from a few to a few handsful, and making a contribution to the eye as well as the tongue.

Green-lipped: the New Zealand or Kiwi green-lipped mussels arrive on the half shell because it best shows the iridescent green lip. They are farmed, processed within minutes of being harvested, and deep frozen. Some are smoked and especially good.

The pale ones are male and the orange are female. Sexual confusion has no place in that country. Increasingly available, green-lipped mussels are good just as they are in salad and seafood platters. If used in hot dishes they must only be warmed through as they are already cooked and will shrink and toughen if heated further.

OYSTERS: it sounds rather fun being an oyster. They start life as one sex and from time to time become the other, much like a modern novel. In the UK they were once a staple of the grateful poor, but like many simple local foods they have become rare and expensive and likely to be served fancifully and badly.

Canned: when only in brine, canned oysters make great additions to classic dishes in which they once featured, like Lancashire hot pot or in steak pies, when they should be laid just under the pastry so their savour is enjoyed the moment the crust is cut.

Fresh: the oysters of most European and American sources have been transplanted, cross-bred and artificially brought-on to a degree that has eroded some of the ancient clear-cut distinctions of flavour.

The original European oyster, the native *ostrea edulis* is immediately recognisable for having a flat and only lightly ridged shell. But this is rare for it has been decimated more than once by disease. It was first replaced by the *portugaise*, which isn't a true oyster but *gryphea angulata*, and, when that too succumbed to disease, by a Japanese variety, *crassostrea gigas*, often called a *creuse* by the French. Whatever the variety, people who like them eat them just as they are; lemon juice, vinegar and shallots are for wimps or those with palates destroyed by chillies.

Smoked oysters: usually in tins from Japan but ruined if served in the filthy cottonseed oil in which they are preserved. They should be fully drained and then sprinkled with the smallest amount of lemon juice. For special occasions I would take the trouble to pat them dry of oil with kitchen tissue and then present them in a nice, gentle lemon juice and oil mixture.

Smoked oysters may be treated with a little more abandon than more plainly canned ones. Minced or chopped, their flavour goes a long way to savour sauces for garnish or filling puff pastry cases. Or make the most of their flavour to replace bacon on skewers of seafood for your grill or barbecue.

PILCHARDS: often described either as a type of herring or a type of sardine, the pilchard is cleverly both. A timid member of the herring family, it is an adult sardine. Now being marketed as Cornish sardines they are increasingly popular as a fresh fish, as they should be.

If we can get past seeing canned pilchards used as cat food, we should eat them as part of an Italian-style mixed antipasto and present them to doubters as grown-up sardines. The type in tomato sauce, mashed with a little vinegar or lemon juice and soft butter or sour cream, can make a fish paste to go nicely on hot toast. Chopped capers, olives or anchovies, those enchanted saviours of anything fishy, might all help.

PRAWNS AND SHRIMPS: although different from one another, prawns and shrimps look alike enough to be called by one another's name. In the United Kingdom you are safe calling little ones shrimps and big ones prawns. In America they are all called shrimp, but the giant Pacific variety is often called a prawn for the sake of alliteration.

Canned: astonishingly good and

cheap compared to fresh or frozen. Those from Malaysia are often shrimps, tiny and floury but other sources offer cans packed with moist plump, pink, crustacea, their shells removed. The initial outlay might seem high but the value for money is comparable with frozen prawns. *Frozen:* there are pitfalls. Some have a protective ice-glaze, which means you are paying for water rather than seafood, and in the case of some Indian prawns, the water is highly salted. I have ruined a very fine sauce for 100 people by adding these prawns, liquid and all.

It is important to defrost frozen prawns very slowly, or you will lose flavour, texture and moistness. The best way is to leave them in their bag in the refrigerator overnight. They will then be moist and plump and have retained most of their natural juices. If they are then to go into a hot sauce, first bring them to room temperature. Then they can be put into the sauce just for the few minutes needed to cook them or heat them through. They do not need to be piping hot and the sauce should never be boiled.

You should carefully consider the size of prawn you want to use. Generally larger ones look better and they behave better if they are to be served hot. Prawns will inevitably shrink when cooked or when reheated. If cooked or heated for too long they will also toughen. Bigger is always better.

You can extend prawns with cheaper seafood, especially mussels, frozen or canned, as long as they have been canned in brine rather than vinegar. The two are especially good in pasta sauces, or in hot sauces to stuff vol-au-vents. Other flavours which go well with prawns are horseradish, tomato, garlic, basil, ground cumin and coriander, sweet or hot paprika and, of course, cucumber.

Potted shrimps: these are a special variety, the brown shrimp, with a distinct nuttier flavour and firm texture. Potted shrimp bought commercially are very good and easily copied at home, for they have simply been packed in butter flavoured with a little spice, mainly mace.

Read the label. They should be served warm but not hot, with the seasoned butter in glistening pools. Even famous fish restaurants, unwilling to make potted shrimps themselves, cannot read the labels on the ones they buy frozen and then infamously serve them ice-cold with limp toast of plastic bread. Asking if you can have your potted shrimps served warm in melting butter is a great way to ascertain if the restaurant has a chef who understands the business he or she is in.

ROE: it comes as a shock to many a bachelor or spinster to learn their favourite supper of soft roes is the milt or sperm of male fish. Hard roe is the eggs of fish females.

Roe of both sorts are popular right round the world. In the Occident, the general agreement on flavour, in ascending order, is: mackerel, herring, and then shad and carp equal first. Most of the soft roe sold in fish shops or in cans is cod roe, but it can be herring, too.

Greeks are especially partial to the eggs of the grey mullet, and this is the proper basis for *taramasalata*. But try telling that to a thousand deli counters. Although smoked cod's roe is a good substitute for that of mullet, this blushing *taramasalata* is usually only an emulsion of low-grade bread and oil with some little amount of roe and a great deal of colouring.

Botargo (Botargue in France): it should be the salted and pressed whole roe of grey mullet but sometimes of other fish. This is one of the oldest and simplest delicacies but now inevitably one of the most expensive. It is found in many Mediterranean countries but belief in the disinfectant and protective qualities of the salting and drying process is ill-founded. As botargo is eaten uncooked, perhaps with oil and lemon, you also eat whatever contamination it has collected. Most definitely a case of buying only the highest quality from the most reliable source.

In New Zealand look for the firm smoked roe of both snapper and blue cod; the latter when smoked was described by André Simon as being like Finnan Haddie gone to heaven. Served unpretentiously in thin delicate slices, accompanied by a perfect light vinaigrette and a garlic mayonnaise, it is worth getting off a jet to experience.

Salmon, cold and hot-smoked

NEED TO KNOW

Atlantic salmon are found naturally in the rivers and cool seawaters of all Northern Hemisphere countries on both sides of the ocean including eastern North America; there is only one variety.

Canadian and Pacific salmon live in the rivers and cooler Pacific waters of western North America: there are five indigenous varieties; Chum, Chinook (King), Pink, Sockeye and Coho.

Atlantic salmon is considered the finest flesh and best flavour.

Pacific salmon are coarser fleshed and have a much higher fat content than Atlantic.

Both types are farmed in salt-water sea pens but concentrated excrement beneath their pens creates environmental problems.

Canada is moving to ban sea pens.

Japan and other countries are developing inland farms using fresh water and sophisticated waste management.

Wild salmon do not feed when they return to fresh water to breed and quickly lose condition. Farmed salmon are closer to prime condition ocean fish, something tasted by very few in the past.

Smoked salmon was originally kippered salmon; herrings adopted and took over the term.

Traditional salting to reduce moisture followed by cold-smoking was developed for longer storage and to transport salmon safely before railways, refrigeration or, later, vacuum packing.

Old-style smoked salmon has a very firm, slightly salty flesh and noticeable smoke flavour: lemon was justified to counteract the bitterness of the smokiness.

In London, processors used milder salt and smoke levels, the London cure, because consumption was localised.

Most modern smoked salmon uses even less salt in curing and lighter smoke, giving a softer texture and lesser flavour—but greater weight for sale.

Today's softer, wetter, blander styles of smoked salmon require new ways of serving and eating, including using much, much less lemon juice, if at all.

Only big mature smoked salmon are tasty enough to be sliced transparently thin; it's always better to go for thicker slices these days.

The Canadian/US habit of eating smoked salmon with raw onion should be a capital offence.

Hot-smoked salmon is cooked and smoked at the same time; it is rarely salt-cured but can be.

Hot-smoking salmon pieces until very dry and chewy is a traditional speciality of Native North Americans: Canadians add maple syrup to make addictive salt-sweet bites.

Yes, you can domestically hot-smoke fresh salmon over wood chips—or in a wok over tea.

Gravadlax means buried salmon, so using weights to express moisture is vital to dill-pickling, otherwise you get only salty dill salmon.

How to serve hot-smoked salmon

Although a meatier choice than most fish to serve cold with hot or cold potato and in salads, hot-smoked salmon fillets excel when served warm. The microwave is the best way to do this without damaging the texture or drying it out. Don't let it get hot because the oil runs and farmed salmon is fattier than wild salmon caught up river because they don't feed in fresh water. Canadian salmon varieties have an even higher content, some off-puttingly so.

Serve a small amount as a first course with sweet chilli sauce, mustard, horseradish or a smart, sharp salad of ingredients not normally seen, like fiddleheads, or wild asparagus or the very best tiny rocket leaves. Or flake into big pieces to serve instead of tuna with the same ingredients as a Salade Niçoise, or with black beans, poached cucumber arcs and salted lemon.

Hot-smoked salmon makes a filling and satisfying main course when served with anything made from potatoes—a mash with a truffle oil, baby potatoes not cooked with mint but turned in fresh mint after cooking, a potato salad vivid with mustard and pickled cucumber.

More millennial would be a sprinkle of *baharat*, strips of salted lemon and fresh coriander leaf.

How to serve cold-smoked salmon

The best Scotch smoked salmon is pink-red and firm in texture; when it is cut, it should be slightly transparent and waxy. The smaller fish, the grilse, have a more delicate flavour and need to be sliced thicker. Only mature adults have enough flavour in them to be sliced finely.

The heavy and bitter smoking of the past needed quelling by lemon juice, for only acid will counteract bitterness; sweetness doesn't do it. Today's lighter smoking means lashings of lemon juice are mistaken, because when smoked salmon is so drowned you generate only a fishy acidity in the mouth.

Taste what you have paid for by grating lemon zest directly onto the plate, over or under the salmon, an improvement I've heard described as 'life-enhancing'. The slight acidity of soured cream or crème fraîche or top-class black pepper also balance things nicely and you will taste the smoked salmon: a touch of caviar, even lumpfish completes the ideal trio.

A disquieting but better idea is judiciously to sprinkle on neat gin or vodka, perhaps with fresh dill leaf. You get just enough bite to contrast with the fish and the smooth texture of the alcohol is strangely complementary; many of the subsequent compliments will be equally weird.

Small smokehouses, in Scotland and Ireland particularly, still process and smoke salmon by hand and eye, the old way, and are likely to favour a firmer flesh and more savoury smokiness. If you find one, encourage them, but also look carefully at labels in supermarkets; blind tastings have found inexpensive, supermarket smoked salmon, made with Norwegian salmon and processed and smoked in Poland is exceptionally well textured and flavoured.

For ambrosial scrambled eggs with smoked salmon, slice the salmon into fingers and throw them over the eggs as you are serving them, or lay them thickly on the toast on which the eggs are presented. Don't chop it into the eggs when cooking and don't smother the eggs and smoked salmon with the acid rain of chives. That is scrambled eggs with smoked salmon and chives, another dish entirely.

Smoked salmon makes a wonderful addition to sauces for plain fish. It transforms cauliflower cheese, if there is not too much cheese in the sauce: it's better to make a cheeseless white sauce with wine and cream, and meanwhile to tuck buffalo mozzarella between cooked cauliflower florets, to strew these with thick-sliced smoked salmon strips, and then to pour on the sauce, sprinkle liberally with breadcrumbs mixed with lemon zest and chopped parsley and then to bake until very lightly browned. You might be happier doing this with chunks of hot-smoked salmon but you *will* be happy.

SALT COD: the importance of salt cod to our universally Catholic ancestors is hard to believe, considering the difficulty of buying it in the United Kingdom today; the first American colonies were founded to ensure supplies of cod.

West Indian communities and good Portuguese, Spanish, Italian and Greek shops should sell slabs of salt cod. Sadly, like herrings, it is considered too cheap to be fashionable, yet it is commonly published as worth the attention of any true gastronome. Maybe I am a false one, for I have never yet enjoyed it, not even when it was specially soaked and washed over three days for me; there remained a back taste I found nauseating, but perhaps it's the fault of the truculent trait of my palate that is revolted by goat cheese when others are smacking their lips.

There is a Norwegian salted cod called *stockfish*, which is especially popular in Germany, Belgium and Holland; once prepared, the classic English way to serve salt cod is predictably boring, boiled and served with a sauce of hard-boiled eggs. It is only in looking at the kitchens of Brazilians, Portuguese, the Spanish and Creoles that salt cod appears to be remotely exciting. In Provence they make *brandade de morue*, a warm, fluffy mousse of olive oil, potatoes, milk and salt cod and even that can be foul; my discovery is that it is superb if you use smoked cod instead of salt cod.

SARDINES: these are increasingly available in olive oil again, a style that almost disappeared. They improve with age and are the better for turning, which keeps the oil evenly distributed. Only refined almost tasteless olive oil is used, and even the very superior canners of Portugal say that after an ideal six months in the can, sunflower oil gives virtually indistinguishable results and flavour. They are then ready to enjoy.

There are three ways to test if it has been worth the wait. When opened, none of the skin of the top ones should adhere to the lid; this means they were too fat and badly chosen or packed. When you scrape back a little of the skin you should see a wine-coloured layer, indicative of fattiness and flavour. Now turn back a fillet. If the flesh is white and creamy, the sardines were caught and processed quickly; if it is pink or red-tinged they were frozen before packing.

Eat direct from the can on hot toast, mashed with a tiny amount of Sherry vinegar. Or grill one side of thick, fresh white bread and then turn it over and put sardines on the untoasted side. Put this back under the grill and the bread will soak up the oil and juices and sizzle and brown with them. Simple but splendid.

SPRATS: when you find smoked sprats from Baltic countries, give them a try. They make a welcome change when arranging mixed seafood platters.

STURGEON: rarely available cold-smoked; it is pale, interesting and startling, mainly for the price.

TROUT, SMOKED: the creatures we buy here, farm-bred and then artificially coloured and smoke-flavoured, are a wee bit pricey for the pleasure they might give but better as a basis for a first course than avocado and prawns, a case of the bland leading the bland I've never understood.

Farmed trout that have grown into comparative monsters and then cured and kippered like smoked salmon, look the same and have much the same texture and flavour, but at a price advantage.

TUNA: now the world appreciates that netting tuna kills dolphins and that canners have agreed to line-fish, this truly delicious fish is back on the menu. Like sardines, tuna is subjected to all manner of iniquity in cans, packed in totally unsuited mediums. Go for brine or water packed rather than a vegetable oil, so you might drizzle with olive oil, or incorporate it into a salad with a decent dressing.

Albacore: the rarest tuna with very pale flesh and is sold in the United States as Chicken of the Sea. It is more finely textured than other varieties and very delicious indeed. Spanish packers often include it in their range and it is one of the first things I look for when judging delicatessens.

Lomo: a thick, air-dried fillet of tuna, enjoyed and served very much as a superior ham might be, especially in tapas.

Smoked: made the same way as smoked salmon, but with a richer colour and flavour.

Ventresca: oil-rich belly cuts from the yellow-fin tuna, prized above all other cuts and species of tuna. Spanish canners are best for this.

WHITEBAIT: in the UK and many other

countries this means fish fry up to 50 mm/2" long, often young sprats, which are floured, fried and eaten entirely. The crunch of the bones and stare of the eyes have turned many a colonial's thoughts to home faster than snow and ice ever did. That's because in New Zealand, whitebait are barely hatched, transparent and threadlike, very like the baby elvers of Northern Spain. Caught largely in river mouths for a very short season they are cooked as thin fritters, best when made only of egg with no flour. The flavour is unique, both nutty and fishy.

I once broke boundaries and made a very thick whitebait fritter only with egg yolks and sweet wine, which was served in warm wedges with the same wine, chilled. If there were a *haka* to celebrate whitebait fritters, all would have stamped and shouted and stuck out their tongues.

Fruit, Nuts, Vegetables, Dried Mushrooms, Truffles and Sea Vegetables

As hunters and gatherers the seasonal progression of wild fruits, nuts and vegetables kept us going between rare feasts of meat; indeed, without fruits, vegetables and nuts, we could never have gathered the strength to go hunting.

Modern transportation and genetic manipulation mean more and more fresh produce is available all year round. Yet, there remains a place for canned, frozen or dried fruits and vegetables in every cupboard, sometimes offering flavours, textures and colours different from the original, but better.

Fruit

APPLES

Canned: as well as excellent apple sauce, apples come in unsweetened segments or, better, as a thickened pie filling. When dished up under pastry or a sponge, steaming hot, spiced and buttery, there will be few who could tell you took the easy route. Deep frozen ones might have a better texture.

Dried: they retain Vitamin C content and 500 g/1 lb of dried apple is the equivalent of 3–4 kg/6–9 lb of fresh fruit. Rather rubbery when dried but chopped into smaller pieces make a worthwhile addition to muesli. They rehydrate nicely, often becoming rather fluffy and therefore good for purées. A good stretcher of other fruits in pies, crumbles and so on.

Dehydrated apple crisps are a perfect snack food and excellent as something to crumble over breakfasts or desserts.

Frozen: for pies and sponges but also pancakes or crêpes; spread liberally with butter and ground cinnamon or mixed spice plus a dark sugar and then roll in pancakes and lightly douse with rum, brandy, Calvados, Drambuie or an orange liqueur. Bake about 20 minutes, so the edges of the pancakes crispen, basting once to ensure the butter/alcohol reaches maximum potential.

APRICOTS

Canned: these usually have more flavour than fresh because, like pineapples, they do not ripen more once picked. Canned ones are tree-ripened. With a little lemon juice, and perhaps some crushed macaroons or amaretti, which are flavoured with apricot kernels, they make an excellent pie or crumble filling.

Dried: always dried without their stones, whether whole or halves. 3 kg/ 5½ lb of fresh fruit yield 500 g/1 lb of dried. I once found them drying under trees in Ibiza, directed thence by the wondrous scent on the air, attended by a single black-swathed woman. Now that site is a hotel or two. Apricots are more often dried in hot air after exposure to sulphur dioxide, which gives a brighter colour. My favourite dried fruit, they are best of all when soaked overnight in fresh orange or apple juice. Thin slices improve muesli more than anything else.

Sheets/armadine: buy thin sheets of armadine in Middle Eastern, Turkish, Greek and Cypriot shops. This is dried apricot purée with a full sharp flavour helped by citric acid. Rehydrate over low heat in a little water or wine, melting it into a purée to serve chilled with cream and ground almonds as a smooth apricot cream.

Chopped into small pieces armadine, can be stirred into ice cream or sorbet mixtures. It adds rare flavour and colour to stuffings for baked apples or to an apple pie, is terrific in or with chocolate cakes, brownies and ideal for fruit and nut breads.

Combining apricot and mint is basic to the cookery of the Eastern Mediterranean. Snip armadine into pieces and combine with fresh or dried mint in stuffings, pilaffs, stuffings for meat or for vegetables. Just as remarkable in pork-based forcemeats for lamb, chicken or turkey, that include sweet spices and mint.

BANANAS, DRIED: golden brown, very sweet and chewy, and naturally sundried. 1 kg/2 lb of bananas make 250 g/½ lb of dried ones. Soaked in water overnight then to eat chopped or sliced with lime, orange or lemon juice, they make a fascinating addition to cereals, hot or cold, and to breads, cake and puddings.

Chips: dehydrated thin slices of banana are crisp, creamy coloured and honey-coated. A terrific breakfast time addition if you don't mind the calories.

BILBERRIES: related to the blueberry, but smaller, so also with waffles, in batters, on ice cream, in ice cream, in soufflés. Dress up with sweet spices, with a little liqueur or citrus juice. Or thicken the can's syrup with cornflour, return the fruit and use as a sauce or bake in pastry, turned with thick slices of apple and lots of cinnamon and nutmeg.

BLUEBERRIES: the wildest picked blueberries will frustrate, because canning dilutes their sharp-sweetness. Eat just one fresh blueberry and you'll never bother with a blueberry muffin again. There is a huge variety of different tasting blueberries harvested worldwide. Find sharp but fulsome fresh blueberries and they might repay being baked, might.

CHERRIES

Black: higher quality canned ones, ready stoned, are life savers as a filling for chocolate cakes, mixed into sweetened chestnut purée and whipped cream, or heated in red wine or brandy with bay and a little spice to serve with pork. Puréed and very slightly thickened with arrowroot or cornflour and then flavoured with black rum, they make a sensational chilled sauce for profiteroles. Probably the better cherry for Black Forest gateau. Available frozen.

Glacé: candied/crystallised cherries, usually the red morello, used for cake decorations or in fruit cakes. As vital to find in Christmas puddings as a silver sixpence.

Morello: red and less sweet than black cherries, morellos are thought tastier in their sharp way for inclusion in chocolate cake fillings and better for baking in pies and pastries. Drained of most syrup, added to white wine, heated with spices and lightly thickened with cornflour or arrowroot, they make an attractive sauce for pork, chicken, duck and partridge; sharpen with lemon juice.

Pie filling: more likely to be red/morello cherries. Instead of a traditional cherry pie of short crust, bake large or small squares of buttered phyllo also scattered with cinnamon and make fly-away pies, with filo top and bottom.

CITRON: this type of citrus has a thick yellow-green peel and little flesh or juice. It is usually seen as candied/crystallised slices, perhaps because it is too expensive to use in mixed peel. Needs a sharp knife to cut but the lemony results are good in baking.

CITRUS PEEL: candied or crystallised, these are an ancient way to preserve and use the flavour of citrus year-round. Mixed tubs of chopped peel might not have the best flavour, so I always hope to buy each variety separate. Orange is by far the best, used in the light ricotta filling of Italian cannoli or Easter cheesecakes as well as in heavy English steamed puddings and fruitcakes. Be bold and strew orange peel widely—roll it into pastry for tarts or stir into fruit pies, particularly apple or rhubarb, or in a bread-and-butter pudding with orange blossom water. And then there is citron—see above.

CRANBERRIES: last for ages in the freezer or refrigerator because of their high Vitamin C content.

A handful in a stuffing for poultry, lamb or fish lends an attractive sharpness, as it does to apple pies and apple sauce.

Dried: always sweetened and a useful spark of colour and flavour to eat as is, or in salads or to rehydrate as they cook in curries and fruit pies.

Sauces: you are missing out if you serve cranberry sauce only cold and only with turkey. It is excellent hot with all game, with ham, with duck, with well-flavoured, garlicky sausages, and hot or cold tongue. Even better when you make your own.

Commercial sauces are not bad but sweeter than they need to be: fix that by adding unsweetened apple purée and orange zest and then serving hot. Don't stop there. Add green or roasted black peppercorns, a cinnamon stick, mace or lemon zest. Add black rum, vodka or whisky. Add fresh or dried mint to serve with duck or lamb. Add juniper berries or gin (at the very last minute) for hot tongue, goose or guinea fowl. Stir in grated orange zest, a little cardamom and cognac—serve with almost anything.

Homemade cranberry sauce: use red or white wine with some orange juice and a little very finely grated zest: about 100 ml/3.5 fl oz liquid to 250 g/½ lb cranberries. Stir in sweet spices including a cinnamon quill and cook until the cranberries begin to burst. Only then add sugar or you toughen the skins, as happens if you do this too soon with marmalade; about 100 g/4 oz is right, muscovado, golden or white. Add a little sweet wine, port, cream sherry or Madeira and keep a rugged texture, so they know you made it, and think about adding any of the suggestions above. Serve hot rather than cold.

DATES

Fresh: super-sweet fruits that caramelise naturally on the palm. The sugar content ensures a voluptuous soft, moist texture that lasts for years. The perfect, transportable energy-snack, fresh dates add greater interest to baking and to savoury cooking than dried dates.

Add slivers to chicken sauces and gravies, even for roast lamb with mint and spices. Do the same to breads and sweet loafs, in bigger pieces than for dried dates. Wonderful surprises in rice, tapioca or bread and butter puddings and better if there is cinnamon too. Grateful surprises with curries, tagines etc, either in them or in the rice or couscous.

The biggest and fleshiest is the Deglet Noor, followed by the Medjool but increasingly other varieties are marketed.

Dried: rather superceded and no bad thing as the skins can be leathery and the texture too compressed. These must be rehydrated before use, but this can still leave skins paper-dry and flaky, the ruin of too many date scones and date loafs. Avoid packs that feel hard or that have noticeable white patches of sugar, a sign of advanced age.

FIGS, DRIED: other than in steamed Figgy Puddings and in occasional dried fruit salads, dried figs seem most used medicinally to ease constipation. Called *anjeer* in India, where they make a popular smoothie. A better thing might be *Bombones Valcorcheros,* dried figs stuffed with hazelnut chocolate and dipped in white or dark chocolate.

FRUITS OF THE FOREST: a frozen life-saver to have on hand all year round, especially if you are short of the essential haunting flavour of blackcurrants for a Summer Pudding. They need need no further heating because the contents are juicy and slightly softened by blanching. Set with gelatine or thicken lightly with cornflour or arrowroot for delicious jellies or a jelly layer in a sponge. Perfect mixed into apple for a pastry pie or topped with a vanilla, orange or chocolate sponge mixture for microwaved sponge pudding in minutes.

LYCHEES: as good canned as fresh, with almost the same texture. Improved by being slightly chilled, they have an astonishing affinity with rose water and thus also with raspberries. If you liquidise a drained can of lychees, strain that, and then reduce the drained sugar syrup from the can over heat until just five or six dessert spoonsful, mix them together and flavour with rose water, you have a show-stopping sorbet. Reheat during freezing and fold in a whipped egg white, which improves the texture.

Drained of syrup and sharpened with lemon or lime juice, or soaked in vodka or dry sherry, lychees are a magical pearlescent ingredient in stir-fried Chinese dishes or served with roasted duck.

MANGO

Canned: snap up cans of mango slices or purée if from India and the Alphonso variety, considered the most fragrant and satin-textured. There are many others and in the fresh season, the honey-mango follows the alphonso. The texture of canned is softer than fresh, but right for fruit salads, smoothies, into or onto ice creams, for fools and for tropical trifles. Bathe with lime zest and juice to use as a luminous garnish, from roast duck to curries, particularly rich, layered biryanis.

Dried: highly flavoured chewy slices to chop into mueslis as is, add to curries and rices, or to soak overnight for mango smoothies whatever the season.

Frozen: the variety is not always noted and the texture is between fresh and canned but frozen mango chunks are an original and sparkling standby. Add to fruit salads, to pasta, to lentil or bean salads, to chilled duck and seafood dishes and reliably to zest up breakfasts.

Or make a bewitching Moghul Fizz. Liquidise mango, using lime or orange juice to get a light texture, and whisk in a very small amount of clear honey. Put into a tall glass and top up with champagne or sparkling wine, swizzling as you do.

Now that smoothies are such a popular health drink, supermarkets have increased the range of frozen fruit. The best combines mango, pineapple and papaya; defrost overnight and sprinkle generously with oatmeal for an instant tropical muesli or serve at room temperature with ice cream, perhaps adding lime juice and zest or a few drops of pure lime oil.

PEACHES: soaked only in water they can seem floury, so I always use orange juice and that is a great success: see *Khoshaf* on page 163. Soaked peaches are aromatic companions when subsequently grilled, which caramelises them here and there. Ham, duck, turkey all enjoy the company, as do waffles or pancakes with hot maple syrup and smoked bacon.

PINEAPPLE: although a world away from fresh, the yellower, sweeter canned pineapple products from Hawaii and from Malaysia are worth seeking out. Canned pineapple is likely to have been riper before harvesting, after which they do not ripen further.

Chunks and rings: pineapple chunks or rings will caramelise when fried in butter and then make a sparkling sweet-sour friend to bacon and eggs and to baked pork chops, roasted pork or chicken, spread with a little mustard for more interest; slices or chunks are always popular when singed by the barbecue and then added to outdoor hamburgers. All are infinitely better if you grind black pepper coarsely onto the pineapple a minute or so before taking from the heat, an extraordinary flavour affinity.

Do I have to say that canned pineapple rings are better than fresh for Pineapple Upside Down Cake? I always add caramel, as for Tarte Tatin. My Norfolk Island relatives bake pies of pineapple chunks and Christmas mincemeat.

Pineapple has a special affinity with gin. Gin-soaked pineapple pieces make bright, sharp cake decorations and can be poked into muffins after baking, or popped onto meringues or into profiteroles; few will recognise the mysterious flavour you are offering.

Crushed: a standby of cooking and eating in Australasia and should be a basic in every store cupboard. Drained (or otherwise) it can be used in ice creams (with coconut?), in cakes, in batters to make pancakes or fritters, or thickened with spices and butter to make sauces sweet or savoury. It can be set with gelatine in flans or on cheesecakes, or used in unbaked cheesecake fillings; fresh pineapple cannot be set with gelatine.

PLUMS: drained and puréed canned plums of any colour make good bases for fools, ice creams and sweet or savoury sauces. Make a tremendously good plum sauce for light meats, game or fowls by adding to the purée some red wine, a spike of mellow vinegar, cider or sherry perhaps, and then tomato purée and ground allspice or cloves. Some brown sugar if you'd like sweetness. It's a sort of smooth, instant plum chutney.

Canned plums are good for pies and sponge puddings and crumbles, but they are already cooked so keep cooking times to an absolute minimum.

Plum Ice Cream
Judged by the number of written requests, a can of Victoria plums was the basis for one of the most successful recipes I gave on BBC TV Breakfast Time. No internet then.

Pour the contents of a 400 g/15 oz can of plums into a sieve, saving the syrup. Force the plums through the sieve using the back of a soup ladle.

Beat a very well chilled, small can of sweetened condensed milk for a few minutes and then add a small carton of chilled double (heavy) cream and keep beating until it thickens and looks like lightly whipped cream. It takes a while.

Fold in the plum purée and flavour with two or more tablespoons of lemon or orange juice. No need to reheat during freezing.

The reserved syrup may be reduced over heat and served warm or cold, but will be pulsating with calories.

The recipe works with up to 300 ml/½ pint of any sweet fruit purée, especially of properly ripe banana. For apple strudel ice cream, add canned apple sauce, cinnamon, raisins and breadcrumbs fried in butter.

SOFT FRUITS

Canned: soft fruits do not react well to canning and strawberries or raspberries are worst, often needing colour added. Some darker berries like loganberries and boysenberries are better.

Frozen berries: individually or as a mixture, another absolute standby always in my freezer. The very best of these are summer-fruit or Fruits of the Forest mixtures. Having been slightly blanched and thus softened and a little runny they make very good Summer Pudding fillings without further cooking and most have a high proportion of essential black currants.

My best results have been to put most or all of a packet of raspberries or of mixed soft fruit under a plain or chocolate sponge pudding mixture, which will cook in minutes in a microwave rather than hours over boiling water.

You might or might not want to turn such a pudding out before serving, as the bright colours and differing textures can be very startling when seen hot, steaming and *en masse*. When I did this live on QVC television, I heard a hissed intake of breath in my ear piece,

followed by 'Road kill!'.

Frozen blueberries are disappointing, as are all cooked blueberries.

Khoshaf—dried fruit salad
One of the greatest culinary treasures is having a melange of dried fruits, your own or a ready-made mix. Soak a medley in liquid overnight or longer and the varied fruits swell and exchange flavours and the soaking liquid voluptuously becomes thicker and more scented.

The original Middle Eastern kho-shaf is soaked only in water and has sugar added. Instead, soak in orange, apple juice or pineapple juice, giving richer spectrums or flavour and needing no sugar. Peaches are especially good and I sometimes add extra. Mango is not included in dried fruit mixtures but I recommend you add some.

When all is swollen and tender, I sprinkle in orange-flower water and/or rose water but not too much as khoshaf is as wonderful for breakfast with yoghurt as it is in the evening, when such sensual scents are more fitting, perhaps. Toasted almonds and pistachios are recommended garnishes.

I make this a few days before Christmas and then keep it in the refrigerator as an any-time snack, palate enlivener and lively accompaniment. It never fails to excite guests and visitors, who can pick different fruits each time. Because clotted cream shares ancestry with khoshaf, the combination is memorable.

PEARS, DRIED: in Alsace dried pears turn up constantly in savoury dishes of meat and game, and I put them under chicken or game birds while roasting, so they swell with the cooking juices.

Small intensely flavoured, dried Williams pears may be macerated in alcohol, either an economical brandy or the unflavoured *eau-de-vie* you buy in French supermarkets. It takes three months for the sugar and scent of the pear to interbreed with the alcohol and make something falling between a *marc* and a liqueur; the softened fruit is addictive. Pears and raspberries have an astonishing affinity and your plumped pears and scented alcohol should exploit this fully.

PRUNES: prunes are dried plums and the finest are the French *Pruneaux d'Agen* and it seems a pity to muck about with them, but people do.

Carlsbad plums: an historic and famed speciality, they are a type of damson, crystallised and robed in dark chocolate. It's cheaper to buy an orchard.

Elvas plums: preserved greengages from Portugal, with a texture and flavour that justify the expense. A real treat.

Sliwka Naleczowska: a Polish secret of stoned small plums filled with a delicious soft toffee, coated with chocolate and decoratively wrapped. By far the most rewarding to eat and to give, because everyone expects them to have cost the same as Carlsbads.

VINE FRUITS: dried vine fruits have eight times more invert sugar than fresh fruit: as invert sugar is pre-digested sucrose, the body is able to use it quickly, hence the usefulness when labouring or having an adventure. Generally, 500 g/1 lb of dried vine fruits began as 2 kg/4 lb of fresh.

Currants: not dried blackcurrants but a special type of seedless black grape, originally from Corinth in Greece, and so 'raisins from Corinth' in old cookbooks.

Raisins: dried red grapes of several types, sometimes seedless. Muscatels are the biggest and sweetest and can be found without seeds if you look hard enough. Muscatel raisins dried on the stem are a marvellous thing at the end of a meal, and stand their ground with opinionated cheeses. Most often seen around Christmas time, when they ache to be eaten with perfect Stilton, but Stichelton is better.

Sultanas: dried white grapes. They were a speciality of Smyrna, now Izmir, in Turkey and also known as Smyrna raisins. Sweeter and more aromatic than raisins, they are a guarantee of a rich, mellow flavour, so add rather more sultanas than raisins in mixed fruit cakes and puddings, especially British styles made for Christmas.

Glacé fruits

Moist, succulent and screamingly sweet, glacé fruits are the ultimate example of technique and texture triumphing over taste. The way they are made pledges that few fruits survive to taste of much more than sugar. That starts when fruit is picked before fully ripe, so it is not too fragile to withstand the processing. Stored in brine, the pitted and destalked fruit is then soaked in increasingly stronger sugar solutions that replace the fragrant natural fruit sugars with sucrose. Some are lightly baked, creating an outer layer that clouds and flakes as it becomes pensionable. A light deposit of sulphur can slow this, acting as a further preservative.

Thus, each fruit is essentially sugar in a clever shape and with negligible flavour reference to the original. Apricots come out of the process better than most.

Does the marron do any better? Are marrons glacés worth the expense? I'm inclined to think not, even when made traditionally from true marrons, a type of chestnut that does not split in the shell but stays a single, flat cone shape. If you have time and chestnuts, the internet will tell you how to make your own, if only so you can add real vanilla, rum or brandy to the syrup.

Nuts

NEED TO KNOW

Pistachios have the lowest fat content.

Macadamia nuts have the highest fat content, followed by the Brazil nut.

Pili nuts might have even higher fat, but this is still to be proved.

Brazil nuts are still harvested from the wild, mainly in Bolivia.

Brazils, cashews, peanuts and tiger nuts are not nuts.

Almonds are the only alkaline nut.

Almond milk was first written about in English in 1390.

Commercial nut milks are diluted, sometimes 'fortified', usually sweetened.

ALMONDS: probably the world's favourite nut, almonds are relatively alkaline and thus help with digestive problems, notably reflux or heartburn. They also create a feeling of satiety, making them useful for controlling your diet.

Amlou: in Morocco *amlou* is a fragrant, golden-brown spread of toasted and ground whole almonds mixed with honey and rare argan oil. Used on breads, scones, waffles and pancakes, *amlou* has a largely unexplored spectrum as an accent or garnish on fruit and vegetables.

Bitter: one or two heighten the essential flavour of sweet almond without intruding but they are harmful eaten in quantity because they contain deadly-poisonous prussic acid, 'given away' in detective stories by its lingering smell. Use cherry or apricot kernels for similar but lesser flavour.

Californian: a new type grown only in California with advanced techniques and irrigated orchards. Used mainly by confectioners.

Californian nonpareil: the principal variety grown in California; it is of medium width but quite flat.

Flaked almonds: one of the most useful of ingredients in a kitchen. You need very few to add flavour and texture to an extraordinary variety of food. They are better toasted but for use in cream sauces can be left their natural colour, although a quick flash in a microwave firms up their texture without changing colour or flavour.

Toasting is usually done under a grill or dry-frying in a non-stick pan but both give uneven results, often colouring the outside but leaving the insides untouched. The answer is to toast in the microwave, where they brown all the way through, making them even more delicious.

Their crisp sweetness complements all fish and seafood and they are wonderful garnishes for potatoes, peas, beans and squashes. Creamy tomato sauces, white wine sauces and richer pasta sauces containing cream are all better with a few toasted, flaked almonds.

Smarten up a cold fruit pie or mousse with toasted almond flakes folded into whipped cream flavoured with orange-flower water. Or add untoasted flakes to a meringue mixture and bake a little longer than usual. The flakes toast and flavour the meringues, which are all the better for being flavoured with such liqueurs as Mandarine Napoleon or Crème de Cacao.

Flour: almonds ground as fine as wheat flour and that can substitute for it in equal proportions but you usually need to add extra egg for binding. Best follow a recipe rather than experimenting. Almond flour is not almond meal.

Ground almonds: also called almond meal, these add unequalled richness and moistness to fruit cakes, make superb custards and tarts, transport stuffings into heaven, enrich sauces, and generally lift the ordinary into the extraordinary. Make every effort to buy the freshest and highest quality. See *Milk.*

Jordan: sometimes called the finger almond as their long, slender shape resembles the little finger and are also the ones with which the eyes of Oriental beauties are compared. Jordan almonds are the sweet dessert kind and extensively used in cooking. Graded according to size, large Jordans are sold retail, and the small ones go to confectioners to make sugared almonds.

Milk: made for centuries by soaking ground almonds overnight to make something richer, creamier and more pure than new commercial varieties. Expensive then and expensive now but essential to use the real thing when recreating recipes from medieval to Victorian times, after which it became less common. Commercial versions are diluted and, well, read the label.

Slivered and nibbed: these fancier shapes, one long and thin, the other short and sort of fat, are mainly recommended for special decoration or where you want to add texture to a vegetarian or vegan nut loaf, when they are better for being microwave toasted to a greater or lesser degree, which gives better flavour and texture.

Valencia: flatter, heart-shaped nuts, with a rougher, tougher skin and less sweet flavour. Sold mainly for cooking, they are usually blanched and skinned and used widely for cake decoration, especially for Dundee cakes.

Whole blanched or unblanched halves: used mainly for cake decorating when they are all the better for being lightly micro-toasted, and in some Chinese dishes, notably with deep-fried seaweed. If you are going to use them in cakes they should be micro-toasted first, so they retain texture and flavour.

BRAZIL: it's not a nut, most come from Bolivia and it's also called the butter-nut, cream nut, castanea, and para-nut. The nut's rich flavour promises very high fat content, currently rated the second highest of the nuts, and it contains thiamine, a vitamin that prevents you going nutty. They cannot be cultivated so must be collected in tropical forest, from wild trees that grow up to 35 m/115 ft, and so are resolutely and immutably organic. The harvesting season is January and June, which is how they get to us so nicely for Christmas. Brazils are not much used in cooking but are very good with chocolate, a not unexpected thing when you consider their common birthright.

CASHEWS: raw cashew nuts have definite vegetal flavour and the pallid, wrinkled look of anaemic distress. When roasted they reveal a generous heart of sweet, full flavour with unique appeal, with or without salt, one of the most gratifying snacks.

The Chinese use toasted cashew nuts in combination with chicken and pork, at least those living in London do. An Indian curry uses raw cashews, but I think roasted ones are much tastier.

Milk: said by vegans to be the nicest and most useful of commercial nut milks, but few seem to have read the labels.

CHESTNUTS: the only nut we treat as a vegetable and because they contain the least amount of oil and most starch of any nut, they are the most digestible and can be turned into a useful flour.

Flour: almost exclusively used in Italian kitchens. It makes a gluten-free non-elastic dough and this is made into fritters, porridges of various kinds mixed with cream, milk, water or oil and an extraordinary yeast-leavened cake flavoured with aniseed. It is also used for a chestnut-type polenta.

Dried (dehydrated): an excellent standby in the larder of any imaginative cook. Soak them in warm water until they can be bitten through or cut with a knife; but you can be more inventive than that. Reconstituted dried ones have more flavour than those found whole in cans, possibly because of the particular variety. I simmer dried chestnuts in red or white wine spiced with cinnamon, nutmeg, a little orange peel and bay leaf and serve those as a hearty vegetable. Or I'll cook them with red wine, garlic and small pieces of fatty smoked bacon, because chestnuts take to fat and smoky flavours like anything. Either way, reduce the liquid until it just covers the chestnuts. These reconstituted and reflavoured chestnuts are then ready for roughly chopping into stuffings and sauces, to add to Brussel sprouts, or to serve whole with roasted meats and poultry.

Chestnuts are good foils to rich winter stews with pieces of bacon fat, and wonderful with pigeon, duck, turkey and pork dishes of all kinds. Dried chestnuts make excellent additions and stretchers to casseroles, put directly into the cooking liquid. This way they contribute to the overall flavour and also absorb the flavours of the cooking medium.

Purée, plain: not something you might use a lot of, but its concentrated flavour and delicious rich colour is useful. Mixed with breadcrumbs, chopped celery green, some brandy and a little onion or garlic it makes a simple moist stuffing for veal or poultry, although this is better baked as forcemeat balls cooked around a roast. Or incorporate the purée in a pancake mix together with buckwheat flour to make fritters to go with all manner of vegetarian, poultry or meat dishes. Mixed with egg it can be baked to make a chestnut polenta, which is good with roast duck.

Purée, vanilla: one of the most delicious things you can buy in a can. It's too rich and sweet to eat as it is, so fold it gently into equal volume of whipped cream, and then add a tot of brandy, cherry brandy or Pedro Ximenez sherry. Cram that into profiteroles, top a cheesecake adding black cherries, sandwich meringues or chocolate cakes or millefeuilles, layer in sundaes or top summer fruits, especially raspberries.

Vacuum packed: available year-round, these packs are inexpensive and something to have on hand to serve as is or with roasted vegetables, especially butternut and other squashes, to bulk out stews, add to stuffings or to turn in lightly caramelised sugar, butter and a few spices.

COBNUTS: also known as Kentish or Kent cobnuts, are a commercially developed and grown variety of hazelnut but are now grown in ever fewer numbers in ever fewer orchards. When developed but not ripe they have an attractive, slightly acidic milkiness than can be addictive; traditionally, some enjoy them with a little salt. They are also eaten fully ripe, when they look and taste more or less like other hazelnuts and can be used the same way.

COCONUT: if you don't fancy coping with whole coconuts, the meat and liquid products can be bought in several forms but a solid block of creamed coconut is the most practical to have on hand.

Cream: the thickest richest part of coconut milk that rises the way cream does from milk. Used instead of cream almost anywhere you want richness and don't mind the coconut flavour. Make your own by pouring boiling water onto dessicated, shredded or flaked coconut until well covered, then leaving it several hours. Put into a sieve and use the back of a soup ladle to force out as much liquid as possible. This is thick coconut cream and can be further diluted to make coconut milk.

Creamed: a solid block, sometimes called coconut butter and which is a paste made from the dehydrated flesh. It lasts for ages, is pure, and can be reconstituted into coconut cream or milk by dissolving an amount in hot or boiling water. The thicker it is the richer, obviously, and as both thick cream or thin milk it can be used like the dairy product. Thick coconut cream separates and 'oils' if heated to boiling point and this is done deliberately in West Indian, Malaysian and some Thai cooking.

Thick coconut cream spread on top of a grilled pork chop or roasted chicken gives an interesting and instant lift to otherwise ordinary food. Even such basics as vanilla ice cream, sliced oranges or grilled bananas are magically transformed; and used with care in association with finer fruits like strawberries or the wonderful mango, thick, chilled coconut cream makes child's play of creating new desserts during hot summer months. I always keep coconut cream in the refrigerator.

You don't always have to eat it; coconut milk is terrific in long summery drinks with rum and fruit juices—a hot evening, a barbecue, some friends, some coconut cream, assorted fruits and alcohols and you'll have a memorable party—or, if you are really lucky, a party that no one remembers!

I like to finish a spicy, gingery curry sauce by leaving solid coconut cream to melt in the liquid, and it can add new dimensions of flavour to the most unexpected vegetables, like butternut squash, aubergine and green beans.

Desiccated, shredded or flaked coconut: these are the same thing, but shredded or flaked coconut are both marginally moister. Particularly popular in Australasia, where desiccated coconut is put into or onto more sweet and savoury dishes than even Dame Edna Everage could deride. Lamington cakes are squares of sponge coated with chocolate syrup and coconut and are as essential at a Down Under christening as the vicar or, these days, the celebrant. Coconut bumblebees, coconut ice and coconut-sprinkled fruit salads and curries will be as life blood to the newly named child. Actually, it is very good in all these foods, especially in curries with which it can also be served as a condiment.

Flour: a relatively new kid on the block, coconut flour is made from what is left after coconut milk-cream is pressed from the nut. Once a waste product, it was discovered in the Philippines to be useful when ground fine into high fibre, gluten-free flour. It absorbs a lot of liquid, so using it in baking requires thoughtful adaptation; use about quarter the amount of plain flour and add a little liquid, too. A bigger problem is that it tastes highly of coconut and this is hard to hide.

Milk: the liquid pressed from fresh coconut flesh or made by soaking dessicated or flaked coconut or by diluting solid creamed coconut. I think you'll like sliced aubergine baked gently in coconut milk spiked with a few rings of green chilli peppers.

Rice cooked in coconut milk or cream is a revelation, and so is coconut cream as a dressing for crunchily cooked green beans, or on lettuce, both creations of my Pitcairn Island relatives.

Water: the natural liquid found in

coconuts can be drunk directly. It's more plentiful and more delicious in young, green coconuts but becomes bitter and is absorbed into the flesh as the coconut ages. Although there are health benefits, the huge new industry selling coconut water must process it to do so, never an advantage. There are two types, sold as coconut water or as pressed coconut water. Both can have additives and be sweetened. Neither is quite what they say and both are likely to have been pasteurised.

Pressed coconut water is obtained by pressing the nut flesh to obtain a liquid that is then pasteurised and must be sweetened, too.

GINGKO NUTS: mildly flavoured and with a strange starchy-rubbery texture, these small buff-coloured productions of the gingko tree are used as garnish or ingredients in all types of Chinese dish. Best bought canned in brine.

HAZELNUTS: hazelnuts are cobnuts as Kent cobs are filberts; the differences are technical and determined by the relative length of the nut to the husk, cobs usually being rounder and filberts somewhat longer. In the United States all types are called filberts.

Hazelnuts are essential to the finest traditions of European cake making and confectionery. There is some argument as to whether hazelnuts, almonds or both go into praline. I think only hazelnut gives the better result.

Hazelnuts taste better when lightly toasted. Microwaving is a faster and better way to do this, ensuring they are browned all through. Lightly toasted and carelessly crushed hazelnuts are good to sprinkle over fruit dishes, in cereals, muesli, yoghurt, cream and with green vegetables. They are specially good with the aristocratic mangetouts, or with broccoli, particularly if also bathed with garlic-ridden butter.

Toasted hazelnuts, whole or chopped, crushed or ground are quite one of the best additions to stuffings and dressings and make a fascinating addition to meat gravies and game sauces. Serve strawberries dolloped with whipped cream or crème fraîche stiffened with chopped toasted hazelnuts.

HEMP SEEDS: hemp seed and hemp oil are used a lot in the US—you'll find hemp milk, ice bread, butters, cheese and beer. Related to the variety that gives marijuana, the seeds have an amino acid count almost as high as soy beans but are blessedly less 'windy'. The taste is similar to sunflower/pumpkin seed, and is more delicious and nuttier when toasted. One of the few things that can work as a substitute for pine nuts.

LINSEED: the small, reddish-brown or golden-yellow seeds of the common flax plant. They are likely to be recommended as a vegan and vegetarian source of an important, single Omega-3 fatty acid, usually found in fish oils, but the accessibility of this ingredient can be affected by association with other constituents and it's best to take specialist dietary advice if this is important. Linseeds add marked dietary fibre and should be added to diets in modest amounts and with increased liquid intake.

MACADAMIAS: from an Australian tree native to Queensland and New South Wales, the macadamia probably has the highest calorie content of any nut. Generally very expensive, partly because the shell is extraordinarily tough to get into. The shucked nut looks like a pale, fat hazelnut and has a curious, fatty, waxy texture and a light buttery taste that is usually aided by coconut oil.

Hawaii is mad for them, so pop into a macadamia shop on Waikiki Beach and taste one or two free samples of their multifarious and surprising macadamia plus confections.

PEANUTS: not nuts but legumes, and also called groundnuts, earth nuts, monkey nuts ... and goolers. Traces of peanuts have been found in ancient Peruvian mummy graves and from their native South America they have now spread to India, Indonesia, China, West Africa and the United States giving peanut oil, peanut butter, salted peanuts, spiced or dry-roasted peanuts, and the peanut sauces that make Indonesian foods so original and full of flavour.

Pound for pound, they have more protein, minerals and vitamins than beef liver, more food energy (calories) than sugar and more fat than double cream.

They need to be cooked, because raw they are feral and one dimensional. Only after boiling and/or roasting does their virtue shine.

PECAN: from North America, where Native Americans ate it and ground it to make a milk for use in gruels and maize cakes, a combination that would be very good. One of the highest calorie contents.

Pecan halves and pieces are good in sweet pies, vegetable purées or dessert pastries that include spices. Although said to be interchangeable with walnuts, the pecan has a richer, more elegant flavour, without the acidic bite walnut so often has, perhaps because it is staling.

PEPITAS: the insides of pumpkin seeds, either toasted as nibbles or used in some versions of *mole sauces* q.v.

PILI: hand-harvested, buttery nuts from the Philippines that are teardrop shaped and also called the Java Almond. It's likely they have the highest fat content of any nut, supposedly over 90% but it's hard to verify. Not well known but were judged Great Taste Awards Supreme Champion in 2018.

PINE NUTS/PINE KERNELS: the usual source is the stone pine, but other pines provide them, too. The quintessence of beguiling and luxurious ingredients for the food of the eastern Mediterranean, and North Africa, as well as Italy, Turkey and Greece. The small, moon-coloured nuts, slim and elongated, are rich and oily and taste of the merest whisper of pine resin. Bigger, fatter and proportionally shorter nuts will be from China.

Pine nuts are basic to pesto Genovese, pounded with fresh basil, garlic, oil, Parmesan and a pecorino cheese into a famously fragrant sauce for pasta, tomatoes and roasted vegetables, fish—for almost anything good you eat in summer.

The combination of pine kernels with currants is ancient, seen in pilaffs, with baby soles in Venice and with chard in pies in Provence. You can't go wrong. PISTACHIO: the green one, rich and decorative in its wine-red skin, is grown from Afghanistan to the Mediterranean and in the United States, where it is particularly popular as a flavour in ice cream. The very best are agreed to grow in Bronte on the slopes of Mt Etna, and when these are roasted and used in ice cream or gelato by Italians who know, you'll recognise the superiority at once.

Pistachios are sold in split kernels because this happens naturally on the tree and they can be roasted and salted without further processing. A popular snack, the pistachio has a low-calorie count and the time taken to shell each one is said to contribute to a lesser intake. Really?

For culinary use they are available shelled and unsalted. To ensure a bright green colour, boil the nuts in water for 30 seconds and then peel away the skins; if the nuts do not brighten, they are not of the best quality. Roasting fresh ones makes a great flavour difference.

Pistachios are invaluable for decorating, chopped finely over sweet or savoury food, hot or cold, essential in dishes that also include saffron and toasted pine nuts. Finely chopped pistachios are part of the fillings for *baklava* q.v., those siren-like Greek, Turkish and Arabic pastries and are also excellent in poultry stuffings.

Europe and the USA have never really taken this nut to their heart—or stomach—so it's more common as pistachio 'flavouring' that is more like almonds, which is a terrible let down. PUMPKIN SEEDS: at least as addictive as salted pistachios and quite as messy. You have to break the outer shell to get at the green-black inner meats. A way of life in Turkey and many near and Middle-Eastern countries, and endemic in Mexico and South America, whence pumpkins and squash came to the Old World. Used in Styria to make a military-green oil. See *Pumpkin seed oil*, see *Pepitas*.

TIGER NUTS: not nuts but tubers that look like a cross between shrivelled peanuts and extruded, dried dog food, they are the Spanish *chufas or alchufas*.

Mainly eaten as a snack they have an extraordinary chewy texture and flavour, not unlike coconut crossed with brazil nut. They were very popular in Britain before the last war but disappeared with corner shops.

In southern Spain you drink rather than eat them, in a popular beverage called *horchata*, a refreshing tiger-nut milk served chilled and if you've ever wondered what people do in a Spanish *horchateria*, now you know. Tiger nuts are rarely used in cooking, but when soaked, apparently go well in apple pie. WALNUTS: black and butternut walnut varieties grow in the eastern states of North America; the English or Persian walnut is common throughout Europe, the Middle East, China and has been introduced to the United States. The nut of the English variety is the only one commonly picked green and dried or ripened off the tree.

Fresh walnuts are creamy, rich, fascinating and don't have a background sharpness or bitterness: those that do are rancid or well on the way to that state, but this is the way most of us eat walnuts most of the time because it happens very quickly.

The walnut is particularly versatile, found successfully in sweet and savoury dishes throughout the world and is used in pasta and vegetable sauces from Italy to the Caucasus, where its astonishing affinity with tomatoes is celebrated in a sauce that combines them. The simplest 'gourmet' dish of all is a bowl of sliced ripe tomatoes invested with slightly chilled walnut oil, a dusting of salt and plenty of roughly torn flat-leaf parsley—and even those last two can be forgone without diluting the pleasures. Adding walnuts increases the pleasure.

Pickled: made from unripe walnuts that have little flavour but great bitterness and are then ambushed by malt vinegar, so not widely acceptable to the modern palate. New versions made with gentler vinegars and warm spices do little for a product with so little intrinsic flavour.

Canned and Bottled Vegetables

ou are missing out if you think canned or bottled vegetables have had their day. Some are simply better when bought this way; others can only be bought this way.

Once again the advice is to read the label. Many unusual vegetables, particularly from Asia, are canned with acetic acid or vinegar that changes their character and virtue too much to be used in any traditional ways. That's why such as pea aubergines are not included here.

ARTICHOKES

Hearts, coeurs d'artichauts: an excellent addition to hors d'oeuvres, or sliced into hot or cold pasta dishes or potato salads. Served solo they should first soak an hour or two with a good olive oil vinaigrette with lemon zest, very finely chopped garlic and parsley.

Bottoms, fonds d'artichauts: the little caps of solid, nutty tasting artichoke flesh with no attached leaves, taste as good from a tin as fresh, as long as they have been canned in brine rather than something acidic. Labels can be consciously opaque about this. Sliced and dressed they make the basis for a high-class salad, ideally with a few cold peas plus any or all of orange segments, black olives and a few anchovy fillets.

Slice in to salads of the Niçoise style, a chunky tomato, hard-boiled egg, green-bean style. Grandly they are served filled with a vegetable purée. Green pea is most traditional but anything with the bite of lemon or garlic will work, celeriac with crushed hazelnuts, Brussel sprouts with nutmeg, carrot with allspice or thyme.

ASPARAGUS: although cooked to a softness we would never entertain in fresh asparagus, canned green asparagus spears are addictive when rolled in thin, buttered white or brown bread. Asparagus rolls are even better if you also butter the outside of the bread and then brown and crisp them in the oven. Prosciutto or pancetta rolled in with the asparagus makes these disappear even faster.

Fold a sieved purée of canned asparagus into mayonnaise for cold fish or poultry, or stir it into a béchamel to make a sauce or soufflé base.

White asparagus: blanched in earth banks to keep the sun from their thrusting stems, they have an insipid somewhat bitter flavour not much to the British taste, even less appealing when canned. Those who cleave to European tastes no matter what, serve them with smoked or unsmoked ham, often baked in a cheese sauce.

BAMBOO SHOOTS: canned in ivory-coloured chunks or large slices and if the odour seems pronounced, rinse well or blanch lightly. Mainly used as a squeaky/crunchy contrast of texture in Oriental dishes but the deep woodiness of flavour marries with such earthiness as wild mushrooms in creative Occidental salads. Keeps a long time refrigerated in water.

BANANA LEAF: a common wrapping for cooking food that is not expected to add flavour, yet long cooking will encourage a leafy, tea-like flavour to be passed to the food. Very useful for barbecuing and grilling fish, which might otherwise burn or stick or both: even if the leaf chars it takes a long time actually to burn away.

Folded and pinned with water-soaked wooden cocktail sticks, banana leaf works very well in the microwave, to wrap fish coated in a curry sauce perhaps. Or as a simple fascinating seal on ramekins in which something sweet or savoury is being cooked or warmed. The leaf is lightly oiled before use, and the older it is the less flexible it will be. Banana leaf is never eaten.

BORETANNE: small, flattish speciality onions from Italy, with a pale, yellow flesh and natural sweetness. Like *lampascioni* q.v. they are a civilised pickled onion. Usually grilled and then stored in balsamic vinegar, making them a smart sweet-sour addition to *antipasti*.

CELERY HEARTS: indistinguishable from home-cooked fresh celery. With plenty of butter and chicken or beef stock, they reheat wonderfully. Equally good in a rich cheese sauce or in something Mediterranean, with tomatoes, black olives, capers and whole garlic cloves.

HEARTS OF PALM: Millionaire's asparagus. Each heart is the central young stem of a special palm tree, which dies when this heart is removed, hence the expense. The ivory-coloured, embryonic leaves have a delicious and unusual sweetness enveloped in woody, earthy flavours, and a texture that can squeak as you eat.

Serve chilled with vinaigrette or mayonnaise as though white asparagus, and often with prawns, or lobster, which appreciate the sweetness. Better if you bump up the tropicality, so flavour either type of dressing with lime, and here's a definite place for angostura bitters, with restraint.

The hearts can be woody and fibrous and rather unpleasant, so if you are serving them for a special dinner it is wise to check each piece individually, and to have a spare can on hand. They don't seem to take to being served warm or to being further cooked.

As a substitute for white asparagus, palm hearts easily earn their keep through novelty value and taste better, also providing additional glamour to smoked salmon, to gulls' or quails' eggs and with smoked fish.

JACKFRUIT: the new darling of vegans and vegetarians—because you can treat it like meat? Yes, you can, although using vegetables to replace or replicate meat is the aspect of vegan and vegetarian life I do not understand.

You must buy only young or green jackfruit in cans and only those in brine; if this is too strong soak or blanch quickly. Jackfruit pieces look like a curious, pinkish cephalopod, taste a bit like artichoke and have a soft fibrous texture that holds its own—hence its popularity as pulled meat because it shreds easily into strings. A greater appeal is that jackfruit absorbs other flavours, so with a good sauce of any kind it gives a satisfying eat. You soon forget its funny shape and texture.

LAMPASCIONI: commonly sold as wild onions but these are the bulbs of wild hyacinth that flourish in Puglia. They look and taste a bit like shallots, and are chargrilled before preserving in olive oil. Best thought of as a pickled onion with airs and graces, so good with cold meats and salami or cheese with a strong presence.

LOTUS LEAF: the lotus leaf of Asia and the Orient gives a subtle extra flavour, when used as a wrapper especially to rice, pork and poultry. More likely to be used for steaming than boiling, and thus flavour exchange will be minimalised. Usually bought dried, the leaves should be soaked in warm water before use. If you grow your own, dip them in very hot water, both to wilt and to rid them of unwanted animal matter. They are never eaten.

LOTUS ROOT: recognised easily as the slices with the holes in them. Crisp, crunchy and slightly sweet, for mixing into stir-fries, or into your own creations for discreet sensation.

LOTUS SEED: now popped to offer a protein-rich snack with less fat and calories than crisps or popcorn.

Mushrooms: don't bother with canned mushrooms, whatever ubiquitous home economists/nutritionists say. Ignore hideously expensive bottled ones too, which are just as unsatisfying.

Look instead to dried wild mushrooms, later in this chapter.

PADRON PEPPERS: although fresh rather than processed in any way, padron peppers should be a mainstay of any speciality food shop. Originally from North-West Spain, they are green, pointy and slightly curved and taste like a sweeter, green capsicum. You cook them quickly in very hot olive oil until browning and wrinkling, then drain and salt liberally to eat while warm. Delicious anyway, they add frisson to any occasion because about one in 15 or more will have the heat of chilli. Tons of fun and addictive. Always buy twice as many as you first thought.

PEAS: apart from mushy, or processed peas, made from dried marrowfat peas cooked with baking soda, canned peas have been cancelled out by the frozen.

Petits pois à la francaise: cooked with baby onions and some lettuce retain a following based on nostalgia rather than inherent quality. Much better fresh.

POTATOES: small and waxy, canned potatoes make salads that do not fall to pieces. Cut into big chunks and then heat slightly before dousing with vinaigrette and garlic, even if you are later to mix them with mayonnaise. To ring the changes, dress the vinaigrette-flavoured potatoes with soured cream and dill, or with a mixture that's half yoghurt and half mayonnaise plus prawns.

RED PEPPERS: these have generally been char-roasted and skinned before processing and so are both sweet and convenient. For general cooking buy only those in oil or brine, not in vinegar or other acid. Drain well, dress with garlic and good olive oil plus a splash of lemon juice or vinegar for a simple but robust accompaniment to plain grilled lamb chops, chicken or pork dishes. Good mixed with slices of artichoke bottoms, too, with capers, with excellent mozzarella, perhaps anchovies. They finish a salad far better than raw ones, can be added to scrambled eggs, puréed for stuffings, added to pasta, added to almost every sandwich, toasted, grilled, wrapped, rolled or made with sliced white.

Piquillo: a type of red pepper unique to the Lodosa region of Spain, it is sweet and rich with a hint of heat. Those of DOC quality are baked, lightly smoked, peeled and packed by hand in only their own juice, and are worth every bit of their keen market price. A slab of piquillo pepper, with a hot, split, sweet chorizo, a handful of biting rocket and generous arbequina olive oil on a split and chargrilled bread roll is one of many reasons to go to Brindisa in London's Borough Market.

SOTT'OLIO: the catch-all for a wide variety of vegetables cooked and preserved in oil, or under oil as the name suggests. All are great for forking directly out of the jar and onto a plate, into a sandwich, wrap or roll, onto pasta or pizza.

SWEET CORN: whole kernel or cream-style, these taste just about as good as you would cook from fresh. Creamed, whole or a mixture, sweet corn makes the best fritters for breakfast, with chicken, ham, bacon, or with barbecues; a little smoked paprika or chili compound lifts them high.

TOMATILLOS: fundamental to much Mexican and South American cookery, these look like small green tomatoes, but the flavour is fruitier and more intense, much like physalis or cape gooseberries; if you grow tomatoes you can grow tomatillos, too. A subtle, fascinating difference in tomato sauces.

TOMATOES: good food is barely possible without tins of plum tomatoes processed in their juices. And now we have chopped tomatoes, chopped tomatoes with any number and style of flavourings, and passata.

Passata: any of the above put through a sieve. If you have to do this, use the back of a soup ladle in the sieve rather than a wooden spoon. Great time saver and you get a much bigger return.

Paste/purée: the professional secret is always to cook-off purée in a little oil before using, so the sugars caramelise and concentrate. This can be done separately or when you are frying and softening onions or vegetables to start a dish. Some advise cooking until a richer red, others say the tomato should turn brown. The amount you concentrate and caramelise is up to you, but even a short pre-cook opens a fuller flavour.

Sun-dried: from being inescapable, sun-dried tomatoes are scarcely visible, dismissed as though another fad. They are better than that, much better. The intrinsic flavour of the tomato variety matters and too many inferior products were marketed too quickly. Some are over-dried and too caramelised, others pale and not interesting.

Excepting individual preferences, my recommendation is to avoid those hydrated in oil or any other liquid and to buy dried ones with the greatest care, avoiding anything with detached skins, browning or broken shape. Many have not been dried naturally but are oven-dried and you can do the same, but only with good-tasting tomatoes.

VINE LEAVES: vacuum-packed, bottled or canned, these will have been lightly cooked and stored in brine and should be well soaked before use. They add a slight honey-like flavour to any food with which they are in contact for some time. Unlike the previous two, these leaves are eaten, but require fairly long cooking. As a wrapping for fish, for roasts or for baked pâtés they may add their flavour without being eaten. Fresh vine leaves from any type of grape may be used after quickly blanching in boiling water.

WATER CHESTNUTS: a walnut-sized bulb covered by a tough russet-coloured skin; the meat is white and crisp and stays that way whatever you do. Usually sliced for stir-fries and when chopped give stuffings and fillings guaranteed texture, particularly those including Chinese mushrooms.

Flour: water chestnuts make a flour into which you may dip ingredients for deep frying: it gives a really light and crunchy texture, and may also be used to thicken sauces.

Why Delia and her assistants are wrong about microwaved vegetables
If you find, as Delia Smith says she did, that microwaved vegetables have lost their soul, then both she and you have overcooked them, simple as that.

Microwaved vegetables are the tastiest and most nutritious possible, officially up to 85% more so, because their flavour and goodness have not been dissolved into cooking water or leached by steam that does the same thing, seen in the water beneath. The flavour of microwaved vegetables has been concentrated and thus often needs less or no salt. Other than potatoes, they don't need the addition of water, as they cook in the steam they produce; if you add water, it will leach out nutrition and flavour.

Dried mushrooms

European and North American

The dried mushroom is an absolute must, used for everything from saving a mundane soup or stew to being served in a Madeira-based sauce with brioches or darkly to flavour a Venetian-style risotto that is perfectly *all'onde*.

It is sad so many are imported and expensive when Britain fair groans with wild mushroom varieties that could be eaten fresh or dried.

CEP, CEPE, PORCINI, STEINPILZ: cep is the English name for *boletus edulis*, better known as porcini, the Italian name. When fresh the cep can be bland and slimy, even after baking has concentrated its flavour; but when dried it is totally different, quite wondrous with a robust earthy-sweet flavour that is unmistakable.

The best qualities are sold in dried slices taken through the cap and stem, but chopped segments or broken pieces are cheaper. Check both for damage by bugs, either before or after drying.

Because dried ceps/porcini are expensive, opportunists offer cheap 'wild mushroom' mixtures with minimal porcini content. Read the label to see where *boletus edulis* comes in the order of ingredients, remembering they must by law be in descending order of their presence. Other types of boletus have nothing like the bold flavour of true cep. It's as dishonest as selling 'truffles' and finding only Summer Truffles *tuber aestivum* plus flavourings. The worst culprit is porcini powder: an Italian brand was spectacular but a French brand I bought in Borough Market was almost tasteless, perhaps why it did not have a list of ingredients.

Dried ceps must be rinsed in cold water in a coarse sieve or colander to get rid of the inevitable grit. The liquid in which they then rehydrate is invaluable and should always be used. If the mushrooms are to flavour a stew or soup or a stuffing, don't pre-soak them, chuck them straight in after rinsing. Otherwise cover with liquid and put over a low heat, which does it faster and gives the stock greater colour than steeping in cold liquid. The microwave is fastest of all. I particularly like to use an amontillado or oloroso sherry or an equivalent Madeira, but anything alcoholic is better than mere water. For a fast rich sauce, rehydrate by simmering in double cream, reduce and finish with a spot of Cognac or brandy.

CHANTERELLES/ GIROLLES: these gorgeous apricot-coloured small parasols have a delicate fruity flavour when fresh but very little when dried.

FAIRY RING: see *Mousserons.*

MORELS, MORILLES: the pointy wrinkled ones, alarmingly like any image you might have conjured of the exposed brain of an alien. They are expensive but repay that with huge flavour, which is definitely mushroom but also of meat and of bacon, particularly. Their appearance, flavour and cost mean they are more used as garnish or to finish a sauce and are a much better bet than truffles in any stuffing.

Morels take longer to rehydrate than ceps but the use of cream, wine or sherry rather than water is well recommended. I've eaten wild-gathered ones just outside Toronto with ricotta-spinach pancakes and once made a savoury Tarte Tatin of celeriac, morels and cream. Wondrous. Fletcher Christian's grandmother's 17th and 18th century cookbook from Netherhall in Maryport, Cumbria, combined morels with sweetbreads and bacon cubes to stuff a boned chicken, served in luscious pastel-coloured slices with a sauce of cream, wine, lemon, mace and a dash of anchovy.

Some people react badly to morels, not a dangerous full allergic reaction but they can feel very unwell.

MOUSSERONS: the French name for Fairy Ring mushrooms, which are also native to North America. These tiny parasols pack extraordinary flavour when dried, at least as powerful as ceps and morels and with similar flavours. BUT there are a number of mushrooms that make rings and variants are sold that have much less flavour but look the same. *Marasmius oreades* is the true variety. Great to throw into stews, soups and pasta sauces.

OYSTER MUSHROOM/PLEUROTTE: not usually dried but this is the fan-shaped one sold as a wild mushroom when it is neither: it's cultivated and it's a fungus. The French name, *pleurotte*, is a clue that these weep copiously when heated and so should be cooked very quickly indeed. They can be eaten raw, which gives you a better return for your money, and are available in other pastel colours, pink or yellow or blue.

TROMPETTES DES MORTS: more sensitively called Horns of Plenty rather than Trumpets of Death, these taste a little like chanterelles when fresh and of nothing much when dried. Better thought of as black garnish than as an ingredient that might add flavour.

Asian mushrooms

Asian mushrooms might be dried or canned and most favour texture over flavour.

GOLDEN NEEDLE/ENOKITAKE: cream rather than golden, but always a long, slim stem and a tiny cap. Usually sold in clumps, they are delicious when raw and so make one of the easiest and prettiest of edible garnishes. The Japanese use them in clear soups, added at the last minute.

HONEYCOMB: a fungus rather than a mushroom, and equally known as honeycomb, white ear or snow ear fungus. It's usually sold dried and needs to be reconstituted by soaking in warm water, with or without the inclusion of rice wine. Before use, the tough central core is removed and the remainder chopped or sliced. It's one of those Asian ingredients eaten as much for its gelatinous texture as anything else, yet there is a mild honey scent and taste, but only if eaten raw or very lightly cooked. The frilliness remains when its cooked, so it's added at the last minute for visual and textural interest.

MO-ER/CLOUD EARS: a speciality from Szechuan province. A crinkly, thin tree fungus, that should be soaked for 30 minutes before cooking. Any hard core should be removed. Adds a curious chewy crunch to stir-fried dishes and stuffings; the sort of ingredient that confirms you are not eating a fry up at the local caff.

SHIITAKE: the very best Oriental mushroom and a much bigger flavour when dried than fresh. They look like ordinary mushrooms except for the speckles or geometric shapes which so prettily pattern their caps. The colour varies from a black to a speckled brown or grey and it is said the medium sizes have the best flavours.

The very best grade is a 'flower mushroom', with star-marks on the cap, and will be fearfully expensive. All must be soaked in warm water for up to 30 minutes before cooking, so that they will resume their normal size and shape and become soft again. The stems will always be tough, and always discarded, although you could use them and the soaking water to make stock. They don't need to be cooked but can be braised. Otherwise slice or chop them into stir-fries, into stuffings or to throw into sauces.

STRAW: small yellow mushrooms with pointed black caps, sold in cans. Use within a few days of opening, as their delicate taste is lost soon after exposure to air.

WOOD-EAR & CLOUD-EAR FUNGUS: eaten for their texture and unruly frilled appearance, as they have negligible flavour. Most often encountered in stir-fries or where there is a mixture of other mushrooms. Usually bought dried, they are soaked in warm water until softened.

Truffles

NEED TO KNOW

Truffles should be eaten raw or with minimal heating.

Bottled and canned truffles have lost most special savour because of heat processing.

Freezing preserves truffles much better than other processes.

Don't cook with fresh truffles but add as a garnish or to finish sauces.

Black truffles are widely cultivated but costs are still high.

Eggs and rice will absorb flavour when stored with fresh truffles.

Summer Truffles, tuber aestivum, *have only subtle flavour, reduced more by processing and thus invariably have flavourings added: read the label.*

Black truffles are ripest after Christmas in the Northern Hemisphere.

There is more than one variety of black truffle.

Italian truffle varieties span a greater season than French.

Most truffle oils and truffle products use synthetic 'flavours' or 'aromas' to replace what has been lost.

I n the 19th century a truffle hunter could come home with a kilo, hence the dazzling frequency with which it was used—handsful to stuff a turkey. Now, finding one or two is thought a triumph but, as truffles have cycled in abundance through history, there will be more in future. The 20th century solution to the dearth was the discovery that these fungi could be cultivated and now they are harvested from truffle farms across Europe, Canada and the USA as well as in Australia, New Zealand and China. Not unexpectedly the mysterious effects of *terroir* have created flavour differences once never imagined.

Types of truffle

BLACK TRUFFLES: the mesmerizing scent and flavour of *tuber melanosporum* is found in nothing else—indeed it isn't found in truffles most of the time. The scents and flavours are oniony, sappy, fruity with notes of chocolate and much more. When a noted but now dead food writer said they were scrotal, many eyes widened with discreet agreement. The aroma is experienced more than the taste but truffles are easily overpowered and expected to perform tasks of which they are incapable.

Little of their famed appeal is left when they are canned and bottled, when they are better used for decoration. Black olives can do that.

Small or large, a black truffle looks like a wrinkled potato and the inside is more a very dark brown than black. When young you will see white veins that get browner as the truffle ripens.

Although widely known as coming from Périgord, the true black truffle grows in an area ranging from there to Italy, especially in Norcia, in Spain, Provence, Piedmont and Tuscany.

Natural black truffles are gathered between the end of November and mid-March or so. They are probably at their best in January, thus the rush to use truffles for Christmas cooking is generally pointless because they are unlikely to have reached maturity. In Provence I was told they were grated over salads on Christmas Day, 'but only because they were the first, we did not cook with them yet'.

Slicing or shaving over food is the best way to use them, although a brief amount of heat when added to a sauce will encourage a growth in flavour. Available on line seasonally, but it's hard to trust a purveyor who recommends they are cooked.

BIANCHETTO: a white to orange smooth-skinned Italian truffle harvested mid-January into April. A few white veins and a pungent smell that's garlic like.

BRUMALE: an Italian lesser black truffle with several variants, including the Muscat truffle. It is recognised once cut because it has fewer veins than a *melanosporum*. It's thought by some to be unpleasantly like turnip but always to be musky. I've never found them either. Always a captivating distraction in pastas or salads, where Italians most use it.

DESERT/SAND/HONEY TRUFFLES: found wild over a huge area of arid and desert conditions, from the Kalahari desert north into Europe and everywhere east of that into China. They are very mild, made milder by processing and cans of them can be found in Middle Eastern shops. A pinky-cream colour, once sliced they are like a textured, mild mushroom. Very cheap compared to black and white truffles and come in large cans, often in Middle Eastern stores, so you can be lavish.

SUMMER TRUFFLES: the very much lesser flavoured *tuber aestivum* or Summer Truffle has very little culinary pleasure to offer, and is the subject of opportunistic marketing, for how many know what *any* truffle tastes like? The Summer Truffle is clearly marbled when cut, and a paler brown than the *melanosporum*.

Most commercial truffle products not labelled as black truffles are processed Summer Truffles with added 'flavours' or 'aromas', sometimes as defeating as vinegar and onion. You do not get what you pay for, even more so if you expect black truffle because that's all you know. It's the basis of one of speciality food's biggest rip offs. Reading the label could never be more important.

UNCINATUM TRUFFLES: an autumn

version of the Summer Truffle, very widespread in Europe but specially associated with Burgundy. It is mild in flavour compared to the black or white, but has more to offer than the *aestivum*. WHITE TRUFFLES, TUBER MAGNATUM PICO: the white Piedmontese or Alba truffle has a penetrating scent and overwhelming flavour, redolent of every possible perversity and prohibition and impossible to describe because it is like nothing else. All you might do is to follow what it makes you think about, and then, like me, keep that to yourself. White truffles have long been granted aphrodisiacal properties, and even been called 'testicles of the earth'.

White truffle is never cooked but grated or very thinly sliced indeed over risotto, over pasta or onto hot brioche, a speciality of the sidewalks of Florence. It is more difficult to cultivate than black truffles and so far there has been little success.

Although associated so publicly with Alba in Italy, white truffles are also found in the Savoy, particularly around Chambèry. They may be frozen and defrosted most successfully and repay better than black truffles the ploy of storing them amidst eggs or rice or both, provided everything is very cool or refrigerated.

The man who began the white truffle fair in Alba used to send one to famous people around the world. Marilyn Monroe wrote back to him, saying: '*I have never tasted anything more taste-ful and exciting. Thank you so much for the pleasure that you procured me.*

Your faithful and affectionate, Marilyn.' Procured?

Sea vegetables

Except for laver, seaweeds come dried and will rehydrate in cold water in five minutes, after which they may be boiled to be served hot or cold, although I should be very certain of your guests' tastes before you dare either. Small amounts boiled in water make very good sea-scented stocks for cooking fish.

AGAR-AGAR: a vegetarian substitute for animal gelatine, especially for setting anything with fresh pineapple or kiwi fruit, as these contain an enzyme that prevents gelatine setting.

AUTUMN DULSE: a dark red colour and full shellfish/seaweed flavour. Once soaked, dredge with seasoned flour and deep-fry for frivolous, arresting flavours in snacks or garnishes.

DABBERLOCKS/WAKAME: accessible un-seaweed flavour of green nuts and young peas. It's olive green, good in chicken stews and soups.

DULSE: greenish red coloured and a definite marine/shellfish flavour, but less so than autumn dulse.

FINGERWARE/FINGER KOMBU: olive green with a meaty, beefy flavour that is nonetheless uncompromisingly marine. Limited in solo use but good mixed into salads and other vegetable mixtures, or in stuffings. Boil 20 minutes and then grill to crispness to garnish fish dishes.

GROCKLE/ HERB KOMBU: like a fleshy,

cooked vine leaf, it has a slight astringency behind a chestnut-marine flavour. Fry in egg batter as tempura or deep fry in seasoned flour.

KOMBU/KONBU: dark green or brown sheets of the giant kelp that should have a sheen, a powdery surface and are thick. They should be wiped rather than rinsed. Cooked quickly with dried bonito flakes, *katsuobushi*, to make dashi, the basic Japanese stock.

LAVER/SLOKE/PURPLE NORI: can be red or black depending how it is cooked. Has an iodine-like back taste easily balanced by good vinegar or citrus juice, but rarely is.

Welsh laverbread is sold ready prepared after cooking for hours, and may also be bought in cans. Cooked for hours until a pulp it was served with cockles and bacon or rolled in oatmeal to make little fritters.

NORI: essential as wraps for sushi, this is dried Japanese laver, and is usually lightly toasted before use; it may be crushed and sprinkled as a condiment. Can be bought ready-toasted.

SPIRULINA: a freshwater algae or seaweed that grows naturally in tropical and sub-tropical lakes. Because it is a supplement rather than a mainstream food, spirulina has not been as deeply researched as major food stuffs. It offers the full spectrum of amino acids (proteins) but is not considered to be as complete in other nutrition as milk, eggs or meat. It's also many times more expensive than other protein sources and its contribution as anything more than occasional novelty value has not been established.

There are currently no industry-agreed systems that will guarantee spirulina crops are not contaminated by other organisms or types of water-based weeds.

SUGAR KELP/ SUGAR KOMBU/GIRDLE TANG: a delicate-looking and tasting seaweed, not unlike a salt-sea version of spring greens. You can do almost anything with it. Once rehydrated it makes a jolly good wrapping for fish that is to be baked or steamed.

Grains including Pasta

NEED TO KNOW

True grains are the seeds of grasses from the Poaceae botanic family.

Amaranth, quinoa and buckwheat are not true grains.

Wild rice (Zizania) is not a true grain and is not related to rice.

Grain's greatest nutritional contribution is starch (carbohydrate), the basic energy source for our body.

No grain has enough amino acids to replace animal protein proportionally; the legume soy bean is the closest plant-based source.

Petit épeautre/einkorn, amaranth, quinoa and wild rice have high amino-acid/protein content, but not the range or quantity to replace animal protein.

The germ in a grain is what sprouts, but contains oils that easily oxidise.

Vegans and vegetarians wanting complete plant-based protein should balance 30% grains to 60% beans, peas or pulses: e.g. wholemeal toast with baked beans; chapati with lentil dhal; rice and beans.

Maize is the least nutritious grain; relying on it as a staple without beans and pulses leads to pellagra and kwashiorkor.

Wheat has the most gluten, which stretches to leaven bread dough.

Barley, oats and triticale contain gluten but less than wheat.

Flours from gluten-free-grains can be mixed with wheat flour to make breads.

Gluten-free wheat flour can be raised with baking soda or baking powder.

Stone-ground whole or white wheat flour is more nutritious than roller-milled.

UK regulations mean refined/white flours always contain supplements to ensure they are as nutritious as wholemeal flour.

G rains are largely the seeds of a family of grasses, and principally responsible for the success of *homo erectus*. The encampments, villages, towns, cities and empires that arose on a platform of cultivating grain stimulated the cooperation that shot men from the plains to the planets. It signalled the change from semi-independent, nomadic hunting and foraging to a settled, community existence.

Grain needed continuous care. The newly-formed groups who gave it were rewarded with a staple that could also be stored for use in winter. Thus 10,000 years ago a new balance was created as hunting became less crucial to survival; instead, humans domesticated the animals on which they liked to feast and ate fewer of them. While man ate grain, the cattle and other animals ate its straw. Babylon, Egypt, Ancient Greece and the Roman Empire were founded on the cultivation of wheat, barley, rye and oats; in the Far East it was millet and rice; in the Americas, maize. There, quinoa and amaranth helped, too, but are not true grains.

The leaders of those ancient civilisations learned by observation or intuition that grains only supply *most* of our nutritional needs. To get the complete range of protein necessary to replace meat, dairy and eggs, they knew to eat grains with such pulses as beans and lentils.

Wholegrains supply significantly more nutrition than crushed grains or wholegrain flours. For once a grain has been crushed or ground, the vitamin-rich oils in the germ begin to oxidise and lose food value, eventually becoming rancid and sometimes dangerous. Many commercial products made of grain are de-germinated precisely to avoid oxidization, giving long, trouble-free shelf life at the expense of nutrition.

It is worth soaking many kinds of grains before use, especially wheat and rye. The prime reason is not to shorten cooking time but to improve flavour and usefulness to the body. Soaking in water begins the germination (malting) process, activating a digestive enzyme similar to that in our mouths. This process converts starches into sugars—maltose particularly—making the grain sweeter and tastier and promoting fuller and more efficient assimilation. Once cooked, some grains continue to sweeten and improve in flavour, the result of a broadly similar process.

Types of grain

AMARANTH: of the many indefensible acts of the Catholic Church in South and Latin America, banning amaranth as a food not only interfered grossly with established rituals but nearly starved the societies that relied on them.

If the church had instead spread the good word about amaranth, Europeans might have been much better off, too.

The tiny, sand-like seeds offer twice as much calcium as milk, three times more fibre than wheat, have a couple of elusive amino acids and because amaranth is so digestible it is an excellent source of nourishment for the poorly. Oh yes, and the leaves, raw or cooked, are a better source of iron than spinach.

Jenni Muir's amazing research for *The Cook's Guide to Grains* tells us that in ancient civilisations from California down to Peru amaranth was mixed with honey and human blood, a recycling of sacrificial by-products, which was then shaped into human figurines and eaten. Appalled Christian conquistadores banned eating amaranth in any form, forgetting they were presumed to be eating the actual blood and flesh of Jesus every time they took communion. The Catholic Church admitted defeat only in the 20th century, but then only allowed amaranth in Christian ritual— the seeds were even incorporated into rosary beads. Jesus would have turned in his grave. If he had one.

Amaranth has a pleasing warm and mild flavour but can go sticky rather easily. The seeds are ground for use as additives in breads, biscuits and cakes and when popped over heat can be made into sweets and snacks, even into a breakfast cereal. There are over 60 varieties, many of which are edible leaf and seed crops. Love-Lies-Bleeding is one of them.

BARLEY: although one of the earliest grains eaten and cultivated, barley is much less eaten nowadays. Yet it is still important. Without barley we would not have Scotch whiskies, beer or malted milk shakes. Half the world's barley crop feeds livestock, making meat eaters dependent on it second hand.

Barley grows in northern countries, where fickle wheat would not, so it was vital when few could afford food that was not local. Today, barley is still a staple food in much of Eastern Europe and in parts of Africa. Being almost gluten-free, it makes heavy, moist bread that cannot be leavened without the addition of wheat flour but a little barley meal added to bread dough gives a warming flavour.

It's good to soak barley overnight before use. And, wonderful trivia. Edward II decreed in the 14th century that the standard English inch measure was three grains of dry, round barley placed end to end.

Barley couscous: a Moroccan staple served mainly within the family; wheat couscous is reserved for visitors. The pearl-grey colour and delicious sweetness of barley couscous make it a hit with stews and with roasts and it reacts well to such additions as dried apricots, ground cardamom, coriander seed, orange zest and parsley or fresh coriander leaf.

There is a green-barley couscous too: *marmez* in the north east of Morocco and *zembou* elsewhere. It's browner and has a rather forward and grainy flavour, much like fine burghul. And that's what these are, barley burghuls rather than couscous.

Barley flakes: lightly rolled grains, usually of pot barley. Makes a special breakfast porridge, soothing, chewy and satisfying. Make it with milk rather than water and sweeten with a natural brown sugar or maple syrup.

Barley meal and barley flour: difficult but not impossible to find. Terms are confused and transposed but generally meal is coarser and made from pot barley and flour is finer and made from pearl barley. Makes an especially good sourdough starter, otherwise simply substitute 20-50% in your bread flour, to add a sweet and wholesome flavour and heavier texture. A recommended addition to soda bread.

Barley sugar: twisted and golden, is increasingly hard to find and probably isn't the real thing anyway. It was a superior boiled sweet made with barley water; saffron gave the golden colour and subtle extra flavour.

Barley water: to make this old-fashioned treat, put 50 g/2 oz pearl barley into 600 ml/1 UK pint of cold water. Bring to the boil, simmer 15 minutes, drain, and then replace drained liquid with 900 ml/1½ UK pints of boiling water. Simmer until reduced by half. Strain. Sweeten or dilute according to taste, and add traditional flavour with lemon, orange or lime juice.

Bere: probably our oldest grain, in continuous cultivation for over 1,000 years until the late 19th century when high-yielding varieties swamped it. Now bere is again grown in the north of Scotland to produce bere meal (flour) for baking bannocks and breads as well as for brewing. It is credited with giving unique, complicated fruity flavours to whisky.

Black barley: developed from an Ethiopian variety, it is said to differ in flavour from ordinary barley the way wild rice differs from white rice. Not yet widely available.

Pearl barley: the most common form, invaluable for thickening soups and stews as it has a natural affinity for fatty liquids, both in performance and flavour. It is the barley grain, husked, steamed and then polished to give the characteristic rounded shiny appearance. The dark line down one side is a remnant of the husk. Increasingly used again as a pilaff to complement rugged stews or roasted game, perhaps finished with flamed whisky and more flavourful if first lightly roasted or butter-fried.

Pot barley: also called Scotch barley, has only the indigestible part of the husk removed, so is extra nutty and nutritious. Can be used the same way as pearl barley but takes longer to cook.

BUCKWHEAT: buckwheat is the fruit seed of an herbaceous plant related to dock, sorrel and rhubarb. It thrives in a harsh climate, so has been a staple in Asia and Russia and northern Europe for untold centuries. Known in France as black wheat (*blé noir*) or Saracen wheat (*sarrasin*) as it is thought to have been brought to this part of Europe by returning Crusaders.

Buckwheat is available natural or pre-roasted and both are often called *kasha* but this is incorrect. Kasha is the collective name in Eastern Europe and Western Russia for almost any grain-based dish, whether porridge-like or dry and puffed up in the manner of a pilaff;

it just happens that most kashas are made with buckwheat.

Buckwheat flour: this gives a speckled effect and a remarkable flavour to batters and bread doughs and nicely complements such assertive flavours as game. You only need a few spoonsful in a basic pancake or bread dough to enjoy its warm, haunting flavour. It is the major ingredient of Brittany's *galette*, a huge, thin, savoury-filled pancake. When included in the small Russian *blini*, made to accompany caviar, it is perhaps the noblest buckwheat pancake of all, but the English eccentrically feed buckwheat to pheasants.

The Dutch introduced it to the American continent, when they founded Nieuw Amsterdam in the 17th century, and there it has remained very much in favour, as buckwheat pancakes served with syrup at breakfast. Buckwheat flour has no gluten content, so it must always be mixed with wheat flour in yeast-baking.

Buckwheat groats: coarsely-ground and thus cooked faster than whole. Available roasted or unroasted although the first is undoubtedly tastier and also makes an interesting addition to all kinds of baking, including bread.

Soba: a Japanese buckwheat spaghetti eaten chilled in summer but hot in winter.

CORN: in modern English, corn means types of maize, but the word was once used as a collective noun for all bread-making grains, including wheat, thus explaining Corn Markets built centuries before this grain came to the UK. Corned beef was so called because the salt used was the size of wheat/corn grains.

Corn/maize is native to the Americas and was the basis of the extraordinary civilisations of the Mayas, Incas, Aztecs and other almost unknown peoples of Central and South America. The smaller tribal societies of North America also relied upon it and in all parts of the continent it was worshipped. Maize has been cultivated so long it can no longer self-seed, but must be planted by man.

This is the least nutritious of grains because it is the one most lacking in essential amino acids and if eaten as a sole staple is a primary cause of the nasty disease pellagra, caused by a lack of niacin. Native North Americans knew to grow and eat beans with the grain, to give full vegetarian meat-equivalent nutrition, so grew beans up cornstalks and then ate them together. Further south, societies treated corn with wood ash or lime (calcium hydroxide or slaked lime), as they still do in Mexico to create *masa harina*, and this unlocks niacin.

When corn was taken to Africa in exchange for slaves neither the beans nor the niacin-releasing treatment went too. Africa's ills were exacerbated by the very food supposed to prevent them and they still are. If you are too poor to add the complementary protein of bean and pulses plus vegetables, a corn-based diet can kill you. Not until the 20th century did Western medicine make the link between corn-based diet and pellagra, so millions of American immigrants died in pellagra epidemics that were thought incorrectly to be germ based.

As well as the familiar yellow, corn can be red, purple, orange, white or blue. Blue corn flour, muffins, chips are crisps are enjoyed for the extra depth of slightly smoky flavour but the inky-chalky colour is always a surprise.

There are essentially three types of corn—sweet corn, eaten as it is, maize grains used to make flours or as animal feed, and popcorn.

Baby corn: specially bred miniature sweet corn cobs eaten whole, largely in Oriental and Asian cuisines.

Corn flour: known as cornstarch in the US, it is a lump-free thickener that is gluten free, light and sweet, especially good for custards, blanc-manges or baked puddings as well as sweet and savoury sauces.

Corn flour should always be slaked in a little cold water before being stirred into something hot. When first added it makes any liquid cloudy, but cooking on gives a vivid clear sauce; it is much used in Chinese cooking to collect up cooking liquids expressed during stir frying in a wok. It can also be used instead of arrowroot. Corn flour sauces will thin if cooked for too long.

Mix one part of corn flour to three of plain flour to make lighter baking.

Cornmeal: made from several varieties of gluten-free maize that are ground to a meal or flour, sometimes still called maize meal and maize flour. The coarsest meals are used for fast, non-yeasted breads and make a delicious addition to wheat bread if used sparingly, as they tend to produce a crumbly, cake-like texture. American breads made only of corn-meal are usually eaten by the spoon-ful straight from the shallow pan in which they are baked, hence the name spoon bread. See *Dent corn/ Polenta*.

Dent corn/feed corn: a variety that develops a dent in its top as it dries and that is most commonly fed to animals. Not a natural way for cattle to fatten but very good for poultry. Dent and *flint corn* q.v. are both cooked in Latin and South America with an alkali—seashells, wood ash or slaked lime—which releases the tough hull and changes the grain's chemical composition so its niacin and protein content are more easily available and this makes it safer for human consumption. This is *masa harina*, used in Mexican *tortillas*, *tamales* and their many relations.

Flint corn: the variety used in Europe to make polenta and also used to make *masa harina* in Mexico and her neighbours. It is called flint corn because the small grains are particularly hard and difficult to grind but the labour is rewarded with big, rich flavour.

Flour corn: a soft sweet variety used

for making an elegant corn flour or into a somewhat coarser meal especially suitable for corn breads.

Grits: coarsely ground dried maize, usually dent corn. Yellow grits are popular in the southern USA and made from the wholegrain. Served as a mush or porridge, boiled or baked in the oven and, like hominy, leftovers are often incorporated into other baking and cooking.

Hominy: is whole dried dent corn without its yellow hull and was the chief food of the enslaved African-American. Cooked in water until the white grains are very soft and swollen, and eaten with gravy and meat, with milk and sugar, or with salt and butter, it is still a great favourite throughout the southern United States. It is the basis of *pozole*, a stew with pork chillies, cumin and a big variety of other ingredients or toppings. Cooked hominy is added to muffins and cakes or fried in lard.

Indian corn: a popping corn, close to the original strain of corn grain and recognizable by its high proportion of bright red kernels. Undoubtedly prettier, it is less good for popping than the newer, all-gold strains.

Masa harina: corn cannot make a malleable dough. If it is cooked with alkaline slaked lime or wood ash and then rinsed of the alkali taste, it forms a dough used as it is and is also dried into a flour. The process releases niacin, which prevents such disease as pellagra. *Masa harina* is the basis of tortillas, tacos etc. and

also of *atole*, a soupy drink often flavoured with chocolate, sugar and spice.

Mealie-mealie: finely cut grain with most of the vital bran and germ removed. It is an important staple food in Africa that is cooked into a rather noisome porridge but unless eaters can afford to serve it with other types of protein and vegetables the diet leads to progressively worse health and, even, death. See *Chakalaka*.

Polenta: although the terms are interchangeable, polenta is not a type of corn/maize meal, but a specific dish made from bright yellow flint-corn meal. It is so common in northern Italy that the chief ingredient has been given the name of the dish. There, polenta is a corn porridge, usually flavoured with Parmesan and butter or olive oil. It is very time consuming to make and splutters vengefully, landing the hottest and most blistering blobs all over your person—which is why it is traditionally stirred with a very-long-handled wooden paddle. But that effort is now behind us.

Instant, which means pre-cooked, polenta is available, ready to eat in five minutes or so, but longer cooking does give a sleeker texture and is well worth doing. The microwave is a godsend but you must cover the container, as ever.

Polenta is traditionally served three ways. It may be served hot as a thick mush, left to go cold and then sliced and fried or grilled, or baked with savoury ingredients which add flavour—small birds roasted in polenta is a great favourite of the Veneto.

Its possibilities are being further explored as the smoky, grilled base for everything from fish to roasted vegetables, and can be layered with many of the same good ingredients, covered with cheese sauce and baked again. Thin polenta mush is an excellent basis for cooking thinly sliced vegetables, finished with chunks of good mozzarella or tiny chunks of Parmesan, and dribbled with a jolly good olive oil, one of those mushy, mucky one-dish meals that can be so gratifying.

Although sniffed at by traditionalists, serving soft, creamy polenta, perhaps instead of mashed potato, can be triumphant, singlehandedly justifying your new microwave; it's very good dotted with dolcelatte cheese as a base for pink slices of roast lamb.

Popcorn: the kernels have a skin under greater tension than other varieties, hence its propensity to explode dramatically when heated.

Homemade popcorn can be cooked in hundreds of interesting ways, though this form of corn gives even less nutrition than the others. Still, it's fun to run up a batch of garlic-and-herb-butter popcorn to serve with roasted chicken and then watch your guests' faces. Is it their first course or their last, and if it is either, what the hell is it doing on the plate now?

Sweet corn: widely known as corn on the cob in its natural state. Soft and succulent, it is eaten as a vegetable rather than as a grain. It degenerates in goodness and sweetness with breathtaking rapidity; native North Americans taught that you should walk to a cornfield and run back to the pot. Continued cross-breeding—it is one of the most genetically manipulated species on Earth—now gives us super-sweet corn that remains sweet even through the supermarket system and is perhaps too sweet to be believable as a natural, soil-grown product.

Best flavour comes from always cooking cobs in their outer green layers, first having peeled them back to remove the purple silk; this stops the kernels charring before they are cooked on the barbecue and adds delicious extra flavour when they are boiled in water.

The outer leaves of corn are equally good for other barbecuing, baking or grilling, especially for such fish as a whole trout or sea bass. Lightly oil them if they are a bit dry and cobble together with soaked tooth picks or satay skewers. Pumpkin and sweet potato are really good cooked in corn leaves.

Otherwise, cut off the raw kernels by running a sharp knife between the kernels and the cob, retaining as much as the milky sap as you can; these can be microwaved or quickly fried as they are or with such additions as butter, olive oil, garlic, chopped capsicum peppers and almost any herb, especially parsley, any kind of thyme and fresh coriander. Excellent made into fritters, especially with pork or poultry and *de rigueur* with fried Chicken Maryland.

Creamed sweet corn is used to make fritters but more usually served as a hot vegetable. In Australasia you might be offered it on toast for breakfast.

KANIWA: a high-protein relative of quinoa that does not need to be rinsed of soapiness.

MILLET: millet is the staple grain for almost a third of the world—from northern Manchuria to the Sahara and especially in north China, India, Pakistan and North Africa. The third most important grain after rice and wheat, millet is a generic term for a variety of small-seeded grains, all of which have the unique property of being alkaline rather than acid. Its light, sweet appeal makes it an excellent foil for strong flavours and spices.

Millet is blessed with a significant advantage to poorer nations—it hydrates astonishingly, so that 500 g/1 lb of kernels will easily feed eight people when cooked. The wholegrains are reputed to store up to 20 years without fear of insect infestation or change in nutrition.

A recommended way to enjoy millet is to cook it in the liquid of your vegetables or meat to create a main dish or substantial pilaff. This way you keep all the goodness of all the ingredients. It's no surprise that most such recipes come from Russian peasant cooking.

Millet is served whole as the pilaff base for stews, curries and so on. It mixes well with oats for an interesting porridge and in English cooking was once used for a baked pudding. It's nicer if it is lightly toasted or roasted before cooking.

Millet flakes: simple additions to porridges or to muesli, where the alkalinity is an advantage.

Millet flour: mainly used to make a flat bread, such as *Teff*, the national loaf of Ethiopia. It goes off very quickly.

OATS: oats probably originated somewhere in the east and slowly worked their way westwards as a weed. Their hardiness and very high, sustaining fat content appealed to the hardworking and cold inhabitants of northern regions; hence the appeal to Scots. Heavy oat breads or porridges lie longer in your stomach, warming and strengthening as you toiled in icy mines, fields and highlands.

Oats are bought as wholegrains, rough cut (sometimes called groats), or fine meal, or as flakes.

Bran: claims for oat bran are justified. Its soluble fibre helps to lower bad LDL cholesterol but maintains protective HDL cholesterol, also supplying protein, energy-giving carbohydrate, the B vitamin thiamin, and contributing to the maintenance of glucose levels in diabetics.

It is widely incorporated in muffins, muesli, breads, cakes and biscuits and is a good sprinkle on yoghurt and fresh fruit.

Oatmeal: widely used to mean both rolled or steel-cut oats but this can be confusing for there are also types of meal, oats that have been ground coarsely or finely.

Fine oatmeal is best for pancakes, for flouring grilled herrings or making a thin, gruel-type porridge.

Medium oatmeal is best for mixing with other flours to make scones, bannocks and such or for including in breads, perhaps after some soaking.

Groats are coarsest and best for thickening stews or broths and for oatcakes.

Quick-cook: grains and flakes steamed and cooked longer before being dried.

Rolled or flaked: rough-cut oats or groats steamed to part cook and soften them and then rolled. Eaten as is in such as muesli or cooked to make porridge in minutes in a microwave and always tastier if soaked overnight. Add up to twice the volume of water, milk or a mixture, tell the microwave what to do and in minutes it is done. Shower while it's cooking, because microwaves obediently switch off. Great to cook individually as people arrive and it can be eaten directly from the cooking bowl. No more burned or sticky pot to scrub.

Steel cut: considered superior nutritionally to rolled oats, as they have not been subjected to any heat during processing. They take longer to cook.

QUINOA: one of man's oldest grain-style foods, fittingly called Mother Grain by the Incas and by the many civilisations that preceded them over thousands of years in the long thin lands between the Andes and the South Pacific. It is not a cereal grain but the seed of a herb related to spinach and chard. It contains the complete range of proteins needed by the human body but in very small amounts, so should not be considered a plant-based equivalent to meat or dairy foods.

Quinoa looks and tastes a lot like millet but with a kick of sesame. The small seeds should be rinsed before cooking or they easily go soapy. A true fast food from the ancient past, it cooks in about ten minutes. When cooked there is slight bitterness, easily mollified by something acidic; a squeeze of lemon juice will do it. There's a little crunch from their equatorial bands that cutely uncurl during cooking.

As well as creamy-yellow it comes, like jelly-beans, in green, pink, orange, purple, red and, just as well, in black.

You have my encouragement never to say *keen-wah*, a posturing approximation of the indigenous name. We don't say *Paree* or go to *Wien* or *Roma*. It's *kwin-oh-a*.

RICE: the world's most important grain and food source, rice supports the cultures of China, Japan, India, South East Asia and much of the Middle East.

Its origins are in the Far East, and an ancient Sanskrit word for it means 'sustainer of the human race'.

The beauty of wholegrain rice is its high content of essential carbohydrate, protein, oil, vitamins and minerals in a soft, digestible bran that allows it to be cooked and eaten as whole kernels, with only the husk removed. Even so, it is not the perfect plant-based protein source and needs to be eaten with legumes and vegetables to be so.

Every one with a saucepan thinks they know the best way to cook rice. I prefer the absorption method and recommend electric rice cookers and microwave rice cookers.

Leftover cooked rice, brown or white, makes an excellent addition to yeast-leavened baking.

It is easy for the layman to identify and enjoy a variety of rices, thereby ringing dietary changes with ease. The basic choice is between brown and white, long, medium or short grains. Even in the West, many brown and white rices are available, each with a flavour and cooking performance peculiar to itself. Even brown rice, too easily associated with the drearier side of vegetarianism, now offers a remarkable range of imports, from the elegant, pale, long grain of Surinam and fragrant brown basmati to a choice of new shapes and flavours from California.

Long grains: give the separate, fluffy grains enjoyed as an accompaniment, in stuffings and in pilaffs and birianis, where the rice is layered with other ingredients.

Medium-length grains: are nearly always used for dishes where the starch in the grains is expected to lend a creamy richness to a sauce made from its own cooking liquids, as in the true risotto.

Short grain rices: are particularly suited to the long slow cooking of milk puddings and in South East Asia and in Japan starchier varieties are vital to many specialties, including sushi.

Types of rice

BASMATI: one of the world's great rices, originating in the Himalayan foothills. It has an elegant, some would say dainty, long grain and an appealing fragrance. Its inherent sweetness is the perfect foil and balance to spiced foods and also makes it an excellent choice for stuffings and rice salads. All kinds of Indian dishes seem better with basmati, especially rice-based birianis.

Properly, basmati rice should be aged, at least a year some say. It's also the only rice I have seen sold by grower, district, region and year, as though a wine. These are a connoisseurs' nirvana but rarely found outside India.

Whatever basmati's age, ignore the ignorant supermarket instructions on packaging to cook and then drain, thus throwing away all that is delicate and superior in flavour; cook only by the absorption method. The addition of bay leaf to the cooking water, especially for rice salads, underpins the flavour of the basmati beautifully. Brown basmati is commonly available, but the husk masks the finer flavour nuances.

BROWN: all rices could be brown, for it is merely rice that has been dehusked, leaving behind the layers of nutritious, fibrous bran. Brown or wholegrain rice is altogether a healthier food, with more protein and vital ingredients than white rice. In spite of its nutty, sweeter flavour it is bland to many and requires both longer cooking and more chewing. If you always cook it in stock, or add soy sauce or miso to the cooking liquid, you'll find it more readily accepted.

Brown rices should always be cooked by the absorption method so you lose none of the vitamins and minerals and generally need 2½ to 3 times their volume of liquid, to allow for the inevitable evaporation. Even so, thiamin is fugitive and up to 30% can be lost even when using this technique.

Belief in brown rice as a complete food is misguided. To be so it must be eaten in balance with pulses and legumes or as an accompaniment to such animal-protein sources such as eggs, milk, cheese or to plant-based soy products.

CALASPARRA: a Spanish rice with extraordinary absorbency and the first to gain DOP status. From the province of Murcia between Valencia and Andalucia that includes Benidorm, which has some of the best food supermarkets in Europe. It absorbs liquid at least 2.5 times its weight, some say up to four times, but doesn't go mushy. It's the favoured paella rice and when fat with its many flavours is arrestingly good. The best paella will be produced by a man on Sunday, cooked over a wood fire so some smoke is absorbed by the rice.

CAMARGUE: comes in two colours. White rice from the Camargue in South West France has IGP status. More interesting is the brick-red natural sport discovered in rice fields there. Only sold and served as wholegrain rice, it gives a bold, gratifying flavour. It should come with an AOC or DOP rating on the packet.

CAROLINA: once a specific but now a generic for American long-grain rice, so a New World version of Patna rice. Can be used for sweet as well as savoury dishes.

CONVERTED/PAR-BOILED: it sounds a lesser rice but is quite the reverse. It has been part-cooked before being husked and milled. This forces thiamin and nicotinic acid/niacin into the grain so that even though it looks white it is closer nutritionally to brown rice, satisfying both society and sense.

CRISTALLO: is par-boiled arborio rice.

FRAGRANT: particularly popular in China and Thailand with a truly wonderful fragrance, and often also called jasmine rice. The best flavour comes from cooking it by the absorption method, but note this rice cooks up to one third faster than other types.

GLUTINOUS/STICKY: types of rice that go slightly jelly-like when cooked and thus stick together. They contain no gluten, so glutinous is rather a misnomer, but merely have a very high starch content, especially liked in Asian countries because the stickiness means they are easier to eat with chopsticks. Sushi rice is from this family.

Sticky rices are a little sweeter and much used in puddings and cakes of great variety, often fluorescently coloured and flavoured with coconut or jasmine and wrapped in banana leaves. One of the highlights of the Thai year is eating sharp and nutty slices of green mangoes with cold mounds of sweet sticky rice. The unpolished or brown version is very dark, almost black, rather like wild rice. The most usual preparation method is to part cook the grains in boiling water and to complete the process over steam.

JASMINE: see *Fragrant.*

LOUISIANA: undistinguished long-grain rice grown in the State and essential to the gumbo, a local style of soup served over a tightly packed mound of rice. Also cooked in rich brown stock to make Dirty Rice and with mixed meats and vegetables in the one-pot Jambalaya. The famed Crawfish Pies combine the crustaceae with rice and the Creole/Cajun Holy Trinity of peppers, onions and celery.

PATNA: a generic term for Asian white rices, less used now in favour of the all-encompassing 'long grain'.

PECAN RICE: a US variety claiming to taste of pecans.

PILAFF: a pilaff is a pulao, pilau and a ploy or plov and are often confused with risottos, but should not be. All are dishes using long-grain rices in which the grains remain separate. Might be

flavoured with spices, and will contain other ingredients like India's birianis, which cook rice in the liquid of stews to make a one-pot dish. Often baked rather than cooked on the hob.

POPCORN: sweet and appealing flavoured varieties developed in southern US states, especially Louisiana.

PUDDING: a comforting term for short-grain white rice used for oven-cooked rice puddings. It swells and joins up but never goes sticky if cooked slowly enough. The same result can be achieved slightly faster on the hob, the way of many variations made over the length of the Silk Road; with saffron and crushed cardamom seeds and continuous additions of milk to make it exceedingly rich, it is served hot or chilled sprinkled with rose water and chopped unsalted pistachios. Clotted cream, made as *ashta* throughout the Middle East, is the perfect accompaniment.

RICE FLAKES: made by steaming and rolling whole or white rice and used for a faster cooking porridge, for baking and for muesli.

RICE FLOUR: may be used in bread and cake making but gives a dry, rather flat product. It is better combined with wheat and corn flour mixtures. Otherwise used to set interesting milk and fruit puddings and delicacies.

RED RICE: see *Camargue rice.* Italians also market one as *rosso integrale.*

RISOTTO: a medium- to short-grain rice known generically in Italy as superfino. They are all rather fat and chunky with a hard white core you can see. This stays firm when cooked properly, whilst the rest of the grain leaks starch into the liquid to make a velvety sauce that is the sign of a proper risotto, the result of whisking while cooking so the stock, the butter and the starch of the rice form a voluptuous emulsified sauce. Risotto is finished by stirring in butter and Parmesan cheese to polish and further thicken the sauce. Venetians call this *mantecari*, a word based on the Arabic for butter, just as *mantequilla* is in Spain.

Modern chefs, including me, have disproven the adage a seafood risotto should not have Parmesan added. It can and is wonderful, just as when you put fish into a cheese sauce or grill Lobster Thermidor with Parmesan.

How often you whisk a risotto divides households. The microwave makes a notable risotto, with perhaps only two whisks, although there is little time saving.

To Venetians, risotto should be too wet to eat with a fork: they call it *all'onda* or wavelike. Other Italians like it so a fork planted into it will stand its ground. Both must have a clearly seen emulsified sauce that bathes the rice and binds it together. If the grains are separate, that's a pilaff.

Arborio: is the best-known risotto rice and has the biggest grain but does not absorb as much stock.
Carnaroli: is probably the favourite with professionals.
Vialone Nano: is the smallest superfino rice and is preferred in the Veneto; it absorbs more stock and

has high starch so gives an ideal creamy result.

STICKY: see *Glutinous.*

SUSHI: a speciality short-grain rice used for sushi, which is starchy enough to hold together when lightly squeezed in the palm of a sushi-master.

SWEET: see *Glutinous.*

VALENCIA: medium-grain rice from Valencia, Spain, that like its neighbour, *calasparra*, absorbs a lot of moisture without breaking down. Perfectly suited for making most sorts of rice dishes as well as an accompaniment.

WHITE: brown rice but with the husk removed. Considered a status symbol in the same way white bread was once. If a major staple it encourages such diseases as beri beri and pellagra, caused by deficiencies of thiamin (vitamin B1) and niacin respectively. This is easily balanced by adding animal or such plant-based protein as soy products.

WHOLEGRAIN: another name for *brown rice* q.v.

WILD RICE: the immensely beautiful, deep mahogany to black seeds of an aquatic grass not related to rice. Once collected only by hand from canoes in a few northern US states by Native Americans, wild rice has been tamed. It is widely farmed in the Americas and Europe.

Nutritionally, wild rice has a much higher protein content than true rices and an excellent range of vitamins. But it does not have the equivalent of the complete protein spectrum of meat or soy beans or of such soy products as tofu.

Wild rice has a deep nutty flavour and takes about the same time to cook as brown rice, depending on size and quality; the finest quality will be the darkest, longest, most lustrous and evenly graded grains. The grains are cooked when butterflied, that is when the skin has split and the grain has slightly burst and opened out from its central seam. If undercooked it will be sharp enough to puncture tongues, gums and throat, something I have seen in more than one restaurant.

As the flavour is so strong and pervasive, you can mix it with up to two or three times the amount of white or brown rice and it will still be fully appreciated, but these must be cooked separately. I think it is more enjoyable to eat wild rice in such combinations than on its own, whatever your finances, largely because it's tiresome to eat solo as it requires major mastication.

RYE: a very important bread-making grain in Scandinavia and the former USSR, rye can be cultivated in conditions where other grains fail. It used to be sown with wheat, so that if the wheat failed there would be something to harvest. The mixture of wheat and rye was known as maslin and used with no regard to the proportions of each. Wheat and rye never crossed but this has now been achieved by science and the new grain is called triticale.

Bread making is the most important use of rye but a loaf made with 100% rye flour is dense, dark, nutty and dry, for there is not enough gluten in rye to allow a high absorption of moisture or a good rise from yeast action. Thus, rye flour is mixed with wheat flour and even when used minimally in a light rye loaf, adds a heartening breadth and warmth. A high rye content loaf, so-called black bread, is often further coloured and flavoured with molasses and caramel. Caraway seeds are common additives, widely experienced in the light rye loaves used for salt-beef sandwiches.

Pumpernickel breads are usually based on rye and other wholegrains but the name is loosely applied to a range of breads and said to be onomatopoeic of the noise of the intestinal wind they famously create.

Rye flakes: good in mixed-grain porridges or in muesli. For general use I think they are best when used in or on bread doughs, after soaking and cooking.

Rye flour: useful in bread making if you use about 15% rye to 85% wheat, giving a light-coloured and tasty loaf. You might use rye flour for your sourdough starter and then use wheat flour for the rest of the dough. Rye flour is used for unleavened Scandinavian crisp breads.

TRITICALE: this artificially created grain combines wheat and rye and gives a higher yield of protein, amino acid balance and food value than any wheat variety. It has a gluten content higher than rye but lower than wheat. It is fragile, so only knead a bread dough with feather-light fingers. Otherwise, use triticale like other wholegrains to add interest and nutrition to pilaffs, porridges, mueslis, breads and biscuits.

WHEAT: over 90% of the flour consumed in Western Europe, the United States and the countries of the old Commonwealth is made from wheat. It is the West's most important grain, and always has been. Archeological evidence shows wheat has been cultivated since about 7,000 BC, which suggests its use for a much longer period. It is a grass of the Triticum family, the true origins of which have never been determined.

For nearly 9,000 years man cultivated wheat in exactly the same way, introducing new varieties rarely, and usually by chance. It was never cheap or plentiful enough to be a universal food; neither would it grow in northerly climates where oats, barley and rye were the staple grains.

In the 19th century the Turkey Red variety was introduced into North America. It produced mammoth crops easily, so wheat farmers everywhere wanted part of this bounty. So did the public, keen to signal their improved social position by eating only wheat bread, ideally white. Next, Russia and Australia developed heavy-cropping wheat strains especially suited to bread making, the so-called strong wheats. Wheat growers had to change every agricultural, cropping and milling technique to cope with the size of the crop and the demand.

Wheat milling

Milling breaks open grains to expose the endosperm, the starchy heart and the wheat germ within it, the component that sprouts to create a new plant. Interaction with the starch and a liquid allows you to make a dough, batter or porridge.

Stone-grinding: eons of labour-intensive hand grinding with the small quern were replaced by the establishment of the windmill. Central milling was also based on two circular stones, but now huge ones of a special granite, each weighing well over one tonne, did the work. The bottom is stationary, the top revolves and both are corrugated or grooved. The grain is fed in to the centre and is then sheared finer and finer as it works its way out and then falls from the apertures at the ends of the grooves in the bottom stone. The top stone may be raised or lowered to control the fineness of the grinding, that can only produce 100% wholemeal flour. The heat and pressure generated distribute the wheat germ and its vitamin E evenly through the flour and they cannot then be separated, the nutritional advantage of the stone-ground flour.

You must sift or bolt the bran to make white flour, taking time and reducing the volume there is to sell, why only the rich and the clergy could afford it. White stone-ground white flour is more nutritious than roller-milled, because it retained the goodness of the wheat germ but this easily oxidises and makes the flour rancid, so it does not store as long as roller-milled flour.

Roller-mills: roller-milling breaks down grain in a series of processes, rather than the single operation of the stone method. First, the grain is cracked to separate the endosperm and wheat germ from its bran coating and then closer and closer set rollers reduce it to flour; meanwhile, the bran and wheat germ go their separate ways to similar processes. Having no wheat-germ content, roller-milled flour lasts longer than stone-ground.

White flour made this way does not have the vitamin or mineral content of the germ or bran. UK legislation ensures some are replaced; these vitamins are usually synthetic, but not known to be less good for that.

In many countries, roller-milled wheat is also bleached, artificially creating what happens to fresh cream-coloured flour when stored for six to nine months, when other natural changes occur that improve its performance in baking. White, very white, flour is what the public has come to demand but having hundreds of thousands of tonnes of flour sitting about waiting to whiten is not an idea that appeals to big business. Bleaching it is. French flour is not bleached and consumer interest means stone-ground and unbleached white flour are increasingly available.

Types of wheat product

ALL-PURPOSE: the US name for plain flour.

ATTA: Indian wholemeal flour, used for chapatis and other breads.

BURGUL OR BULGHUR: although commonly called cracked wheat, burgul is quite different from that. It's a precooked processed food, probably the world's oldest.

Berries of the local wheat in Middle Eastern countries are cooked to a mush which is spread out to dry, sometimes after straining. When crisp and dry it is broken into varied textures. To use it, pour on twice the volume of boiling water or stock and allow it to be absorbed and swell. Faster in a microwave.

Burgul is the perfect Millennial fast-food replacement for rice. For inspiration, Middle Eastern websites and cookbooks use it in highly individual and often exciting ways. Simplest is the salad known as *tabbouleh*. The most esoteric is *kibbeh*, made with raw lamb.

CAKE FLOUR: plain flour that is mainly soft and low in gluten, as that is not needed when mixtures are raised with baking soda or baking powder.

COUSCOUS: not a grain but a type of pasta, the national dish of much of north-west Africa, based on semolina, each particle of which is rubbed patiently by hand to coat it in very fine, lightly moistened flour, creating a film that helps keep the pieces separate during steaming.

Then comes long laborious steaming rather than boiling and this takes ages over spectacular stews in sauces redolent of ground ginger, cumin and coriander, and that glisten with fats and butter (including long-fermented *smen* in Morocco) and burgeoning with meats and or exotic vegetables.

Two things you should know. First, couscous tastes exactly the same whatever you steam it over, including plain water, as steam cannot carry flavour with it. Steaming couscous over a stew in a two-tiered couscousière is an economical way of using one heat source instead of two. But look at the label again. More and more commercially available couscous is pre-cooked, so all you need to do is add liquid. It steams and cooks to perfection in minutes in a microwave, in seconds if you have poured on hot stock or water.

Second, without accompanying stews and sauces couscous is fairly boring. Butter is the key, not olive or other oils. There are other types of couscous offered but apart from *barley couscous* q.v. these are more properly a type of burghul and made with grains other than wheat.

CRACKED WHEAT: wholegrains are cracked under the pressure of roller milling. Similar to kibbled wheat, which is broken up a different way. Once cooked it is added to bread doughs or used as an excellent base for stuffing or any way you might use burghul, but with more texture and nuttier flavour. Good in vegetable salads or as a pilaff, especially with game dishes.

DURUM: a variety of strong wheat specially used for commercial pasta making and that naturally gives a golden colour. Although high in gluten it is not very elastic, hence the difficulty of using it to make pasta at home.

EINKORN: see *Épeautre, Petit.*

EMMER: see *Farro wheat.*

ÉPEAUTRE, PETIT: also known as *einkorn.* One of the most nutritious of wheats, this extraordinary and ancient wheat variety *triticum monococcum* is vigorously being restored to production, particularly in Provence, where it has been known for millennia. It is harder to thresh but its drought-resistant qualities are behind its new popularity. Keep an eye out for the growing number of products made with *petit épeautre,* which include beers. *Le Grande Épeautre* is *spelt* q.v.

FARRO: also known as emmer, it is thought to be the wheat carried by Roman legionnaires. It has IGP status, which guarantees it is still cultivated without synthetic help and is then stored without the addition of pesticides. Perhaps the best for making pasta.

Farro is commonly confused with spelt, but there are differences. Farro must be soaked but spelt may be cooked directly; farro keeps its texture but spelt cooks to a mush.

Farro della Garfagnana (triticum dicoccum): has been grown without interruption in districts around Lucca, in Italy.

FREEKEH: this ancient Middle Eastern staple is made from green wheat heads to which some of the stalk is attached. Tied bundles are dried and then burned. The moist, green grains don't burn but are left with a delicious smokiness from their charred husks, which are then easily rubbed away.

Cooked like rice, freekeh is nutty rather than starchy to eat and is particularly gratifying; you need half the amount you'd eat of rice to feel well fed. Freekeh was also made with barley.

FRUMENTY: an ancient mainstay source of carbohydrate energy, it's a porridge of cracked wheat, finished with milk, nut-milk or stock, egg, dried fruit and honey, sometimes with alcohol, rum latterly. The rich might include saffron, and sprinkle with cinnamon and sugar, as a special addition to a Christmas feast.

GLUTEN: see *Seitan*.

HARD WHEAT: another name for strong flour, which indicates a high gluten content.

KAMUT/KHORASAN: this is a branded wheat grain developed by an organic farmer in Montana. The grain is twice as big as normal varieties with both protein and gluten in higher than usual proportions. There is a growing belief that those with wheat malabsorption problems (far more common than 'allergies') can tolerate Kamut wheat in a varied diet.

KIBBLED WHEAT: a kibbler pricks the wholegrains, splitting them into small pieces, different from the way cracked wheat is made. Commonly used after cooking to finish breads or included in the dough but delicious as a bigger-flavoured pilaff.

MAFTOUL: a Palestinian staple that should be widely known and used, it is made like couscous but is flour wrapped around particles of pre-cooked burghul rather than uncooked semolina. The small wheaten balls thus reconstitute in minutes, even faster in a microwave. Use like couscous or rice to accompany stews, as the basis for herb-rich salads or as addition to soups.

MOUGRABIEH: couscous as big as pearls, up to 6 mm/¼ inch in diameter. Some call it Israeli couscous because it's exported by that country. It's Lebanese, so let's call it Lebanese couscous if we do not call it mougrabieh.

Traditionally it is steamed over a stew, like couscous, but don't serve it naked and pearlescent, because it looks like raw tapioca or the forbidden eggs of an endangered fish. Some is bought ready-toasted, which is a clue to what I think is the tastiest method. Pan roasting it in butter makes it tastier before simmering in stock or gravy. Or boil it like pasta and then brown in butter or butter and oil before finishing with such a fragrant Middle Eastern spice mixture as *baharat* and masses of roughly torn flat-leaf parsley.

You could cook them in an oxtail, chicken, duck or beef stew, too, like small, oh-so-chic dumplings.

00: an Italian indication of general purpose, medium-ground flour, usually a mix of hard and soft, and that is available in different types. Yellow is more suited to making pasta and white is for general baking. 0 flour is coarser, closer to a fine semolina.

PLAIN FLOUR: called all-purpose in the US, it's a varying mixture of strong (hard) and soft flours to make it widely useful. Although the gluten level is lower, averaging 8–11%, it still makes light yeasted breads and is recommended for home-made pasta because it is easier to roll thinly: see *00*.

SEITAN: pure wheat gluten, this is plant-based protein extracted from several types of wheat flour by a kneading and rinsing process, after which it is boiled. Used for many centuries as a vegetarian substitute for meat and fish throughout China, Japan and some neighbouring countries and is now increasingly used in the West by vegans and vegetarians. It is *not* a full dietary substitute for the protein of meat, dairy products or eggs but must be complemented with pulses in the usual way.

Seitan is quite flavourless but like tofu absorbs other flavours readily. Available in slightly chewy pieces to lightly puffed shapes, or in a powder. Sometimes offered flavoured and is found as an ingredient in many commercial vegetarian products.

Powdered seitan is mixed with water, lightly kneaded and then ready to use. The pieces can be used as you would meat, in stews, stir-fries, soups and broths. It is a very good addition to bean and pulse recipes of all kinds, as the finished dish will then offer close to the full protein requirement of humans, in quality if not quantity.

SELF-RAISING FLOUR: plain or all-purpose flour with a raising agent like baking powder. To make your own add a half teaspoon of baking powder to every 100 g/4 oz of plain flour and mix very well.

SEMOLINA: often, but not always, made from durum wheat, semolina was once the boltings of flour—the hard unground pieces of wheat endosperm that did not pass through the sifter. Now, semolina is de-husked wheat rollered to a size of coarseness that allows it to perform as expected. It is the basis of couscous and was once regularly used for a baked pudding.

SOFT WHEAT: soft wheat grows in more temperate climates and is lower in gluten (7–10%) than strong or hard wheat and thus will not give the same rise when leavened with yeast. But it is higher in starch, which contributes to the light foamy texture desirable in cake and scone making, when chemicals are used to give the rise. Soft flours also absorb less moisture, so baked goods with a low-fat content will quickly become stale.

French bread, especially the well-known long shapes, are made with soft flour but this makes only a minor contribution to the special flavour and fast staling of these loaves. A long slow rising gives the characteristic holes and flavour, and the special crisp crust comes from being baked in commercial ovens with controlled bursts of steam: baguettes and the like were never produced domestically and cannot be.

You cannot reproduce an authentic French loaf without proper French soft flour, but if you use soft, unbleached white flour, prove the dough very slowly indeed, bake with a pan of boiling water in the oven, and then eat the bread almost immediately, you get close.

SPELT/ LE GRAND ÉPEAUTRE: the undisputed leader of born-again wheat varieties, spelt was commonly the staple grain grown throughout Europe. Although of the same genus as common wheat, spelt has a different genetic structure providing more protein per grain, a greater concentration of minerals and vitamins, and a propensity for adding unique flavours to breads which also have the property of not crumbling when sliced.

Modern farming, commonly at odds with good food, changed that ancient dependence because although the close husk of spelt gives it superior protection against pest and disease, it is difficult to thresh mechanically and thus loses out to the winning appeal of modern varieties which have looser husks.

Canny organic farmers are more impressed with spelt's disease resistant qualities which guarantee a decent harvest and thus don't mind the extra work in husking.

There's also a growing view that the protein in spelt does not cause as many problems to those with gluten intolerance and may indeed allow those sufferers to eat wheat produce, provided they introduce it into their diets slowly. Spelt is being grown again in Britain and, should it or spelt bread be offered, it will be well worth your interest.

STRONG FLOUR: strong or hard wheat has a higher proportion (13-14%) of gluten-producing protein, essential for the lightest bread doughs.

TRAHANA: not an East European car but a rustic wheat-based food from north-west Greece. It's a dried and broken paste of flour, goat's milk and eggs rather like a desiccated crumble mix and is cooked in water to make a creamy but textured porridge. Thin, it is soup into which Feta cheese, herbs and olive oil are added. Thicker, it is a rude polenta or a cooking medium: small chunks of mixed greens cook in the prepared trahana in five minutes or so; add Gruyère or Feta.

There is a sweet version too, and like burgul, trahana is an unusual wheat product that even the inexperienced cook will conquer easily.

WHEAT BRAN: the husk of the wheat grain, added to other foods as a good source of dietary fibre, it has many useful vitamins and minerals.

WHEAT FLAKES: made by rolling steamed and softened berries under pressure. They make a delicious wheat porridge, solo or with oats, and are a choice for inclusion in such cold-grain breakfasts as muesli.

WHEAT GERM: found in the central endosperm of wheat grains, this is like an egg yolk, for from this will germinate new life. A popular additive to many foods, but as it contains oil it easily goes rancid if not kept cool and dark. Vitamin E is an important component.

WHEAT GRASS: the young shoots of wheat, *triticum aestivum*, contain much chlorophyll (the green stuff) and other vitamins and minerals. But is it better than anything else? Rather like bean shoots, it depends who you ask and, particularly, who is selling it.

The NHS and The British Dietetic Association disagree with the common message that a shot of wheat grass juice has the same nutrition as 1 kg/2 lb of vegetables and says that weight for weight its dietary contribution is about the same as spinach or broccoli. The quantity usually taken doesn't even count as one of your 5-a-Day. The broadly accepted medical view is that wheat grass is no better or worse than other fresh produce, and like all foods taking an excess of it can be dangerous.

WHEATMEAL: a rarely used term now and it cannot legally be used for a type of bread. Although it sounded like wholegrain flour, it was an extraction flour meaning that 15 to 19% husk had been sifted out, giving flour lighter in colour than wholemeal and that gave lighter results. Adding some wholemeal flour to white bread dough gives an equivalent with a sweet flavour and attractive look and texture.

WHOLEMEAL: flour made by grinding the wholegrain. Bread made with 100% wholemeal flour should not be kneaded, because interaction of the wheat germ with the bran reduces the elasticity of the gluten.

Pasta

NEED TO KNOW

Pasta is wheat flour and water: eggs or olive oil might be added.

Soft flour is used for domestic pasta making: hard or durum flour by factories.

Traditional pasta is shaped through bronze dies and is then dried slowly. It looks dull and feels sandy to the teeth: the packets say bronzato or similar.

Bronze-extruded pasta absorbs more sauce.

Pasta shapes extruded through plastic are shiny and smooth, sauces slip off.

Properly, sauces are a clingy dressing for pasta, not a pool for paddling.

Cooked pasta should never be rinsed in water, hot or cold.

Pasta should steam dry for a few minutes before adding sauce; this makes it more absorbent, especially traditional bronzato pasta, giving greater eating pleasure.

Italians use 20% of the volume of sauce added in the UK but it is much more concentrated.

Al dente or slightly chewy pasta is more easily digested than very well cooked, because it mixes with saliva when chewed.

Al dente pasta absorbs about 1.25 times its weight of water: 100 g/4 oz of pasta will weigh 225 g+/7 oz cooked; longer-cooked pasta absorbs around 1.5 times: 100 g/4 oz pasta will weigh 250 g+/8 oz.

Oil on cooking water does not stop pasta sticking together.

Pasta never sticks if it is cooked in enough water.

Ideal proportions are at least a litre/1.75 pints of boiling water per 80 g/3 oz dried pasta; more is better.

Salt highly so the pasta absorbs it during cooking.

Smooth pasta shapes are meant for thick but smooth, clingy sauces.

Grooved, folded and twisted shapes trap thin sauces and sauces with lumps, clumps, vegetables, seafood and such.

It is not traditional to add pasta-cooking water to a sauce; only do this if a sauce has been over-concentrated but beware of upsetting the salt and starch balance.

Pasta to be eaten cold should be lightly tossed in oil when steamed dry but still warm; also add garlic, citrus zest, flavoured oils, especially lime or truffle, or tomato paste now, so they penetrate and flavour the pasta.

Most flavoured and coloured pasta does not deliver what it promises, as both of these are extracted by the cooking water.

Even though an Italian word, pasta is about as exclusive to Italy as palaces and royal families are to Great Britain. Marco Polo did not bring it to Europe from China—that is a 19th century American fabrication.

Pasta's origins are the same as those of cheese—no one knows when, where or by whom. Ancient Etruscans, Greeks and Romans enjoyed it— indeed the *noodles, nouilles and knudeln* of modern Europe are clearly rooted in the Roman *nodellus*, a word which means little knots and describes what happens to long strands of pasta when on your plate. Arabs had their own *noodles*, the *trii*, which they introduced to Sicily long ago, in sumptuous recipes.

Pasta was rarely eaten in post-Roman Italy until the middle of the 19th century when new wheat strains increased wheat flour's availability. Even then, those who ate it lived in the south. Rice was the staple of the north, hence risotto.

Only after the 1870 unification of Italy into a kingdom did pasta and the tomato sauces of the south change the style and flavour of northern Italian cooking. All of Italy ate more pasta and the North created *salsa Bolognese*.

Neapolitan immigration to the United States led the modern march of pasta and then popularised the idea of pasta as a main course, which it never was. Italian purists say pasta is eaten as a first course and only at lunchtime. Someone in the US invented canneloni, tagliatelli with cream, ham and peas, carbonara sauce, and the notion of cold pasta salads. Chances are these innovators were Italian and not all progress is bad.

The Encyclopaedia of Pasta (University of California Press, 2009) describes 310 types of pasta but the number available commercially is likely to be a tenth of that. Take the trouble to buy old-fashioned *bronzato* pasta if you never have. When cooked *al dente* and allowed to steam dry, these soak up much more sauce. Like salad dressings, there should never be leftover puddles on the plate.

Pasta families

FLAVOURED: with black pepper, beetroot, squid ink, pumpkin purée, orange, walnuts and almost anything else, these have cerebral and visual appeal rather than culinary. Once plunged into boiling water the flavour you paid for is diluted into insignificance. The solution is to flavour the cooking water highly with the same ingredient—pepper, beetroot, squid ink etc. Isn't it simpler to make a decent sauce with the flavour you want? Sweet pasta should be cooked in sweetened water.

GNOCCHI: although most seen made of potato and flour, this is an ancient family of dumplings, perhaps the earliest forms of pasta, often made then and now with a portion of stale bread. The mixture can include chestnut, squash, spinach, potato or pumpkin, sometimes egg, sometimes cheese. The dumpling shape most seen is a small oval that has been folded over the tines of a fork, so it is ribbed or serrated. Very good hot or cold as a side or a salad base when fried golden-brown. Sometimes found stuffed with such as basil pesto.

In Lombardy *canederli* are made of bread mixed with egg, left over ham or prosciutto, cheese, and herbs, rolled into quite big balls, dredged in flour and then boiled. Can be served in soup or as an accompaniment topped with breadcrumbs browned in butter.

PASTA ALL'UOVO/PASTA WITH EGG: flour is mixed with a proportion of egg, never less than one per 500 g/1 lb of flour.

PASTA CORTA/SHORT OR CUT PASTA: best known are the rounded, hollow pastas, usually cut on the bias and which may be smooth or grooved, like *macaroni, rigatoni, penne* and the comparative newcomer, *canneloni*. Also included are the shapes and shell types for holding sauce-juicy chunks of meat or seafood; elbow shapes, *lumache* (snails), *conchiglie* (shells), *fuselli* (twists). *Orzo*, shaped to look like barley is popular as a rice alternative, hot or cold.

PASTA LUNGA/LONG PASTA: from the tiniest *cappelli d'angelo* (angel's hair) to thick and broad *lasagne*, with every type of *spaghetti, vermicelli, linguine, ziti, fettuccine* and *tagliarelli* or *tagliatelli* in between. With or without holes.

PASTA RIPIENI/STUFFED PASTA: *ravioli* in all different sizes are the best known but *tortellini* and bigger *tortelloni*, which look like belly-buttons, and *cappelleti* looking like head scarves tied on the chin are more fun. *Angolotti* and *panzerotti* have joined these on ready-made meal shelves. There are many other varieties of stuffed pastas seen these days as fresh pasta sits firmly beside other easy-to-prepare but rewarding dishes in the supermarket. Ravioli might be served in butter, especially browned butter and others in cream or tomato sauces. *Vareniki* are Russian little pillows of pasta, stuffed with cheese, with cabbage, with fish or strawberries or poppyseeds or almost anything.

Pasticcio, pasticcio, pastizzu or

timbale: a very special family not of pasta but of pies of pasta in a baked crust. The fillings can be plain shapes in a *ragu* of pork, beef or giblets and cheeses, or such stuffed shapes as *tortellini*, again in a rich sauce.

PASTINA: these tiny pasta pieces seen as egg drops or squares are made for serving in soup and now include such novelties as alphabet pasta, tiny animals and visitors from outer space. *Tarhonya* are small Hungarian pellets of egg pasta, fried to good colour before boiling in water. Great with anything paprika-rich.

WHOLEMEAL: a century ago most pasta would have been more 'brown' than white because of milling processes, but by the time it became internationally popular, white flour was universally available. The Veneto, around Venice, still offers *bigoli*, a thick type of spaghetti made from whole flour. People who should know, like Valentina Harris, guffaw at the idea of serving wholemeal pasta, saying it is eaten only by the infirm and the costive, and only when prescribed by doctors. That might be true, but it doesn't mean we shouldn't find other ways to eat wholemeal pasta—if only to show the Italians they don't know everything.

Further reference: Flour (Absolute Press) by Christine McFadden reveals over 40 culinary flours including cricket, coffee, lupin and sesame, with recipes.

Herbs,
Spices
and
Natural
Flavourings

Herbs are always leaves, and thus usually green.

Dried herbs are usually twice as strong as fresh.

Flower petals are used as herbs.

Spices broadly include seeds, pods, buds, bark, stalks and roots.

Natural flavourings include extracts, distillates and oils.

T he golden rule for dried herbs and spices is to buy as few as possible and store for as short a time as you can. The heat close to a cooker will hasten their deterioration. Light destroys them, too, so although pretty and homely, it's no good thing to hang sprays of herbs in a warm kitchen. Find somewhere cooler and darker and they will be longer lasting, better tasting and more rewarding. For ground spices and for particularly aromatic whole spices, like cardamom, a plastic box in the refrigerator is by far the best idea.

Herbs and spices can be used to make a remarkable number of interesting drinks, hot and cold. The rule is that leaves and flowers are usually infused in boiling water and roots, barks, stalks and so on are boiled for a few minutes. The former should always be brewed in a cup with a saucer over the top or in a teapot; the saucer or lid keeps in the essential fumes and keeps the drink hotter. See *Herb teas and tisanes*.

ACAI BERRIES: the berries of a South American rain-forest palm, also the source of hearts of palm. Acai taste of soft fruits and chocolate but with a metallic after taste. Like all newer foods there are extraordinary health claims but the effects of eating them in bulk for a long time are unknown. A sedilla under the 'c' suggests it is pronounced ay-sigh.

AGRETTI: saltwort, also known as monks' or friars' beard. It's a marsh plant with long leaves very like samphire but not segmented and without as much salt. It's a little minerally and must only be lightly cooked and then can be used as is or mixed into pasta, especially with seafood.

AJOWAN: tiny, power-packed seeds tasting like a combination of thyme and black pepper. Just the thing to add lightly crushed to savoury baking, like cheese biscuits, or to thread through bread dough and an intriguing sprinkle on every type of grain, starch or vegetable, but most arresting when scattered on or rubbed into something made of fish or seafood.

If you have used thyme in a dish, ajowan seeds offer a contrasted and textured way to brighten the flavour when serving. Another ingredient that supposedly deflates flatulence and colic, and is credited with adding to a 'husband's enjoyment in middle years'.

ALLSPICE: allspice is the dried, unripe berry of a myrtle-related tree discovered in the New World by Christopher Columbus. The bright, spicy smell and taste is a mixture of the sweet cloves, cinnamon and nutmeg of the Old World, thus its name, a single spice that tastes the same as a combine of all the others. Often called Jamaica pepper or pimento or pimento pepper, but it must not be confused with pimiento, which is the vegetable we call capsicum or red/green/whatever pepper.

Turkey has notably adopted it for meat stuffings that might also contain fresh dill, parsley and coriander. Pounded or ground allspice goes well in rice stuffings for poultry and lamb, is essential in pork or veal-based pâtés and welcomed by such sweet vegetables as carrots, parsnips and pumpkin, and in fruit pies and sauces. Pickles and curries benefit pointedly.

AMCHUR: an alternative to lemon, lime juice or tamarind to donate acidity to curries and fruit chutneys. It's dried green mango, sold as slices or ground, sometimes as green mango powder. It has a tenderizing effect, so it's good in marinades for cheaper cuts of meat for barbecues.

ANARDANA: dried pomegranate seeds that, like fresh ones, are syrupy, crunchy and wonderfully sweet-sour. Add dry to curries, pulse and vegetable dishes, to pickles and chutneys. Once soaked they develop a lighter texture and can be strewn over almost anything, as their delightful texture and sweet-sour balance enhance everything. I like them with grilled fish.

ANGELICA: every part of the tall angelica bush can be eaten. The celery-flavoured leaves make a tisane or herbal tea, sometimes in conjunction with juniper berry. The root may be boiled for a tea, and root or seed oils flavour liqueurs and wines. The best-known use is candied stalk and leaf stem for cake decoration, easy to make at home.

ANISE/ANISEED: one of the oldest known aromatic seeds, it has a sweet, liquorice-like flavour with a broad spectrum of uses in marinades and fruit salads, cakes and pickles. It's very good with cabbage dishes hot or cold, or scattered on bread dough before baking.

The tea, made by steeping the seeds in boiling water, is a good digestive after a large meal but so is aniseed liqueur— *anisette*. The Dutch candy anise seeds, as *muisjes*. Anise is the flavouring of pastis alcohols, and discrete amounts nicely flavour fish dishes and anything with dried fruits.

ANNATTO: small red seeds ground to give a light, musky flavour and colour to rice and marinades in Mexico. Worldwide, the dried fleshy outer covering of the seeds colours cheese, cheese rinds and, sometimes, butter but is so diluted there is no discernible flavour lift. It should be the red colouring on Chinese barbecued pork. Heat seeds in a little oil and you have red colouring to brighten up roasted meats and birds and such.

ASAFOETIDA: *hing* in India, this is the gum from a variety of giant fennel with a repulsive, invasive smell, rather like rotting garlic. Yet it is blessed by Brahmin, Jain and other Indian sects that eat neither garlic nor onions, for tiny amounts add similar savour without either of those. For the many millions of other people who can't or won't eat raw or undercooked onion, asafoetida is a Godsend, and Indian cookbooks that dismiss onions and garlic as intimates of the Devil are revered. Well, they are by me. Quite why I think onions ruin more food than they ever help is another book.

Used discreetly, asafoetida's savouriness adds an edge to vegetarian dishes far better than undercooked onion, dusty mixed herbs, celery salt and a surfeit of miso or soy sauce. It lifts fish dishes, where onion or garlic would be too coarse. And there's more. Asafoetida is a great defeater of intestinal wind, recommending it for inclusion with lentils and beans.

Asafoetida bought as a yellow powder has been diluted with flour and turmeric, a reminder to use it scantly. If it is a brown powder it will smell quite a lot for it is just ground brown gum. The real thing, the gum, comes as red-brown lumps. The fresher the gum, the more pungent, for its volatile oil escapes easily and its essence fades. Asafoetida gum is as anti-social and divisive as durian. Seal hermetically, at least double wrapped, or the house smells like yesterday's garlic. The powder is much the better way.

BARBERRIES: tart, fruity and like fresh red currants, but barberries can be eaten without sweetening. Related in flavour to *sumac*, q.v., they come as dried dark red berries and rehydrate quickly. The Iranian word is *zereshk* or *zershk* and you'll find them commonly fried in butter, with or without a little sugar, and then topping a saffron pilaff or plov.

BASIL: the essence of summer. Although a native of India and Persia, basil is particularly associated with Italian cooking, and is also important in South East Asia, Thailand in particular. Yet its name is Greek, and means king. New varieties seem to appear every summer but these are the basics.

> *Bush basil:* has a small habit and leaves with a citric taste, making it more like marjoram.
> *Holy basil:* is not Thai basil and the two are regularly confused. In India it is *tulsi* and sacred to Hindus and used widely in medicines. Leaves are up to 5 cm/2" long and are green or red. There are three varieties, all very pungent with mint and citrus added

to underlying anise and other spice flavours.

Opal: is the one with purple leaves developed in the 1950s and is milder tasting than sweet basil.

Sweet basil: also called Genovese, is the most common variety. Intense anise/clove but with mint, pepper and citrus there, too. Basil's peak of culinary achievement is its simplest—freshly torn on slightly chilled slices of rich, red, knobbly tomatoes, perhaps with dribbly buffalo-milk burrata. The one to use for pesto Genovese and any tomato dish, hot or cold, including pizza and spaghetti sauces. Dried basil is a big disappointment.

Some don't add herbs to ratatouille, but a combination of basil and sweet marjoram gives enticing extra Mediterranean elements. If you grow your own, pinch it out and use it regularly, because lush growth dilutes the pungency.

Thai basil: the darker, smaller leaved variety used in Thai cookery. It has a stronger anise flavour than sweet basil and is chosen there to cook with meat; sweet basil can be substituted but doesn't have the same oomph.

Creative cooks should look beyond the initial anise-like flavour of basil and think meeting and taking further its citric notes, and the peppery ones, so, fresh basil leaves with raw oysters or with oysters briefly warmed in buttery Chardonnay and served in split brioche...

BAY LEAF: the boards of a stage upon which most savoury flavours perform better, bay is indispensable in red-meat dishes and the sauces that go with them, gravies included and has unexpected sweet uses.

Knowing cooks use two or more times the number specified in recipes. When fresh, check the underside for nasties. Fresh or dried, bay leaf has a remarkable aromatic flavour that is much underused. Unsuspected realms of taste and pleasure reward you for stuffing fresh bay leaves under the crackling of roast pork, or under the breast skin of a chicken. When you add a wine or stock to a roasting dish, also add some torn bay leaf to pull together the gravy flavours.

Appreciate the unappreciated spectrums of bay leaf by using it to flavour rice; use two big dry leaves or four fresh ones, torn roughly, to 225 g/8 oz or 1 cup of uncooked rice. Served with plain or spiced food it adds a truly individual and much appreciated flavour. Basmati rice cooked with bay leaf is by far the best way to start a rice-salad or to improve beyond blandness rice that is going to be used in a stuffing.

Prunes plumped with abundant bay leaves, red wine, spices and a little brown sugar become the most unctuous accompaniment to poultry, pork and game dishes; simmer until there is just enough liquid left to cover the fruit, then remove the leaves and whole spices. Bay-flavoured custard is an old favourite with baked apple, and very elegant when chilled; simmer leaves in milk, then remove them and proceed the usual way.

Bay rum: beloved of 'gentlemen's hairdressers' this is made of bay oil with essences of orange and clove, plus black Jamaican rum.

Golden-leaved bay: is rare and a more ornamental small tree. The leaves are more fragrant and elegant than the green, echoed by the flavour.

Powdered bay/ground bay leaf: is very useful in pâté mixtures and in spaghetti sauces, but it must be very fresh and fresh or dried leaves are more reliable.

BERGAMOT/BERGAMOT OIL: this is the true flavour of Earl Grey tea q.v., and has nothing to do with the plant below. The brilliant, robust and incisive combination of orange, lemon and lime flavours comes from the thick skin of a large citrus particularly associated with Reggio Calabria. The skin's flavour is too powerful for most as a single-source marmalade, but makes a captivating addition to Seville or other orange marmalades, used instead of lemon and up to equal portions, although I prefer less.

A culinary grade oil is available on line, offering great opportunities savoury or sweet. I think custards and ice cream, but also a faintness of it with seafood or a whisper with fine zest on tropical fruits or on apricots, white peaches or plums—perhaps in jams made of these?

BERGAMOT, FLOWERING PLANT: also known as Bee Balm, because its scarlet flowers are popular with honeybees. The crushed leaves give a citrus-like fragrance with exotic overtones, and the flowers are good in salads. The leaves are brewed into a tea and this comforted American patriots after the Boston Tea Party deprived them of green tea from China.

BITTERS: angostura bitters are the best known. Originally a fever cure, the bitterness is quinine, but there are also tropical spices, citrus and some rum. Far more useful than for pink gins, especially added to the sugar syrup for a fruit salad. Angostura bitters are comfortable with creaminess and thus for finishing sauces for fish, for chicken and for pork. Guaranteed to get conversation going.

There are many more bitters, some of which are 'flavoured' and although largely used in cocktails, have many culinary uses. Orange bitters, made from Seville oranges and spices, changed my life when I discovered the Hoffman House martini at London's Corinthia Hotel's Bassoon Bar. Named for an extinct Fifth Avenue hotel-palace, it was four dashes of orange bitters in four fluid ounces of gin and a little vermouth; other proportions are proposed. Transcendental, as orange bitters are in fish, veal and chicken dishes.

They are as good in a fruit salad as a dash of angostura bitters and perhaps in icing for orange or lemon drizzle cakes, or a banana cake. I've not got past the martini. Members of the UK Guild of Food Writers also proposed rhubarb, grapefruit, spiced chocolate and Carpano Botanic Bitters. Best UK source seems to be Gerrys.UK.com.

BORAGE: the cucumber-like flavour tells you to sprinkle the vivid blue flowers over salads, use them in sandwiches, layer in jellies and to put a noddy sprig into long, cold summer drinks—especially Pimms.

A salad of borage flowers and strawberry halves is extraordinary, as good as it is unusual. Best not to use the challenging hairy leaves unless very finely sliced.

CAMELINA: an ancient oil-seed crop, the seeds of which can be used as a sprinkle and have very high omega-3 fatty acid content as well as other good nutritional contributions; slight almond flavour. Camelina oil is used as bio-fuel in jet engines.

CAPILLAIRE: the flavour of maidenhair fern, popular towards the end of the 19th century but almost unknown now; it's described as faintly aromatic tending to bitterness. The fern was used to garnish sweet dishes the way parsley is on savoury ones. Capillaire syrup-flavoured drinks were 'improved' with orange-flower water and saffron. They were often mixed into Victorian cure-alls.

CARAWAY SEEDS: the tiny grey sickles of sharp aniseed flavour that populate seed cakes and some rye breads and that are much disliked by many. Can be used in moderation on hot vegetable dishes and cold salads; a few sprinkled on buttery carrots are nice and they suit coleslaw and beetroot salad very well.

Caraway has an affinity with apples, both raw and cooked. A baked apple pie is much emboldened if you add the zest of half an orange and then brown sugar, butter, nutmeg and few, very few, caraway seeds. Kummel liqueur relies on these seeds for its flavour and digestive qualities.

CARDAMOM: one of the most aromatic and pungent spices, native to south India and Sri Lanka. It has a distinct whiff of eucalyptus and camphor behind an otherwise concentrated sweet fragrance. Because it grows in shady forests some way above sea level, cardamom is an interesting and easy plant to cultivate, perhaps even indoors. Its luscious leaves can be chewed for pleasure, to sweeten the breath, or to slice finely into sweet or savoury foods.

Best way to use cardamom is to bruise the pod, slightly cracking open the fibrous casing and lightly splitting the long, rippled seeds, so the pod still contains them. Otherwise you must remove the seeds and crush them very well indeed; if you do not reduce them to a powder your dish will look as though a loose-bowelled rodent has passed through.

A sprinkling of ground cardamom over hot coffee, morning noon or night, or a few bruised pods in the coffee pot, is often the cause of more comment than the most complicated and original dish.

The Vikings introduced it to Scandinavia, where it remains the saviour of their commonly bland food. Cardamom gives elusive appeal to good Danish pastries, and can also go into meatballs, marinades, curries and fruit dishes. Cardamom's most sensual use is combined with saffron and rose water in voluptuous warm rice puddings: see *Rice*. The same combination is mixed into thick yoghurt along the coast of the Maghreb, and then served chilled.

Green cardamom: the basic and most elegantly flavoured.

White cardamom: these are bleached by sun or other processes, and are not as tasty as green ones.

Brown/Black cardamom: a bigger seed pod with the same sort of flavour but more of it. Not inferior to green cardamom but different and its unique additional woody and smoky flavours are invaluable aids to any Indian foods cooked in a tandoor oven. Cardamom of this kind is native to the Himalayas. There is also a Chinese variety, with bigger pods, up to 3.5 cm/1½"; it is less smoky and more medicinal seeming than the Indian.

Ground cardamom: although available is not recommended. Cardamom is so expensive you should get every last bit of goodness by crushing your own whole seeds and anyway, as it loses strength quickly. A coffee grinder will do the crushing for you. Absorb the oil left behind by then grinding rice and mixing the result into your store of rice. Otherwise, a mortar and pestle do nicely, and a wodge of bread or ground rice will collect up the oil left behind.

Cardamom extract: very strong and superb for adding entrancing flavour when you want to be beguiling, unfathomable, mysterious. I've whipped it into butter to flavour filo pastry, used it with rose water, of course, in a rose-tea ice cream and a bread-and-butter pudding, stirred some into a spiced-chai cake mixture, sprinkled it judiciously into a tropical fruit salad, tossed buttered rice with a little and rubbed some into a young leg of lamb and let that sit around for a few hours. It might be dripped into after-dinner coffee but you must be lean with it.

CAROB: made from the abundant locust bean, carob is a chocolate substitute for those who want the treat but none of its accompanying fat, calories or caffeine. The seeds are held in a sweet pulp, and this makes one of the syrups thought to be meant by the Biblical 'land of milk and honey'.

Once dried the pod can be chewed, like a fruit leather. Otherwise, it is cooked and then roasted, caramellising the natural sugars present and giving a cocoa-like reddish brown colour. Once ground, the flavour is chocolate-like, with fudgy, caramel overtones more like milk chocolate and because it is naturally sweet it can't be a substitute for dark or bitter chocolate.

Use in cooking like a mild sweetened cocoa. To replace low cocoa-solid or milk chocolate, substitute a couple of dessertspoons of ground carob per chocolate square.

Carob molasses: which you'll find in Lebanese or Syrian shops, can be used as a sweetening or a pour-over syrup for waffles, pancakes or ice cream.

CASSIA: the bark of the cassia tree is sold as 'Chinese' or 'bastard' cinnamon and can be used as a substitute for the real thing, but is stronger and coarser. Easily identified because when curled into cigar shapes it is redder and rougher than true cinnamon; read the label, as much is sold as cinnamon with no descriptive.

Cassia buds: are sweet and tangy, like cinnamon and cloves combined, and especially good with cherries; you will see them specified for Hungarian cherry soup. Even when preserved in salt and sugar, these tiny yellow flowers have a wonderful fragrance, presumably because cassia is of the jasmine family.

Traditionally used for scenting teas, wines and sweet dishes, and I remember the buds ingeniously used in a duck sauce at the 1993 Hong Kong Food Festival.

CAYENNE: a mixture of sweet capsicum (paprika) and just a dash of heat. Indispensable to cookery and cookbooks in the early 20th century and into the '80s, it was inevitably used to finish egg, cheese or fish dishes. Sprinkled for colour rather than flavour, it gave an elegant jostle to the palate, rarely menacing fine food or wine in the way of raucous *chilli* q.v.

CHRYSANTHEMUM: the fresh petals with spicy, fragrant flavour garnish an aristocratic Japanese soup. One or two flowers infused make a tea, hot or cold; can also be added to your usual tea but not for long or bitterness prevails.

CITRIC ACID/SOUR SALT: a pinch of citric acid gives as much acidity as the juice from half a small lemon, or from a lime, and gives a cleaner, fresher flavour than using concentrated juices, which have been deadened by heat processing. A standby in northern and eastern European countries where citrus fruit is or was rare and is very good in such as beetroot borscht, cheesecakes and the like. It's not expensive, so is a great larder standby.

CITRUS OILS: I feel naked without bottles of pure cold-processed lime, lemon and orange oils from Boyajian of New York. They are direct, exact and magical when something isn't working, and the tools to make magic.

When pasta is drained and allowed to steam dry for a few minutes, I toss it in a mixture of olive oil and lime oil. The dried pasta surface sucks it up and voila! Lime-flavoured pasta, extraordinarily good with anything tomato-y and enthralling as the basis for a cold pasta salad with prawns or roasted vegetables or just about anything. Something different in a chocolate cake or in brownies? I add lime oil in the proportions they suggest and voila! Again. And if I forget, I mix some in to the icing.

You really need these in your refrigerator, if only to add a whiff to gin or vodka, with or without tonic, which lime oil does magnificently. It adds wonder to rum and coke, and to most other rum-based drinks, but be very sparing. Boyajian do other pure, direct flavouring oils, but start with the lime. You'll find them on the web but check the prices as these vary enormously.

CELERY SEED AND SALT: ground in a pepper grinder, the seed is used as a condiment. It is common to use too much, which is why many vegetarian dishes smell and taste the same. Nonetheless, it is a very handy helpmate when bland dishes need resuscitation and is too much overlooked.

Celery salt: a mixture of salt and ground celery seed, it is potentially a culinary lifesaver but over beloved of vegetarians and sorely missed by drinkers if not included in a Bloody Mary.

Celery seeds: good as a condiment for but not in fish, soups, tomato, potato salad, eggs, cheese and vegetarian nut dishes. Ground or whole seeds add an interesting lift to a marinade if you heat the liquid slightly to stimulate the extrusion of fragrant oils from the seed. Never serve the whole seed in food: the flavour is coarse and you are better off with chopped celery greens or the more subtle flavour of dill weed, even though not exactly the same.

CHERVIL: like a fragile parsley, chervil tastes of aristocratic drawing rooms and parterres, rather than of something from a bucket at the back door. Its appeal is the discreet flavour of anise, a thin resonant thread of the finer notes of French tarragon. Sometimes called French or (in America) gourmet's parsley.

Chervil transforms the mundane into something serious: crushed *belle de Fontenay* potatoes with a little cream and chervil as a bed for seared scallops comes to mind, thanks to super-chef Jean Paul Novelli. Eggs cooked any way but fried, and all salads, are improved immeasurably, as are vegetables and vegetable soups, even if only garnished. Like the related flavour of tarragon, chervil has an affinity for chicken in hot or cold dishes. Butter sauces for firm white-fleshed fish or for lobsters are both very good places to find chervil. It is an important component of *fines herbes*.

CHILLI/CHILLIES & CHILI/CHILIES: first, hear the diamond advice of rock-star Joe Perry, of Aerosmith. In *Bon Appétit* magazine he said:

> *'I found a lot of chillies ... bury the flavour of everything else. A really strong habanero flattens your taste buds. It's like listening to really loud music all the time. You don't hear any of the nuance anymore.'*

Wise words I hope you will heed. The extraordinary battle by chillies to take over the world and banish flavour in favour of hot vulgarity is almost lost, particularly as more and more people believe 'spicy' means hot, when it should mean spiced. And why? Because chillies create an addiction as real as nicotine or hard drugs. The more you use, the more you need and your palate dies. Here's how.

Chilli heat is neither flavour nor culinary ingredient; it is mouth trauma. It burns your tongue and once you go beyond a certain point, which differs from person to person, the brain recognises the trauma and releases endorphins, natural opiates. These do little to dull the pain of the injury, but make you feel great. This opiate euphoria becomes addictive and is the saviour of many poor people around the world. The same is true of unfortunates with few taste buds, slow tongues, who include many 'celeb' chefs and once great recipe writers who are ageing and don't understand their palates have faded or know how to brighten food without further dulling their tongues with the burn of chillies.

Look carefully and chillies really are the refuge of the poor, used most lavishly where there is little else to eat. A bowl of rice with scraps of vegetables does little to make the belly or body feel good. Add the heat of the chilli and at least you get some pleasure, some buzz from eating.

Like all drugs, the more chillies you eat, the more you must eat to get the euphoria. In the meantime, you are scarring your tongue deeply and so taste less and less of everything; the only pleasure left in eating comes not from flavour or texture but from an opiate high caused by chillies.

Most travellers visiting India, say, Thailand or Nepal, return believing that to continue eating authentically, they must burn and sweat, because that is the sort of food they were served there. Not so. There they were eating a chilli content measured for those who have eaten it all their life and who have become increasingly immune because of long-scarred tongues. If you were to have very little chilli indeed, you would more accurately approximate what those locals experience. Never mock someone who asks for little or no chilli, for not only are they respecting their palate, they are the ones eating most authentically.

The seeds in fresh chilli peppers hold only about 3% of the capsaicin oil, which is the hot content in chillies; the pale vertical membranes or placentas contain a great deal more. Thus, you must remove both the seeds and the membranes from fresh chillies, and then the fire is reduced considerably: Mexicans think of this as emasculation, and call such chillies capons.

And here seems the ideal place to tell you what to do if you have burned your mouth with chilli. Don't gulp water, beer or wine, which spread the burning oil about, often straight down to sear the unprotected intestines, which makes everything worse tomorrow, or sooner. Rice, sugar or banana will quickly soak up the fiery oil and milk or yoghurt also absorb it. So do cheese, butter and ice cream.

Those who use chilli a lot in ethnic dishes rarely drink when they eat. You shouldn't either, but eat rice in equal proportion to what else goes in your mouth, mouthful by mouthful, not one of one and then of the other. Any soup on the table should be sipped discreetly throughout the meal and never gulped before the meal.

Every man and woman, with or without a dog, has their version of what is chili and what is chilli, or chile or chille. My research in places where such ingredients are grown or used, and together with my conversations with Elizabeth Lambert Ortiz, one of the greatest writers on South American food, has a solution.

An 'i' or an 'e' at the end of the word doesn't matter. Otherwise, chilli with two 'l's is the basic ingredient, the fruit of the chilli plant, whether fresh, dried or ground. Easily remembered, because unadulterated chilli is likely to be as hot as hell, which also has two 'l's.

Thus, chili with just one 'l' is any dish that includes chillies or the mixed spice with which you make a chili/chile, explained below in Mixtures. Not knowing the difference between chili and chilli is why so many recipes called a chili con carne turn out to be nothing but burny mince and beans.

Chili powder: should be a mixed spice, based mainly on ground cumin with oregano and garlic plus chilli powder as a lesser or greater inclusion. The mixture is sometimes sold as 'chili compound' but read the label to be sure. To make a chili con carne or any other style of chili/chile dish, you must use this mixed spice. Adding such other spices as turmeric or coriander make it a curry.

Chilli powder: should be only ground chillies and is only one of the ingredients in the mixture used in a made-up dish called a chili.

Dried chillies: drying spreads hot capsaicin oil throughout the flesh. Shake out what seeds you can and develop a relationship with the texture of those you can't.

Fresh chillies: it is generally true that the smaller the chilli the hotter it will be. As a double check, look at the colour of the inner membranes,

the placentas, where the seeds adhere. An orange-yellow stain is an indication of elevated heat.

Classically, fresh chillies were measured on the Scoville chart but this has been simplified into The Official Chilli/Chille Pepper Heat Scale of 0–10. As this changes often, check on the web if you need to know.

Types of dried chillies

Commonly available dried chillies in ascending order of their heat quotient, simplified into a scale of one to ten. Note that heat is not 'spicy' and that some chillies change their name when dried.

Generally, dried chillies are reconstituted in a warm liquid (milk, water, beer, wine) weighted down to keep them submerged and then they are puréed. The purée is a more controllable way to add chilli without the risk of overdoing it. But you can cut them into strips, mince or stuff them and also use them whole or crushed. Dried chillies can be toasted for extra flavour, but it is a hazardous business because the fumes damage your eyes in a blink, and you risk burning the chillies, which makes even worse smoke, and turns them bitter.

What you do with each variety depends on the thickness of their flesh.

Choricero: 0. A sweet mild chilli, that's wrinkly and a gorgeous rich brown colour. Can be stuffed whole, or used in sauces, soups and stews.

Ancho (dried poblano): 3. Usually big enough to stuff, it has a full sweet flavour with mild heat. Good in general use, as above, and is partial to being served with chocolate, a nudge for creative cooks to start experimenting with sauces, cakes, cookies, brownies, ice creams and the like.

Guajillo: 3. The mahogany-coloured guajillo (little gourd) brings a bright tannic flavour, not unlike green tea. Very good with tomato and anything else that would make a chili, a pizza or a pasta sauce.

Mulato: 3. Deep, herbal flavours that combine well with root vegetables and mushrooms, in sauces perhaps, or cut into strips and tossed with the cooked vegetables.

New Mexico Red: 3. A tangy sweetness good with tomatoes and garlic and very good in chilis or soups.

Cascabel: 4. There's a nutty woody flavour accompanying the increased heat of the brown cascabel (little rattle), and that combines well with lime, lemon or orange in sauces for meat, fish or all kinds of pumpkin and squash.

Pasilla: 4. Herb and dried-fruit flavours and a brown-black colour explain the pasilla name, which means little raisin. Can be snipped into rings for garnish and is happy with seafood and lamb. One of the traditional ingredients of *mole* sauces.

Chipotle (smoked jalapeno): 6. Now it's getting hot and chipotle heat lingers on the palate. Smoky, nutty and with some bitterness but very useful to add flavour depth and width to anything wet—soups, sauces, stews salsas, etc.

De arbol: 8. Close to searing but still with a discernible clear, clean flavour. Red and small and good to store in oil or vinegar to give teeth to either or both.

Piquin: 8. A definite sear here, but with a nut and corn flavour. Small, so can be used as the de arbol, or simply to add heat.

Habanero: 10. Intensely, threateningly, fiercely hot. These orange-brown chillies still pack a good fruity flavour, and so are good with tropical fruits, tomatoes and the like, raw in salsas or cooked in sauces. But why?

Thin-fleshed smooth skinned chillies: de arbol (8), piquin (8). Can be soaked or used dried and may be scrunched, crushed or used as they are, to remove from cooking when the desired height of heat and flavour. Can be toasted for richer flavour.

Medium-fleshed, smooth-skinned chillies: New Mexico reds (3), guajillo (3), cascabels (4). All these are better for being puréed and sieved, getting rid of the tough skin. Then add to sauces, soups, stews and gravies. Mayonnaise or butters are good too.

Thick-fleshed, wrinkly, thin-skinned chillies: ancho (3) mulatto (3) pasilla (4) choricero (0). After soaking and puréeing these do not need to be sieved and so the purée can be used as above. All can be cut into strips before being soaked, then used in batters, breads, stir-fries, sauces, pasta and so on. Chipotle (6) need to be stewed whole in water until very tender. Pull off the top so any internal water can escape and then use in stews and casseroles.

For Habaneros (10), once you are kitted up in long rubber gloves and protective goggles to stop you touching your eyes or being damaged by the acrid fumes given off by the soaking water, you drain them and use them as is or lightly crushed in cooking. It is usual and advisable to remove them once they have added heat and flavour to your dish, for very few people actually want to eat them. Those who do need counselling.

Much of the information on dried chillies came via the great generosity of spirit of www.coolchile.co.uk, who do all the above and more by mail order.

CHIVES: I doubt the place of raw onion flavour in serious or subtle cooking. Chives are culinary acid rain, thrown thoughtlessly into or onto dishes but without mentioning them on a menu. Scrambled eggs with smoked salmon is quite a different thing from scrambled eggs, smoked salmon and chives. I send that combination back if I have ordered the former. What happened to soothing parsley? Even when chives are the most robust ingredient on the plate they have rarely been considered in the creation of the dish but added, sometimes for 'colour', but no understanding that they change the character and flavour profiles of the dish.

If you disagree, you'll use chives chopped over chicken soups, on sour cream garnishes, in omelettes and cheese dishes and, if you ape most chefs, over everything else.

CINNAMON: the main spice for which the New World was discovered and reliably the most comforting down-home, all-is-well aroma and taste. British soldiers in the Afghanistan desert sought US encampments, to beg, borrow or swap what they could for their cinnamon-heavy doughnuts, sweet rolls and more.

True cinnamon (see *Cassia*) is the inner bark of a fragrant type of laurel. The best comes from Sri Lanka and is sometimes sold as Ceylon cinnamon to distinguish it from cassia.

Ground cinnamon: multifarious in its usefulness with fruit, cakes and pastries; try cinnamon sprinkled on thick, chilled slices of a blood or navel orange and a few drops of orange flower-water—strikingly simple and unbelievably good. Arabs might sprinkle cinnamon over poultry, with rose or orange-flower water.

Egg dishes, sweet or savoury, marry seamlessly with this warm, comforting flavour, as in the American breakfast combination of cinnamon-coffee cake with eggs and bacon. Rice stuffings for lamb or whole fish benefit from cinnamon, especially if ground almonds and a little, very little, sugar is also included.

Quills: slim roll-ups of true, dried cinnamon bark, quills are slightly pliable, pale and creamy-brown rather than reddish brown. Wonderful swizzle sticks for coffee or hot wine, for hot chocolate and, surprisingly, for hot tea, a combination that is soothing and delicious. Quills are important ingredients in stews and curries but should be removed before serving. For cinnamon in syrups, creams, ice creams and custards, steep broken quills in warm liquid milk or cream rather than using ground cinnamon. You get a truer flavour, no discolouration and no chance of reduced or off-flavour because the powder has oxidised.

CLOVER BLOSSOMS, RED: dried or fresh, the honey-like flavour of clover makes a delicious tea and steeped in warm milk or cream makes delicate creams and ice creams.

CLOVES: Chinese courtiers were once obliged to have cloves in their mouths when addressing their Emperor, to sweeten their breath.

Clove comes from the French *clou* meaning nail, for these unopened buds of an evergreen tree look like shrivelled nails and seem as hard. I regularly reach for ground or whole cloves when cooking pork, rubbing some into roasts or incorporating either form in casseroles and pâtés, where I think them most important, with beef stews, too. With fruit, marinades, spiced biscuits, rich fruit cakes and mulled drinks, cloves work best combined with such sweeter spices as cinnamon.

Orange has a special affinity with cloves, so in hot cross buns, Christmas puddings and Christmas cakes, add extra ground cloves to the mixed spice and incorporate grated fresh orange peel. Cloves and lemon together tastes medicinal.

Ground cloves lose flavour quickly. Out with the old.

CORIANDER SEEDS AND LEAVES: the taste of the leaves and of the seeds of coriander are totally different.

Coriander leaves: look like flat parsley but are something else entirely. Fresh coriander is usually sold with its roots attached, a way to tell it from flat-leaf parsley. They have a bitter-sweet and haunting flavour endemic—some would say epidemic—in countries as diverse as Thailand, Mexico, Spain, Greece and Cyprus. It is used as basic flavour or an almost inescapable garnish in the first two countries where life can be very difficult if you don't like it. When the late Peter Leggat MBE wanted to ban fresh coriander from his Bangkok table he was threatened with losing his entire staff. Romans called it the bed-bug plant, for the smell of the leaf is apparently that of crushed bed bugs.

Although the stems are almost tasteless, the roots are a powerhouse of flavour, yet only Thailand uses them regularly. They are scraped free of skin and threads and pounded with garlic and black pepper as an essential flavouring Trinity. I do the same but poach the garlic first, add coriander leaf and whiz it all together to make a powerful, fragrant pomade to use as a marinade, to fold into mayonnaise or other sauces or, best of all, to spread over fresh white dough instead of tomato as the base of a Thai-style pizza, topped with sliced lemon grass, tiger prawns, coconut cream, basil leaves and so on. Well worth exploring.

Coriander seeds: the orangey bite of coriander seed is an unsuspected way to brighten up almost anything. Mix equal quantities of coriander seed, black and white peppercorns for a taste better than either one to enhance most savoury foods and plates. Not bad as the base for a baking spice mixture. Together with cumin, coriander seed is the backbone of Asian curries. If you discover a curry mix is boring or just plain horrid, add a mixture of coriander and cumin powder in the proportion of two to one. You might even reverse the proportions.

Crushed coriander seeds add interest to marinades, to pâtés and sausages and sausage rolls. Ground coriander adds delicious warmth to breads and biscuits and in custards. Peas, carrots, lentils, squash and pumpkin go well.

CREAM OF TARTAR/TARTARIC ACID: made from powdered dried grapes, it is an ingredient of baking powder. The combination of baking soda and tartaric acid with liquid and heat creates rising for cake mixtures using soft rather than high-gluten hard flours. Unlike the immediate action of baking soda, baking powder works only when heat is present.

CUBEB PEPPER: native to Indonesia, these look like comic-book bombs as each peppercorn has a tail. They are as pungent as a good black peppercorn, but the scents and flavours add camphor and pine forest. Best used with other peppers or in spice mixtures, such as *ras el hanout* q.v., particularly in pâtés and sausages, where they either complement or can substitute for the allspice you would properly use.

Cubebs are comfortable with fattiness, useful in cheese dishes, even sprinkled into a cheese topping. I mix cubeb with black peppercorns and long pepper in a pepper grinder and this gives exotic, ever-changing scents and tastes highly evocative of faraway places.

CUMIN SEED: together with coriander seed, the basis of curry mixtures, and one of the most important spices throughout the tropical belt of the world, New and Old alike. It is essential to chilis.

Cumin seeds have a sharp, attractive lemon flavour and are very useful to add zing to almost anything, especially to aged or jaded palates or for those who do not tolerate citrus juice. Sprinkle them in salads, on eggs, into baked potatoes or as a condiment over almost anything. Cumin whole or ground works well with tomato in sauces and seafoods: prawns bathed in a pink sauce of tomato and cumin are wonderful. Moroccans combine cumin, sweet paprika and tomato, which is magical. It is strewn on bread doughs, yoghurt and bean dishes and its special tang brightly complements chickpeas, cooked whole or made into a purée. Find it featured in za-atar and see coriander for advice on how to zip up a boring curry powder mixture.

Cumin and coriander make a good flavouring for rice salads, and I think that whereas coriander and clove work extra well when orange is present, cumin reacts well with lemon—and this marriage should always be arranged when possible.

Toasted cumin seeds are invaluable to have about. Toss them gently in a non-stick pan until they smoke lightly; it is a little like burning old rope or those fat, hand-rolled cigarettes of the Sixties. It's more controllable if you do this in the microwave, arranging the seeds in a circle around the edge of a plate and mixing and reshaping them every minute or so until done, lightly or deeply. You can crush these, of course, but slightly crunchy sickles of bright roasted flavour are perfect strewing material, on bread, salads, sandwiches, fish, poultry and meat.

CURRY LEAVES: leaves that smell and taste of curry, funnily enough. Available both fresh and dried. Fresh leaves are lightly fried at the start of cooking. Dry ones are added once the cooking liquid is in. Arguments rage over whether or not bay leaves may be substituted; the consensus is not.

DANDELION: a great wild food if you can pick young leaves from somewhere dogs don't parade. Ideally, find dandelion in your back yard and put a garden pot over a young plant to blanch it.

Add just a few of the slightly bitter raw leaves to a salad, or blanch green ones quickly in boiling water, drain and flavour with salt, pepper and good olive oil to serve warm or cold. The French *pissenlit* salad wilts dandelion leaves with hot bacon fat in which garlic and croutons have been fried.

DILL SEED AND WEED: the famous foundations of Scandinavian cookery, but also found in Turkey and Greece, whence they originate.

Dill seed: lightly crushed seeds are sharper and more pungent than dill weed, and can be used in rice dishes and breads, with fish and with cucumber. A condiment in Russia.

Dill weed: the feathery fronds of dill are absolutely wonderful to use, quite different from anything else in the basic repertoire of flavours. When dried and sold as dill tips it has almost the same flavour as when fresh. Dill is superb with fish of all kinds, and on anything to do with cucumber, yoghurt, vegetables and, surprisingly, with meat. The Turks make delicious stuffed courgettes and aubergines, filled with dill-flavoured mincemeat and cooked in a sauce of tomato and butter.

Dill is basic to gravadlax, the Swedish dish of lightly salt-pickled salmon, and Swedes cook their crayfish feasts with festoons of the weed. It's a delightful if unexpected flavouring for spinach and feta in Greece's *spanakopita*, their superb filo pastry spinach pie. An unexpected affinity is with black pepper, particularly if you macerate the two in vodka for some time.

ELDERBERRIES: like elderflowers, these usually find themselves made into wine. Provided you use a recipe that incorporates spices like nutmeg and cloves, you will, after several years of patience, be rewarded with a wine that can develop much of the elegance and nobility of a fine Burgundy. Unlikely, but true.

I've never eaten elderberry jam, but believe it to be very good. What I have done is combine elderberries with apple in a pie and that was very successful.

ELDERFLOWERS: the honey-scented, muscatel-flavoured elderflower is largely unknown as a flavour even to those who have a tree in the back garden. It has been enjoying a renaissance in such drinks as elderflower *presse* or cordial but most offer so little flavour you can barely detect it. Proves once again, you can't eat or drink labels.

Traditionally elderflowers made delicious muscatel-like sparkling wine. It improves dramatically with keeping and makes a refreshing chilled apéritif or a mixer with other drinks, like ginger ale or sparkling white wine. I prefer to make a strong elderflower syrup, then to dilute with fizzy water, prosecco or champagne. The syrup wonderfully flavours whipped or pouring cream and I can't think of anything better than fragrant red-fleshed strawberries with a little concentrated elderflower cordial over them.

Elderflowers grow happily in city surroundings and even in Central London it's amazing the harvest you can make on a short walk. Each flat head should be smelt as it is picked for some have a distinct catty smell that, like all bad things, dominate the rest no matter how much or little you have.

Classically, elderflower is cooked with gooseberries, but gooseberries ripen just as the flowers fade and you can miss out. When cooking gooseberries for a fool, one or two heads of rinsed elderflower will be enough to add the required flavour. Gooseberry and elderflower jam or jelly is particularly recommended, as is apricot and elderflower.

Cream perfumed by soaking elderflower in it overnight is a lovely surprise with all sorts of summer fruits, strawberries and raspberries included. It's a very ancient thing to mix the tiny florets into a cheesecake mixture or to stir them into a pancake batter. One of the most successful hints I gave on BBC TV Breakfast Time was to stuff a head or two of elderflowers into a bottle of medium dry or Germanic white wine overnight. By morning you have a Muscat wine to drink chilled as an inimitable apéritif. Judi Dench, well before damehood, told me live on air how much she enjoyed it. It's also now used to flavour gin.

EPAZOTE: a Mexican citrus-like herb, with distinctive notes of its own. The flavour of the raggy-edged epazote leaf falls between parsley and coriander but is easily too strong and unpleasant by itself. It is rarely used fresh, although it is an interesting minor player in salsas of tropical fruit, tomato, avocado and a little chilli.

Epazote is essential in *mole*, and in Mexican black bean stews, but that might have something to do with alleged flatulence-beating properties. Can be happily used with cheese, fish and pork. If you buy it dried make sure you are getting leaves, because the stems are sold to brew up a medicinal tea.

ESPELETTE (PEPPER): although sold as a pepper, espelette is a unique chilli variety, as its full name shows, *Piment d'Espelette*. Grown only in the French Basque area, it is only mildly hot but does have a clean, fruity flavour widely used in cooking and when making Bayonne hams. There is an Espelette Pepper Festival in the last week of October with traditional Basque cultural and sporting events.

FENNEL SEEDS AND FRONDS: similar in taste to liquorice-like anise and dill seeds, and somewhat interchangeable, fennel seeds are especially useful in cooking such oily fish as mackerel as they cut the richness, and are good in snail butters. Their greatest height comes combined with pork, always a high point of Italian fresh sausages and salami. The effervescent British charcuterie scene recognises this and most make a product with fennel seed and reckon it is their most popular.

Fennel is *finocchio* in Italian, a vulgar name for flaunting homosexuals, presumably because both are highly scented. Look for the word in connection with anything pork and you will not be disappointed.

Fresh fennel fronds and stalks should be used lavishly: red mullet and other oily fish should be stuffed full and if you have a barbecue, put dried but soaked stalks onto the charcoal to smoke and smoulder just before the fish. You can put the sticks to burn under the mesh of a grill tray, if you do not have a barbecue.

Root fennel, F. vulgare dulce: is a different animal and quite one of the world's most delicious vegetables, cooked or raw.

FENUGREEK SEEDS: the name means 'greek hay' because Ancient Greeks used it to sweeten hay. The bitter-sweet taste is used in the curries of southern India and Sri Lanka and over-used in many commercial powders, giving a characteristic damp, stale smell. The flavour is more appealing if first dry roasted or microwaved. Very little, ground and sprinkled over vegetables, can be appealing. In Greece fenugreek seeds are eaten raw or boiled with honey. The seeds are also recommended for sprouting and make a good ingredient in or on breads, as they do in Egypt and Ethiopia.

FILÉ: sassafras leaves are ground and made into *filé*, a green powder with a haunting flavour that's a cross between eucalyptus and marijuana. Used to thicken hot liquids with great care or the results are unpleasant and stringy. The defining ingredient in *filé* gumbos, a staple rice dish of Creole kitchens.

FINES HERBES: in contrast to the robustness of a bouquet garni, fines herbs combine three or more sweet delicate herbs, such as parsley, tarragon and chervil, and, if you really, really must, chives. They go very well with eggs.

FISH SAUCE: think of this as liquid salt with added flavour and you'll find it more acceptable. *Nam pla* is the Thai version and *Nuoc mam* is fish sauce from Vietnam. Both are salty seasoning made by fermenting whole small fish in salt, the way Romans made their indispensable garum. Worcestershire sauce is made rather the same way, if that helps.

Fish sauce is the essential salt/savouriness of South East Asia, and like shrimp paste is missed when not there. If ever offered a tour of the pits where fish and salt ferment, plead poverty, insanity or both, to avoid it. The hotter the day, the greater should be your pleading.

FIVE SPICE/FIVE FRAGRANCE POWDER: a powerful mixed spice with a predominantly anise and cinnamon flavour but that may combine any of star anise, cinnamon, cassia, fennel seeds, cloves, liquorice, nutmeg, Szechwan peppercorns and ginger. Many Chinese mixtures contain six or seven, but the flavour of the first two must predominate. Especially used in marinades, in poultry and pork stuffings, or rubbed well into their scored skin before roasting.

FOOD COLOURING: generally, if you can do without food colouring, I think you should because most of it is artificially based.

A few years ago, I experimented to find how one might recreate the medieval requirement of brightly coloured pastry without having to find sandalwood, woad and such. It was easy. Once you put pastry on your pie, paint it with undiluted food colouring. When the colouring has dried, cover with the usual egg glaze, let that dry and then bake away. Lighter colours are fugitive so if using light greens and yellows glaze only for the last few minutes of baking: the same advice goes if the pie will bake for more than 30 minutes, glaze for just the last ten minutes. The simplest stripes look good; diagonal stripes of bright green and saffron yellow on, say, a chicken, lettuce and cucumber pie.

For a wedding reception in a grand country house, I cooked a ten-course banquet for 60 people in evening dress, them not me. The *pièces de résistances* were hot game pies, gilded and decorated and painted by an artist from Paris, who gave each pie crust her style. A sensation. For Glyndebourne I made a peach and rose-geranium pie decorated with roses, leaves and vines of pastry and painted them carefully, leaving the crust its natural colour. Others on the Glyndebourne lawn came to take photographs and it is still mentioned with awe, perhaps, I like to think, because it also tasted good.

It is far more fun for a child to have their name or portrait on a cake than to be faced with over-decorated cupcakes.

A commonly used colouring is

caramel or gravy browning, but good cooking technique should make this unnecessary. Use minimal flour and make sure your meat is very well browned before adding liquid. If you need browning, then cook white sugar until it turns golden brown and then dilute it with a little water to keep the mixture concentrated: keep that bottled until you need it. Commercial gravy browning is the result of an extraordinary process that incorporates ammonia and some authorities recommend it should not be used as human food.

GALANGAL, KHA, LAOS ROOT: a highly fragrant root, with distinct overtones of camphor and that looks like a thinner, paler, pinker version of ginger root. Recognised by knowing a ginger root looks like a foot but galangal looks like a hand, and is often tinged with a delicious rose colour.

Galangal has a crisp, less fibrous texture than ginger, so is sliced rather than chopped or squeezed. Must be used with moderation, even though the flavour lessens when heat is applied. It is important in Thai cooking, pounded into curry pastes of different colours. My instinct was to combine it with fresh ginger, but Thai mentors teach never to mix the two, and that ginger is rarely used in Thai cooking.

Galangal is an important flavour in Tom Yam Goong soup, the sour-hot-citric soup you sip throughout a Thai meal. Kai Tom Kha gives the flavour of galangal a solo starring role, in a soup with chicken and coconut, which can be supremely elegant.

Galangal is the galingale that so often appears in the sumptuous ingredient lists of medieval cookery, but it was then used dried and ground. Dried galangal has little of the fresh root's flavours and edginess.

GARLIC: like the onion, garlic was supposedly one the chief nourishers of the thousands of men—probably volunteers for a sort of national service, rather than slaves—who built the pyramids and was the common food of the Roman labourer and soldier.

From a pariah state in the 50s and 60s, when only foreigners and people who ate by candlelight in bistros knew about it, garlic is now common. It can be used with more foods than you could imagine. All meats do better with garlic and all birds should be rubbed over with a cut clove whatever else you are going to do with them: duck à l'orange is far better when the crisp skin yields the scent and flavour of garlic.

It is a peculiarly European warning not to brown garlic because it will become bitter; sometimes this is true, sometimes it's not, and most times it just doesn't matter. Thai cooks regularly brown sliced garlic to use as a last-minute garnish or tempering, and very good it is. Be bold, brown your garlic. The trick is to do it over low heat so the natural sugars caramelise, rather than turn to cinders.

Bitterness is a common problem with the fashion for roasting whole garlic cloves, because the process goes too far. It is best done by slicing the top off a whole bulb, dobbing in some olive oil and then slowly roasting, often on a bed of coarse salt that does nothing but keep it upright. Sweeter and more subtle results come from blanching the bulbs once or twice before roasting. Otherwise, unpeeled cloves of garlic are slowly roasted until browned through, but should have been taken from the oven when still cream-coloured. When I want to serve browned garlic cloves, I first poach them with their skin on and they are always sweet.

Poached ones stay a bit anaemic but roasted garlic cloves turn an old-ivory colour and develop unctuous-ness close to mayonnaise; they may be tossed in olive oil and lightly grilled to give the skins a little cosmetic colour-ing and then used in warm salads, or as a condiment—you squash out the flesh and mix it into other foods and sauces as you go. Otherwise, throw whole unpeeled garlic cloves into stews and casseroles as they cook and serve a few to everyone, so they enjoy their cream of garlic as and when they like.

The simplest use of garlic is to fla-vour butter, melted or otherwise and blanched garlic is far superior for this, so the garlic does not go off. I add lemon juice and chopped parsley for hot cobs of sweet corn, as a dip for arti-choke, with fresh asparagus and with broad beans. Hot vinaigrette sauce with garlic and parsley is a welcome boost to simple salads of hot or cold pulses, potatoes or mixed vegetables. If you are saddled with someone who says they loathe garlic, use it anyway and simply

say it is 'a secret ingredient from Turkey or Brazil'. It's astonishing how many people do not recognise garlic when used subtly and in profound incognito.

Websites push amazing claims for hundreds of types of red, white, purple, violet, small and large. Most is imagina-tion, for science decrees only six vari-eties: rocambole, porcelain, Asiatic, purple stripe, marble-purple stripe and artichoke. As with grapes or tea or coffee, perceived differences are a result of *terroir*. The answer is indeed in the soil.

Aioli, alioli etc: the most famous garlic dressing but not a mayonnaise into which garlic is added. It must start with pounded fresh garlic, two or more cloves per eventual serv-ing, so there is a startling, rugged bite. Used in many famed dishes, including to finish Provencal white-fish *bourride*, on the bread gobbets in *bouillabaisse* and for the mixed-veg feast the French call *aioli*. Superb with crisp, slim French fries, with bloody côte de boeuf, baked salmon and everything from the barbecue, potatoes to lobster.

Black garlic: an old Asian condiment and cooking ingredient, made by carefully aging whole bulbs of garlic, during which they naturally cara-melise, becoming softer and gentler in flavour. They are not fermented.

Dried minced garlic/garlic powder: these never quite work in my opin-ion, usually giving an unwelcome bitterness.

Elephant garlic: a worthwhile variant

with individual cloves that can be as much as 5 cm/2 inch across. It is a gentle giant, for even when raw it is milder than other types.

Garlic salt: useful for final hints of flavour but you must remember it is largely salt—many don't. Make your own by mixing three or four parts salt to one of garlic powder and use it to flavour mashed potatoes, gravies or seasoned flour. You are better off with real garlic and less salt.

Smoked garlic: use anywhere you would expect the flavour of smoked bacon—in stews of beans or pulses—but be unexpected too. I like it poached whole, squeezed from its husks and then whisked in to mashed potatoes or in salad dressings.

Wild garlic: colloquially called ransoms, brightens up woods and is increasingly available commercially and used professionally. The green tops (not the bulbs or flowers) have a garlic-like flavour delicious to find in salads and sandwiches. But beware, very beware, if you are foraging. The leaves look like three toxic plants, including lily-of-the valley, and there are serious poisonings every year. It's a shade tolerant plant and it's safer and simpler to grow your own.

GERANIUM LEAVES: scented geraniums have many uses in the kitchen for someone who likes exotic but traditional effects without fuss. My favourite is the genuine rose geranium. It grows as easily as you blink from any old bit of it stuck into any old bit of ground, and in the right place can even make a scented hedge. It should be encouraged to spread over the pathway so passersby brush the leaves, and this releases the scent even on quite chilly days. On sunny days the heady, spicy scent travels and concentrates in your garden where you least expect.

The pointed, herbaceous rose aroma of the leaves was used to flavour plain or chocolate sponges by putting overlapping leaves on the base of the baking pan before the cake mixture. A little rose water in the icing completes this transformation of a basic cake into something special.

Otherwise slice up four or five or more lusciously scented bigger leaves, picked early in the morning for maximum intensity, and then slide these into a bottle of relatively inexpensive gin or vodka. In a few weeks you will have something very special to drink as cold shots or to sweeten and serve as a chilled digestif. It's a thrilling way to flavour the cream for summer fruits. Or make rose-geranium sugar: slightly tear some leaves to help release the oils and then mix with caster sugar in a screw-top jar. After a week you'll have a scented sugar that is good on soft fruit or in baking, and far more interesting than vanilla sugar. The little orange-scented leaves of the Prince of Orange geranium are good for this, and so is a combination of them with rose geranium leaves.

I like to chop a few rose geranium leaves into soft fruit salads just before serving, and after pressing torn leaves onto the side of pats of cream cheese left overnight, the result is a wonderful accompaniment to raspberries. Macerated in cream and then strained out, they make a sexy panna cotta. Orange-, lemon-, mint-, nutmeg-, apple- and coconut-scented geranium can be used too.

Tunisia makes rose-geranium water, subtler and more complicated than rose water.

GINGER: grown all round the world, ginger is very different dried from when it is fresh. Although many herbs are used both dry and fresh, it is rare for spices like ginger to be so used. Jamaica is a prized source, as is Australia's Queensland.

Crystallised ginger: pieces of ginger impregnated with sugar and with a light dusting of sugar on the outside. It's very good for chopping into baking, from cakes and shortbread to banana cakes, just perfect for adding to ice creams, trifles, grown-up jellies, fruit salads or for the cream that accompanies them. Chopped very finely, it's an intriguing addition to sweet and sour sauces, and in gravy for chicken, duck, goose, salmon or lamb, particularly if you also add sliced fresh dates.

Dried ginger root and ground ginger: fire but less fragrance, and I do not use dried ginger very much, as it can add a dimension that is medicinal rather than culinary. It is *de rigueur* in cake making and then I like it enormously. Gingerbread can be many things—from a rich treacley dark cake to unique chewy, thin Grasmere gingerbread, made and sold only in that Lakeland village. Unusually, ground rather than fresh ginger is correct in Moroccan tagines and other cookery.

Fresh/green ginger: peeled and sliced thinly, the intoxicating mix of pungency and perfume is fabulous with stewed rhubarb, wonderful with beef, excellent with chicken and almost indispensable with fish of all kinds, particularly when poached. Always use a little more than you think for the pungency cooks out.

For an original condiment, chop fresh ginger root and squeeze it through a garlic press, then use this enticing juice to refresh sauces just prior to serving or offer it as a dip for something oriental or fishy. The garlic press extracts useful juice when ginger is too fibrous to use in slices or to chop, so use this tasty sap to flavour a chocolate ice cream, a chocolate custard or mousse, or in a butter cream to paste together a sponge you will top with cream and strawberries.

If you have good stock, cook it for five minutes with matchsticks of ginger plus four or five other contrasted vegetables—cucumber, green pepper, celery, carrot, radish and so on and you'll have an elegant oriental soup. For authentic flavour in Chinese dishes add finely chopped fresh ginger and garlic a few minutes before serving.

Pink sushi ginger: the subtle sweet-sharp flavour and crisp texture are invaluable once discovered, pickles for aristocratic palates, for this holds its place with caviar. Carrots with grated green ginger are good, but elevate when strewn with strips of pink sushi ginger, especially white or purple carrots. Sushi ginger is heavenly served with fish of all kinds, even the most expensive smoked salmon, which you will find superior to a lake of lemon juice. I stir some into any sort of seafood risotto just before serving—it is fugitive when heated. Terrific in salads, fantastically good to enliven ham sandwiches and good with poached fruit.

Baking would over power it in fruit pies, so I chop it into cream to go with such as apple pie, adding enough sugar to temper but not disguise the acidity. 'Yummy pink stuff' said great-nephew Daniel, aged four.

Preserved ginger: the one in syrup, can be used in ways that enhance its sweet tang. Elizabeth David recommends its use in white dough to make ginger tea breads, and it enhances many ice creams—vanilla, chocolate, coffee and strawberry, for example. The syrup is a more elegant friend to chilled melon than an eye-watering dust of sugar and ground ginger.

Young ginger: thinly sliced and lightly pickled in Chinese white vinegar with a touch of sugar, is used as a condiment and as you would any other pickle.

GOLDEN NEEDLES: dried day-lily buds with a musky-sweet flavour. They must be soaked, rinsed and have their knobbly ends picked off. Over soaking can soften them too much; 30 minutes is enough. Add to stir-fries for the last few minutes and to hot/sour soups particularly. Some say these are made from tiger lillies and perhaps they are but as day lilies are commonly eaten fresh, those seem more likely.

GOMASHIO: a flavoursome Japanese condiment that can cut down on salt if you like the taste of sesame. Toast sesame seeds, mix five parts of seeds to one of salt, crush or grind and keep in an airtight container.

GRAINS OF PARADISE: also malagueta pepper, and often called for in older recipes. They have a strong sharp flavour, with the eucalypt/camphor tones of cardamom, and the best equivalent or substitute is a mix of cardamom and black pepper. The real thing has a sting like that of the Szechwan or Australian mountain pepper, that numbs as well as bites. This spice is integral to Voodoo charms and love potions, otherwise the grains can be chewed to sweeten the breath and are used to flavour Swedish Aquavit.

GUARANA: a small Amazonian berry that looks like a madman's eye. Used indigenously for centuries as a stimulant as it contains both caffeine and theobromine, the exciter in chocolate, and like acai powder is commonly used in health and other drinks. Another with great health claims and some contradictory opinions.

GUM ARABIC: a natural, edible gum from select varieties of acacia trees with virtually no scent or flavour that's used as a fixative and binding agent in scented foods and breads. If you are sybaritic enough to want scents wherever you go, mix one part (a tablespoon, perhaps) of powdered gum arabic to three parts rose water, or almond oil, vanilla extract or something equally aromatic. Mix until a thick paste forms, and then use your palms to roll small beads that harden overnight. They can be threaded and worn close to the skin or carried in a warm pocket, whence they will dispense their headiness. Your favourite commercial scent can also be used and it's worth experimenting with powdered spice mixtures.

To crystallise flower petals, mix one part gum arabic with three parts rose water, brush them all over with this solution, sprinkle with caster sugar, and dry on a rack in a dry, warm place.

HONEYSUCKLE FLOWERS: the woodbine's intense, sweet perfume can be captured and used to flavour creams and syrups, including ice cream. Dried honeysuckle is less successful.

HORSERADISH: this habitué of English railway cuttings is used more as a condiment than a flavouring but start to experiment and you'll be impressed. It is called a horse radish because the root can grow as long as 25 cm/10 inch, very big compared to an ordinary radish, and horse is commonly used to indicate excess size, as in horse mushrooms, horse mackerel and so on.

The distinctive super-pungent, tear-jerking aroma and taste-heat only happen when the root is grated or scraped, for this breaks down the cells allowing two components to form a volatile oil, the same oil as in black mustard seeds. When freshly grated, the taste is severe, the fumes alone making your eyes water and nose run.

I'm not fond of it freshly grated and mixed with vinegar or a little milk to accompany roast beef—it overwhelms. A few scrapings folded into crème fraîche, sour cream, whipped cream or mayonnaise, perhaps also with garlic, is a much better thing and also good with fish, especially smoked eel, mackerel or salmon. Or, buy a tube of *pepparots visp*, a preparation of horseradish and cream the Swedes use to smear on thin slices of reindeer meat. Next time you serve cold meats, make a gentle horseradish and cream sauce and just see how good it is.

If prepared with a very light hand, horseradish and cream sauce can be served very successfully with grilled lobster or salmon. And if not on the salmon then stir both horseradish cream and cream into crushed potatoes, with garlic too, and a few scrapes of nutmeg: that goes with almost everything but is best with grilled steak or roast beef. Cuisine brute.

An easily available Polish condiment mixes horseradish with beetroot, as *krajne* or something similar. However it is said or spelled, little is better with smoked trout, salmon or smoked mackerel, or indeed with any smoked or salty meat.

IRISH MOSS: also known as carrageen, this seaweed-based product is very good for you, and is used to set liquids in the same way as agar-agar.

JAGGERY: see *Palm Sugar.*

JASMINE ESSENCE/EXTRACT: called *mali* in Thailand, where it is used to perfume sweet syrups and custards. You should do the same. Add it to thick coconut cream and serve that instead of dairy cream with tropical fruits or, wondrously, with strawberries and it can be used in anything milky or creamy, in ice creams, cakes, icings and biscuits. Wonderful stuff. It is sold in Thai shops, where you might also look for *essence of pandan*, q.v.

JUNIPER BERRIES: their ancient reputation as an appetite stimulant is probably why the English and Dutch flavour raw spirits with the juniper berry, thus giving us gin in its many guises. The unique flavour of juniper—half resinous, half fragrance—is very important in marinades for game or if you want to add gaminess. Pig's liver, usually too strong to eat by itself, becomes very good if soaked in milk overnight and then in a marinade of white wine and crushed juniper berries, with which it is baked whole.

The berries can be used to make rabbit taste like hare, and lamb like mutton, although I'd rather have those meats untampered. Better use the berry to complement rather than vanquish venison and other game animals.

The juniper-based flavour of gin is not used a lot in cooking because it is fragile when heated, but if strengthed with crushed juniper berries you get good results.

Gin has an amazing affinity with pineapple, something to do to pineapple served in a prawn or other seafood cocktail, and decoration for a cake or trifle. Serving fresh pineapple doused with a slug of gin is mystifyingly wondrous. I know nothing else so magically different from how they both began.

KAFFIR LIME: see *Makrut.*

KAPI: see *Shrimp Paste.*

KATSUOBUSHI: shaved flakes of dried bonito (tuna), a basic of Japanese cooking, used with kombu seaweed to flavour dashi, the basic stock. Sold in flakes, these lose flavour very quickly, so keep them well sealed and buy only as much as you expect to use quickly. Tear jerkingly expensive.

KATSUO DASHI: liquid bonito extract—a simpler way to make dashi, used by itself or with kombu dashi, which is liquid kelp extract.

KRACHAI: a rarely used Thai ingredient, this is wild or white ginger and has a fascinating flavour, rather citric at first but perfumed enough to be confused with galangal. It is used in *kapi* balls, an essential part of Khao Chae, the extraordinary dish of iced jasmine rice that is the basis of a Royal Thai banquet. There's a recipe in GC Tastes Royal Thailand, the book that accompanied my TV series.

KOKUM: little known outside southwest India, kokum is also called fish tamarind. You soak it and then use the refreshingly acidic liquid rather than the kokum itself, as if lime or lemon juice. It has particular cooling qualities and kokum sherbet is grateful relief to locals during stultifying days of summer. The dried, halved fruit is purplish, like shrivelled plums, and the darker the colour the higher the grade. Grain-queen Jenni Muir says the aromatic pink liquid was topped up with gin (she thinks) to make the best cocktail she's tasted before or since.

LAVENDER: the musky overtones lavender has over rosemary are addictive. The spikes and leaves will replace rosemary in almost any recipe, especially with fish and veal. Lavender and carrot soup is special.

Use the flowers or the leaves. Lightly, lightly is the rule but beware. The only lavenders you should use in kitchens are English lavenders, *lavandula angustifolia*. English lavenders do not have that butterfly thing on top—those are French lavenders and far too bitter. Only very few varieties of *angustifolia* are powerful enough: the dusky-dark darling Hidcote is very good, but best of all is the old variety Dilly-dilly.

Countless lavender farms with cafés serve lavender scones greedily guzzled. To me they were always inedible, for lavender flowers, often French ones, had been mixed in, so your tongue was nastily assailed by bombs of bitterness. It's the oil you are best advised to use and to eat. Culinary lavender oils are available, as are instructions to make your own but be sure you are using *angustifolia*.

Store flowers in caster sugar to make very useful lavender sugar. Make lavender tea the same way. Simpler is to store lavender sprigs with tea bags in something air tight. Otherwise, gently simmer masses of English or French lavender flowers in water to make a concentrated lavender essence. Don't use this for cooking, but dilute it and use it to spray linen when ironing.

LEMON BALM: regarded as a weed, for it is more prolific than rabbits. That's a good thing, for then you can use it in greater quantities. Enjoy its clean citrus flavour instead of, or in tandem with, lemon; in stuffings for poultry or fish, finely sliced in salads (very good) and to add a tang of taste and colour to fruit salads. Strew bunches in your bath while it is running and you'll be rewarded with a heavenly smell. It makes delicious tea, too.

LEMON GRASS: particularly associated with Thai food, this citric grass is also used in Sri Lankan, Mauritian and other tropical cuisines. Its fragrance is closer to lemon balm than lemon and there is thus a hint of sweetness. It works best when fresh, although dried versions of the finest quality make an exceptional tisane.

The best flavour of fresh lemon grass is in the fleshier bulb end, but precisely how much and which part you use depends on the dish. When used fresh, perhaps to finish stir-fried prawns or to flavour a Western-style salad, the bulb end only is crushed and very thinly sliced, and even so it can be woody. In long-cooked dishes, the whole stem is more likely to be bashed flat and used whole, and then removed before serving. Then thinly sliced fresh lemon grass will be added for the last few minutes to freshen the flavour. Thai cooks usually combine lemon grass with other citric flavours, including lemon zest and lemon juice, lime juice and *makrut* q.v. In Sri Lanka it is likely to appear in their sensational white curries, based on coconut milk and cream and gentle spices.

Lemon grass is a natural companion to fish but its extraordinary range of affinities is still being discovered in the West. It goes anywhere lemon or lime might. It is terrific on tomato salads and a spritely change from basil. When macerated in cream it makes a terrific custard or crème brûlée, but you must be bold with it.

LEMONS, SALTED/PRESERVED: specially associated with the heights of Moroccan cooking, the skins of salt-preserved lemons offer one of the world's most intensely fragrant and perfumed flavours. But only if they are the correct kind of lemon, those that are thin skinned, short, fat and have a pronounced pointy-outey navel at one end. They should not be cooked too long or used finely chopped, but there are exceptions.

Preserved lemons should be sold in the brine in which they have been preserved but are so salt laden they survive a very long time out of brine; I keep them in a sealed container in the refrigerator, even a plastic bag will do. To use, rinse well under running cold water and then extract the insides; these are not traditionally used but in fact make a perfectly good, salty ingredient for inclusion in stews, soups or stock. Taste, and if still too strong, soak in cold water for a short time.

The skin is then sliced into strips, quite wonderful added to fish sauces or to melted butter for fish. It adds the affinity lemon has with fish without dousing it in lemon juice, often done to excess. The only time to chop salted lemon finely is to shower caviar or oysters, neither of which are eaten with lemon juice by people who (a) know what they are doing and (b) like the flavours of caviar and oysters. The choppings do well in salads or on hot or cold poached salmon or any other fish, but this is not as luxurious as strips. Chicken sings whenever salt lemon is combined with it, as does anything in mayonnaise, especially Coronation Chicken. It's a revelation in potato and tomato salad.

The best are sold loose from bowls of brine in Moroccan and Middle Eastern shops, but avoid any pale coloured, that are too firm, have thick skins, or that do not have the extruded navel.

In Morocco the favoured varieties for salt preserving are *doqq* or *boussera* lemons, *citron beldi* in French, and the best Western variety is the Meyer lemon, actually a hybrid with other citruses, which explains its sweetness. No variety gives an inedible or bad result and instructions for making your own are easily found.

LEMON VERBENA/VERVEINE: often macerated in *eau-de-vie* as a digestive with kick, this leaf has a sharp citric flavour with overtones of lime. It makes a fragrant herbal infusion and an excellent addition to stuffings, under the skin of roasting chickens, in any kind of fish cookery or like lemon balm, used in great profusion to scent a bath—even a foot bath is invigorating.

LIME LEAVES/KAFFIR LIMES: see *Makrut.*

LIMES, DRIED: a basic of Iranian food, cooked in meat dishes to give another experience of the wide spectrum of citrus. The flavour is like lime, higher, thinner and sharper lime, with a fragile woody note, and these blossom into richer flavours once in the same saucepan as anything buttery or sweet. I've used them with all manner of vegetables, most notably a couple of dried limes cooked with pumpkin, apple and potato made a very superior soup.

LIQUORICE/LICORICE ROOT: a natural sweetener that contains no sugar, it can be used to stir drinks or made into a sweetening brew by boiling in water. The active sweetener is so powerful that one drop can be detected in 50,000 drops of water. Liquorice is having a renaissance as a natural sweetener in herbal tisanes. A mixture of liquorice and mint was awarded Three Gold Stars at the Great Taste Awards—mint tea with no need of extra sugar or calories. Heaven.

Chewing liquorice instead of sweets is said to have helped many give up smoking, but it's also thought to be an infallible aphrodisiac, especially for women; it does contain traces of oestrogen.

Liquorice ice cream has been appearing in restaurants for a few decades now, but has always seemed bizarre. The solution, suggested by great-niece Natalia, was to chop liquorice allsorts into a softened, simpler flavoured ice cream and then to refreeze that, and this works exceptionally well.

LOCUST BEANS: see *Carob.*

LONG PEPPERS: whole ones look like small catkins and like cartwheels when cut across. The better ones are from Java, and have an extraordinarily evocative aroma and taste; peppery-hot yes, stingingly so, but also supremely sensual, for there are clear notes of frankincense and iris, perhaps even of Parma violets, suggestive of the stew of harems. Javanese long peppers can be up to 2.54 cm/1 inch long: Indian long pepper is shorter and not quite as stirring of the senses, Cambodia makes Kampot red long pepper, very good with anything eggy.

LOVAGE: looking like huge celery and having something of the flavour, all parts of the lovage plant can be used. Mainly it is added to soups and stews.

Gin is now flavoured smoothly with it and in the West Country they make a cordial, which, mixed with brandy, is said to be the best soother of upset stomachs. Make your own by steeping the root in brandy. Supposedly good in baths; the leaf I presume.

MACE: the lacy outer covering of the nutmeg kernel and altogether more elegant. Largely overlooked now but essential in Georgian and Victorian kitchens. Used instead of nutmeg, mace brightens and lightens fruit cookery, pork sausages and pâtés, chocolate dishes and has a special affinity with the cherry. As whole blades or ground, mace should be a pale yellow-ochre—the paler the better.

MAIDENHAIR: see *Capillaire*.

MAHLAB: these are cherrystone kernels and can be bitter or sweet. Found in Greek stores and probably Turkish and Middle Eastern ones, too, they give a great density of almond/cherry flavour, and are a basic of Turkish Delight. Russians use mahlab when making cherry kissel, and the Greeks use it to flavour their large Easter loaves—Tsourekia.

MAKRUT *previously Kaffir Lime leaf:* the fleshy, dark green, shiny leaf of a knobbly variety of lime used almost exclusively in Thai cookery, but with a great deal to offer to others. The zested skin is transporting, perkier, brighter and more nuanced than other citruses. Both zest and leaf lend captivating full, rich, citric flavour but with overtones of brilliantine and thus must not be overdone; especially good in conjunction with lemon grass.

Each leaf is a figure of eight; Thai recipes mean the whole, double-lobed thing when they specify a 'leaf'. Unless very young, remove the central spine before use and ignore older, coarser leaves anyway. Makrut leaf is available fresh in Thai shops, and freezes very well, so buy a bag when you see it but I've never found dried ones worth using.

When flavouring a stock or a stew, tear leaves into big pieces, a visual reminder these are not meant to be eaten. Once done, fish them out, and replace with fresh leaves tightly rolled and very finely sliced, which freshen the flavour dramatically and can be eaten. Scissors are better than knives for the slicing.

Western cooking has much to explore with makrut. It has a spectacular affinity with lamb, so stuff plenty of rolled leaves under the skin, the way you would rosemary, roast the ordinary way; remove the leaves as you slice. Amazing hot or cold, so resolve to do the same to chicken, turkey or duck, particularly. Razor-thinly sliced young leaves are excellent on tomato salads and in potato and seafood salads.

Pounce on any makrut fruit you see. They are the size of other limes but very, very wrinkled. There is next to no juice, but the zest is other worldly. Using this grated directly over something, so the almost invisible oils are caught, can be enough to convince guests you have been cooking all night and day. It keeps its flavour very well when cooked. Be bold. Use makrut everywhere that you would have used citrus. A makrut crème brûlée served with tropical fruits perhaps, or in a chocolate sauce for ice cream, or in a ganache for chocolate cake or grown-up fairy cakes; and think about macerating them in cream for an ice cream, for the milk for a bread-and-butter pudding, in a baking-powder loaf made with makrut rather than orange, or dare I say it, as the zest in madeleines. Think skate wing with makrut rather than orange zest in the scorched butter, a rabbit pie served with grated zest—or makrut butter on lobster or scampi or turbot or snapper or ...

The trees need only a temperate climate to flourish, and so make a good addition to an English orangerie or sunny terrace, as long as they come inside when frosts threaten. The little effort is vastly repaid if you raise fruits as well as leaves.

MALI: see *Jasmine essence.*

MARIGOLD: not commonly used now, but the dried petals are recommended as an interesting alternative to saffron for colouring stews and casseroles, soups, breads and buns. The slight flavour can be rather exciting with poultry dishes and the fresh petals make an excellent addition to mixed salads.

If you are a butter or cheese maker, marigold was the original colouring before annatto was imported. It can still add life to cream or cottage cheeses.

MASTIC/ GUM MASTIC: mastic has the resinous overtones you would expect from the natural gum of a tree; the precise tree is the lentisk, a type of Pistacia. The flavour is fascinating when used in moderation, but is bitter and unpleasantly haunting when over used—a little is amazing in rice pudding and it is also used in cakes and sweet breads. Mastic marries well with rose water and orange-flower water, and so with all their sweet-spiced friends, when it adds a hint of resinous mystery.

Although related to the flavours of ouzo and retsina wine, mastic is a different substance from the ones used in those. The Greek island of Chios makes a rather special liqueur called mastica, flavoured with the gum from their variety of lentisk, unique to the island; the Turks use mastic to flavour their fire water—raki. If Greeks come bearing gifts of gum mastic, always accept because it can be hard to find. If you find the Greek has delicious breath, he or she may well have been using mastic as chewing gum.

MARJORAM: closely related to oregano, sweet or knotted marjoram is used with grills, tomatoes, poultry and fish. The flavour is reminiscent of thyme, but warmer, slightly spicy and definitely sweet. Although it can play an important part in flavouring such vegetable dishes as ratatouille, I don't think it works with red meats like beef or game. I use it in smoked mackerel pâté, helped by tomato. It is quite fugitive and should only be added to hot dishes shortly before serving. Pot marjoram is another name for oregano.

MINT: the large family of flavoured mints provides a simple and accessible way to start experimenting with herbs and herb teas. Any decent plant nursery will have a variety of them, most of which can be used for culinary purposes.

Dried mint is one of the few herbs that tastes the same as when fresh, but both dried and fresh mint reduce in flavour alarmingly if heated for any length of time, so always use at least twice what you first thought of when cooking with them and then think about refreshing the flavour with fresh leaves before serving if you can.

I loathe 'traditional' mint sauce, even though it is one of the few survivors of medieval sauces; the idea of dousing sweet lamb meat in sugar and vinegar is appalling, and emerged only mid-19th century. Before that lamb was rarely eaten and then served with jellies or sauces made from the berries that grew on the same hills it did. Mutton was the thing and the forequarter considered infinitely better than the hind leg. Once New Zealand began to send Britain plenty of cheap frozen lamb in 1882, budgets and good sense persuaded a national change of taste. At the same time the growth of the cities meant it was more likely you had a patch of mint at the door than a rowan tree. Convenience rather than culinary sense meant acidic mint sauce, which perfectly complemented the strong meat of mutton, was thoughtlessly served with the sweet flesh of lamb. Horrid.

Stuff lamb with sprigs of mint, roast it on a bed of mint, and serve it with a spoonful of the juices you have pressed from that bed, and you have something quite superlative. This works sensationally with chicken too, and cold minted chicken is the most marvellous picnic food. Mint leaves are generously crushed for the mint julep of the southern United States, and are essential in a powerful Pimms, doubly good and dangerous made with champagne rather than lemonade.

Dried mint works well in grain-based stuffings; it makes a tantalising, original contribution when added to Eastern combinations that also include currants, dried fruits and nuts.

Pennyroyal: a wild variety of mint that has extra dimensions of flavour.
Peppermint: thought to be a hybrid, has a definite extra fizzle on the tongue, has a reddish stalk (the darker the better) and is the proper one for mint tea.
Spearmint: is mellow and usually has a green stalk.
Other mint flavours: include eau-de-cologne, pineapple, lemon, orange, apple and champagne. These smaller, whole leaves are perfect for salads, for decorating or perfuming cakes and fruit dishes (see *Geraniums*). Eau-de-cologne mint is pungent and needs to be used with great discretion but is wonderful in summer salads and drinks.

MIRIN: a sweetened Japanese rice wine rarely used for drinking but added to marinades and grilled dishes when it is combined with soy and other sauces; Chinese rice wines, like Shao-Hsing are equivalents, but these are also used for drinking. There are processed and flavoured varieties, known as *aji-mirin*.

MONOSODIUM GLUTAMATE (MSG): don't stop reading! MSG is potentially one of the most important and useful ingredients in your kitchen, particularly if you have a heart problem. Like salt, MSG does not alter the flavour of food but stimulates the flavour buds of your tongue, so they can taste what is in the mouth.

Unlike salt MSG has no flavour, so those who say they can taste MSG are quite wrong, but they may detect the effects of its over-use, for then the taste buds will be stimulated to such a frenzy of sensitivity they will taste aspects of food, even of saliva, never encountered before. If salt stimulated such a reaction you would taste only salt, and probably vomit.

Forget MSG allergy, now largely replaced by other 'allergies'. Used properly, MSG is perfectly safe, even for babies according to the United States FDA, one of the world's toughest food safety agencies. There will be a few who have unfortunate reactions but this is particularly rare and orange juice is more likely to be a culprit. The problem is that in the West we misuse it.

A large amount of MSG on an empty stomach upsets almost 50% of the world's population, including the Chinese. Chinese soup is likely to have the highest amount of MSG on the menu, to make weak stock taste stronger and this creates an immediate problem if the soup is eaten as a first course on an empty stomach. Yet eat soup the way Chinese do in the middle of the meal, or sip it during the meal, and it is unlikely there will be a reaction.

Bad chefs do over-use MSG, and that is to be deplored. But would you ban chips because sometimes they are served too soggy or oily and made you feel sick?

MSG is a glutamate. Our body manufactures glutamates, and they are naturally in many foods, tomatoes and roasted meats in particular. Indeed, it may be their very presence that makes them so enjoyable and differs us from animals. A school of thought thinks appreciation of the glutamate flavour in roasted meats was one of the first steps from ape to man. That savour is called umami and has been added to the basic tastes of food: sweet, sour, bitter, hot and salty. Chinese call it *jian* and have also added *jiang*, translated as the fragrant or aromatic flavours of wine and spirits, garlic, spring onions and spices.

MSG is very widely used in processed foods as a flavour enhancer because of its ability to make the tongue taste more flavour when less is actually there. It's a great contributor to anyone with a slow tongue or with heart problems. Lazy taste buds require more salt to get flavour of any kind, and can demand so much that salt is all that's tasted. Take the salt away, perhaps on the recommendation of a doctor, and they get so little gratification from eating they are bound to slip from their diet. The secret is judicious amounts of MSG. It has far less sodium than salt and is, anyway, used in far smaller amounts; by helping the subject to mouth gratification they will be likely to stay on their diet.

A broad rule is to use a quarter to half the amount of MSG you would of salt: for those who merely want to cut down a little, a mixture of MSG and salt works wonders. Even for those with no health problems, MSG can be a boon. If you have created something you know tastes terrific, but is fairly light on flavour, don't add salt. Add small amounts of MSG, and that will greatly enhance what you have created. But remember, that is only in your opinion. To some it will be over-flavoured, to others it will still require seasoning to make their tongue work. But at least the MSG will help prevent your food tasting only of salt.

For more about tastes, tasting and your tongue, see my book *How to Cook Without Recipes* (Portico).

MUSTARD: white, brown or black mustard seeds are from plants of the cabbage family. Combinations of ground seeds or mixtures of the coarsely crushed seeds together with a variety of liquids are what give the broad palette of mustard flavours.

Although introduced to Western Europe by the Romans 2,000 years ago and thought of as basic to English cookery, it is actually used very little other than on our plates and for devilling. The introduction of sweeter American mustard that coincided with the invasion of the hamburger has done more to create interest in mustard in the United Kingdom than the increasing tiers of gaudy prepared mustards.

Mustard heat and flavour develop only when the crushed or ground seed is in contact with water. Mustard powder, even when used to flavour, say, a cheese sauce, should first be mixed with water and left to develop for ten minutes.

It is also important to remember the hotness and flavour of mustard disappears with time and cooking. If you want the heat rather than the flavour of mustard, you should add to sauces or casseroles just before serving, or use a great deal. If you use too much you simply cook longer, if you can. Your reward is a remarkably fragrant flavour that is savoury and fascinating and more profound than expected. Seeded mustards are commonly added to finish sauce for rabbit, but are also marvellous in sauces for leeks, in cauliflower cheese, to flavour baked salmon or other fish, or in a sauce to go with them. Mixed generously with yoghurt it is a great marinade for chicken or pork, and this can be used as a barbecue dip, too, perhaps with a squeeze of garlic.

Having a germicidal action, mustard acts as a preservative in vegetable pickles and preserves. The seeds, or lightly crushed seeds, keep their virtue relatively longer than does the powder. It is called for to start mayonnaise because mustard is a wizard at keeping emulsions together.

American mustard: sweetened with sugar and made only with the milder white mustard seed, this is a creamier consistency spread with a nonchalance that would strip your mouth if it were the English type. It can contain a lot of additives, largely unnecessary in view of mustard's preservative abilities. It's the only mustard to eat with hamburgers or frankfurters, and an interesting base for sauces.

Bordeaux mustards: usually have herbs added.

Dijon mustards: should be mixed with grape juice and can be almost as hot as English; either is excellent for spreading on steaks or other meats before grilling or roasting, and give a touch of interest when mixed into a good mayonnaise.

English mustard: sold as a powder or ready prepared and usually made of brown and white mustard seeds, with the addition of wheat flour if it is for the United Kingdom market. Prepared English mustard is not quite as strong as the freshly-made kind but English mustard sold in the United States is hotter than in England, because it is pure ground mustard seed.

Mix mustard powder with cold water and leave to stand for five to ten minutes, which allows the pungency to develop. Salt and vinegar both inhibit the development of flavour, as will very hot water. If you then mix in milk or cream the flavour is mellower and more complementary.

Hot mustard disguises flavour in other foods and the appeal is the serotonins released when you burn your tongue. Those who insist on ruining their food and palate mix mustard with malt or wine vinegar and even add horseradish, which is what they do to Tewkesbury mustard.

Making your own mustard powder is easy with a pestle and mortar: use a variety of mustard seeds and grind some into powder, some into pieces. Honey goes very well in mustard mixtures, but isn't a good idea if you are going to coat meat or fish for grilling, as it will caramelise and burn.

French mustard: a broad term, covering many mustards that in general are far less strong than English types, mainly through being mixed with other aromatics, thus lessening the proportion of heat to flavour. See *Dijon*.

German mustard: usually mild and sweet, often with herbs; *Austrian mustard* might be tarragon-flavoured.

Grain mustards: popular to the point of swamping the market are mustards made with whole or crushed grains and add visual interest as well as flavour. Use them liberally in stuffings particularly for salmon or trout (the heat largely cooks out, remember) or in vegetable purées.

Mustard oil: essential for authentic Bangladeshi, Bengali and Punjabi cookery. It is very hot, but is a good way to get a controllable heat plus interesting base flavour for curries when used rather than bland vegetable oils. It is used in commercial styles of Italy's *mostarda di frutta*.

NAM PLA: see *Fish sauce*.

NIGELLA: a southern Indian seed with a complex, onion-pepper flavour in each tiny black seed, often mistaken for onion seed. Dry roasting or microwaving brings out more of the nutty pepperiness. Used as a sprinkle over rice or vegetables particularly potatoes and specially good in bread or tossed onto South Asian or North African flat breads.

NUTMEG: must be used sparingly and should always be grated from a whole nutmeg, for it loses its flavour and develops a soapy, thin flavour when ground and stored. It is extraordinarily flexible, equally at home in sweet and savoury dishes. You can buy nutmeg graters, but it's simple to run a kernel up and down the finer side of a grater or to scrape with a knife.

There are few cheese dishes that do not benefit from the addition of nutmeg; only those that include tomato, like pizza, are better without it. Fondues, soufflés, sauces, rarebits, cheesecakes, salads and sandwiches all benefit.

Nutmeg is a prime ingredient of mixed spice and important to cake, biscuit, or pastry cooking, particularly in association with apples. Hot green vegetables are good with nutmeg, particularly green beans and spinach. It is very good with many meats and excellent in pâté; fine-textured sausages like frankfurters and Bologna sausages invariably include some.

ORANGE-FLOWER WATER: a standby of my kitchen, as it was in every British kitchen well into the 20th century. After the trauma of the First World War, both this and rose water fell from favour after a reign that lasted from the days of the Crusaders. Distilled from the flowers of the Seville or bitter orange, it seems to some to have an off-putting brilliantine scent, a warning it should be used with discretion. Once it is sprinkled over food this scent softens and becomes as fragrant as moonlit nights in orange groves, and quite as sensual.

Arabian, Moorish and eastern Mediterranean kitchens use it lavishly on every conceivable type of meat dish, in breads, pastries, cakes—and you. In Morocco, servants sprinkle guests with orange-flower water after dinner. It is diluted and served as 'white tea', said to be a soporific, especially for young children.

Orange-flower water is also called orange-blossom water or bitter-orange water. Equally you will see citrus-flower water, usually from somewhere Greek, where I suspect lemon blossoms are included, heightening the brilliantine effect, but not badly. In Egypt or Morocco, the water seems softer and richer and I recommend buying it there but read the label—it can be made with imitative chemicals.

Orange-flower water combined with almonds, pistachios, rose water and honey gives exotic flavour to baklava, layered pastry confections found in every country once part of the Ottoman Empire, from the Balkans to Egypt and the Maghreb. It is transformative with anything creamy, from cream to rice puddings, panna cotta, egg custards, crème caramel and, yes crème brûlée. In the days before vanilla, my great-great-great-great-great-great grandmother Mary Senhouse (Fletcher Christian's granny) wrote in the cookbook of Netherhall that such puddings weren't worth making if you did not have orange-flower water. She put caramel under baked custard as well as on top of it and that is very good.

Peaches or strawberries with

orange-flower water are extraordinary. Sprinkle the cut or sliced fruit with caster sugar and then dash with orange-flower water. Leave the combination at room temperature for a couple of hours or in a refrigerator overnight, turning from time to time as the syrup develops. Adjust for sweetness or voluptuousness just before serving. It will be more difficult to convert you to sprinkling orange-flower water over lamb stews, over chickens and over roast kid, but once you've tried it ...

Then move on to rose water. You might make these discoveries in reverse; rose first. With both in your cupboard you are master/mistress of a thousand new flavours, all by varying the amount of one to the other. Other than with strawberries I can think of nowhere I don't mix rose and orange, to blend a different exotic each time. Together or separate they offer the most effective way to stun or impress. The only way to go wrong is to use too much orange-flower water—but who is to say how much is too much? Pretend something excessive is your norm and others will follow. The fashion world relies on this principle; why shouldn't you?

OREGANO: the *rigani* of Greek cooking and the proper, perhaps only, herb that should go on pizza. Wild oregano from Epirus is available on line and something transformative in the kitchen, sprinkled on eggs fried in olive oil, to finish anything with tomato in it, on moussaka or something cheesy. You might forget you have other herbs and spices.

ORGEAT: rarely seen nowadays but once a standby at balls and for summer teas, this is a base for cordials and syrups based on barley-water flavoured further with almond milk and orange-flower water.

PANDAN/PANDANUS: a heady, perfumed flavouring, which is as suggestive, seductive and outright sexy as its other name, screw pine. Look in Thai books for uses, or use sparingly in cream or whipped cream for luscious fruit desserts, for which it also makes an outstanding ice cream. Available as an extract.

PAPRIKA: there are dozens of flavours of paprika, all from two varieties of capsicum or red pepper, one hot and the other sweet.

A recipe that includes paprika as an ingredient but that does not say whether it should be hot or sweet is no recipe. Where paprika is indigenous to cooking a single choice is unlikely, as most houses mix the two to get a taste to their own liking. The combination I like most is three parts of sweet paprika to two of hot.

You might find so-called Spanish paprika is marginally sweeter than so-called Hungarian paprika, which might be slightly hot. Sweetness is sometimes added with sugar, which is why some sweet paprikas tend to caramelise easily. If you wish to add heat to paprika, mix in cayenne pepper, or straight chilli powder.

Recipes call for a lot—20-30 ml/ 3-4 tsp for 900-1200 ml/1½-2 pints of liquid is nothing. I put in half the specified amount when starting and add the rest ten minutes before serving, and this gives more vivid flavours.

Both paprika types are excellent with tomato-based sauces and in Morocco are mixed with ground cumin, a delicious combination. In Sri Lanka they use paprika to pep up the red-colour reading in a curry based on red chilli peppers, but where fewer than usual have been used, to lessen the heat. If you use too much paprika and the dish is too bitter, add acid of some kind and not sweetness; instead choose a touch of dry sherry or balsamic vinegar, lemon, lime or orange juice, pomegranate molasses or, even, tamarind. Soured cream also aids this amelioration, which is why it is found with some but not all paprika-flavoured recipes.

Smoked paprika: newest paprika kid on the block. It's not really new but has been discovered as a 'next big thing'. There are sweet, hot and bittersweet versions. The smoke does pick up and run with some of paprika's inherent flavours, but also emphasises bitter compounds, which is why not everyone likes it.

To show how easy it is to be wrong about the cuisine of other countries, here is an official definition of Hungarian foods flavoured with paprika. Note beef in a rich tomato sauce finished with soured cream, which we all know and love as goulash, doesn't exist. What's more, paprika only became popular in Hungary a century ago.

Goulash or Gulyas: more a soup than a stew, made with beef or veal, onion and chunks of potato and sometimes with small pieces of pasta too. No soured cream.

Porkolt: a meat stew braised rather than boiled, with masses of finely chopped onions that become a thick sauce.

Tokany: fewer onions and only a little paprika, finished with mushrooms and soured cream.

Paprikas: this is the proper name for dishes made with paprika and finished with soured cream or sweet cream. A paprikas is always made with white meats—fish, fowl, veal and lamb. Red meats and fatty birds like duck and goose are never traditionally used.

PARSLEY: the only things you may not already know about parsley are: (a) the best flavour is in the stalk so use that for flavouring stocks, soups and so on and (b) chewing parsley neutralises the odour of onion or garlic on the breath.

Don't ever use dried parsley; it nearly always has a hay-like quality, the antithesis of its appeal when fresh.

Flat-leafed parsley, also known as French parsley or petroushka, looks much better than curly parsley and offers a more flamboyant flavour spectrum but its leaf looks similar to coriander leaf. Most markets differentiate by leaving the root on coriander bunches, but cutting it off parsley, but not all do and supermarkets rarely do.

Thinking of parsley as an ingredient rather than a garnish adds terrific zest to your table with negligible effort or cost. Chop up masses and swirl it into a mash—of anything. Pluck leaves from the stalk and toss them through a salad, even if only of tomatoes. Save leaves for garnish or mash or gravy, but ensure a supporting cast of flavours by roughly chopping the stalks to use as a base for anything you're roasting. Crush the juices from them before straining them out.

Parsley shines in sandwiches and wraps and rolls. Little is as refreshing as the clean, green taste of parsley with otherwise drab cheese or ham: yet it can be the height of elegance with salmon, masterly in hot or cold pasta dishes. Or find a recipe for Burgundian ham, chunks of good ham set willy-nilly in a firm, off-dry, white-wine jelly with masses of parsley. In these freer days you might use a fruity Beaujolais instead.

PEPPERCORNS: possibly the most important spice in the world, certainly the most widespread in use. Native to India and the Far East, peppercorns were the basis of the earliest trade between East and West, and at one time public debts, dowries and rents could be paid in them—hence peppercorn rent.

Black, white, and green peppercorns come from the same climbing vine, and variations are due to the manner and timing of harvesting. For more fascination than you ever thought possible I thoroughly recommend *Pepper—the Spice that Changed the World* (Absolute Press) by Christine McFadden. She also generously helped with tasting notes for less usual peppers but emphasises that, like wine, cheese, tea, chocolate and coffee, changes of climate will affect *terroir* and resultant flavours year on year and thus what might happen in your mouth. That's the excitement.

Espelette pepper is actually a chilli; see page 236.

Black peppercorns: aromatic, sharp tasting, and beloved of thoughtless recipe writers who demand freshly ground black pepper with everything. These are whole peppercorns picked when slightly underripe and then dried and sold in their entirety. Black pepper is indeed very good but it is dangerous in the hands of those frightful people who screw it over everything before tasting what is before them.

We are used to two flavours of pepper, that of long cooking and freshly ground. In cooking, the pungent piperine oil oxidises and diminishes after about five minutes of cooking. When you grind on fresh pepper to eat the dish, you enrich the thin flavour left after cooking.

There is a third experience, the complex result of heating ground black pepper for just a short while to finish a dish, which brings the many flavour components into full, bursting vitality. Stir coarsely ground pepper into anything hot no more than three minutes before serving and the flavour becomes zingy and fresh and complicated. Stir it into a stew, grind it on to grilled or pan-fried fish, chicken or meat and then keep cooking but for not longer than three minutes before you serve it. Include it in a rarebit mixture rather than putting it on afterwards; it's especially good added generously to a garam masala, the mixed spice that is properly used to temper a curry, that is to be added just for the last few minutes so that all the spices are enlivened. Such a good trick, and another of those that make people think you have been cooking for days.

Pepper guru Christine McFadden says peppercorns are never roasted, not in India, anyway. I find this an intensely interesting and flavoursome way to double your culinary repertoire with little effort and no added expense. The microwave is the surest way to do this without burning or added oil, as the peppercorns roast in their own oils and brown throughout rather than just outside. Arrange them on a circle on a plate and check every few minutes; the technique is the same for micro-roasting nuts. Micro-roast peppercorns lightly or quite dark and ideally keep both styles on hand.

A ham or a tomato sandwich with roasted black peppercorns is quite different from those with plain black pepper. So are salads, vegetables, eggs and, of course, all manner of stews when you are stirring them in for the last three minutes of cooking. It may not be the done thing in India, but roasted black peppercorns have gone down very well everywhere else in the world I have demonstrated or served them. They make a wondrous difference to a gravadlax you make yourself.

Brazilian: aromatic and very hot with piperine. A robust, all-purpose pepper.

Indian: generically a hot pepper with less aroma and character, and useful in cooking but not as gratifying fresh.

Madagascan: aromatic and hot; an excellent substitute if Brazilians are unavailable.

Malabar: mid-quality and with coarser pungency and flavour than the Tellicherry.

Tellicherry: widely thought the Rolls-Royce, with a comparatively mellow bite but full complex flavour experienced only when crushed or ground.

Sarawak: the mildest, sweetest and most fragrant and by far the most rewarding to use freshly ground on vegetables and salads, and for tossing into sauces just before serving, which dramatises their flavour.

Vietnamese: now dominant on the international market, these offer elegant, scented flavour.

GREEN PEPPERCORNS: exactly what they say they are, under-ripe peppercorns, and most delicious. Quite soft, so they crush into butters or marinades where the colour is useful and the mild heat comes with a unique green, prickly aroma. Buy green peppercorns packed only in brine; those packed in vinegar lack elegance and usefulness. The brine from green peppercorns is a useful flavouring agent itself, just right for adding a dash to a stock or sauce, particularly for fish.

To keep green peppercorns, turn into a screw-top jar and just cover them with a medium-strength brine solution. They will last for months in the refrigerator and that brine will soon take on their flavour. It may go black, but the peppercorns will be fine once rinsed; make more brine and recover them. It is simpler to replace the brine with vodka, of course, and a sip of the vodka is a remarkably stimulating thing when you're out of cookery ideas.

Steak au poivre made with green rather than black peppercorns is delightful: I'm tempted to think this is the proper way to do this overdone and often palate-searing dish. Green peppercorns go very well with fatty meats and thus complement well a duck or goose.

> *Dried green peppercorns:* need to be ground or crushed and don't have the subtle overtones or flavour of the softer, tinned ones.
> *Fermented green peppercorns:* Cambodia ferments green peppercorns under salt, giving a rare combination of heat with fruitiness and spice.

RED PEPPERCORNS: the rare fully-ripe peppercorn, for the crop is usually harvested earlier to avoid the risk of ruin by too dry or too wet weather. Said to include flavours like pineapple, banana and toffee, these are lost if brined like green peppercorns. Cambodia ferments them.

WHITE PEPPERCORNS: these are whole peppercorns left to mature and redden on the vine and then soaked to remove the outer husk. The creamy corns underneath are hotter than black pepper but do not have its beguiling perfume and flavour. They are rarely fermented, which converts their natural sugars into acids.

White peppercorns are appreciated where black pepper would look nasty, as in béchamel sauce, in scrambled eggs, cream soups, quiche mixtures and so on; you can always grind on black pepper afterwards.

PINK PEPPERCORNS: let the colour warn you—these can be dangerous. Pink peppercorns, which quickly became the *ne plus ultra* of 70s nouvelle cuisine in the United States, never caught on in the United Kingdom, and just as well. Still, I found the flavour perfectly wonderful, something truly new, and my excited broadcast in the early days of London's LBC Radio is still remembered for having hundreds of people scouring the shops in vain. Those pink peppercorns were not peppercorns at all but the processed berries of a pesky Florida Holly, a relation of poison ivy. They could cause nausea, giddiness and fainting, and stimulate excruciatingly large and painful haemorrhoids.

Pink peppercorns are something quite different these days, the berries of the *schinus*, that most fragrant and beautiful of weeping trees, commonly called a pepper tree because of the pungent oil expressed when you crush leaves, something I remember doing on my way home from my first day at Owairaka Primary School in Auckland.

POMEGRANATE MOLASSES: fresh pomegranate juice is a refreshing balance of sweet and acid, a natural sweet-sour sauce but that stains fearfully. Pomegranate molasses is the juice boiled down, so thicker, sweeter, more acidic and luscious. It goes brown if baked or boiled, so best use it as an instant sweet-sour finishing sauce. Baked or grilled fish love the stuff; deliver something different by adding a few olives and buttered couscous. Chicken and pork are great friends of pomegranate.

Combining the molasses and fresh pomegranate seeds gives entrancing spectra of flavours, colour and texture, at its simplest, added to a salad dressing. And don't forget sweet treats. Pomegranate molasses are very good with hot apple pie, indeed with all baked pies or roasted fruits. You can never go wrong with scattering pomegranate seeds over anything. Pomegranate syrup is another name for the molasses.

POPPY SEEDS: the mild, nutty flavour becomes very rich when mixed with eggs, almonds and sugar as fillings for middle European or Russian cakes and breads. The seeds can have a bitter taste that stays on the tongue, but this supposedly disappears if you roast until a light golden brown. Roasted poppy seeds are interesting when incorporated in salad dressings or in dips. They can be added to rice or included in cream sauces for noodles and pastas.

Commonly they are sprinkled, unroasted, over unbaked bread, bread rolls and savoury biscuits, in which case they are usually first mixed with salt or sprinkled with strong brine to add extra flavour. There is a white poppy seed used in Indian cooking.

I think them best when combined with orange zest or glacé orange. Polish Christmas recipes mix cold pasta shapes with roasted poppy seeds and glacé orange, so good you wish for a month of Christmas Days.

RED CURRANTS: the classic accompaniment as a jelly with lamb and game birds, in sauces and gravies. Bar-le-Duc in France makes perfect jellies and preserves with pitted currants at great and justified expense. Rather than buying or making a jelly, just lay a perfect bunch on each plate, and savour each explosion as you crush them one by one in your mouth. When dinner parties lag, ask if anyone remembers the word for taking red currants off the bunch by running the stalk between fork tines?

Pretend not to remember until the last possible second; it's strig.

RIGANI: see *Oregano*.

ROSES: if petals smell good, eat them. Add rose petals to a salad, strew pink petals on Summer Pudding and rose-petal jam is ambrosial with a traditional cream tea or added to the cream of a Victoria sponge with raspberry jam, but use orange-flower water with strawberry jam. When using roses for eating, trim away the lower, white part of the petal, which is bitter. Red damask roses were traditionally best but there are now so many strong-scented varieties that rules are pointless. Also espouse roses as rose water (see next) in authentic Turkish Delight and as a perfect partner in *Rose Pouchong tea* q.v. Rose-flavoured vinegar is excellent and Fortnum and Mason's Rose Petal Jelly, made once a year from English roses is entrancing with scones and clotted or whipped cream.

ROSE WATER/EAU DE ROSE: this brings the entrancing glory of the rose to your recipes and has done so for centuries. Classically distilled from the most fragrant red Damask roses, it was hardly possible to cook throughout the Ottoman world and Europe right up to the death of Queen Victoria unless you used this. Now almost forgotten in Europe, it is still vital in the Moslem world, sprinkled into everything and over you.

Before reading on, please promise to slap anyone who says rose water tastes of soap. Such nonsense. If anything, soap is hoping to taste like rose. It's ok to say you don't like rose water, but it doesn't taste of soap and how can so many billions be wrong for so many centuries?

Rose water tastes like it smells, very rosy, spicy and slightly smoky, too. Its ultimate expression is an affinity with raspberries, for it makes them taste powerfully more of themselves, one of the ultimate culinary aspirations, that of making one plus one equal four or more, yet still remaining true to themselves.

There is no rule about how much you use, sometimes I like to use very little and other times I get away with making the flavour very strong indeed, directly on to fat ripe peaches, into a syrup or cream for sliced oranges or recreating the Shaker habit of incorporating it in baked apple stuffings or in apple pies. Florentine curd pudding is an old English curd cheese, spinach and egg-custard tart with currants, sweet spice and rose water. When did you have rose-flavoured spinach for pudding?

Old-World rose water is amazing with New World chocolate. Flavour a rich chocolate soufflé with rose water, served baveuse and with a hot soft-fruit purée—loganberries would be very good. Perfume a mix of crushed raspberries and cream for a chocolate, vanilla or orange roulade. Serve soaked dried fruit with chopped pistachios and lavish sprinklings of rose water and orange-flower water, almost embarrassingly sensual, served hot or cold, in the morning, afternoon or evening.

Rose water marries well with cream cheese or cream and, as with orange-flower water, will transform the well-known. I once made a croquembouche wedding cake of profiteroles stuffed alternatively with orange and rose-flavoured creams; pouring cream was scented with rose water and the tower was scattered with rose petals. The scents and flavours were bewitching, tantalizing for guests to identify.

Rose water offers the pleasure not only of recreating the food of our forefathers, but also of creating new classics with the broader range of ingredients available today.

ROSEMARY: the thin spiky leaves of rosemary have a camphorous, piney, smoky flavour, particularly liked in Italy but often hated elsewhere. Some food writers—Elizabeth David, I think—don't like rosemary at all and others worry about the spikes 'getting' everywhere. I like it very much when fresh and used with great discretion: I dislike it very much when it is dried.

The warm, smoky but nicely sharp flavour of fresh rosemary is quite unlike anything else and makes an incomparable contribution to good eating. I like to plunge a whole branch of the fresh stuff into a tomato sauce for 10-15 minutes; this is more than enough for its perfume to be transferred, and then I yank the branch out leaving only a few potentially offensive bits. If I'd used a dried twig it would leave a mess of spikes behind.

Rosemary twigs are better or best for perfuming barbecued or spit-roasted food.

A small sprig of fresh rosemary is excellent when brewed with Indian tea—very good for relieving tension headaches. Rosemary is for remembrance and where it grows it is said to show the woman rules the house. It makes dense, aromatic hedges, seen surrounding holy places in the Moslem world, but it's rarely used in their kitchens.

ROWAN: the wild-gathered bitter, bright, scarlet-orange berries of the rowan or mountain ash also fruit in villages, towns and cities. Forage them to make gorgeously red jelly that retains acidity, has a hint of bitterness and a light, distinctive flavour. A favourite with lamb and excellent with game and birds.

RUE: this bitter aromatic herb is not fashionable in the kitchen nowadays, and was used only in great moderation with lighter flavoured red meats and poultry, sometimes with potatoes. The only time I've enjoyed it is in grappa, the fiery Italian equivalent of marc, a spirit distilled from what's left after wine has been pressed—skins, pips and pulp. Sardinians put a long stem of rue into each bottle of their grappa, for rue is thought to be a digestive aid. *Grappa con rutta* turns a pale green and has a more appealing perfume and flavour.

SAFFLOWER: this flower can give the same colour as saffron but it doesn't have the profundity of flavour. If saffron is offered cheaply it will be safflower, as I learned in a market in Old Jerusalem.

It was used by Native Americans to colour breads and porridges, by Japanese courtiers to dye their lips, and is used in Mexican food. It is also known as American, Mexican or fake saffron. Safflower is more important as a source of a low-cholesterol cooking oil.

SAFFRON: saffron comes only from the stigma of an autumn-flowering crocus. They must be picked by hand and it can take between 370 and 470 hours of work to produce 1 kg/2 lb of dried threads. Iran produces most, followed by La Mancha, Spain. Saffron is also grown in Kashmir and in northern Greece, whence outstanding saffron-based teas are marketed.

Trying to describe its mysterious flavour is a challenge, as saffron has the property of being all and everything but different to everyone. The flavours are earthy but hay-like, with a nuanced floral sweetness, and a final taste of bitterness. Saffron changes mercurially, lighter or darker used with nuts or cream, with rice or in breads, with sugar or spice, with dark or light meats, fish or seafood.

Whole saffron stigmas have a dark top and a pale yellow or white base. The colour and flavour are in the dark part, so saffron that includes the culinarily useless lower part means a lesser result and should mean a lower price. Stigmas are often sold in glass wrapped in a golden-red or yellow film, precisely to hide the excessive amount of white you are buying.

High-quality saffrons are Iranian *sargol* and Spanish *coupe*, both indicating the white has been cut away, also known as cut saffron. That undiluted colour is mystical, a dark vibrant, red-black you've seen nowhere else: the scent also tells you of its superiority—it doesn't do to try to think what it reminds you of, what perfumes you detect, like a desperate wine buff-babbler.

Saffron goes particularly well in yeasted doughs, and saffron cakes and scones and breads are specialities as far apart as Sweden and the West Country, Russia and Spain, Italy and Armenia. French bouillabaisse, Spanish paella and risotto Milanese are impossible

without it. It's also important in perfumery and is found in Czech and Speke's Dark Rose.

Saffron powder: used for quicker results, because it can be stirred directly in to a dish. Mix into egg yolk to paint a roasted turkey, chicken or goose or onto the peeled top of baking apples. Often thought to be adulterated but I've never found this so with mainstream brands.

Whole stigmas: these can be added to food as is but you get a greater result from soaking and using the resultant powerful brew. Some suggest you should lightly toast or dry the stigmas but no suppliers I know think it a good idea, as this has usually been done before marketing. They also recommend longer soaking than often recommended, using hot but not boiling water and leaving 20 minutes. The stigmas can be strained out but I find people like to discover them.

Zafferello is a superior Limoncello enriched with saffron stigmas.

SAGE: the time-honoured flavouring in true blue British sausages, but few contain it. It is one of the most difficult herbs to use, for its pungent herbalness and overtones of eucalyptus and mint go rank and stale very easily, developing features of damp rooms and bad disinfectant, an effect often found infecting mixed herbs and a jolly good reason never to use these. Used with restraint, pork, veal, goose, tomatoes and cheese, are its best friends. Fresh sage is interesting under pork crackling but better in Italy's saltimbocca, in which thin slices of veal sandwich ham and fresh sage leaves.

SALT: if there is but one truism in the food world, it is that you cannot, absolutely cannot, tell someone else how much salt they need.

Rather than working on food to 'bring out its flavour', salt stimulates our taste buds to discern what flavour is possible. The more salt, the greater the stimulus and the greater the flavour reward, except the more salt you use, the more you taste salt rather than food.

Someone who uses more salt than you will not always have a saltier taste in their mouth. They may have a slow or dull tongue because they genetically have fewer tastebuds or have lost sensitivity by growing old; like most important body parts, tastebuds deteriorate. Thus, some need a higher degree of salt stimulation to experience the same taste as others. Others are super-tasters and rarely use salt. Again, you cannot tell someone else how much salt they need to experience the same flavours you do. The risk of high salt intake because of age or slow taste buds is that the salt taste becomes paramount, and that is bad for you and boring for the cook.

One proven way to reduce salt intake is to microwave vegetables, covered but with no added water. This way the natural salts and flavourings are concentrated rather than being leached out, and many discover this increased harvest of flavour needs less or no salt.

Much better nutrition too.

A pink salt from the Himalayas or an Hawaiian island, from South Australia's Murray River, a blinding-white but yielding *fleur du sel* from France and a sun-dried one from the Dalmatian coast can all taste different, but the differences are additives, some natural some not. Detectable if dabbed directly on your tongue, differences when salt is diluted by cooking water or chewed with food are as likely as you becoming Pope. Sprinkling salt flakes or chunky salt grains onto food will give different textural effects in your mouth but then you eat more salt than is good or needed.

Salt behaves strangely when deep-frozen. Salted butter keeps far longer than unsalted butter in a refrigerator but frozen salted butter lasts safely only a month, and unsalted butter can be stored three times as long. The salt content is why dishes containing bacon cannot be frozen for very long periods. Strange, isn't it?

Bay salt: see *Kosher salt.*

Celery salt: salt pounded with celery seed. Beloved of vegetarians and very delicious if used with restraint.

Flavoured salts: sometimes called seasoned salts, these are traditional for spicing meats but were usually made at home with preferred mixtures of cloves and nutmeg, peppers, and some of the sharper, sweeter herbs. Grated lemon or lime zest make an excellent salt. In fact, pound any fresh or dried herb with salt, and once you have a favourite, they will keep a long time. All are better as condiments as few retain their virtue in cooking water.

Fleur de sel: the first and finest flakes of sea salt, whipped by the wind onto the shore or the edge of saltpans. Weather conditions, tides and temperatures are said to produce different flavours and they might directly on the tongue but there is rarely enough concentration to taste these once mixed with food.

Garlic salt: check the label as it also might also contain monosodium glutamate and other ingredients. Fresh garlic and whatever salt you have to hand will taste better.

Himalayan: blocks of this pink-tinted salt are used to line dry-hanging rooms, especially for beef. Ionisation keeps the air pure and dry, and the meat is tastier and more tender.

Iodised salt: iodine salts have been added as a necessary dietary supplement in some countries as defence against goitre. It has a definite taste but this disappears when diluted by cooking.

Kitchen or common salt: made by extracting underground salt, once by mining and now by dissolving it in water, pumping this brine out, and evaporating the liquid.

Kosher salt: sometimes Bay salt, is specified in much US cooking as something special but is only a cruder form of sea salt, often rather greyish. The difference between this and common or kitchen salt is a larger but lighter grain size. Where kosher salt is specified, use half the volume of other salts to get the same effect, one teaspoon to two of kosher salt. It is called kosher because this size was deemed best for koshering meat, that is, draining it of blood, so some sources say it should be called koshering salt. It is commonly the salt used for preserving and brining and to dry-salt fish or meat. The airy crystals give better results, perhaps because they dissolve faster. Large grains used to salt meat in the UK were the size of corn, once the collective name of wheat and other grains, hence corned beef. Common or kitchen salt is the same thing but finer and sea salt is the same but often in flakes.

Rock salt: mined in ready-formed crystals, the deposit of a long-gone dried sea or other waterway. It is invariably mixed with a great number of other tastes, some of which you may not like, so it is worth tasting rock salt before you buy.

Sea salt: evaporated from the sea and thus includes trace elements and chemicals that will change according to location. The broad spectrum of complementary ingredients is what recommends sea salt to health experts. I just prefer the direct more complex flavour.

Smoked salt: I'm not sure if you can tell the difference between apple-wood smoked salt or manuka-smoked salt because it will inevitably be so diluted by whatever you are eating, but it's a great marketing ploy. Whatever the wood, the salt needs to be highly smoked or it is pointless. Hickory-flavoured salt is a favourite in the US.

Table salt: the purity is interfered with by the addition of starch or other chemicals to promote free running. The battle between the salt and the bland additives makes its flavour pretty boring but this is no bad thing if it makes other ingredients sparkle more.

Vanilla salt: salt with ground vanilla bean is extraordinarily good with fish, but as a finishing shower rather than an additive to cooking water or stock.

SAMPHIRE: samphire—*salicorne* in French—is crisp, brilliantly green, long cylinders joined together to make a low many-branched bush you find on salt flats. It looks like a miniature desert succulent. You can eat it just as it is, and each segment bursts in the mouth with pointed brininess that's mellowed with a grassy sweetness.

Served with fish or seafood it's a sensation, and I often put it into the microwave just long enough to warm it and turn it an even brighter green and hand that around with drinks. Very good in smaller pieces in salads. If you heat it too much or think to cook it, samphire goes floppy and loses colour.

Although commercially grown and imported, native samphire is one of the few genuinely wild treasures left to us, and should be eaten as close as possible to that natural condition. Unfortunately, the French and some folk in England pickle samphire, which destroys its colour and flavour, replacing its natural zing with vinegar.

SANSHO: a Japanese condiment, made from a small berry with a high pepper/citrus taste and with the same numbing effect as Szechuan peppercorns.

SAPA: see *Vin cotto.*

SARSAPARILLA: the root of a plant indigenous to tropical America from Mexico to Peru, sarsaparilla flavours a drink with so-called tonic properties and that usually includes winter green.

Like *sassafras* q.v., sarsaparilla is one of several root beers that were once the currency of Temperance bars. They have been rediscovered, together with dandelion and burdock, and increasingly available all over Britain. London's few traditional pie and mash shops often sell sarsaparilla.

SASSAFRASS: the bark of the aromatic sassafras tree can be made into a warming drink and is a flavouring for *sarsaparilla* q.v., but sassafras is a recognised carcinogen and although legally able to be used, you need a licence and so most makers of root beer don't bother. Creole cooking grinds sassafras leaves to make *filé powder* q.v.

SAVORY: often confused with thyme, summer savory has a more peppery taste and the leaves are longer. Particularly good with beans and often grown between rows of broad beans to repel black fly. What grows together gets eaten together and the French are very fond of savory with broad beans; I think you should try it too, otherwise use it where you would thyme. It is *sarriette* in French and deliciously coats a *mi-chevre* cheese, a half-cow, half-goat milk cheese. Winter savory is inferior.

SESAME: sesame seeds have high nutritional value and a sweet nutty flavour that comes with puckering bitterness; this is counteracted with something acid, usually lemon juice or vinegar. Maple and other syrups or sugars do not do this, but add sweetness after the bitterness is counteracted. The seeds can be made into a milk, but are generally used as a sprinkler over breads, in casseroles, sauces, pie crusts, puddings, and so on. When browned lightly in butter they are excellent on almost every type of vegetable or on plain noodles. Sesame seed bars make terrific snacks as long as you have good teeth. See *Gomasio*.

We are probably more familiar with sesame in halvah and as *tahini* q.v. Halvah is a Turkish/Greek/Israeli confection of ground sesame seeds, honey and flavouring. The Poles make excellent halvah and their chocolate-flavoured one is particularly good. Low-grade halvah will have an inescapable bitterness.

SHAO-HSING WINE: a yellow wine made from rice that tastes like minor sherry and is always drunk slightly warm. Even the highest quality can seem barely drinkable to European palates but all grades are used in Chinese cookery, sometimes first to intoxicate live prawns. It's a good dressing on Chinese greens or to finish fish or fish sauces—dry white wine is the last thing fish needs.

Drunken Chicken is captivating, strips of poached or microwaved chicken breast drowned while warm in a superior Shao-hsing wine, chilled at least 12 hours and served very cold. Forbid it to children, teenagers and teetotallers, for nothing has diminished the alcohol content.

SHRIMP, DRIED: the great divider, and one of the principal flavouring agents of South East Asia. Like most dried fish they have a penetrating cheesy smell that nauseates many, although in mitigation they never taste as bad as they smell. As a base flavouring, they must be soaked in water for 30 minutes before using, but may also be soaked overnight; sherry or rice wine makes them less noxious. Dried shrimps are often pounded and are the basis for shrimp paste/*kapi*, the noisome but necessary flavouring paste of Thai cookery.

SHRIMP PASTE: *kapi* is the Thai version of an extraordinary ingredient endemic to South East Asian cookery. Repellent to many, this paste of fermented and dried shrimps quickly becomes addictive. The paler the colour, the higher the quality and the more freshly it is likely to have been made: some versions can be very purple, because of dye in the black eyes of a variety of shrimp.

Sometimes shrimp paste is roasted before use, always done in a wrapping of banana leaf or aluminium foil. Put the air extractor onto maximum and toast under a slow grill until inspection shows it is evenly dark in colour.

SORREL AND WILD SORREL: acidic leaves that are steps to rare gastronomic heights but rare as hen's teeth in stores, even though found wild everywhere.

Sorrel looks like small dock or anaemic spinach and has a tantalising oxalic-acid-based sourness backed with herbal greenness, a bit like raw rhubarb. Cultivated leaves grow quite big but the wild is usually no bigger than a man's thumb. Used raw in salads for a lemon-citrus contrast, it is mainly a superb flavouring for sauces and as a soup, but this is likely to be a thin white sauce with sorrel in it, pointless and horridly khaki. Sorrel shrinks prodigiously, a couple of handfuls of small leaves, trimmed of stalks, end up as a puddle on the bottom of a saucepan and then you make a sauce according to the recipe book you most trust and that uses a lot of butter or cream.

Sorrel sauce is outstanding with fish, especially eel, salmon and sea trout. It is excellent with sweetbreads and with eggs and young green vegetables. I put it into the choke-free centre of baby or teenage artichokes, as a dip. If not too strong, sorrel sauce makes a nice change on asparagus spears.

STAR ANISE: an important base note in much of China pork and poultry cookery, this warm liquorice flavour easily overpowers and becomes sickly. Best used in combination with other flavours, as it is in *Five-spice powder* q.v.

Ground star anise can seem to be full flavoured, but it's likely only to be an echo of its original aromas. It's better to break off one or two of the points of a single star to get the right amount of flavour; sometimes you need only use star anise for the last few minutes to finish a dish.

SUMAC: next time you reach to scrape lemon zest into or onto anything, use sumac instead and it will rekindle the recipe, especially fish and salads. Sumac has a wonderful fruity flavour with delicious acidity and is the ground berries of the stag's horn sumac bush, a relative of the cashew and that grows easily in temperate climates.

A staple in Iran, sumac is used throughout the eastern Mediterranean and Middle East as an all-purpose seasoning on almost everything; a little on-line research will make you wonder why it is not better known elsewhere. Sprinkle on rice, noodles or mashed potatoes, use it on green vegetables, in green salads, on carrots ... a small bowl of sumac on your table will quickly become something you don't like to be without. A surprising 'secret' ingredient in salt and pepper squid.

SZECHUAN PEPPERCORNS/FAGARA/ BROWN PEPPERCORNS: nothing to do with peppercorns, but the berries of Prickly Ash. They have a pungent, slightly anise smell. They must be roasted and crushed because only the petal-like husks have flavour. In the mouth they numb rather than burn— Australia's mountain pepper and New Zealand's horopito have the same curious effect.

To roast them, toss lightly in a dry

non-stick pan until smoking slightly, or do the same in a doughnut shape on a flat plate in the microwave; when cool crush roughly. Some will strain out the kernels but this is a little fanatic. A common seasoning used as a dip for deep-fried food or anything else which needs a little zip of flavour is mixed roasted Szechuan peppercorns and salt: mix one teaspoon of the peppercorns with three tablespoons coarse salt and dry-fry over low heat until the peppercorns are lightly smoking and the salt is lightly browned. Cool, crush and keep in an airtight bottle. This can also be done in a microwave.

Less common but terribly useful for adding imprecise fascination to bland dishes, is to steep roasted Szechuan peppercorns in vegetable oil; a few teaspoons to 300 ml/½ pint is about right and the process is considerably speeded if you add the oil to the pan after the peppercorns are roasted and apply gentle heat for another 10–15 minutes; it's either a frying medium or a discreet condiment.

TABASCO: simpler, cheaper and more controllable than chillies, Tabasco allows you to cook richly flavoured food without heat, and then to allow others to add it to their plate. Better to look the other way while one person massacres your food than facing a table of guests pretending they are not in pain.

Tabasco in the kitchen means you can add a little heat to almost anything, as the idea appeals. To cheese scones, for instance, to a chocolate cake or chocolate icing, to brighten up a chili to which you have added too much cocoa or chocolate, into poached, stewed or grilled stone fruit, Moroccan tagines, stir-fries, chocolate truffles, whatever.

The best thing I ever did was to add Tabasco to a punchy Mocha-Rocky-Road ice cream on BBC-TV. You didn't know it was there until the ice cream slid down your throat, and then a pleasant minor warmth of chilli seemed to clear the palate for the next spoonful.

The original Tabasco is made from the company's own variety of chilli but now there is a choice of 12, including green made from the milder Jalapeno pepper, a Habanero Tabasco that is hotter and a smoky Chipotle.

TAHINI: sesame butter, ground sesame seed with nothing added or subtracted. It is inescapably bitter and is usually used with citrus to counteract this, but the taste is never fully dulled. Some brands will have used processed seeds to make them more mellow, but there's no reliable way to know this without tasting. Used to flavour salad dressings when thinned with a little oil and lime or lemon juice, or to flavour dishes like hummus, a paste of chickpeas. Vegans can use it as a butter substitute in pastries and bread, for sesame makes one of the best oils for cooking. If offered a tahini darker than you expect, this may have a lower oil content and it's possible a portion of commercial tahini is made from seeds previously processed and crushed to extract oil.

TAMARIND: an Asian and Oriental way to add acidity, like the use of lemon juice. Dried tamarind is soaked in very hot water, strained, and then only the liquid is used. You can reduce it over heat if the volume would disturb the texture of a dish. A walnut-sized lump in 300 ml/½ UK pint of hot water for 20 minutes is about right. Excellent in all curries, otherwise throw in a halved or quartered whole lemon or lime. Well worth experimenting with, say, to flavour a sauce for fish rather than using lemon, to sharpen a tomato sauce for pasta, in a vegetable soup or as part of an oriental-style salad dressing, with soy sauce and chopped toasted cashew nuts.

TANGERINE PEEL: a common yet expensive Chinese flavouring ingredient; its expense means it is often not tasted in a dish but has been used as a menu come-on. You can make your own equivalents using any citrus except grapefruit, which interacts badly with many modern drugs. You can use roughly shaped pieces but fine slivers are better and either way you then scrape off the pith. Dry in a slow oven or by following the dehydrating instructions that came with your microwave. Keep the dry peel in glass in the dark. It will slowly turn to black, but this is an advantage, as provided it is kept dry, it will improve in flavour for several years, at least.

The dried and aged peel is commonly discarded before serving yet I have never had complaints when I have left it in. It is particularly good in a sauce tending to fattiness or sweetness, say an oxtail stew or boiled tongue. Provençals use fresh orange peel in stews, so I add the dried version to many stewed, braised or boiled meat dishes, more usually as background fascinator rather than a forward flavour.

Finely chopped peel can be used to flavour sugar and is a fragrant final addition to a stir-fry, even better, if first softened in rice wine or sherry. Iranian shops sell dried orange peel. While there pick up an Iranian cookbook and be prepared to faint with pleasure.

TANSY: an old-fashioned herb with the peculiarity of making rhubarb taste sweet, perhaps because the bitter-sweet of the herb cancels out the high acidity of the rhubarb. It's traditionally been added to sweet omelettes and puddings, sometimes with apples, and often these were called tansy puddings.

Because it keeps flies away, tansy was rubbed over meat before it was cooked, and planted by door ways to repel ants. It's also a reliable preserver of corpses.

TARRAGON: a necessity in every herb garden and kitchen, basic to French cooking, and to anyone who cares about fine flavours. It is warm and aromatic but must have both bite and an air of liquorice. There are two sorts, the Russian and the French, but grow and use only the French for the Russian will add a flavour no more useful than fresh lawn clippings. I can't understand why garden centres sell it.

Tarragon's great affinity is with dairy products and with eggs, hence its appearance in classic sauces, and savoury soufflés. It is extraordinarily good with melted butter over virtually every vegetable but does have a special relationship with courgettes/ zucchini. This also applies to chicken, and chicken roasted only with butter, a little lemon and fresh or dried tarragon is really hard to beat. When you combine chicken, courgettes and tarragon in the same dish and then finish it with cream, the result is astonishing.

A lesser-known affinity is that of tarragon with lamb, another recommendation; so is lobster baked with tarragon. Tarragon is essential to sweet, mixed herbs and wonderful in a herb mayonnaise for serving with cold fish, especially salmon, when the bite of the tarragon is a good foil for the smoothness of the flesh.

Tarragon vinegar is one of the finest of all the flavoured vinegars and adds instant elegance to almost anything. Vinegar is often overlooked as a finisher for casseroles and sauces, but shouldn't be.

Tarragon is better for being grown with lots of sun, because its flavour is changeable, affected by the slightest variation in soil and climate. No two plants taste the same so always test the strength on your tongue when using tarragon. Don't even think about using Russian tarragon.

THYME, LEMON THYME AND WILD THYME: a favourite herb of such long standing the ancient Greeks used it with incense to purify their temples. For quite as long, thyme has been a favourite of bees, and thyme honey from Mount Hymettus is regarded as amongst the best. Lemon thyme makes one of the best citrus-like tisanes imaginable.

There are many different thymes, most of which are useful in cooking. Basic and wild thyme are related in flavour, with the wilder being the headier. Lemon thyme is more citrus than plain thyme and its fresh flavour gives a clue to one of thyme's greatest affinities—lemon. One of my earliest cookery successes was Egyptian Chicken, from a Robert Carrier book: crushed garlic, lemon zest and juice, olive oil, butter and masses of thyme sprigs, all in great abandon, used to marinate chicken pieces, which are then cooked in a hot oven. It's still a favourite. Some rarer thymes have the flavour of caraway and should be used with great discretion.

Thyme loves tomatoes and tomato sauces, goes well in savoury sausages and stuffings and indeed is fairly basic in my opinion. Dried thyme imported from the Mediterranean may be very much stronger than fresh but weaker stuff from a damp English garden. You have to be careful. White flesh, rabbit, veal and poultry go well with the slightly sweet-sharp flavour and it is good with garlic. Nearly all vegetables like thyme, but carrots are its best and prettiest companions.

Thyme is one of the original strewing and paving herbs, for it doesn't mind a bit if you stand on it, so releasing its fresh pungency.

TONKA BEANS/TONQUIN BEANS: a flavour that hovers on the edge of being 'discovered' every few years. The dried bean looks like a small leathery thumb, and has a heavy, sensuous aroma of woodruff, a scent so like vanilla it has been used to extend vanilla or as a substitute, even in tobacco. The problem is the major flavouring ingredient coumarin is suspected of being poisonous and carcinogenic, but not if used in small amounts. If you live somewhere tropical, coumarin essence is extracted by soaking collected beans in rum for 24 hours or so.

TURMERIC: the intense smoky-gold colour and pungent flavour of turmeric are basic to piccalilli and curry but well worth exploring in their own right. Related to the ginger, it is the plant's ginger-like roots, called fingers, that are used and sometimes found fresh. They are quite thin and small, rather like psychedelic babies' fingers because when fresh are very orange.

The flavour is mellow, perhaps peppery but has exotic layers of fascinating earthiness. If you use too much the flavour goes flabby and can taste like wet cardboard, not a good thing to discover after serving. It can dominate a bad curry mixture the same unpleasant way.

The inexperienced cook should use turmeric as a colouring rather than a flavouring but used with restraint can add interest on or in rice dishes, in stews, fish dishes and in kedgeree; mixed with a little butter and garlic it makes an interesting enlivener of vegetables.

Sometimes turmeric is suggested as a saffron substitute but there is absolutely no similarity in flavour at all. I spit on any book that reckons to substitute turmeric for saffron, and so should you.

VANILLA: this ultimate of sensuality is the flavour of the sun-cured and fermented seed pod of a climbing orchid native to Mexico but now grown throughout tropical areas, including India, Indonesia, French Polynesia, Madagascar—even on Pitcairn Island. A 2017 cyclone destroyed much of Madagascar's production, increasing the price of vanilla dramatically.

Vanilla is now so common it is barely regarded as a flavour; how often do people say 'plain' when they mean vanilla? It is so popular it is largely replaced by cheaper vanillin. This is the source of vanilla flavour in the bean but can be made artificially from wood, pine bark and cloves. It's the same thing but does not have the complicated, complementary micro-flavours of vanilla from the bean.

Vanilla flavours milk, cream, sauces or sugar syrups for hot and cold fruit or desserts, and is used successfully in savoury dishes, particularly with fish and seafood, where its unique rich but discreet sweetness is an unsuspected advantage. *Larousse Gastronomique* recommends vanilla as an ingredient in fish soups and in Mauritius it makes wondrous vanilla black tea. Otherwise, vanilla has the most serene of unshakeable relationships with chocolate, originally from the same broad geographical area.

Wherever they grow, most vanilla beans are the *planifolia* variety and develop characteristics according to where they grow, *terroir*, and how carefully they are processed.

India: now a major producer of vanilla of very good, complex flavours.

Indonesia: its vanilla is spicy and a little smoky. A blend of Madagascan Bourbon and Indonesian vanilla is recommended for baking: a good tip is always to cream the vanilla into the butter or other fat, as the globules protect it and give a better, bigger ultimate flavour.

Madagascar or Bourbon: the better-known vanilla is Bourbon vanilla from Madagascar, so-called because French interests introduced it to Reunion and the Comoros Islands, then called the Bourbon Islands. Bourbon vanilla has lots of perfumed body without the spicy notes of Mexican, and is preferred by many pâtissiers, not least because the supply is usually more reliable but also because it seems to work best with ice cream and creams and such. Pieces of Madagascan vanilla are best for pot-pourri and other room fragrancers.

Mexico: produces a full rounded vanilla flavour with hints of coffee and cinnamon and which calms the acidity of tomato in sauces, including chilis. The US company Nielsen-Massey buys a big portion of the limited Mexican crop and so is the most reliable source if you want these nuances.

Tahitian: an evolution from vanilla *planifolia* into *tahitensis*. It has fatter, sweeter pods and is strongly perfumed, earthy and fruity with less natural vanillin but more heliotropin, hence its common comparison with cherry—heliotrope plants are known as the cherry-pie plant. Tahitian vanilla is particularly good at supporting fruit flavours in sauces and frozen desserts and is also that targeted by the fragrance industry. Its true home is not Tahiti but the island of Taha'a, twinned with Raiatea, once as commanding and revered as the Vatican City and that drew worshippers from all points of the Polynesian triangle. It is also grown in Papua New Guinea, which you'll identify from PNG as a prefix.

Vanilla beans: graded according to size and appearance, and smooth-ribbed appearances and good lengths usually get a higher price. Some sources are better than others in producing a thin gloss of tiny white crystals on the beans called *givre*, French for hoar frost, and a sign of elevated quality.

If stored in a closed (not airtight) jar, vanilla beans improve with keeping, and if they dry out are easily plumped by soaking, even in water. A more classic ploy is to make your beans pay for their keep by flavouring something else. So, store your beans with caster sugar to make vanilla sugar: as you use it, put more sugar in, shake it all about and soon it will be back to strength. Use the flavoured sugar wherever you want a sweet vanilla flavour, to add glitter to fairy cakes, to bake cakes especially cheesecakes, in cocktails, on poached or grilled fruit and about one thousand other things. You can grind them to mix with sugar, even though it's not recommended to eat the beans—but see *Vanilla powder*. Up to you.

Vanilla essence: unless mislabelled, this is based on vanillin, a 'nature identical' flavouring that has little of the flavour resonance of vanilla from the bean. It is designated on labels as C811803.

Vanilla extract: the real thing, originally made by soaking vanilla pods in alcohol, which you can do with most spirits and still use the pods. Black rum seems the best choice.

Vanilla paste: a useful blend of the tiny black seeds that is used more easily than scraping them from a split pod.

Vanilla powder: ground whole vanilla pods, used as approximately ½ teaspoon to a pod. No additives and a great time saver if you are happy to eat the pods.

Vanilla sugar: sugar in which vanilla beans have been stored. As you use the sugar, replace it, for the beans go on giving for ages. Good as a garnish and for baking if it is strong enough. Vanilla sugar is very good in coffee and surprisingly so in tea: in fact, vanilla tea is outstandingly good, luxurious and calming in flavour, but only if it is real tea with pieces of vanilla bean chopped up in it rather than added 'flavouring': vanilla tea makes great ice cream.

VERJUICE: verjuice (green juice, vert jus, verjus) is an ancient acidifier, an alternative to lemon juice or vinegar or tamarind. It was never something to be used in volume as a cooking medium, meaning most verjuices marketed are nothing of the kind and have none of the correct characteristics.

In Britain, verjuice was made from unripe grapes or from crab apples. It was a default crop, made only after a bad summer, when an entire vintage was made into verjuice because the grapes did not ripen. Verjuice was not something you planted vines to make.

Verjuice went out of use for a long time, possibly because lemons became more easily available. Modern, mellow grape juices, fermented or not, are far from verjuice and should be called something else. They are honeyed and velvety, delicious enough to drink, but in no way an acidifier, for they don't have the spine. One taste of rugged old-style verjuice and you'll know they are too well bred to do what verjuice is supposed to do. True verjuice is produced in Iran and exported. A label I treasure says 'Unripped grape juice' and the back label calls it 'sour grape juice'. It doesn't rip your tongue with acidity, but it has a damn good go, with unrefined flavour, a long-lasting, cleansing, acidic feel in the mouth and few fruit or honey tastes; you can taste its relationship with vinegar.

When most modern verjuice is specified in recipes, lemon juice is invariably added, a culinary contradiction. A notable UK exception is made by Verjuice. com only from unripened grapes and although milder than vinegar is clearly a 'green juice'. I hope there are others.

VIETNAMESE MINT: a relatively new kid on the Western world's block, with a nice heart shaped-leaf and fresh flavour that mixes well with other exotic herbs. There is some mint flavour but it tastes more like basil in party mood, warm but zingy, sharp and acidic but still aromatic, and then a definite tongue numbness develops.

It shines in such 'wet' foods as soups and laksa, can go into any green salad, but is greatest for the refreshing lift it adds to Vietnamese rice-pancake wraps.

VIN COTTO, MOSTO COTTO, SAPA: grape juice (must) that has not fermented, but has been cooked. In the southern Italian province of Lecce, the grapes chosen are the tasty Negro Amaro and Malavasia Nera. First left to wither on the vines for about a month so a degree of raisin flavour develops, they are then pressed. Boiling reduces that juice by half and the result is aged in oak barrels. This is a similar process to balsamic vinegar, but made with different grapes and not aged long enough to develop the acidity to be a vinegar.

Vin cotto is easily lost in complicated recipes and best used as a dressing rather than an ingredient. Sweet vegetables, like parsnips or turnips or carrots become perfectly heavenly and special interest is added to grilled meat, fish and seafood. The best I've tasted is vin cotto spooned over anything plain and creamy—like a chilled Petit Suisse.

Some vin cotto are flavoured with figs, with raspberry and other fruits and delicious by themselves, as a treat by the teaspoon; chilled poached figs with fig vin cotto, raspberry on raspberry sorbet or some combination. Rather than stirring an orange or mandarin-flavoured vin cotto into a gravy or sauce for duck, spoon it directly onto the carved meat.

Fruit fools benefit from vin cotto ladled upon them, as do rice puddings. A slice of aged cheddar, or a soft blue cheese, eaten with a few drops sprinkled on to them, could out do those wonders. They are wonderful dips for thin biscotti or for warm madeleines. For something colder, pour vin cotto or a sapa into a tall glass and then fill with champagne or a top sparkling wine. I'm thinking gin with a good splash, too.

Sapa: is the same thing from the Marche, on the east coast, opposite Tuscany, where they recommend it with poached quince, and also eat it with polenta.

WASABI: one of those Japanese ingredients particularly associated with their most sophisticated dining, but which does not stand up to close scrutiny this side of the globe, not mine anyway. Wasabi is a very hot, green, Oriental form of horseradish, used grated fresh or dried and mixed with water to form a paste. More aromatic than ordinary horseradish, it gets right up your nose and then scours your sinuses and then does it again. It is very hot indeed, yet served exclusively with sushi, or sashimi, exceptionally delicate raw fish, which is considered best when almost flavourless.

If sushi or sashimi are soaked in soy sauce into which a little wasabi has been whisked it may as well be a wodge of white bread dabbed with fish paste, for all else you will taste. But that's the Japanese way.

To me, wasabi is the Japanese equivalent of serving raw onions and cooked eggs with caviar, an ancient way to conceal all possible shortcomings of age and condition in food too expensive to throw away. In the modern world of fresher, safer ingredients wasabi is just not needed with sashimi and sushi: the freshness and texture of ocean-fresh fish needs no thuggery to hide the fragile flavours they offer. I guess addiction to endorphins has won again.

In any case, read the label. Most 'wasabi' is anything but the real thing, and artificially coloured too: you'll find it more likely to be a fluorescent paste of horseradish powder, mustard, and blue and yellow colourings, revealed in the ingredient list usually printed on the crimped edge of individual servings and so particularly inaccessible. Not what I would want to put on cooked fish, let alone raw.

As an alternative to chillies for mixing with other rugged flavours in Occidental foods, genuine wasabi is worth exploring but not, perhaps, as deeply as the wasabi panna cotta and wasabi soft cheeses I have encountered.

Wasabi has many defenders, who think its flavour far more complex than horseradish. Make up your own mind but take teeny-tiny baby steps or you won't get your nasal passages back for ages.

ZEDOARY: also called wild turmeric, and with its bright orange flesh you can see why. It is related, adding camphorous notes to make it more like galangal, but it's warmer, with an acidic finish and a fragrance like ripe mangoes.

Zedoary is one of the spices the late and lamented Mark Steen of Seasoned Pioneers called sultry, such a good word. The light bitterness it can leave on the palate means it is not used as often as ginger or galangal these days, but it's useful to add interest to curry mixtures, especially milder ones for seafood and lamb and is used fresh in the Indian kitchen. It is another credited with aiding digestion and absorbing flatulence and colic.

ZERESHK/ZERSHK: see *Barberry.*

Compounds, mixes, seasonings and powders

The Internet is greatly to the advantage of creative cooks, for the range of special mixes available is far greater than in any shop. Here are some mixtures to make life more interesting, in your armchair kitchen at least.

ACHIOTE: these sauces and marinades for barbecues in Mexico mix powdered *annatto* q.v. with herbs and chillies and combine this with citrus juice or vinegar. The Yucatan mixes achiote with orange juice for roasting, baking or barbecuing.

ADVIEH: an Iranian mixture of cinnamon, cardamom and cumin with rose petals, boiled with rice.

BAHARAT: this Seraphim-bright spice mixture is from the Gulf States and is also used in Iraqi cooking. Its particular appeal is reliance on sweet and fragrant cardamom, cassia and nutmeg with heights of cloves, the note that gives such unusual appeal. Originally it did not include chilli but many versions now do.

Think of chilli-free baharat as a primer for ras-el-hanout, as a rugged country cousin but from an equally noble family. It's just fantastic with lamb or mutton, especially if you add dates to the gravy.

Baharat enhances roasted vegetables or root vegetable mashes, and roasts and stews, too, a sophisticated, chilli-free sort of curry and is a real hit in steak or steak and kidney pies. It makes scrambled, poached, boiled and other egg dishes truly exotic and different, and nicely livens tomato sauces for pasta. Some commercial varieties offer too high a chilli content, which you can adjust by adding much more of the sweet spices; look for chilli being the last listed ingredient.

BERBERE: from Ethiopia can be searingly hot, but is better when it is not. Its base is roasted and coarsely ground cumin, coriander, fenugreek and allspice berries, heated up with ground ginger, cloves and nutmeg plus small and thus very hot chillies. Use this as you would a curry mixture.

BOUQUET GARNI: the fresh version of mixed herbs and much more acceptable. The bouquet should be one or two fresh or dried bay leaves with thyme sprigs and parsley stalks only, other herbs can be added of course. Using two bay leaves as outer covers makes the pack easier to tie together; leave plenty of string or cotton free, so you can tie this to the pot's handle and thus retrieve the bouquet garni easily. I see no reason to use mixed dried herbs as an alternative and this includes the 'tea-bags' of bouquet garni, almost always oxidised and stale.

Have you wondered if one bouquet garni is enough? Or is a bouquet garni another knee jerk, the way so many recipes finish unthinkingly with 'serve with crusty bread, freshly ground black pepper and a salad'? Apart from the two bay leaves, one bouquet garni is rarely enough when you simmer for more than an hour. So, use more or bigger bouquets garnis but also fish out the old and put in a new one about ten minutes before serving, to brighten flabby flavours after long cooking. Such a good trick.

BUMBUS: these wet Indonesian mixtures are available vacuum packed and offer excellent tastes and flavours. A mix of herbs and spices, they typically contain lemon grass, galangal and makrut leaves and so have underpinning citric aromatics. A 100 g/4 oz sachet is right for about 500 g/1 lb of meat, chicken, fish or vegetables and each is finished with stock, coconut cream or water and will thicken as it cooks.

Bumbu ajam paniki: specially for chicken in coconut.
Bumbu ajam pedas: hot and spiced for chicken.

Bumbu babi ketjap: soy-flavoured sweetness and spice for pork.

Bumbu Bali: Balinese heat and spice for meat, chicken or fish.

Bumbu kare: an Indonesian yellow curry that is mild and flavoursome.

Bumbu nasi goreng: for the traditional Indonesian rice dish.

Bumbu redang: a chilli-spiked coconut cream and beef speciality.

Bumbu rujak: for pork or chicken with a true Indonesian tang.

Bumbu sambal goreng udang: gives a rich, spiky coconut sauce for prawns.

CHERMOULA: a rugged purée of herbs and spice that's very big on fresh coriander. Claudia Roden gave me a treasured recipe for chermoula almost twenty years ago for the book I wrote about my first visit to discover the fabulous foods of the Eastern Mediterranean.

Although Moroccan, it has been taken to Israel and become a great standby. It's used as a marinade for meats, but its freshness better suits the spectrum of flavour found in firm-fleshed fish and poultry. Some recipes use raw onion, but I think it intrudes and acidity comes better from fresh lemon or lime juice when serving.

Chermoula makes an original dip for hot breads and to serve with kebabs and can be used, with or without mayonnaise as a terrific binding for a potato salad or a chunky chicken salad to which is added avocado or tropical fruits, say pineapple or mango.

CHILI POWDER, SEASONING OR COMPOUND: confusion about these is why so much chili con carne is only chilli con carne and thoroughly disgusting—undercooked, sour, watery onions and grey mince have been sprinkled with chilli rather than chili, nothing but a bit of heat and no flavour.

Chili powder or compound is a mixture of ground chilli pepper plus spices and herbs, the most important of which are cumin and oregano. Without cumin you cannot have real chili or chili con carne or chili con anything. See: *Chilli/chillies.*

To add greater appeal to dishes cooked with true chili powder or compound or seasoning, the judicious stirring in of cocoa powder or a very few melted squares of very dark chocolate works a treat. This gives the faintest of culinary glimpses into the myriad flavours of *mole* q.v., complicated sauces of spices and chocolate evolved from the cuisine of the Aztecs by those who conquered them.

CURRY: see also *Masala,* the word curry is almost certainly based on a Tamil word *kari,* which means a spiced liquid. If you look, the essential ingredients are cumin, coriander, with chilli and turmeric: the first two for flavour, the third for heat and the last for flavour and colour, but turmeric doesn't have to feature at all. From then on it's up to cooks. Some will say we should not use curry as a blanket term for Indian stews but until something else is in current use, I'll use it because it is so widely understood.

Food made with ready-made Indian spice mixes are astronomically popular. There are as many companies and families that market superb authentic mixes as there are who sell dross. Some of the worst come from the biggest household names, whose ideas of what goes with what, and how many pointless extra chemicals they can add, puts them well to the fore for fantasy writing awards. They usually misunderstand chilli content and confuse chilli and chili, too, as do supermarket recipe developers.

The basic retail rule applies—read the label and if the contents contain something you or an ethnic cook wouldn't have in the kitchen, put it back. Some mixes misuse or misunderstand traditional words and meanings—from curry names to their ingredients, and even wickedly use spicy to mean chilli-hot, when it shouldn't; this seems a battle lost.

For greatest eating enjoyment when a dish is high in chilli—hot, not spicy—every small mouthful should be equal amounts of curry and of rice, or of greater proportions of rice to curry. Believe me, you and your digestion will have a much nicer time. Don't drink any liquid except in very small gulps and if your mouth feels injured, pile in the rice to absorb the chilli or eat something fatty, butter, cheese, yoghurt and the like.

Here is a guide to some Indian dishes loosely called curry, found in old books published in India. I did the same on the ground in Sri Lanka and Thailand, when shooting my TV series in each country.

Indian

Balti: cooked in a balti, something like a two-handled wok thought to have developed from buckets, the idea was popularised in the 1980s and 1990s in Birmingham and is still maintained there.

A balti curry can thus be whatever you like, if it is cooked and served in a balti and should be served with a garnish of fresh coriander leaf.

Bhuna: a mild mixture of up to 20 spices for meat or chicken.

Biryan/biriani: layered rice with cooked or cooking meats and that is turned out to serve. A biryani spice mixture should be notably fragrant, no more than medium hot and can include whole spices. Biryanis are often elaborate and expensive and decorated with real silver or gold foil.

Delhi: should mean mild spicing.

Dopiaza: from northern India, it should be a tomato and onion base plus a clear preponderance of cumin.

Jahlfrezi: a succulent Kashmiri style based on sweet peppers/capsicums and coconut.

Kabuli: from Afghanistan, medium spiced, with cracked black peppers rather than chillies, and with almonds.

Karai: medium-hot mixture starting with the classic cumin/coriander base, and adding fennel seeds and tomatoes.

Korma: the meaning is braised dishes, but is commonly used for any lightly spiced and creamy sauce, often finished with coconut.

Madras: one of the hottest and so it

matters little what else is included.
Makhani: medium spiced and buttery, with fennel seeds dominating.
Moglai: must be very aromatic and include expensive saffron, so should be mild to medium and is usually rich with butter, cream and almonds.
Pasanda: favours the fragrant spices plus the richness of almonds—very good with lamb.
Rogan: a tomato and cumin sauce often used for lamb: thus rogan josh.
Tikka: medium spice and heat, largely flavoured with turmeric and ginger.
Vindaloo: the hottest of all, so Western-style eating is challenging.

Sri Lanka

Curries here are identified by their colour, and cooks can make each of them anything from mild to super-hot. Take nothing for granted but double-check an order is going to be the way you want.

Black: the most common Sri Lankan curry style, so-called because all the spices are pre-roasted to a dark rich brown, browner than you expect.
Pepper: an intriguing survivor of the times before chilli came calling, relying on black pepper for flavour, fragrance and telling heat.
Red: a high content of both fresh and dried red chillies can make these very hot indeed. Some cooks incorporate mild red paprika, to keep the colour but much reduce the chilli content.

White: very mild and liquid, doubling as soup: coriander, fenugreek, turmeric, curry leaves, fresh green chilli plus coconut milk and coconut cream. Specially good made with potatoes.

Thailand

The colour of Thai curries has no bearing on their heat. Although you expect the fresher green chillies used in a green curry to be milder than the dried red ones, the result depends on how many are used.

Thai curries start with a paste including *kapi* pounded in a mortar and pestle. There are no classic recipes in Thai cookery. Innovation and novelty are encouraged within very fluid boundaries.

Don't feel bad about buying Thai curry pastes, as most Thais buy theirs from markets. Look at the ingredient list to identify what you might add or beef up. There's usually something missing and often fresh lemon grass and makrut leaf will do the magic.

Green: green chillies, shallots, garlic coriander root, lemon grass, makrut zest, peppercorns, coriander seeds, cumin seeds and *kapi*/shrimp paste.
Jungle: Kaeng Paa: usually yellow and meant to be made only with ingredients a traveller could find in the jungle, so largely vegetarian and never with coconut cream or milk, which would have to have been carried from the coast.
Musselman/Muslim: the only Thai curry using Indian

spices—cinnamon, cloves and cardamom. Based on red curry paste and finished with coconut milk and cream.

Red: as green but with dried red rather than fresh green chillies, galangal, cinnamon, turmeric and perhaps a little star anise.

Tom Yum: the base for famed hot-sour prawn soup, Tom Yum Goong.

DUKKAH: a mixture of two or three nuts and sesame seeds all lightly toasted and then crushed with cumin or coriander, salt and pepper. Dukkah is culinary magic at a shake. As many ways as you can think of using it, another hundred will tumble in behind them.

The classic use is as a dip with olive oil and good Turkish or other flat bread. It's much better than that. As a finishing scatter it helps everything from salads to roast potatoes; in mashes or vegetable purées it should be added at the last minute. It is particularly good on most pasta, warming up the basic flavours with the toasted nuts and then adding bright notes with spices.

Use it after grilling chicken, lamb or fish, to ensure it isn't over toasted or burned, and it makes fascinating flavours with tropical fruits, particularly banana and fresh, chilled mango: it's just as good with stewed fruits or mixed dried fruit salad, in stuffings for baked apple and sprinkled on sliced oranges. It's miraculous in any salsa you might construct.

When using dukkah with savoury foods, you might add extra sharpness with sumac: with sweet foods, you might enhance with cinnamon or cardamom.

FINES HERBES: in contrast to the robustness of a bouquet garni, *fines herbes* combine three or more sweet delicate herbs, such as parsley, tarragon and chervil, and, if you really, really must, chives. They go very well with eggs.

FIVE SPICE/FIVE FRAGRANCE POWDER: a powerful mixed spice with a predominantly anise and cinnamon flavour but that may combine any of star anise, cinnamon, cassia, fennel seeds, cloves, liquorice, nutmeg, Szechuan peppercorns and ginger. Many Chinese mixtures contain six or seven, but the flavour of the first two must predominate. Especially used in marinades, in poultry and pork stuffings, or rubbed well into their scored skin before roasting.

HERBES DE PROVENCE: just because these mixed herbs have a French accent doesn't mean they are better than other mixed herbs. The variation in content is astonishing, and often nothing to do with Provence, even when bought in Provence. Thyme, savory, parsley, bay and perhaps rosemary are expected. Lavender flowers are commonly included but thought not to be authentic and there to counteract the low quality of other ingredients: this could be true because you should use only the English *angustifolia* types for culinary purposes, as the French ones are too bitter. Can you imagine Provençals importing or using English lavender for a mixture touted as reflecting the scent of their sun-bleached summer countryside?

I might add dried orange peel, used down that way a great lot in stews and as part of the base for a bouillabaisse. Next time, read the ingredients—I'd bet money you'll be more inclined to put it back than to use it to remind you of Provence.

KHEMELI-SUNELI: from Georgia, the country, it unusually combines herbs and spices, usually dill, mint, savory, fenugreek leaves and marigold petals with coriander, cloves and cinnamon. It gives an elegant, multi-faceted and elevated flavour to vegetables and soups but can be used in a marinade or rub for roasting meats and birds.

LAKSA: originating in Indonesia, Malaysia and Singapore, laksa is a spicy, hot nourishing main course soup packed with any of a hundred ingredients plus noodles and with a sauce that is thickish rather than thin. 'A runny curry with stuff in it' seems the best of the many descriptions.

MASALA: the word simply means mixture, so all curry powder mixes are masalas.

Chat masala: meant especially for fruits and vegetables, both raw and cooked and can be cooked with or sprinkled on. It adds a delicious lift to salads of all kinds, even to cold roasted vegetables. There should be very little heat indeed, ideally none, and it can contain few or many spices. *Chat/chaat* is an Indian word for potatoes, which gives a clue where chat masala often shines most brightly.

Garam masala: this should not contain chilli and is not properly added in classic Indian cookery until just before or just after a dish is ready—for no more than ten minutes. It is a fragrant tempering spice mixture, used to lift and refresh flavours after long cooking. It's a waste of a good one to use it at the start of cooking.

MIXED HERBS: the biggest step anyone can make towards being a good cook is to throw away mixed (dried) herbs and never use them again. Ever.

It's not that some mixtures are bad, but that all tend to be put to the back of the cupboard and used well past their life span, which heightens the flabby, mouldy, dank taste. Anyway, there seems no agreement about what should be included. My career in food, much longer than anyone predicted, only took off when I controversially stopped using onion, stopped using mixed herbs, and instead concentrated on making the most of individual herbs and spices.

MIXED SPICE: generally, a mixture of cinnamon, nutmeg and cloves or allspice, a decent mixed spice will include far more than that, so don't be afraid of experimenting. Dill and fennel seeds give liquorice flavour, which is good in conjunction with lifted clove notes. Coriander and cumin both give warmth and can be added together or individually for a sense of orange or lemon. Ginger adds bite as well as flavour, but so could grains of paradise, malagueta pepper. Cassia serves to heighten the cinnamon taste. Fenugreek can also be used, and Elizabeth David added black pepper to her spice mixture. Finally, mace adds unmatched and too often overlooked elegance, and cardamom an unmistakable touch of the exotic but it can easily overpower.

MOJO DE AJO: translated as a bath of garlic, it's more like garlic in a bath. Whole garlic cloves are simmered to softness in oil together with lime and chipotle chillies. Squash the well-bathed garlic into a little of the oil for prawns, fish, mushrooms, as a bread dip and spread. Or over baked beans.

MOLE SAUCES: these most fabled mixtures from South America were supposedly created by Spanish nuns, who combined the intricate Old World spice blends of medieval and Moorish Spain with the challenging ingredients of the New World, particularly chocolate and chillies.

A mole (mol-ay) is profound, thick and packs both flavour and heat. Genuine mole recipes can take days, getting richer and darker as they do; and the one dish you should always try if offered is turkey with a mole sauce, for it is considered the pinnacle of such cookery.

Mole sauce mixes and mole sauce kitsets are offered, containing a mixture of chilli types, cocoa or chocolate, many spices, sesame seeds, almonds, raisins and more. Sometimes a mole will be identified by the chilli that dominates its recipe, as Mole Poblano, and this gives some clue as to how hot or aromatic it will be. There are lighter coloured green *moles*, made with pepitas, raw, green pumpkin seeds.

Do-it-yourself mole makers should look for authentic background and recipes in *The Book of Latin American Cooking* by Elizabeth Lambert Ortiz (Grub Street).

PICKLING SPICE: this mixture of spices, with a few herbs like bay thrown in, has more uses than for pickling onions. I use it to flavour vinegar for my red cabbage, and use it to flavour wine or cider when sousing mackerel, sprats or sardines.

There is no agreed recipe for pickling spice, but a quality blend would have mustard seed as its main component and fragrance and interest can be added with most of the following: coriander seeds, peppercorns, ginger root, allspice, dill seed, chillies, fenugreek, whole cloves, mace and cut bay leaves.

Sousing is a good way to prepare fish, especially sardine and mackerel; long slow cooking with pickling spices and a diluted vinegar allows the vinegar to dissolve the bones which in turn act with the liquid to form a jelly. Wonderful outdoor, picnic food.

POUDRE DE COLOMBO: this Caribbean curry mixture should have no chilli in it, and thus offers clear citric notes over warm spices. Very good with fish, and to make a difference to the mayonnaise or vinaigrette dressing of a potato salad or a mixture of roasted vegetables.

QUATRE-ÉPICES: a backbone of French domestic and commercial kitchens, and used a great deal in charcuterie, it's a mixture of white pepper, ground ginger, nutmeg and cloves.

Quatre-épices, like all ground spices, should only be bought or made in small quantities, kept dry, cool and airtight and used quickly. There is a sweet version used for ginger breads and the like, where the white pepper is replaced by allspice, often disguised by being called pimento.

RAS EL HANOUT: the Valhalla of mixed spice, the blissful, ultimate prize for all the conquering, looting and lusting by Muslim nomad, soldier and proselytiser, a culinary lexicon and souvenir of all the countries they once overran physically or intellectually. It is at once floral and sweet-spiced, sharp but immensely refined, arresting and disarming, sensual but never vulgar, raw, rough or challenging. And never ever included chilli, although most Western commercial mixes now do.

The name means 'top of the shop' for that is where the spice-soukh's merchants will keep their expensive ingredients, far from robbing hands. The average number of ingredients is said to be 27, and unless there are at least 20 it's stretching it to call a mixture ras el hanout.

In the whole spices I took back to London from Fez in screws of Arabic-scripted newspaper, there were six different peppers—Guinea pepper, long pepper, black pepper, grey cubeb pepper, malagueta pepper (grains of paradise) and monks' pepper, which comes from Morocco. Fragrance was given by cardamom, mace, galingale, nutmeg, allspice, cinnamon, turmeric, cloves, ginger, lavender flowers, rose buds, cassia buds and fennel seeds. Orrisroot, cyparaceae, ash berries, bella donna and quite a few untranslatable things were also included. Then to top it all, the metallic glint of whole cantharides, counted carefully and tellingly. I don't think this mixture included hashish but it is an authentic inclusion. None of the ingredients is overwhelmed, all are available to the palate, so much so you use far less than expected and still get a sat-in-smooth hit of hedonistic reward.

Commercially, ras el hanout is becoming a victim of sloppy wordsmiths and populism. It has become enmeshed in the awful belief all exotic spice mixtures should be hot to be authentic, in part because the world has been allowed to confuse spicy with hot—to me spice should mean just that, spiced. Every family and every spice merchant in Morocco has their own recipe and flavour of ras el hanout, and I always found enough heat came combined with flavoursome peppers and ginger. It is self-defeating to pay for such voluptuous fragrance and then to ambush it with chillies and they certainly didn't include chillies in any of the stalls I visited in Fez, Meknes, Marrakech, Rabat or Casablanca on a very recent visit to Morocco. I saw chillies for sale on only one stall in three weeks of looking; they are not traditional in Morocco or in Moroccan recipes and should not appear in ras el hanout.

Ras el hanout is wondrous when stirred into cooked couscous or rice with plenty of butter. It's magical with green vegetables, with carrots, or celeriac root and on roasted beetroot. Anything eggy reacts gratifyingly, as indeed does anything creamy or creamy of appearance and texture—so chicken and duck and turkey for sure.

This is an aristocrat of the most noble breeding, so don't treat it as a rub and then blacken the spices on a barbecue or grill or roast them into a cinder. Fry pieces of chicken or squid to a golden brown and then add ras el hanout, so it is not scorched or blackened.

My latest triumph with ras el hanout was to whisk some into the eggs for a potato frittata, without onion, of course, the most authentic way to many Spaniards.

SABZI GHORMEH: an excellent mixture of dried or fresh mint, parsley, chives and coriander with lime and perhaps some fenugreek, used in Iran in their many stews, or with rice.

SAMBALS: these are Indonesian and, although classically a relish, can be used to cook with and to flavour almost anything from kebabs and satays to absolutely anything served with rice. Fox's Spices sell a variety and describe them as 'breathtaking condiments to liven up any meal!'

Sambal assem: chillies with tamarind, making it hot, sharp and sweet.
Sambal bajak: chillies with fried, deeply browned onions; there is also a bajak extra heat, a version with ever more, even hotter chilli content.
Sambal bawang: chillies with onion and spices; bawang putti adds garlic.
Sambal manis: chillies with palm sugar, warm and sweet as well as hot.

Sambal oelek: the chillies are chopped and salted to make a very hot paste, chilli ferocity for those who don't fancy tasting anything else. Similar to harissa but with fewer layers of flavour.
Sambal nasi goreng: a mild mix of chillies and spices for traditional Indonesian rice dishes and that brightens up stir-fried cookery of all kinds.

SHICHIMI: a Japanese mixed spice with a fascinating flavour if it is not made too hot. It should include sesame and poppy seeds, tangerine peel and a number of untranslatables, plus chilli. Noodle dishes are served with this on the side but it is also used in stews.

TAGINE SPICES: a tagine is cooked in a vessel of the same name. The lid is a tall cone designed to drip condensation evenly back onto the food and keep it moist but not too moist. Moroccan foods rely on thickening sauces by reduction and concentration of their liquids plus emulsification of these with the butter and oil used.

Tagine spice mixtures vary according to personal taste and what is being cooked but that means European cooks often veer far from the real thing. Overuse of onion is a give-away of something not Moroccan as is the dearth of butter. The clue to authenticity in tagine recipes is ground ginger, something that gives Moroccan food a unique culinary place. Chillies are not a classic ingredient.

La kama is a tagine mix and in classic Moroccan style incorporates a lot of ground ginger, this time with pepper, cinnamon, nutmeg and turmeric.

TSIRE: an African flavouring based on peanuts with spices and chilli used on meats and vegetables. Plenty of red chilli with salt, mace and allspice make a difference to the common cumin, coriander and others of the usual suspects.

ZA'ATAR, ZAHTAR: I first met this most delicious of seasonings in the streets of Jerusalem, where although Arabic, it is especially popular baked onto flat breads, or spread onto bread with olive oil when it is toasted.

The ingredients are simple, toasted sesame seeds, ground thyme and *sumac* q.v., but the big flavours and acidity of the latter two have an extraordinary affinity with one another and with the sesame seeds. The palate reward is far greater than you might expect.

Once you have some in your cupboard you'll find it increasingly easy to reach for, in fact wherever you could use dukkah, or perhaps sumac alone, za'atar does equally well but with fewer crunchy nuts and more focussed flavour.

Truly fabulous on grilled or oven-roasted tomatoes and in any tomato sauce including pasta sauces. It's a treat on scrambled or fried eggs especially with ham or pork sausages, and in or on omelettes, when brunches or light suppers allow a bit more flavour on a plate than breakfast might welcome. Plainly roasted chicken legs can do with a coating before going into the oven, and so can a roasting chicken

but don't use it as a rub and then scorch or burn the ingredients in a pan or under a searing grill. I've not done it yet, but za'atar must be fabulous in bread dough.

ZANZIBAR CURRY POWDER: a particularly good mixture for vegetable curries and for roasting vegetables that includes brown sugar and such roasted spices as fennel seed and fenugreek.

Australasia's Indigenous Ingredients
Native or indigenous ingredients from these countries offer new flavour experiences or a new take on those we know. They are not difficult to use and well repay the effort. The opportunity is no different from being a medieval cook in Europe, confronted for the first time with cinnamon or nutmeg or black pepper. There's a real chance for many to make a mark by making these new flavours as familiar as the old.

Outside Australasia you might more easily find these products sold in sauces, jams and the like, and these make a good introduction to the flavours and to the intensity level at which they should or should not be used.

Some ingredients are grown commercially, many are still harvested from the wild. Indigenous ingredients from Australasia should be sourced through Aboriginal or Maori-owned companies or with local agreements.

Australia
BUSH TOMATOES/AKUDJURRA: a fruit of Australia's Central Desert they have

a gutsy, full tomato-like flavour heightened by definite raisin notes and a clean acid finish; an alternative name is desert raisin. The flavour can be considered a wilder cousin of sun-dried tomatoes, and thus can be used in all the same ways—on pizza, in pasta sauces or stews.

When the bush tomato is ground it is sold as *akudjurra* and this is easier to use in baking, where the warm flavour is very pleasing, so bread and pizza doughs and scones are simple ways to enjoy it. It mixes well for rubs etc. with most other indigenous flavours. Bush-tomato chutney gives amazing new life to robust cheeses, and to anything barbecued, particularly kangaroo and other game meats and birds.

DAVIDSON'S PLUMS: damson-sized and flavoured but too acidic to be eaten raw. Yet cook them with sugar, or make a jelly from them, and the wondrous flavour is one of the best of indigenous ingredients. Commercially-made chutneys with Davidson's plums will astonish you and create much talk around the barbecue.

ILLAWARRA PLUMS: the dark red berry of the Brown Pine, a semi-tropical tree found from New South Wales north to Queensland that like strawberries grows its seed on the outside of the fruit. About the size of a grape, they have a rich plum flavour with the resinous overtones of many indigenous ingredients; lemon juice holds the colour and keeps the resin flavours at bay. Used in compotes and sweet sauces for cheesecakes and other

desserts, but also as or in sauces for meat.

KAKADU PLUMS: looking like a miniature quince these yellow fibrous fruits have a vitamin C content 600 times that of a fresh orange, and are found in Western Australia from Katherine to the Kimberley. They make a terrific sweet jelly that adds an evocative new note to cream teas.

LEMON ASPEN BERRIES: another intense lemon flavour that's not acidic but has the common wild-food flavours of honey and eucalyptus: found in rain forests from Sydney right up to the Far North.

LEMON MYRTLE: perhaps the Australian rain forest's greatest gift, and certainly the easiest to use. The leaves taste of lemon with a touch of lemon grass, but then move into a clean, clear citrus flavour all their own, perhaps with elusive hints of makrut and eucalyptus. The flavour heightens when it is dried, but none of the finer notes is lost.

To create a minor sensation, simply use lemon myrtle anywhere you would use lemon, from fish sauces to ice creams and custards but if cooked too long at a high temperature the lemon flavour disappears, leaving resinous and bitter flavours. Found commercially in biscuits, shortbreads etc. and a New Zealand-made white-chocolate truffle flavoured with Australia's lemon myrtle won a bronze medal in the Great Taste Awards.

LILLI PILLI/RIBERRY: a number of these trees have edible berries, but the most stunning is the clove lilli pilli, which offers a concentrated spice flavour with top notes of clove. Excellent when used judiciously for both sweet and savoury concoctions including jams, baking and meat cookery.

MOUNTAIN PEPPER BERRIES: bigger than black peppercorns and with the same flavour profile as mountain pepper leaves, but the berries have both more heat and more of the palate-numbing sensation, so start by using only a tenth the amount of black pepper you would use. I tasted a mountain-pepper alcohol made in Tasmania that seared and deadened my tongue and made my eyes bulge and was first to wake me up to understanding that Australian native ingredients have something important and fresh to say for themselves, or in this case, to yell.

MOUNTAIN PEPPER LEAVES: the flavour and heat of pepper but with more dramatic aromas, and a definite tongue-numbing effect. Native to Tasmania, the leaves have such perfume and flavour they can be cut finely when fresh, or crushed when dried, and added to salad dressing, into a herb mixture for egg dishes, for barbecue spices and marinades. But beware, they are intense, and you should use only half the amount you would of ordinary black pepper.

MUNTRIES: sometimes called a native cranberry and can be used much the same way but with bigger, better apple overtones, too.

NATIVE MINT: curiously refreshing, the leaves look nothing like mint and have the characteristic slight resinous undertone of many Australian ingredients, and of black peppercorn. Extra good to give lamb a fascinating move sideways, and excellent combined with lemon myrtle and mountain pepper. It loves anything to do with garlic.

PAPERBARK: not used to flavour food, but to wrap or carry it. Dampened, it makes a superb way to roll up or fold up anything being cooked in the oven or on the barbecue, fish particularly, for although the paperbark might burn and might suffuse the food with a mild smoke flavour the food is unlikely to dry out or burn. If you cook in parcels of paperbark, serve them whole at table, so every diner gets the full whoosh of aroma when the bark is cut.

QUANDONG: called the native peach, bush or desert peach, quandongs are one of the best-known and best-loved Australian indigenous ingredients, yet are less commercially marketed than many. They have a distinct stone-fruit flavour and sweetness, followed by definite acidity in a silken flesh that is enjoyed fresh and dried. Quandong is quintessential Outback produce and most common in arid areas of South Australia. European settlers used quandong from early days, and made it into jams, chutneys and, best of all, double-crusted pies.

Usually bought dried, what you eat reconstituted looks like the peel of a small citrus, and is a rich red-orange colour. I best liked it when I baked a good handful with apple in a pie topped with lemon-myrtle-fragranced meringue. It must be terrific in salsas with poultry or fish and in chutneys for spreading on decent hams and salamis and the like.

RIBERRY: see *Lilli pilli.*

ROSELLA/WILD ROSELLA: the fruit or calyx of a climbing vine related to the native hibiscus, rosella gives a magnificent magenta-red colour and a comforting flavour that shuffles between rhubarb and red berries. Excellent as a jam, it's also a terrific basis for chutney that's just right for turkey instead of cranberries, and, because of the sweetness, with scallops, mussels and prawns.

WARRIGAL GREENS: used as a spinach substitute, as it was by Captain Cook in 1770, or as a substitute for Asian greens. Only the youngest leaves and buds should be used and should be cooked at least three minutes to reduce their oxalate content. The same plant as New Zealand spinach.

WATTLE SEED: don't try making this at home. Only some wattle (acacia) varieties from west of The Great Divide are suitable—the rest are poisonous. The seeds are lightly toasted to give a flavour profile reminiscent of coffee and roasted hazelnuts that can be used both sweet and savoury. Wattle-seed biscuits are commonplace, as are wattle-seed ice creams, meringues and pavlovas; they bring new zing to anything with chocolate, like tiramisu. Also use them in stuffings and sauces for poultry, mixed with other indigenous flavours for such fatty fish as eel or salmon.

WILD LIMES: about the size of a hazelnut and with an intense, distinct lime flavour, perhaps with a touch of grapefruit too. They make an excellent pickle with Indian spices to eat with cheese, beef, and seafood—almost anything where a citric note is welcomed. Recommended for the innovative.

New Zealand

There are few plant-based flavourings found in the New Zealand wilderness. Instead, emphasis is given to the quality of the produce of its fields, farms, lakes and sparkling seas.

HOROPITO: a perpetually fascinating herb-that-tastes-like-a-spice, obtained from the dried leaves of the eponymous native tree. Its flavour profile is huge, rushing in the mouth from pepper to garlic to celery and many other places before, during and afterwards. It has heat and a degree of numbing effect, too. All in all, something very special but it is not always used with respect or understanding. The flavours are fugitive and most disappear when heated, so horopito rubs, barbecue mixes and horopito pastas are a dead loss. Use horopito as a final seasoning on warm pasta or green vegetables or roasted chicken or scrambled eggs, and then it's a definite winner.

KAWAKAWA: known as native or bush basil, and there is a degree of that flavour, as part of its spectrum of pepperiness; it's related to kava, but the leaves make a tea that doesn't have its narcotic effect. It's an added aromatic in gin distilled in New Zealand.

PIKO PIKO: neither flavouring, herb nor spice, these are the exquisite curled emerging fronds of some of New Zealand's unique species of tree ferns. They are a vibrant green and look like the scroll of an over-embellished cello, but are not much bigger than a big thumbnail. The flavour is vegetal and provoking, asparagus gone bush. They are also marketed with stem or stalk, making them even more musical.

In other parts of the world young fronds from brackens and low-growing ferns are served as fiddleheads. The Maori name is *koru*, symbolic of new life, of rebirth. As a garnish or feature in salads or vegetable mixtures piko piko must rate as one of the world's most beautiful ingredients.

Oils

NEED TO KNOW

An edible oil is an edible fat that is liquid at normal temperatures.

Every natural fat and oil has the same calorie count.

Hydrogenation turns oil into a fat, but creates trans-fatty acids, thought carcinogenic.

Hydrogenated palm oil was widely used to prevent oxidisation and staling in processed foods: this has now largely been withdrawn because of major cholesterol dangers.

Vegetable oils are mainly liquid polyunsaturated fats and linoleic acid, which help lower cholesterol and aid burning of carbohydrate, preventing conversion into fat.

Although earliest man in northern Europe relied on animals for fat, the rest of the ancient world looked equally to vegetable oils. In Mesopotamia sesame seed oil was used and records survive of the 'best quality' being bought for Nebuchadnezzar's palace. In Anatolia it was almond oil; in the Americas oil from the peanut, maize and sunflower; in China and South East Asia they used soya and coconuts. Before the introduction of the olive, you would have used radish seed oil in Egypt, walnut and poppy seed oil in Greece. Poppies of a different type were used in northern Europe, as well as oil from flax and camelina. Where olives grew, olive oil was always first and best.

Not all oils were used exclusively for cooking, nor are they now. Pliny says: 'There are two liquids especially agreeable to the human body, wine inside and oil outside.' I shouldn't think he was speaking of salads alfresco ...

A cook who understands oil has at least three in the cupboard: a superior extra virgin olive oil to use as a dressing and that will never be heated; a lesser extra virgin olive oil or a virgin olive oil for cooking and frying, and that is also good enough to be a dressing, and a third, blander oil for frying or for mayonnaise bases. This third oil could be a 'light' olive oil or one of the vegetable oils. To these basics I would add walnut or hazelnut oil for a delicious change, and sesame oil for finishing Asian and Oriental dishes.

Types of oil

ALMOND OIL: best known as a beauty treatment, but edible varieties are bottled and sold, mainly in France. It is pallid in colour and exceptionally fragile in flavour and if your tongue is sensitive enough it titillates with a slight milky greenness, the same after-effects as fresh green almonds. Perhaps more pleasing outside than inside.

ARGAN OIL: vital to survival of indigenous Berbers in south-western desert areas of the Sousse plain, inland from Agadir in Morocco, it is made from the seed-nut of the ancient argan tree, which has adapted to survive in severe conditions that make lesser plants panic. It has been a reliable source of food oil for centuries, but the 20th century began encroaching. Today, after local agitation and the bravery of protesting women, much of its scant habitat is officially protected and argan production is becoming an important source of income.

The flavour is light, warm, comforting and nutty; many think hazelnut oil is the closest. In Morocco it is sprinkled onto couscous, used to dress chargrilled capsicums (bell peppers), used for frying eggs that will be dusted with cumin, even used to finish gorgeous tagines of meat and dried fruits in their typical buttery sauces heightened with ginger and paprika and cumin. Or it makes *amlou*, a thick mix of ground almonds, honey and argan oil, then piled onto yeast-raised pancakes, or used as a dip/spread for fresh bread. Argan oil is best used and eaten cold or warmed, and never heated or hot.

BERGAMOT: the oil of an intensely flavoured Sicilian citrus, the proper flavour of Earl Grey tea but that can be used in creative ways to startle and gratify.

CANOLA: see *Rapeseed*. A construct based on Canada and oil because that country produces so much rapeseed oil.

COBNUT: this is one name for cultivated hazelnuts. A Kentish company makes cold-pressed cobnut oil that was a sensation when introduced at the Great Taste Awards. Deeply nutty and fresh tasting, it is a great drizzler.

COTTONSEED: widely used in vegetable oil mixtures and in margarines, especially in the United States. It has usually been bleached but when used to pack seafood (especially from Japan) it still has slight colour and, to me, an unpleasant taste and texture, also detectable in the butter substitutes, reminiscent of the oil used in old sewing machines.

FLAVOURED OILS: a range of flavoured oils and vinegars makes the keys of a piano in your kitchen. With their bright, exact flavours plus zinging fresh ingredients you can play a favourite or a new flavour tune in the kitchen whenever the mood hits you. As so often with something that seems lively, worthwhile and new, these are often not what they seem but are oils tarted up with manufactured flavours. Read the label and prefer oils that are infused rather than 'flavoured'. Also see *Citrus Oils*.

Some olive oils are pressed with such ingredients as whole oranges but be aware that such a flavour is likely to be a man-made 'flavouring'. Read the label.

Other commercially available flavoured oils worth considering are those flavoured with Oriental ingredients for wok cooking, like garlic and ginger. But honestly, why pay others to do what is so easily obtained at home? Make flavoured oils the way you would make flavoured vinegar, by macerating. Unwaxed citrus zest, singly or mixed, smoked or plain garlic, any sort of fresh dried or smoked chillies, fresh or dried herbs, fresh or roasted black or green peppercorns, lavender or rose, Thai makrut leaf or zest—and everything else delicious. Dried porcini oil keeps its flavour well in gentle cooking and I make my own by macerating the dried pieces in a light oil.

GRAPESEED: some say delicate, some say dull. Used for margarine and by some in salad dressings but that seems wimpish. If you fancy making flavoured oils, then grapeseed easily absorbs the flavours of herbs, spices, citrus and the like without pushing in.

GROUNDNUT: see *Peanut.*

HAZELNUT, HUILE DE NOISETTES: less common than walnut oil, but worth every centime—it usually comes from France. It has an affinity with tomatoes, although not as strong as that of walnut oil. Heat ruins it so don't cook with it; better pour it lightly over, say, grilled rabbit or game, onto warm artichokes with soft-boiled eggs or green beans into which you have stirred roasted hazelnuts and garlic. Flavour a

traditional bread sauce with this at the last minute rather than with butter: just great with game birds.

Hazelnut oil is considered coarser than walnut oil and more strident, and thus it is commonly diluted with vegetable oil, a lesser olive oil, or, in a sauce with melted butter, but I would always try it neat first, because you might think it just right, as I do. Not unexpectedly, hazelnut oil works very well with berry fruits and thus with such fruit vinegars as raspberry on salads.

The oil must be kept cool and dark once opened, as it oxidises very quickly. In extremis I should refrigerate it, even though it thickens and clouds. See also *Cobnut oil.*

HEMP SEED OIL: a rich green colour and a strong nutlike flavour that is sometimes diluted with other oils and flavours when retailed. Full of flavour and of goodness for you, highly poly-unsaturated, and a definite talking point. Particularly when someone recognises its faint, curious but curiously familiar scent of marijuana; ask how they know that.

INFUSED OILS: see *Flavoured oils.*

LINSEED: culinary grade linseed or flaxseed oil has a rich, buttery taste and is useful to add richness to bland dishes; it can be used as a milder laxative than the seeds.

OLIVE OIL: those who buy the very best extra virgin olive oil and use it for all culinary chores are historically wrong. Heating fine extra virgin olive oils destroys the finest flavours and aromas, the very graces that cost you so much. That is the classic historical advice but things have changed.

Because so much olive oil is today extracted by mechanical means rather than pressure, oceans more cheap extra virgin olive oils are now marketed. A new option for the cook is to have a variety of extra virgin olive oils that are used on the basis of cost and quality of flavour, still reserving the best for dressing and not cooking.

Northern Europeans, the British and North Americans who have still not cooked with olive oil are greatly reducing their culinary highlights. Start by using olive oil to fry eggs or make chips or pour into baked potatoes, baste chicken and fish, smother roast vegetables or to make tomato sauces.

Before we proceed, let's get clear about the official classifications of olive oil. Then it's up to you.

The basic standard for olive oil is virgin olive oil, and that has been defined by the International Olive Oil Council as being:

'... obtained solely by mechanical or other physical means under conditions, and particularly thermal conditions, that do not lead to the deterioration of the oil, and which has not undergone any treatment other than washing, decantation, centrifugation and filtration ... virgin olive oil (must thus be) fit for consumption as it is ...'

Virgin olive oil may be made by the traditional mill's first pressing of a paste of crushed olives, or by the modern, more common and greater yielding combination of hydraulic press and centrifuge, each process without any heat or chemical assistance. Extra virgin means an oil higher than the basic standards, based on lower acidity as well as appearance and flavour.

Olive oils not only reflect *terroir* the way wine grapes do, they also reflect annual differences. The variety of olive grown has a bearing, of course, but so does the weather and humidity on the day of pressing, the time between harvesting and processing and the precise mixture of varieties. Some of the most highly protected olive oil names can officially be made with a bewildering number of different varieties and the balance of these is likely to change by the day, let alone by the month, making the tastes in the bottle you buy as imprecise and unpredictable as that weather.

These variations make nonsense of any belief in precise olive oil flavours produced in an area, just as this would be foolish to believe about wine. If there is consistency in any olive oil it is almost always due to blending, as with champagne. It would be an advantage to consumers for single-source and regional olive oils to have a vintage system that celebrated natural differences rather than pretending they do not exist.

Types of olive oil

EXTRA VIRGIN OLIVE OIL: EVO or EVOO. These must have a maximum acidity of 1%, although most are around 5%. They should be impeccable in every sensory way, called organoleptic qualities, and properly reflect the individuality of the olive variety/varieties and the season in which they were harvested.

VIRGIN OLIVE OIL: maximum acidity of 1.5%, and most are indistinguishable from extra virgin oils.

LAMPANTE VIRGIN OLIVE OIL, REFINED OLIVE OIL, AND OLIVE OIL: descending grades of olive oil processed to make them palatable. The 'olive oil' category once used to be called 'pure olive oil' and is 100% olive oil, but this is no guarantee of flavour or other qualities. Some are very lightly flavoured and make excellent oils for mayonnaise, for basic cooking and for the palates of those who are not yet adventurous.

LIGHT OLIVE OIL: is not lighter in fat content but lighter in flavour and this will be the result of soul and spirit reduction through processing. Its calorie content and imputed health-giving qualities are no different from the finest extra virgin oils.

POMACE: oil obtained by solvents after the main pressing of olives. Although 100%, it might not be retailed just as 'olive oil' because of that process.

And ...

There are two exceptional styles of olive oil not made by pressing the olives.

FLOWER OF THE OIL *FLOR DE ACEITE*: it takes 11 kg/22 lb of olives to make a litre/1.75 pints. Olives are crushed into a paste the usual way but when this is spread on traditional mats the oil flows only under its own weight, with just light pressing to complete the yield, as with Hungary's Tokay wine grapes. Nunez del Prado in Andalucia is possibly the only company making this style.

SINOLEA: a 20th century mechanical method extracts oil by chopping olives with metal blades and harvesting the oil that collects on them, using neither heat nor pressure.

Styles of olive oil

Internationally, about 25% of olive oil is made from the picual olive. It is very herbaceous and pungent with residual bitterness and often thought too strong a flavour, but has a gratifyingly high oil content so makes a solid platform on which to make blends with other varieties that mollify its aggression.

The broad character of each country's olive oils changes as you move North to South and more dramatically West to East. Olive oils are light and green in Portugal, are a fragrant medium weight in France and north-east Spain, get stronger as you go south in Spain and become increasingly robust and sometimes peppery in Italy and get throatier and heavier as you move eastwards across the Mediterranean, or southwards in a Mediterranean country. An extra virgin oil from Spain or Provence may seem positively honeyed and vinous compared to the same quality from Italy, which can be distinctly biting and peppery or from Greece, which will be altogether thicker and powerful, except this will depend on whereabouts in Italy or Greece. It's not simple.

Modern business practice means that an olive variety once identified only with a certain region is now grown elsewhere in the country and even in other countries. The elegant *arbequina* originated in Mallorca and is taken to its greatest aristocratic heights in northeast Spain. Now grown in Italy, its name on a bottle is no guarantee of its Spanish elegance, because the soil, climate and methods differ.

Time, taste and budget are all necessary partners to finding the olive oil you most like. An expensive shop is no guarantee of quality or consistency but should be: a remote hovel is no guarantee of roughness, but could be. Should you find a cheaper olive oil you like, which does not have fancy packing or famous names, you are more likely to be paying for what is in the bottle rather than what's on it. It's just that none of it may have come from where you might expect; much of Spain's olive oil is exported to Italy. An oil bottled somewhere does not guarantee it has also been made there.

Wherever it is from, virgin olive oils should be sold and kept in dark glass and even then be kept out of the light. Oil left on the lip of a bottle or other container should be wiped away, as it will oxidise; oil poured and exposed to the air should never be returned to the bottle.

What follows is a mixture of personal experience, the advice of respected specialist oil importers, and of Anne Dolamore's *The Essential Olive Oil Companion*. I especially like that book because her palate seems to be exactly the same as mine. Yet, do not fear to disagree, for exchange of opinion is the greatest flavouring of food.

AUSTRALIA: it didn't take long for Australia's olive trees to be discovered by the Italians and Greeks who flooded to Australia after the Second World War. A few were in groves, but most had been planted as shade trees by even earlier settlers.

As with NZ, the success of a wine culture changed everything, and in Australia's cities and towns restaurants serve olive oil rather than butter and hardly a hunk of meat goes into mouths without olive oil associated somehow. On the Fleurieu peninsula close to Adelaide, feral olives are collected every year, and these oils are particularly well worth seeking out.

FRANCE: the provinces with a Mediterranean coastline all produce olive oil, and thousands of small olive mills continue to press local olive varieties and make truly individual oils of finesse and delicacy.

In broad terms the expression *Huile de Provence* is generally a guarantee of decent standards. Nyons is the great olive centre, relying heavily for eating and oil olives on the invaluable *tanche*, a small black olive introduced by the Romans; it adds terrific sweetness and fruit to oils. In the village of Mirabel the Farnoux family produces Le Vieux Moulin oil only from such olives.

Because France produces relatively small amounts of her own olive oil you don't easily find it available, but if you are travelling in the south an olive oil tasting and buying expedition is great fun. There are five olive mills just north of Marseilles on either side of the A7; here local varieties *aglandaus* and *saurines* make very individual oils. Head also for Mausannes-les-Alpilles, Mouries, Beaumes-de-Venise, and the famed Les Barronnies, also at Nyons.

The oils of La Lucques in Languedoc are considered quite the equal of Provençal oil, if not better, which will give you something to argue.

GREECE: no one can accuse these oils of delicacy. The generally robust, straight-forward flavour can be neat and clean behind a full, flavoury body—and they have probably been making them longer than most, too. The two main areas of production are the Peloponnese, which includes famed Kalamata, and the island of Crete, where olive trees cover more than half the cultivated land.

You will find organic oils made in remote areas, and a Cretan oil pressed from a particularly small variety of olive with negligible acid content. Kalamata oils are outstanding, but not what you might think. They are not made from the exceptional *kalamata* olive but produced in the Kalamata area from the major Greek oil olive, the *koroneiki*, but then so are most main-land oils, whatever they are called.

JORDAN: the Hashemite Kingdom of Jordan is the world's 10th largest pro-ducer of olive oil, and some very supe-rior olive oils are exported. Terra Rossa is a brand reflective of the iron-rich soil in which their ancient olive trees grow and they market sinolea-style olive oil.

ITALY: the best-known style is largely Tuscan with an exaggerated chilli-type pepperiness given by the *frantoio* and *moraiolo* olives and that appeals to the modern taste for heat on the palate. A gentler oil and freshly ground black pepper would be kinder and more fra-grant on most foods. Some estates that make Chianti Classico wines also pro-duce oils that are *very* robust but with a lesser amount of expected peppery aftertaste. In complete contrast, oils from the Ligurian Coast use only the *taggiasca/cailleter/Niçoise olive*, which gives a medium to light, green-gold oil with accentuated sweetness.

Other olive varieties most found in Italy are the *Ascolera Tenera*, a green eating olive that adds delicate fruit-iness, the black eater *leccino* adding sweetness, the *Coratino* (actually from Apulia) that keeps its rich fruit-iness for a long time and the *Nocellara Etnea* from eastern Sicily that gives a deep green-gold colour and a dis-tinct perfume. The high-yielding *pen-dolino* is self-pollinating and its weep-ing branches make harvesting simple and fast; it's quite grassy and has a tingle that stays in the throat. In Sicily the *cerasuola* olive gives a rich flavour and texture but Apulia in the south, the country's largest producer, con-centrates on the *coratina*; even Italians might agree that this is Italy's best, with a full olive flavour that is bal-anced and has a clean aftertaste but no pepperiness.

NEW ZEALAND: the combination of a Mediterranean climate and an 'I can do that' attitude means New Zealand produces sensational olive oils, but has only done so for the last few decades. Olive trees were introduced by 19th century settlers but olive oil produc-tion was ignored until the country's palate was lit up by its equally late but stupendous embracing of superior wine production.

Now most of the country grows olives and in some places has discovered varieties flourishing in NZ long enough to have adapted and become distinct. Many of the groves are still very young and most, but not all, are associated with wine-growing areas.

Most producers have opted for the richer, grassier and more peppery style of Tuscan oils, yet there are plenty of exceptions, as there should be. Like New Zealand's wines, they are clear, direct, utterly faithful to the olives, and highly recommended.

PORTUGAL: these less-seen oils often have a fresh taste of apples, a more refined way to balance unctuousness than the pepper-heat of Tuscan oils. The oil of Conservas Rainha Santa from Estremoz is wonderfully supple, clear and gratifying in the mouth. A definite destination for serious olive-oil researchers.

SPAIN: Spain is the world's largest olive-oil producer and exporter (especially to Italy it should be noted) and was also the first to declare officially guaranteed areas of origin and production standards for olive oils.

The queen of Spain's oil-producing olives is the *arbequina*, introduced from Mallorca, and now grown particularly elegantly in north-east Spain, Catalonia and thereabouts.

Guaranteed areas of Spanish production are no indication of flavour or style. For instance, the holiday island's DOP Mallorca oil can be almond-like with minimal pepperiness or bitterness, or notably sweet, but with no almond or other fruit flavours.

On the mainland, the *arbequina* and *picual* are grown together, the fruity *empeltre* is widely included, as is the bitter-sweet and fruity *hojiblanca*. Further south the fleshy table olive *gordal* is included. Add hundreds of local varieties and that is Spanish olive oils, none of which will be aggressive and many of which are yellow-gold rather than green and just as often offer a lingering nuttiness.

PALM OR PALM KERNEL OIL: the brilliant red fruit of the oil palm grows in bunches averaging 13–18 kg/26–32 lb in weight and if properly cultivated the tree produces a higher yield than any other oil-producing plant per acre. That is why forests everywhere are ravaged and then replaced by oil palm plantations. You will see claims on labels that palm oil is sustainable but this overlooks the fact that natural habitats and indigenous creatures have been lost to achieve this. Virgin forest and jungle is raped to plant palms so this oil can be harvested. I try to live without anything containing it.

It was once hydrogenated to make a solid fat, widely used because it gave very long life to processed foods but was discovered to cause greater cholesterol problems than dairy and meat. Another solid reason to avoid it.

PEANUT OIL: the nut has an oil content of 45–50%, and as well as having almost no taste, peanut oil can be used to fry at an extremely high temperature without unpleasant smoking or other side effects, so you get crisper food faster because the oil has had no opportunity to penetrate. By far the best oil for deep-frying and for wok cooking and another choice for making your own flavoured oils.

PISTACHIO: pistachio oil is almost fluorescent, a profound green-yellow, and perfectly but lightly pistachio flavoured. It is such a rare treat it should be used without any chance of confusion, dribbled only onto a guaranteed affinity, excellent lettuce or other saladings, perhaps with edible flowers. Segments of room temperature blood oranges to accompany duck scattered with roasted pistachios. Or on perfectly poached slices of salmon served just below room temperature. Or on a warm brioche, in which case I might just have whipped some of the oil into an unsalted butter, cultured or not, a pretty good idea with all nut oils. A minuscule amount of garlic is very good with pistachio oil. If the nuts come from Bronte on the slopes of Mount Etna the oil will be best of all.

PINE NUT OIL: not very immediate in flavour, pine nut oil must be used in quantity to be ensured of tasting it, but also with restraint and discretion as the slightly resinous flavour can be off-putting.

It is good on lightly chilled poached poultry breasts or on salmon, with perfect tomatoes, perhaps dribbled onto small warm rolls to serve with fragrant Moroccan dishes, maybe to finish a Provençal *tian* of spinach or chard.

It's a very good effect to use it as a garnish or dressing with toasted pine nuts.

POPPYSEED OIL: another oil popular simply for its lack of taste, an asset in some sorts of cooking. It is sold as *huile blanche* (white oil) in northern France and Paris, where it enjoys greatest popularity.

PUMPKIN SEED OIL: an initial belief in some relationship with motor oil is not unnatural. It is thick, turgid and terribly green-brown. It has an astonishingly rich, nutty flavour—too much to use by itself unless flavouring a soup or a mash. For salads it very much needs to be diluted with a vegetable oil.

RAPESEED OIL: oil-seed rape is now one of Europe's biggest crops and responsible for those sensational fields blanketed mustard-yellow but that are not mustard. The powdery, musky scent from these acres causes untold agonies of allergy; and the bitterness of its nectar permeates, and to some palates, ruins honey. The oil must be radically purified and refined to make it useful.

If you use something called only vegetable oil, this is what it is likely to be, and why it is taking over Britain's fields. Canola is a coined name, perhaps to disguise the reality.

Cold-pressed rapeseed oil: is something else, a sunny yellow colour with very good health claims, including the lowering of cholesterol levels.

SAFFLOWER OIL: safflower seeds have been unmasked in Egyptian tombs of 2000 BC and even then the crop was grown for its florets, which give a cheap imitation of saffron without any pretension to imitating its flavour. When synthetic dyes began to displace safflower it seemed doomed, but then it was discovered oil from the florets and their seeds has the highest percentage of polyunsaturated oil known, 78%.

SESAME SEED OIL: a very ancient oil, which should be used as a flavouring rather than as a frying medium or as an oil by itself. It can be darkly red-brown or a less assertive reddish brown, depending on whether the seeds have been first toasted. It must be fresh and made to high standards or will be bitter, even on the nose.

Marco Polo was impressed enough to write about it and it is still widely used in India and the Orient, especially in confectionery and bakery. Add a few drops when deep-frying tempura or anything else in batter. Add to marinades, especially for microwaving, or sprinkle onto almost anything to which you would add sesame seeds: prawns, green beans, pumpkin purée, chicken joints, baked hams. It very quickly goes rancid so should be stored cool and dark once opened.

SIBERIAN OILS: hard to believe but Siberia exports 10 cold-pressed oils including pine-nut oil, apricot kernel, sesame seed, sunflower seed, walnut, corn, watermelon seed, flax, rose hip and mustard seed; often they are blended with camelina oil. Worth exploring.

SOYBEAN OIL: one of the top four in the polyunsaturated league and an extremely good keeper. Soybean oil also has an elevated smoking point, which means it will fry or deep-fry at a temperature high enough to ensure it will not pass what little flavour it has onto the food.

SUNFLOWER OIL: the very high percentage of poly-unsaturates in this oil make it very important indeed, and it is widely used as an oil for salads, cooking, fats and margarine. It is very good for frying also but perhaps a little expensive for this use on a regular basis.

TRUFFLE OILS: reviled as the tomato ketchup of the upwardly mobile, but truffle oils are the safest way to be overtly sensual in public. Few if any are the result of macerating these magical fungi in oil, but are 'flavoured' with laboratory-created 'flavourings'. If you overlook their artificiality, the best economically spread the apparent pleasure far wider.

Black truffle: less immediate than white truffle oil but has an earthy, meaty flavour the late food writer Jeremy Round bravely described as scrotal. It is best used without exposure to direct heat, but may be whisked into warm sauces, mashed or scalloped potatoes, poured into eggs just before they scramble, sprinkled onto smoked salmon or worked into whipped cream or butter to go with almost anything— hot or cold ham, when genuine, rather salty ones go orbital. Black truffle oil is just the thing for dressing excellent roasted beef or steaks, sprinkled onto slices of hot, roasted turkey, free range chicken or game birds or in salads which contain them.

White truffle: like the astronomically priced white truffle, the oil has one of the world's most arresting, disturbing and irresistible smells, said to be 'redolent of all possible perversity and prohibition and reeking of every forbidden vice'.

Just as you should never cook with a white truffle, you should never cook with white truffle oil. Thus instead of shaving white truffle over your risotto you simply sprinkle on some of the oil. You could and should do the same to mashed potato or to scrambled eggs. Adding white truffle oil to the uneasy flavours of artichoke make the edgiest of combinations. In parts of Italy raw white truffle is shaved over brioches: to emulate this I'd mix the oil into some melted unsalted butter, pull apart a warm brioche, and pour this on to the two halves. You could, of course, have added the oil to some fearfully thin slices of young mushroom, and put these into the brioche, but somehow the texture gets in the way of full abandonment to the flavour. A white-truffled brioche is not for the faint-hearted, but an extraordinary thing to eat late in the morning, perhaps with smoked salmon.

Once hooked you will think of zillions of ways to use white truffle oil, but beware: the scent plays havoc with some people who can barely be in the same room.

WALNUT OIL, HUILE DE NOIX:
Perigueux, that was the place, on a warm stone wall on the corner of a hot cobbled street. There I first discovered the God-given affinity of tomatoes and walnuts when I poured walnut oil onto a sun-warmed tomato.

Bacon and eggs, gin and tonic, fish and chips? Such are nothing in comparison to this affinity wizardry, and,

just as few additions can improve those, you need little else when you have tomatoes and walnut oil. Perhaps some parsley, that's very good, and maybe a little salt and pepper. But no vinegar, no herbs, no garlic or chives, no million-and-one ingredients, clear-out-the-fridge salad. Just two ingredients that work together to make something bigger and better than either.

There's more to walnut oil. It keeps the slight bite of fresh walnuts and together with its inherent sweetness thus both complements and extends the flavours of light meats, from grilled pork chops to pan-seared pheasant breasts. It's terribly good with fruit as you might expect, so peach halves dribbled with walnut oil after grilling become a much faster and better-tasting accompaniment than grilled stuffed peaches, especially with hot or cold ham. Walnut oil goes well with green salads of course, or add it to mayonnaise made with bland vegetable oil. Added microwave-toasted walnuts make more of the pleasure.

Don't cook with walnut oil, as most of the flavour goes. Most of all, be on the alert for really ripe tomatoes.

Olives

NEED TO KNOW

Olives are green, violet, natural black and processed black.

Some olives are best if harvested early and green; others must be ripe.

Violet olives are half ripe, particularly popular on the North African coast.

Black olives are naturally purple or brownish, not black.

Some olive trees provide both green and black varieties.

Green olives are usually put into a soda (lye) solution, reducing bitterness, softening and lightly cooking and then put into brine for lactic acid fermentation.

Ripe olives may be sterilised before putting into brine and fermented by yeast action.

Oil curing puts ripe olives into salt to dry and concentrate, and then into oil to hydrate again.

Processed olives are alternated between lye and water and compressed air oxidises them to become blacker and shinier with uniformly coloured flesh.

Once cured, olives are stored in brine, vinegar or, rarely, oil.

Finest quality olives, like the Greek kalamata, are stored only in oil, pointed with wine vinegar.

Rare, over-wintered olives are like raisins, wrinkly and concentrated.

The stones of pitted olives are pressed for low-grade oil.

Only a pitted Spanish manzanilla olive properly belongs in a martini cocktail.

It is more important to keep olives out of light rather than refrigerated.

Brine levels should always cover olives.

Sliced lemon prevents mould growing on brine.

Draining, rinsing and coating in oil is the best way to extend life.

Anything you find in pitted olives will scent olives in oil: zests, herbs, garlic, peppers, citrus.

Some types of olive

France
The south of France grows a bewildering number of olives in both colours. As well as plain black or green, the markets of Nîmes make a speciality of stuffed olives. The best black olives in brine are from Nyons and Carpentras; Menton's are especially big and luscious but there are many important local varieties.

Cailletier/ olives de Nice/Niçoise: small, brownish and very perfumed. The proper olive to use in Niçoise cooking, including Salade Niçoise. Sometimes called Taggiasca.

Lucques and petits-lucques: are green, curved, pointed and part easily from the stone, with a notably rich creaminess.

Nyons (sometimes tanches): the best French black olives, a rich plum-black and heart shaped.

Picholine: green, savoury and generously fleshed even though small.

Saloneque: often broken and especially good in cooking where a discreet residual bitterness is welcome.

Taggiasca: see *Cailletier.*

Greece

The majority of olives are black, and these include some extraordinary varieties sweet enough to eat direct from the trees. In Greece it is especially easy to detect differences of flavour given by variety and by soil and climate.

Kalamata: fleshy and succulent purple-black olives widely thought to be amongst the very best from any source. Always sold in olive oil, sometimes with a dash of wine vinegar. Good for eating and cooking.

Mitilini: the island reputed to grow the best of olives eaten from the tree.

Throumba: succulent and mild, wrinkly, over-wintered eating olive made on the island of Thassos.

Italy

A bewildering choice of excellent eating and cooking olives, often oil-cured.

Baresane: light and fresh Puglian olives from greenery/yallery to pale purple.

Castelvetrano: see *Nocelarra del Belice.*

Cerignola: very big and creamy, they can be green or black.

Gaeta: often stored in oil, they have a particular sharp citrus tang.

Nocellara del Belice: mild Sicilian green olives with a creamy texture; recommended as a superior table olive and it also makes a notably superior oil.

Saracena: an ancient cultivar grown on Sicily that produces a fleshy olive judged comparable to the kalamata in fragrance and flavour.

Taggiasca: well-flavoured with fruitness and slight feral undertones, these are from Liguria and crossed the border to France, where they became *cailletier/olives de Nice.*

Spain

Although dozens of olive varieties make Spanish olive oil, some from Andalucia are specially suited as green, eating olives.

Manzanilla: small, paler finer textured and silky skinned, especially good for cooking and martini cocktails, in either order.

Queen: large, deep green, and fleshy, known as the *gordal* in Seville and the *sevillano* in the rest of Spain.

Sauces

Dabbed, smeared, shaken, spread or eaten by the spoonful, each of these is a condiment, used to add spirit and joy, even to food already highly flavoured. The range available commercially changes by the month, even on supermarket shelves. Fashion is specially fickle about chilli-based sauces and whatever is in vogue spawns 'make-your-own' versions on the web.

Some types of sauce

AIOLI: rarely available to buy authentically, this is not mayonnaise with added garlic. It is garlic used as the basis for a mayonnaise, which should be hot with the sting of fresh garlic, at least two cloves of garlic per person. Mustard is a permitted addition at the start as this helps emulsification. In Spain it is *ali oli*.

AJVAR: a purée of roasted and peeled red peppers with some roasted aubergine, and mercifully without onion, this Balkan-ish product is everything from a condiment to a spread to a dressing. A sparkling friend to cheese of all kinds, used instead of butter in sandwiches, in seafood dressings, on pasta or in baked potatoes. Made mild or hot.

ANCHOVY ESSENCE: a concentration of anchovy and salt that should be used with great restraint and that has been relied upon for centuries to add hidden wonder to all manner of dishes. Spread very thinly over lamb before roasting, add to any sauce for any fish and to cheese dishes or sauces.

Anchovy sauce: is more diluted but should still be used with care.

Recommended as a substitute for Asian fish sauces.

BROWN FRUIT SAUCE: date syrup is the base for many, especially HP sauce, but vinegar, onions and fruit of other kinds are also essential. It is easy—and right— to make fun of those who use these and other sauces with no thought for the cook, but like every product that has survived on the market, fruit sauces have their place and time. A good game pie or pork pie is more improved by such a sauce than mustard. Try directly from the refrigerator, which lessens unwarranted sweetness.

CHAKALAKA: made in South Africa with a base of onion, chillies, fresh ginger and curry powder, into which are stirred tomatoes, green pepper/capsicum and carrots, and then topped up with baked beans and cooked until smooth.

Chakalaka was created as a sauce for *millipap* or *mealie-mealie*, the staple township porridge of cornmeal. And that's the clue to the presence of baked beans. Cornmeal is unbalanced and a diet based heavily or exclusively on it leads to protein imbalance and the dread disease pellagra. Yet add bean protein to grain protein and you get a meat protein equivalent: add other vegetables and you have a healthier diet. It is said imminently to be exported.

CHILLI SAUCES: a great favourite to make by artisans and small manufacturers everywhere, so there are dozens made in the UK alone. Whether mild or hot, please don't call them spicy, a word that has no relevance to heat on the palate.

MILD OR SWEET: thickened, sweet sauces with (usually) only a mid-hit of chilli and sometimes of garlic and ginger too. The sweetness makes them a great friend of fish, especially of such oily types as salmon, mackerel and eel, hot or cold. A perfect zester to stir-fried chicken added at the last minute, perhaps with a squeeze or two of lime. They contain stuff you wouldn't normally have in your cupboard, but give a lift when you have no time or inclination for complication.

HOT: every year a different hot chilli sauce from somewhere in the world becomes the fashion but their extreme heat quotients leave little chance of discovering nuances of difference. Some of these are:

Balachuang: a mildish, chewy condiment from Burma with dried shrimp, browned onions and garlic.

Chamoy: something really different from Mexico, made from fruit and chillies specifically as a dip for fresh fruit.

Chimichurri: an Argentinean condiment of oil mixed with pounded parsley, oregano and garlic with varying amounts of chilli, used particularly on grilled meats.

Harissa: a Tunisian mix with olive oil, citrus and spices but these are regularly blown out of existence by the chilli content. Although sometimes included in Moroccan recipes, it is not traditional as chilli is rarely used in that voluptuous cuisine. Rose Harissa adds rose petals that easily disappear and/or rose water, which has more chance of survival, but both are fugitive in the presence of so much chilli.

Katsu/Tonkatsu: a Japanese barbecue sauce based on Worcestershire sauce and soy sauce with other ingredients, even tomato ketchup. Everyone has a recipe.

Sambal Oelek: an Indonesian chilli-based paste with many aromatic ingredients including shrimp paste, so used very moderately it can have something to say in a recipe. There are many other *sambals*, q.v.

Shito: a Ghanaian variation with tomato and ginger underpinned by dried fish and shrimp.

Sriracha: from Thailand, it is mainly chillies with sugar, vinegar and man-made flavour enhancers plus a preservative that Finland does not allow. It can also be found smoked.

Tabasco: many styles of chilli now make a range of *Tabasco sauces* q.v. but all have the advantage of being able to be used discreetly, drop by drop.

Yuzukosho: a fermented paste of yuzu zest, green chillies and salt.

The strong salty combination of this very aromatic Japanese citrus and chilli makes this a striking condiment to electrify soups and stocks, on noodles and pasta or as a marinade for roasts and grills.

Zhoug: a Yemenite paste of coriander leaf (cilantro) and chillies used widely as a condiment with falafel, but you'll probably have to make your own.

FISH SAUCE: although best known as the *nam pla* of Thai cooking, fish sauces are used throughout South East Asia and China. They are a result of the fermentation of fish, a direct cousin of the Romans' garum. None smell or taste of fish if they are any good, but are a lightly coloured and flavoured seasoning, more salt than any other taste. Used to finish dishes and as a table condiment.

HOISIN SAUCE: the one for Peking Duck. Also known as Barbecue Sauce even though its name means fresh flavour of the sea. Made from soybeans, flour, sugar, salt, garlic and chilli peppers, it is dark reddish brown in colour, has a creamy consistency and a sweet aftertaste. Particularly associated with roasted duck and pork and the like but, as the name suggests, also with seafood and fish. It may be used as a simple dip, too, and can be pimped with fruits and nuts.

KECAP MANIS: an Indonesian mix of soy sauce sweetened with palm sugar—or it should be palm sugar. The perfect finisher of microwaved/steamed green vegetables, with fish and with chicken pieces. Invaluable once discovered,

even in salad dressings.

MAYONNAISE: commercially produced mayonnaise is little like the real thing, an emulsion of egg yolk and oil. But products like Hellman's have created a new definition and are used where the real thing would not be right, such as on hamburgers. Enjoy them by all means, but read the label and know what you are eating.

MUSHROOM KETCHUP: one of a few ancient culinary standbys that survive. Salt is sprinkled on mushrooms and extracts the liquid from them. This is heated, flavoured and bottled.

Mushroom ketchup now often contains soy sauce, making the apparent salt content so high that mushroom ketchup becomes interchangeable with anchovy essence. Use mushroom ketchup only at the end of cooking to strengthen or add interest, in the same way that celery, salt, soy sauce, anchovy essence or garlic and ginger juice might do.

MENTAIKO: is a relatively new Japanese condiment, the roe of walleye pollack marinated in salt and chillies. When the roe sac is left whole, mentaiko looks like a skinned rodent, but it can also be bought sliced or mixed down into a purée looking remarkably like taramasalata. Originally the chilli-salt-fish product was intended to be eaten just with rice, but mentaiko can be found on pizza and pasta, on potato crisps, in instant noodles—there are even mentaiko restaurants.

OYSTER SAUCE: a rich, brown condiment or dipping sauce made by fermenting oysters and soy sauce, and thus related to fish sauce and soy sauce, but meatier tasting and more expensive than either. Use to finish a dish rather than as a cooking ingredient. Like fish sauce, only poor-quality oyster sauces will taste or smell fishy.

PESTO: all sauces made in Italy by pounding ingredients into a thick sauce are properly called a pesto. Pesto Genovese, from Genoa of course, is only one of them.

This pesto is of fresh basil, pine nuts, garlic, Parmesan, Pecorino (it should have both) and olive oil. It is bright, pungent and just what tomatoes and pasta need. It is an excellent condiment with grilled vegetables, cheese, steak, roast lamb and poultry and fish—hot or cold.

Commercial pesto Genovese has been pasteurised and most don't taste too bad but the basil has been attenuated and lost its colour and citrus/aniseed underpinning. Balance this by adding fresh basil, chopped or pounded and keep your mouth shut. Pound the basil between two sheets of wax paper or cling film, using a rolling pin, and then be sure you collect the oil left on the film, by rubbing it with fresh breadcrumbs or ground almonds and adding those.

PLUM SAUCE, CHINESE: made from a sour, yellow plum, so is a sweet and sour sort of chutney. Widely used as the start for other sauces: equal amounts of this and tomato ketchup make a basic sweet and sour sauce mix. Sometimes known in America as duck sauce, for the mixture was served together rather than the more usual Hoisin Sauce.

PLUM SAUCE: in the UK and Australasia, plum sauce means something quite different. Spiced red plum sauce or more elegant plum and tomato sauce, as thick as ketchup but darker in colour and infinitely more nuanced in flavour, is common on dining tables, and usually homemade, too. It adds life and interest to the dullest cold meats and hot pies, and behaves superbly when offered with the finest fare, including lobster from barbecues, roasted beef or lamb and the best parts of roasted birds.

PONZU: true Japanese ponzu is a thin, citrus-based sauce. Often mixed with shoyu, when it should be called ponzu shoyu but is usually just ponzu. Know the difference.

ROUILLE: has widely become a mayonnaise or an aioli with chilli, but it shouldn't be. Sadly chilli-hot rouille is increasingly served with bouillabaisse in the belief this is traditional and correct. It is not, but becoming so. Authentic rouille is a style of aioli or mayonnaise extended with breadcrumbs and saffron originally with a background touch of cayenne.

True rouille belongs to the simple and bland bourrides made west of Marseilles; bourride is mixed white fish poached in stock, which is then thickened with rouille. Bouillabaisse is made from far finer fish and, anyway, flavoured with saffron, the world's most expensive spice. Do you really think traditional cooks used saffron and then added chilli so you couldn't taste it?

The problem arose through

restaurants in Marseilles employing chefs and waiters from the poorer Camargue, who brought with them the custom of chilli with everything, once again showing chillies are a refuge of the poor with nothing but bland food otherwise to eat. A rouille that is very hot on the tongue may be to your liking but think again about including it with the expense and the universe of fine flavours in a true bouillabaisse.

SOY/SHOYU SAUCE: the quintessential Japanese flavouring and condiment of Asian cooking. Shoyu is the Japanese name but is often used by food writers to indicate a naturally brewed product rather than the artificially produced product.

The real thing begins with steamed soybeans mixed with malted wheat kernels, that is they have been allowed to sprout and then roasted. Special yeast is added to start a natural fermentation and precisely developed yeasts give this or that manufacturer their particular flavour and style; they are jealously guarded secrets. After three days the mixture encourages a mould or culture on the surface, and then proceeds also to grow aroma and other types of flavour. Some of the sugar and alcohol transforms into acids, which give sharpness to the final flavour. Natural glutamates are also formed, the basis for the sauce's ability to enliven other tastes. After six months maturing, the mixture is drawn off into cloths to be pressed. A deep, reddish brown, clear liquid is funnelled from the pressing machines to be pasteurised and bottled.

The classic process is indicated by the words 'naturally brewed' on a label. Commercial processes make an approximation in a few days by hydrolising soy protein using hydrochloric acid, diluting with salt water and then adding corn syrup, colouring and other additives; there is also a process, semi-natural, semi-chemical, which combines both methods.

Many Oriental ingredients last forever, but not this one. Once opened soy sauce keeps its virtues for about a month, after that it will begin to oxidise and lose most of its subtle complexities; this happens faster and more noticeably if it is exposed to extremes of light or heat. Provided it is well sealed, refrigeration will not harm it.

Dark soy sauce: has a rich dark concentrated flavour that is both sweet and salt. It will colour sauces and foods and this is part of the consideration when using it. Often both dark and light are combined to get precisely the flavour required. *Kecap Manis* q.v. is an outstanding sweet soy sauce from Indonesia.

Light soy sauce: brewed to give 25% of the usual colour, so it will not discolour dishes when adding flavour; it is often slightly saltier than dark soy sauce.

Low-salt soy sauce: is increasingly marketed.

Tamari soy sauce: is made only with soy beans, and is used in sushi restaurants, but rarely in the home.

SUKIYAKI SAUCE: soy sauce mixed with rice wine and sugar, added to water and boiled up as a stock for cooking beef and vegetables: if you make such stock from scratch it's called *warashita*. Can be used as a salt-sweet marinade for grills and barbecues—very good on pineapple: see *Teriyaki*.

TABASCO: see *Chilli sauces*.

TAPENADE: not a Provençal paste of black olives but based on capers; *tapeno* is local dialect for capers, and it is the flavour of these that should predominate over the olive content. Use as a dipping condiment for bread and vegetables, on eggs, to dress pasta and with fish and meat dishes.

TERIYAKI: a Japanese barbecue and grill marinade, baste or dip. It is soy sauce flavoured with wine, sugar and spices; you can make good but individual equivalents by mixing soy sauce with pineapple juice, with mirin and five-spice powder or with plum sauce and ginger wine. Some of these mixtures will be more like sukiyaki sauce.

WORCESTERSHIRE SAUCE: when Asian fish sauces are mixed with such extra ingredients as vinegar, molasses, garlic, sour-sweet tamarind and much more that is secret, you get something like Worcestershire sauce. There used to be many of these spicy, hot, salty sauces, made from recipes brought back by gourmand colonels from the India of Queen Victoria. Some were manufactured for distribution and some were kept as private stocks. Lea & Perrins Worcestershire sauce was first made as a private stock but forgotten about by the owner.

Eventually the barrel was about to be thrown away but it was discovered the long sojourn had transformed a sharp and unpleasant liquid into something with possibilities, and it was made commercially. Thank goodness. It is extraordinarily good for pepping up boring food and for adding unrecognised piquancy and interest to mayonnaise, soups, aspics, sauces for fish, herb butters and mince dishes, especially hamburgers.

You know, of course, that a Bloody Mary is bloody awful without Worcestershire sauce.

XO: reputed to be created in Hong Kong in the 80s and already something of a legend because of both the great depths of savoury (umami) flavour and its expense. It's made of pricy, dried scallops and shrimp plus regional ham, sugar, garlic, shallots and chillies cooked down to a jammy lumpiness or made smooth. Although recommended as an ingredient or as a high-toned condiment it's popular served directly on to noodles or pasta. Quantities of the seafoods vary and some commercial brands can be over-sweetened; there are web recipes to make your own.

Sugars, Syrups and Honey

NEED TO KNOW

Sugar is sucrose, a white carbohydrate with a sweet flavour that is the world's most popular sweetener.

Anything that ends in 'ose' is a sugar: sucrose, glucose, galactose, fructose, maltose, laevulose.

Invert sugar is sucrose broken down into glucose and fructose.

Honey's sweetness is invert sugar.

Unless you are a diabetic, sugar does not cause disease other than tooth decay, but too much of it contributes to obesity and that can have bad effects.

Sugar is mainly obtained from sugar cane and sugar beets.

Other natural sugars are made from maple syrup, palm trees and sorghum, a type of millet.

Beet sugar makes only white sugar.

Brown sugars made from beet are coloured with molasses from cane sugar.

Raw sugar means sucrose crystals produced without bleaching: it is little different from white sugar.

Sugar in cake mixtures keeps the gluten soft and pliable, so it expands to give volume and lightness.

Sugar and honey are preservatives.

Cream, butter and egg yolks freeze better if sugar is added.

Cakes and biscuits with a high-sugar content freeze best.

Stevia is a calorie-free herb with powerful natural sweetening potential.

Agave syrup is a vegan sweetener mainly of fructose.

How sugar is made

CANE SUGAR: first the cane is cleaned and shredded to expose the inner core, which is crushed and sprayed with hot water to form a free-running juice. Clarification comes next, when added ingredients encourage pitching of impurities that are then removed.

The clarified liquid is reduced by evaporation and the condensed liquid, a type of treacle or sugar-containing molasses, is seeded to encourage the formation of sugar crystals, which are then extracted by centrifuge. This first extraction gives the biggest crystals, and at this stage they contain both residual impurities and molasses and also have a very light coating of molasses; this produces raw sugar, golden sugar and demerara.

Two more stages of processing and centrifuge result in the extraction of the remaining sucrose in increasingly smaller crystals, which are darkened by greater concentrations of molasses—muscovado and molasses sugars. Eventually, with almost all the available sucrose extracted, only blackstrap molasses is left.

White sugar is obtained by chemically treating and bleaching the original sucrose-rich syrup, and it is this process that is generally meant by refining.
BEET SUGAR: sugar beet arrives at the factory to be washed and cut into 'V' shapes, called *cosettes*. Mixed with hot water, the cosettes are rotated in a tower or drum to dissolve their sugar into the water. The syrup has lime added to it and carbon dioxide is bubbled through, which forms a precipitate that carries out the impurities. More careful filtration follows, then a sulphur-dioxide treatment and then concentration until you have the final syrup, which can be crystallised into white sucrose.

Types of sugar and sweeteners

AGAVE: syrups made from several agave plants are sweetened naturally with fructose, and can be light, amber or dark according to how much they are concentrated over heat. All are almost twice as sweet as sucrose. The darker each is the more caramel flavours are present, and so they offer a wide range of drinking and cooking choices; they can be used directly from the bottle in drinks and in savoury and sweet dishes. Dark agave syrup has a more distinct vegetal undertone and may include vestiges of agave plant material.
CASSONADE: few French believe it, but this is white beet sugar coloured and flavoured with sugar-cane molasses. The sugar beet equivalent of molasses is utterly inedible, hence why beet sugar can only be white.
CASTER SUGAR: fine-grained cane or beet sugar used for baking, drinks and decorating, where it dissolves faster or looks prettier. In the United States the grain is smaller and called Superfine or Baker's Special.
CITRUS SUGAR: wonderful on fruit, in cream or sprinkled over hot or cold puddings of almost any type and may be flavoured with lemon, lime, bitter (Seville) or sweet oranges, tangerines or any of the new citrus styles marketed.

Rub the zest with sugar cubes, stopping before you get to the bitter pith. As the cube collects the zest and oils and thus slightly dissolves, scrape that off onto a plate; keep everything well away from absorbent wooden chopping boards.

When you have enough, dry the flavoured sugar and zest residue in a low oven, and then crush it and store in an air-tight jar.
COFFEE CRYSTALS: over-expensive and maddening large crystals seemingly planned to ensure you either enjoy coffee in all its bitterness before they are dissolved, or that you drink it stone-cold, by which time some of the crystals might have dissolved.
CORN SYRUP: made by hydrolysis of the corn starch, that is, a chemical splitting

into component sugars together with the addition of water. Regularly used in baking in the United States, it adds sweetness and notable suppleness in the mouth. Indeed, it's the key to success of many American speciality cakes. You can replace it with golden syrup, which will give added colour and flavour but not the all-important mouthfeel.

CUBE SUGAR: produced by molding and pressing selected granulated sugar with sugar syrup that cements the crystal. On drying, it is very hard and is presumably the process that once formed loaf sugar.

DARK BROWN SUGAR: fine-grained white sugar with twice the amount of commercially added treacle than Light Brown Sugar. Used when rich colour and dark flavour is wanted, in gingerbreads, rich fruit cakes or other mixtures containing vine fruits. Like natural muscovado sugar, you can almost pretend it is dark rum you have used.

DATE MOLASSES: a velvety syrup pressed from such semi-soft dates as the medjool. Use wherever you might a syrup, including on yogurt or mixed with yoghurt as a sweet-sour dressing for fruits, on ice cream or to finish gravies. The syrupy texture makes it the perfect vegan alternative to honey.

DEMERARA SUGAR: crystallised from cane syrup that is partly discolourised and filtered during boiling. The large, sparkling, yellow crystals are about 98% pure sucrose and 2% molasses and thus give you some minerals. It takes its name from the county in Guyana where it was first produced. Now there are other types of 'dem' as it can be made by adding cane molasses to refined white sugar, which could thus be beet sugar. It will have exactly the same qualities but its name must be qualified.

Demerara on a packet means it was made from cane sugar in the country in which the cane was grown. Other types, such as London Demerara, indicate it has been artificially made and the qualifying adjective indicates this was done in a refinery closer to the point of consumption.

Demerara is excellent for flavouring cooked or new fruits, and for cereals. It is traditionally used to sprinkle on fruit cakes and biscuits before baking, to give a crunchy topping. It can replace white sugar in virtually every recipe where you do not mind the addition of a little colour.

FLORAL SUGARS: rose petals, jasmine flowers, rose geranium, lavender and orange blossom are the best. Violet is a terrific idea but only if you grow parma violets. The flowers should be perfectly dry and in large amounts and then mixed with caster sugar: the less sugar you use the greater the result. Be specially careful to store away from heat and light. It takes one or two weeks for the sugar to absorb the oils and fragrances of the flowers and when you are happy the flowers can be strained out. Use on berry fruits, or in cream cheeses, yoghurts, whipped cream, sponges and the like.

GOLDEN SUGARS: a culinary oasis of their own between white sugar and demerara. Steam cleaning and careful manipulation of the processing leaves less molasses in the crystals than in a demerara, but has stopped short of complete refining.

Golden sugars may be sold as unrefined because of the molasses content, offering a level of the original vitamins and minerals but there is little molasses flavour and they may be used like white sugar, even in hot drinks.

GOLDEN SYRUP: created in 1883, this is a white sugar plus invert sugar plus colouring from the original sugar syrup that was once discarded. It was an instant success worldwide and still is in confectionery and baking yet nothing betters its use in a golden-syrup steamed pudding.

Golden syrup was once known as light treacle hence its otherwise confusing use in treacle tart. If you cannot easily buy golden syrup, use corn syrup and colour it lightly with brown sugar.

GRANULATED SUGAR: the most common form of pure white sucrose, cane or beet. Although varying from country to country each grain is usually about 1 mm.

ICING SUGAR: powdered or confectioner's sugar in the United States, this is made by grinding sucrose into a fine powder and cornflour is usually added to prevent caking. Its major use is in icings.

JAGGERY: see *Palm sugar.*

JAM SUGAR: blends granulated sugar with apple pectin and citric acid and thus guarantees a good set when making jams and preserves without the danger of overcooking or caramellising.

LIGHT BROWN SUGAR: fine-grained white sugar with a commercially added treacle coating, specially designed to dissolve more easily than demerara and thus ideal for creaming with butter for cake making or for making brown-sugar meringues. It will give marginally more flavour and a little more colour than white sugar. Dark brown sugar has twice the treacle content.

LIGHT MUSCOVADO: a creamier-coloured muscovado with a lower molasses content than true muscovado. It is ideal for cakes and puddings where you want extra flavour, because darker sugars aren't generally recommended for cake making.

MAPLE SUGAR: crystallised maple sugar, it has marginally higher nutritional value than sucrose.

MAPLE SYRUP: the reduced, sweet sap of the North American sugar maple (*Acer saccharum*) varies in sweetness, colour and flavour but this is not a result of processing but because maple syrup naturally gets darker through the season as its sugars change in nature.

The grades are now the same whether from Canada or the US: Golden is the lightest flavour, Amber is richer, Dark is thought robust and Very Dark has a strong flavour but is rarely marketed.

It is best used hot on pancakes and waffles but is regularly served at room temperature, which greatly reduces the appeal. Otherwise, it is a favourite in baking and for ices, sauces and icings. It will always be expensive and thus most on the market are 'maple-flavoured'—read the label.

MOLASSES: the rich, concentrated syrup remaining after cane sugar syrup has been through the several boiling and separating processes necessary to extract almost all the pure sucrose. It contains some sucrose and other types of sugar as well as everything that refined white sugar is missing; 8–10% of molasses has vital minerals including iron, copper, calcium, magnesium, chromium, phosphorous, potassium and zinc.

There are various colours and grades, depending on how much sugar is left in the liquid. The darker the molasses the less sugar it contains. All types can also contain sulphur, which is used in some refineries—unsulphured molasses is usually light coloured and better flavoured. Some cane-growing areas will simply reduce cane syrup over heat and call this molasses; but this is never sold commercially that I know of.

Molasses is mainly used these days to flavour baking, in Creole cooking and to add flavour to the water when boiling hams.

MOLASSES SUGAR, BLACK BARBADOS SUGAR, DEMERARA MOLASSES SUGAR: this is fairly difficult to find outside cane-processing areas. It is a very strong-tasting sugar with high molasses content and a rich, almost black colour. The sticky texture and taste are similar to good treacle toffee.

MUSCOVADO, BARBADOS SUGAR: the most common naturally dark sugar, this is extracted after the mother liquor has made three trips through the centrifuge. It is the last time the producer can extract sugar from the almost exhausted source. The crystals are very small and one-seventh of their weight is molasses, which forms a coating on each crystal.

PALM SUGAR: also called *jaggery* this should be the boiled and crystallised sap of several types of palm tree but most sold is artificially created from cane sugar, easily spotted on the label. The real thing, moist, tawny and fine-grained, has a fudgy flavour that is less sweet than sucrose and an irresistible success when used in place of dark sugars, particularly in baked apples or banana or melted with toasted nuts to top ice cream. Sri Lanka spices it, adds dessicated coconut and stuffs it into small pancakes, served as part of Small Eats with tea in the afternoon.

POWDERED SUGAR: see *Icing sugar.*

PRESERVING SUGAR: large crystals that dissolve slowly and do not settle in a dense layer on the bottom of the pan, meaning less stirring and less chance of burning.

RICE SYRUP: made by enzymic action on brown rice. It might be considered healthier than many sweeteners because its major components are forms of glucose, rather than of fructose, except it has almost twice the calories of an equivalent amount of white sugar, about the same glycaemic index as honey.

ROCK OR CANDY SUGAR: huge sugar crystals, often strung together. Used for sweet making as it does not burn easily.

SORGHUM SYRUP: the concentrated stalk juice of the sorghum plant, a type of millet.

SPICED SUGARS: sugars scented with cinnamon, ginger, aniseed, cardamom, clove or mixed spice are suddenly invaluable once you have them, for pancakes and batters, toast, yoghurts, cake toppings or flavourings, fruit pies, hot chocolate and coffee or the whipped cream which might top them. Use very freshly ground spices and proportions that best suit your taste; one tablespoon of spice to 100 g/4 oz of sugar is a good starting level.

STEVIA: is related to asters and chrysanthemums and yet is a powerful natural sweetener, naturally between four and eight times sweeter than sugar by volume, that is a teaspoon of stevia will give the sweetness of four to eight teaspoons of sugar but with no calories. You can use the dried leaves or, in some countries, buy a refined syrup or white powder. There's a hint of bitterness if you use the dried leaves, but that has been excised in the syrup and white powder. Products using stevia often contain other alternative sweeteners.

Still not widely approved for much commercial use, it could be the next, next big thing.

TREACLE: much sweeter than molasses as it is the full cane syrup with only a proportion of sucrose removed. It can only be made from cane sugar, although golden syrup might also be added to it — the label will tell you. Used mainly for puddings.

TURBINADO: a raw cane sugar that has been steam cleaned and is thus lighter in colour and flavour, so turbinado falls somewhere between light muscovado and demerara in appearance and flavour and thus either of these or light soft brown sugar may be substituted when you are using American cookbooks, where turbinado is commonly specified.

VANILLA SUGAR: one of the most useful sweeteners in any kitchen, this is most easily made by storing vanilla beans in caster sugar in something air tight. The sugar can be topped up as used and the beans removed and used several times for flavouring such as milk and sauces and then dried before replacing.

Honey

NEED TO KNOW

Honey is nectar from flowers, which is made of invert sugar, a mix of glucose and fructose.

On average 300 bees take a month to make 500 g/1 lb of honey from nectar.

One Australian eucalyptus blossom supplies a bee's full load but it is more usual to have to visit up to 1500 flowers.

If bees are fed sugar syrup during winter, none of this is converted into honey.

Honey is flavoured by the oils and essences of the original nectar, which largely survive gentle heat treatment.

The hotter the country, the stronger the tastes of single-species honeys.

Most honey is heat treated; some are pasteurised.

Raw honey is not sterile and can contain hazardous spores.

Raw honey is generally safe for adults and children but should not be fed to babies under a year old: this is especially true of comb honey.

Commercial honey is blended for uniformity from many sources, like tea, oils, wines.

The US produces over 300 varieties of single-source honey.

By volume honey is twice as sweet as white sugar.

The best oils and scents of fine honey are destroyed in cooking: it is better added after cooking, as is or diluted.

To flavour filo pastries, use cold honey or syrup on hot pastries; hot on hot or cold on cold gives sogginess.

Store comb honey standing up, not flat.

E ven without claims for it as an elixir of life, honey has long been one of the world's most important foods. Together with the lowly parsnip and carrot, it was a main sweetener until sugar dropped in price to become more universally available in the late 19th century. Its other use was as a preservative, something it did for thousands of years in Pharaonic tombs.

You may safely dismiss most claims made for honey as sweet nothings. Honey is a concentrated solution of water and sucrose that has been pre-digested into simpler sugars that make 75% of the bulk.

However, recent research indicates that the antioxidants in a daily tablespoon of raw honey have distinct beneficial effects on cognitive performance including memory and thus can help alleviate symptoms of dementia. More contributions to human health are under investigation, all in addition to its known antiseptic and preservative qualities. Perhaps Dame Barbara Cartland was right. She lived almost to 99 and wrote 723 novels, powered she believed by honey; she wrote best-seller *The Magic of Honey* well before there was science to support her beliefs.

To be stored and sold in the retail market, honey has been strained to take away traces of wax debris, but leaving pollen and other minutiae including colloids. It is only these minimal ingredients that could remotely give honey magical qualities. There are substantiated claims that it helps wounds to heal, but essentially, honey is sugar and sugar is calories.

The aristocrats are honeys made from the nectar of a single flower and the rarer the flower the more expensive the honey. Like good olive oils, these should never be used in cooking but enjoyed solo.

Some types of honey

ACACIA: exceptionally elegant, especially from Middle Europe.

AUSTRALIA: a plethora of extraordinary honey with truly independent and often challenging variations of flavour, sweetness and colour. The eucalyptus honeys — blue gum, white gum and so on — are a great place to start as you work up to Tasmanian Leatherwood honey. This spicy, complex honey is unlike anything you think of as honey, and many people can't abide its confrontational flavour.

CLOVER: medium-rich and full of flavour, clover honey is a gratifying universal choice for most people and uses. The hotter climate means Australian clover honey is more robust than an English one and New Zealand clovers are middle-range.

COMB HONEY: if you can bear to chew the wax, this is the most nutritious of honeys, and more likely to contain whatever is said to be one of life's elixirs. But don't make the mistake of storing comb honey lying down. The bees don't. Examine a comb closely and you will see each cell slopes back slightly, so it can stand upright without leakages. This is how you should keep it too. It is always untreated and increasingly expensive. Generally, you buy a square cut from a larger comb, but sometimes the bees have been persuaded to make combs in smaller, plastic squares — an expensive but practical ploy.

CREAMED HONEY: however it is made, the honey's crystal size has been reduced to give a lighter texture and creamier, smoother mouth feel. You can whisk clear honey for a very long time or add a portion of clear honey to crystallised honey and whisk that.

CRYSTALLISED: even the most carefully refined and pasteurised honey will crystallise, depending on the origin; some heather honeys may not begin for up to two years. To make crystallised honey clear again, stand the sealed pot in cold water and slowly bring it to a temperature into which you can just put your fingertips. Keep the water at this temperature until the honey is clear. Cold storage promotes crystallisation so keep honey away from refrigerators. Honey is a preservative and preserves itself best at ambient temperature.

ENGLISH: single-flower varieties can be terribly expensive, presumably because there is so little harvested in many summers. Curious sources offer individual honeys that reflect where it is gathered. Fortnum and Mason have hives on their roof and the bees feed on the blossoms of London's Royal Parks. City Farms and industrious groups of all kinds sell honey made within a defined district, most of them urban or suburban rather than rural, and dependent for individuality on what is in back and front gardens.

Countryside British and European honey making is blighted by the ever-increasing acreage of rape, the nectar of which gives an overbearing muskiness and bitterness, which many find destroys their enjoyment of honey, even when in minute quantities.

GALICIA: awarded honeys from north-west Spain include multifloral, eucalyptus, chestnut and two local specialities; *azamora* is a dark amber with a strong fruity flavour; *brezo* is reddish amber and has curious bitterness accompanied by light floral notes.

GRANADA: a variety of single-source honeys, including avocado, rosemary, thyme, French lavender and, best of all, orange-blossom honey.

LAVENDER: one of the varieties offered by noted *miel de La Alcarria*; look also for rosemary honey from this source.

LINDEN LIME BLOSSOM: notably concentrated and perfumed, even when made in central London.

NEW ZEALAND: outstanding individual honeys sourced from its native trees, many of which are in pristine wilderness and thus truly organic. Best known are:

Honeydew: not honey and not made by bees but an excretion of aphids which live on the bark of black beech trees in the country's virgin Southern Alps: it is untreated and also guaranteed organic. It has a slightly yeasty nose and flavour with an aftertaste of orange-flower water.

Manuka or ti-tree: a dark, full, sharpish honey and its medicinal claims are supported, but only in select styles that are very expensive.

Pohutukawa: made from the gorgeous red flowers of a tree that lines the beaches and blooms at Christmas time. It is white and buttery with a light brown sugar or butterscotch flavour.

ORANGE BLOSSOM: one of the most fragrant and elegant, it offers a lifetime of pleasure to compare those of each country which makes it, which includes Central American countries as well as the Middle East.

PITCAIRN ISLAND: honey made on this remote South Pacific Island is probably the world's purest (a) because it is entirely free from varoa mite or other pests, and (b) because it offers intriguing, probably unique, tropical flavours: available direct from the island at www.government.pn/shop/index.html.

SCOTTISH HEATHER: an exception to the hot weather/robust honey rule, for Scotland's cool moors produce a very tasty, rather direct honey that is particularly well thought of for desserts and cooking in general. Good with thick spreads of butter.

SET HONEY: see *Crystallised*.

THYME: widely thought a queen of honeys, Greek Hymettus, is flavoured with the nectar of wild thyme from the mountain of that name.

WHIPPED HONEY: see *Creamed honey*.

Tea and Herbal Teas

NEED TO KNOW

Tea is made by steeping the tips of cultivars of camellia sinensis.

The tip is a leaf bud and two infantile leaves.

Tea reflects its terroir and is finer flavoured the higher it grows.

There are six styles: white, green, yellow, oolong, black and pu-erh.

Black-leaf teas must be made with freshly boiled water.

Brown leaves give stronger tea than black ones.

Reboiled water gives lesser flavour because it contains less oxygen.

White, green, yellow and oolong teas should be made with water at 95°C or less.

For some green teas, even 60°C is too hot.

Black tea should be brewed once; some green styles can be brewed up to seven times.

Caffeine in green tea is about half that of black tea: black tea has about half the caffeine of black coffee but these are very broad comparisons.

China teas are traditionally rinsed in hot water before brewing: see gong fu style.

Steeping time depends on size of leaf—the bigger the leaf, the longer the brew.

The finest flavours emerge towards the end of steeping.

Do not confuse colour with strength or flavour, as colour comes out first.

Tea brews best in slowly cooling water.

Tea cosies should only be used after leaves or tea bags have been removed or tea is poured into a second pot, as was the custom until mid-20th century.

Tea bags should be brewed for some minutes—read the instructions.

Originally, milk went in first to protect cups before heat-proof bone china and porcelain were introduced.

Milk after tea allows control over strength and was once a sign you could afford bone china and porcelain because hot tea could be poured directly in to such cups.

Milk in first gives a better emulsion.

Milk combined with the tea bag in a cup or mug prevents full flavour because the added water is then not hot enough to brew the tea.

Lemon should only be added to tea to counteract bitterness in low-quality leaves.

Soaking dried fruit in tea is pointless as the flavour is fugitive when heated; it was once done so expensive leftover tea was not wasted.

Iced tea should be made only with cold water, which ensures no cloudy deposits.

Decaf tea is made by forcing heated and pressurised CO_2 through tea leaves, which binds with and removes the caffeine.

Tea leaves can smoke food but don't include herbs, sugar or alcohol, which make no difference.

What must we do to make tea as fashionable as coffee? It is infinitely more variable in flavour, much harder to ruin in the making, and so naturally flexible in caffeine content it is kid's play to match your tea to your mood—an Assam to startle, an oolong to refresh, a green tea to soothe. If only we could be asked which tea we would like, rather than being offered whatever is to hand.

Britain was one of the pioneers of tea drinking in the non-Oriental world, and yet with few exceptions it remains a very difficult country in which to get a decent cup of tea. Low-grade blends, chosen for instant colour and quick harsh flavours, must be mollified with milk and sugar to be palatable. And tea is left to over-stew in pots, tea bags dipped not brewed. Yet merchants and blenders offer a remarkable range of quality teas, including outstanding supermarket products at bargain prices—if they are made and served properly.

Until the late 18th century most tea drunk in England was green tea, although some black types were developed in China to be more reliably robust for the long journey. Used green tea leaves were commonly rebrewed or sold on by servants. From the early 1820s and 30s cheaper black tea appeared from India, followed by much more from Ceylon (Sri Lanka) in the 1870s and 80s. Tea was no longer a rich man's drink but becoming a staple of the poor, both stimulating and safer.

The tea bush

The tea bush *camellia sinensis* is native to a fan-shaped area that starts in Vietnam and expands westwards to Assam and eastwards into China. It has a fragrant white flower and if not kept plucked would grow into a 12 m/40 ft tree. Tea is now grown extensively in East Africa, where Kenya produces tea of notably high quality. There are tea gardens in Cornwall, Australia and New Zealand. The plant is remarkably free with its affections and cross-breeds within its own species with abandon, so, like humans, almost every new bush is different from all others.

In an effort to keep up quality, notably successful bushes have for some years been cloned, giving a more predictable and consistent product than the usual lottery of quality. It sounds like a good idea, but no-one knows what curious ancestral behaviour a cloned bush may suddenly display in ten or 20 years.

Like coffee, the height above sea level at which tea is grown is a major influence on its body and flavour. Low-grown and 'mid-country' teas flourish furiously in lush, humid foothills, giving large volumes of bigger leaves with plenty of colour and body and straightforward, robust flavour without finesse.

At 1200–1900 m/4000–6000 ft high-grown teas produce more slowly in the cooler days and cold nights. The crop is very much smaller but has greatly superior flavour, fragrance and delicacy—high-grown Darjeelings from single estates are thought the aristocrats.

Only the top two, very new leaves and the emerging leaf bud between them are plucked to make tea, something never successfully mechanised; Japanese *ban-cha* is an exception to the definition. The best picking times are called flushes; the first flush is early in spring, the second a little later, and the third flush, after summer, gives speciality autumnal teas. In between is when standard teas are collected. With a growing interest in *terroir*, such companies as Jing.com are seeking and marketing teas from small, remote gardens and wild-sourced teas throughout China and other Asian countries.

Types of tea

All types of tea start by withering the leaf to reduce moisture. From then on, as with wine or cheese, the slightest difference in technique makes more or less of particular characteristics given by variety, soil or climate. This list is in order of amount of processing: white, green, yellow, oolong, black, pu-erh.

WHITE: made only from the smallest and newest shoots covered with a silvery fur and from a specific varietal, Da Bai. Never rolled and never cut, so it does not oxidise. The very pale, yellow liquor has much less 'green' flavour and can be lightly fruity, floral or honey like. There are four grades and those made only of tips are thought best.

Peony white: made from a different cultivar, gives a bigger flavour. That from Fuding can be aged up to six years, developing complexity and flavours of hay and dark honey.

GREEN: the withered green leaves are dried without breaking, so green teas keep their vegetal, grassy flavour. They may then be left flat or rolled into balls when dried. Traditionally dried in a large wok, when they are known as pan-fired teas, a process that can give a metallic sheen, hence gunpowder green tea. Graded according to the size and shape of the fired leaf, the highest grade rolled leaves, sometimes shaped by steam, are the smallest and called pinhead. Country green teas are generally the brightest and freshest tasting green teas.

Green tea is credited with enormous health benefits, often to do with its high proportion of anti-oxidants and has a great deal less caffeine and tannin content than semi-fermented oolong or fermented black teas. They are thus ideal for later in the day and will soothe rather than stimulate. Chinese drinkers put green tea leaves directly into a covered mug, to which they add water again and again. If you did that to black teas, the tannin extraction would be unpalatable.

Whatever green tea you buy, take great care to read the brewing instructions. Some green teas must be brewed at only 50°C or 60°C, and for no more than a minute.

YELLOW: a rare speciality of China's Anhui, Sichuan and Hunan provinces. Its long, slow production gives a mellower, sweeter and riper flavour than green tea, as well as a sometimes startling, cold/ minty sensation that lingers in the throat. The process is the same as for green tea but then the leaves are wrapped or otherwise kept out of the sun or air to thus oxidise very slowly, after which they are fired.

Also known as Imperial tea, yellow tea almost disappeared because of its complexity of manufacture. It is now being made traditionally in just a few places but made artificially in many more. Buy only from established dealers of speciality Chinese teas, like www.jingtea.com.

OOLONGS: to qualify as an oolong, the leaves are only semi-fermented, that is they are roughly torn and fermentation is stopped when much of the leaf is still green. Sometimes little more than the cut edge has browned. Greater or lesser bitterness is an expected ingredient in the spectrum of oolong flavours.

The difference in leaf picked for oolongs in spring and in autumn is greater than with any other type of tea, and the early summer teas picked from late May to mid-August are generally thought the tops. Freak conditions producing one-off results and complicated intermediary gradings make oolongs a lifetime study, so it is really worth taking advice—and spending good money.

Oolongs are always Orthodox tea, with a rather large leaf that thus requires a good long brew—up to seven or eight minutes. Oolongs should never be drunk with milk or lemon, but lower grades benefit from a little sugar. They are exceedingly good after-dinner teas—elegant, soothing and refreshing without being too stimulating, as the caffeine count is low.

China oolongs: noticeably coarser than Formosas, with a distinct earthiness, they are just as refreshing but graded differently and their darker tastes are much more an acquired taste; Kwai Flower is one you might enjoy. Tieguanyin from Anxi in Fujian, sometimes known as Iron Goddess of Mercy tea, is the name for the Fujian family of oolongs, sold according to both the season they are made (spring is the most floral) and how highly they are baked. An amateur cannot easily forecast the flavour of a Tieguanyin offered without further identification but it is a field rich with treasures for the explorer.

Formosa oolongs: Formosas are generally finer and more delicious than China oolongs. The very highest qualities have a distinct fruitiness and a beguiling sweetness, sometimes reminiscent of peaches. Graded from Fine grades to Finest, which are also sometimes called Poppy or Peony oolongs. Then it's on up to Fancy or Peach Blossom and to Top Fancy oolong, often sold as Silver Tips. Peach Blossom and Silver Tips are the teas with the fruitiest nose and flavour.

High-Mountain oolongs: can seem barely fermented at all, with most leaves still green, but this style is highly prized.

The highest grades of tea grown in other regions of the world are made the oolong way but don't say so; in Darjeeling it's commonly indicated by using 'silver tips' in the tea's name.

BLACK: the withered leaf is crushed and cut, the released juices then oxidise or ferment fully, developing colour, flavour and tannin; it is then heat treated or fired to complete drying. The Chinese teas of this type are called red teas, because of the colour when brewed. Indian teas are thought of as orange, hence the use of this word in tea grades. Tea from the finest gardens is marketed in whole leaves or large pieces, usually called Orthodox and that can take up to eight minutes to brew. Modern black tea designed for fast brewing is known as CTC or crush, tear, curl, which produces very small pieces. See *Tea Grades*, below.

PU-ERH: a speciality of the western Chinese province of Yunnan. With very few exceptions, pu-erh is the only tea deliberately aged and sold by vintage. Made from particular tea bushes that often grow wild and are always rather tall, the fully oxidised leaves are very tightly pressed into discs that are thinner in the middle so that ageing progresses evenly. These are matured in special buildings that are airy and dry, so mould cannot develop.

The slow enzymic changes create leaves that brew to give a rich, rounded, dark taste and a notable, silken mouthfeel that drinkers spend as much time describing as wine lovers do with favourite vintage wines. There is a definite leatheriness to the nose and palate, but a challenging one of sweat-infused saddles and riding boots rather than of the interior of a new Bentley. Tobacco and sandalwood, peach or apricot are frequently noted flavour discoveries; there is a syrupiness, too, and always an exceptional ever-changing spectrum of taste and flavour on the palate. Old pu-erh teas create as much passion as great wines and brandies and can cost very much more. There are establishments where the cost of a single cup would feed families for a week.

Classic pressed pu-erh teas are sold as raw pu-erh. That's because the 20th century created a faster way to make pu-erh, involving steam and heat and this is called cooked pu-erh. Cooked pu-erh is sold loose rather than pressed and like all newish food, some styles are much better than others.

If stored badly in humid conditions pu-erh develops a hideous mouldy character that I find too nauseating even to have in a pot on the table. It's something that happens in Hong Kong's climate but is widely accepted there. When correct, pu-erh is renowned for magically creating bonhomie and comfort among guests, particularly after a meal.

Other tea styles

BLENDS: like champagne, black teas that are not identified by garden are blended to give consistent results to customers. This can mean mixing teas from many regions and countries, some to give quick colour, like Bright Flowering Africans, others to give body and flavour.

BRICK: finely powdered black or green tea leaves compacted under great pressure into shiny shapes that are practical to carry and store. Some sport illustrations and calligraphy of the highest standard, so make marvellously useless gifts, unless to a homesick Tibetan. You grate or chop a little into a mug or teapot and add boiling water, which Tibetans believe is improved when they whisk in rancid yak butter.

BROCADES/ FANCY LEAF/FLOWER TEAS: intricately woven, sewn or folded bundles of whole green or white tea leaves to make exotic blooms that are good to look at when dried, and then swell and explode into beguiling fantasy shapes when brewed. Most are created specifically to be brewed in a tall glass, so the unfolding can be watched and enjoyed as part of the tea experience.

They can be searingly expensive, but some can be brewed up to five times, which helps. Those with a high jasmine content seem the most popular.

CTC: invented in 1928, this process crushes, tears and curls the leaf into very small pieces to give a faster, stronger black tea brew—two to three minutes—because boiling water penetrates each particle faster.

FERMENTED: known as *kombucha*, this is sweetened green or black tea fermented by a combination of bacteria and yeast into a slightly effervescent drink with a very small alcohol content. None of the extraordinary health claims for kombucha have been substantiated by science but it seems likely it makes some pro-biotic contribution to better gut health. Unsafe domestic hygiene is said to be associated with serious adverse effects; some disagree. Fruit juice and other flavourings are commonly added.

TEA BAGS: pioneered in 1908 by American tea broker Thomas Sullivan, who took his tea samples around in silk envelopes. If you treat tea bags properly you will get a very good cup of tea, but most people do not; as usual it's a matter of reading the label and doing as it says. Tea bags should be brewed for at least two minutes—if you want stronger tea, use less water, if you want weaker tea, use more or dilute after brewing, but without the full brewing time you get only a speck of what you have paid for. One bag of a strong tea style will make two or three flavourful cups of tea if allowed to brew for two or three minutes—either do it in a tea pot, or brew in one cup or mug, divide the brew between the others, then top up with more water.

When I gave this advice on BBC TV's Pebble Mill at One, a woman wrote to say I had all but saved her marriage as until she allowed tea bags to brew she was constantly insulted by her husband about her tea.

Tea grades

The complicated system of grading tea sometimes uses the same terms to mean a different thing in another country. Some styles of tea have their own categories as do most countries. The grades below are for Indian black teas, as these are the most commonly encountered in labelling.

Orange Pekoe (OP) or Broken Orange Pekoe (BOP) are widely thought to indicate quality, particularly in the United States, but this is not accurate. Those two and all other classifications refer precisely to the shape of the dried leaf. OP and BOP are low categories; higher grades also indicate the proportion of tips (buds) to leaves.

Indian black tea grades divide into four types of leaf descending in size— whole leaf, broken leaf, fannings and dust. Sub-grades of increasing quality of leaf are: Orange, Flowery, Golden, Tippy. These attributes are awarded in the opposite order, so a top whole leaf tea might be graded FTGFOP: Finest Tippy Golden Flowery Orange Pekoe. A broken leaf might be TGFBOP: Tippy Golden Flowery Broken Orange Pekoe.

Below these in size of leaf but not necessarily in quality are grades of Fannings and then Dust grades. Neither were they ever floor sweepings, as was long rumoured about tea bags.

Choosing tea by country

It's a broad view, but the further west you go from Japan, the stronger the tea is in both tannin and caffeine.

Thus, Chinese and Japanese green teas are the mildest. Move south and tea becomes Fujian's oolongs. Go west to find Chinese black teas, all of which are milder in caffeine and tannin than anything from the Indian continent, but stronger than oolongs or green tea.

Sri Lanka offers liquory teas with exceptional fragrance and firm fresh body that comes with still more caffeine and tannin. On up through India until you find Assam, the malty-strong heavyweight of teas.

The exceptions to this pattern are the aristocratic high-grown Darjeelings of Northern India and the world-class teas now coming from Kenya, which are close to Sri Lankans in fragrance, flavour and colour.

Within this broad-stroke picture there are thousands of variations, but it's very useful for assessing a tea you've not met before. With this knowledge you might start the day with a strong black Indian tea and as the day progresses, move down to a Ceylon or Kenyan, on to Darjeeling or a China Black, then to oolongs and finish the day calmly with green or white tea.

China

China's greatest green tea gardens are in the east and Fuzhou (Fuchow) in the south east was the great port whence stirring tea clippers raced to Europe. China is by far the biggest producer of green teas: only Japan and Taiwan also grow them.

Chinese black teas are divided between North China blacks and South China blacks. They never have the astringency or bite of Indians and some are so rounded and full in the mouth they can remind of aromatic chocolate. The Chinese have a well-organised and carefully observed system of numbered quality standards, and thus if you find a tea you like a lot, try to find its number so you can get it again. Jingtea.com specialises in single-garden teas, offering extraordinary, truly unique experiences.

CHING WO: a South China Black or Red Congou, and considered amongst the very best. Gives a reddish liquor, as the type suggests, which is very aristocratic and even the look of the tightly rolled leaves is high class.

CHUN MEE: a common green tea made from young, medium-sized leaves, which roll peculiarly neatly and thinly. Because they then curve to look like pencilled brows it is known colloquially as eyebrow tea. It is the best grade of a style called Young Hyson, all sharper tasting than gunpowder teas.

DRAGON'S WELL OR LONGJING: one of the best, branded green teas, fired flat and with a rich green colour and flavour. It should be made only with the top shoot, hand-picked with no accompanying leaf, no matter how small.

GUNPOWDER: best known of the green teas and instantly recognisable because the leaves are always rolled into balls and given a metallic sheen by wok-drying. The smallest, highest grades are known as pinhead. It is especially good after a spicy or chilli-rich meal. A scatter of gunpowder tea balls encourages greatness in Ceylon teas and the combination of gunpowder with China black was the most common offering when hostesses mixed tea leaves from a precious tea caddy into a personal blend in front of their guests.

Gunpowder green is the base of mint teas in Morocco, although elsewhere mint teas are made of the herb alone.

KEEMUN: from Anhui province and generally thought the best of North China black teas. The best have a naturally sweet, mouth-filling flavour described as orchidaceous, winey or like chocolate and so are always great complements to such very un-Chinese comforts as Victoria and other cream sponges, cream teas, cupcakes, muffins, chocolate cakes, ginger cake and shortbread.

PAI MA TAN: very large-leafed green tea, which is slightly fermented, and thus looks like the aftermath of weeding the herbaceous border. A very acquired taste, but some do. This is often sold as white tea, but it is not.

PANYONG: one of the best South China black teas. These teas from Fujian province are less immediate than Keemuns, more clarets than Burgundies.

SOUCHONG: like Congou and Pouchong, descriptive of a style of large leaf in China teas. See *Rose Pouchong*.

YUNNAN: these black teas from a western province are generally of very high grade and often glow with golden leaf tips. They have a bold earthiness and to some have overtones of smoky lapsangs: a single leaf of lapsang in a potful or Yunnan will magically enhance this.

India

The country has three main styles: South Indian that are similar to Sri Lankans, North Indian which are amongst the world's strongest, and Darjeeling, also northerly but producing a light and fragrant style found nowhere else in the world.

ASSAM: the most important tea producing area of India, in the Brahmaputra valley in the north east, based on *camellia sinensis* discovered to be native there, although bushes were also imported illicitly from China. Strong, heavy-liquoring, malty teas which cream massively, a daunting phrase that means the tannin extraction is so high the teas go creamy and cloudy as they cool. Assams are generally used in blends, especially as the solid base for breakfast blends, good or bad.

Assams do have excellent flavour if you brew them properly—subsequently dilute with more water if you like, but it's not an Assam if you have merely dunked a bag or brewed for a few seconds. The finest grades show a lot of golden tips and may even contain stalk, a characteristic of the teas produced late in the season. Any tea sold as an Assam will mean it has the character of Assam and will contain Assam teas, but has usually been extended and tempered by teas from other areas and countries.

Single-estate Assam teas include vigorous Mokalbari and Hazelbank, which is thought to be particularly rich in flavour; both Mohukutie and Mangalam give the classic 'malty' Assam flavour.

DARJEELING: notably famous for the best having a muscatel flavour, Darjeelings are the only Indian teas that are universally self-drinkers, that is all of them are fine enough not to require blending. They grow in the Himalayan foothills of Bengal at up to 6500 ft and have long been the highest-priced teas sold in quantity. There are three main seasons, first flush, second and autumnal.

Most first flushes are semi-fermented, but the tea gardens would rather say they are lightly fermented; whatever you call it the leaf has not been fully fermented and shows quite green yet gives a liquor that is darker and richer than you would expect, combining body with a unique astringent, grassy freshness and fragrance. The leaf is not as big as oolongs but will still require up to five minutes to brew perfectly. Autumnal teas are delicious, floral, syrupy and with a heavier liquoring. Unfortunately they lose their character very quickly and must be cared for with great skill.

Few Darjeeling teas drunk in Britain have the muscatel character, most commonly found in second flush and mid-season teas (July to Sept). Germans are prepared to pay the premium prices and when I drank a perfect Darjeeling in Munich it was like sipping a voluptuous bunch of scented grapes.

Darjeelings offer tremendous opportunities to taste individual estates: Castleton and Margaret's Hope are famous and expensive and other names to trust are Bannockburn, Chamong; Jungpana, grown at a particularly high level, has one of the finest and most exceptional of muscatel flavours. A Darjeeling Raritat is a blend of fine Second Flush Darjeelings, all said to be grown within sight of Mt Everest.

Darjeeling Phoobsering is a true white tea, made only with the downy tips and, unusually, dried naturally under the sun—June-picked is best. The Singbulli and Margaret's Hope estates both produce an oolong style: the former gives a green liquor with a rose petal character, the latter is floral, peachy and retains its characteristic Darjeeling notes.

Although self-drinkers, Darjeelings have a famed ability to add to other teas and if you are blending at home this is a good place to begin, especially with a fine China Black.

NILGIRIS: the best-known of teas grown in southern India, possibly because they grow at up to 6000 ft and thus are a higher quality than teas from the Madras district. They are quite like Ceylon teas and can taste pleasantly citric.

Indonesia

Generally found only in blends, but highly thought of in the tea trade, and could throw up some individual stars, in the same way coffee does in this region. Sumatran teas are very similar to Assams, but cheaper, and most find their way to Ost Friesland where they like their tea even darker and stronger than the Irish.

Japan

There is much more to tea in Japan than the ritualised tea ceremony, as much about porcelain and frocks as the drink itself. Pan-fired teas are polished in an iron drum giving a whitish sheen; basket-fired tea is a more careful process and gives better taste.

BAN-CHA: the twiggy prunings from shaping bushes at the end of the plucking season. Particularly low in caffeine. You use boiling water and drink directly.

BAN-CHA HOUGICHA/HOJI-CHA: includes fragrant stems and are toasted to turn brown, giving a coffee-coloured drink that is light in every other way.

GENMAI-CHA: an extraordinary mixture of green tea with brown and puffed rice, rather like tipping all your breakfast into a pot, and thus thought very gratifying.

GYOKURO-CHA: the best. Specially selected leaves from reed-mat shaded bushes make a naturally sweet and fragrant green tea. Terribly expensive, too, like anything of quality in Japan. It should be brewed for 90 seconds to two minutes with freshly boiled water that has first been allowed to cool in a bowl for 90 seconds and is thus 60–65°C.

HIKI-CHA: a high grade of ceremonial ten-cha.

MATT-CHA: powdered ten-cha for the tea ceremony; the water should be only 60–65°C, you use about 2 g per teacup and there's a lot of whisking involved to encourage a froth on top. The longer that lasts the better your chance of remaining in top kimono circles. Modern Japanese without a Tea House in their minuscule apartments also make matt-cha with hot or cold milk and with iced water.

Known in the west as matcha, smoky but bright green hues of this green tea are increasingly seen in the West in sweet and savoury sauces (pheasant is a common victim), sorbets and ice creams and pastries. Not sure why.

SEN-CHA: basic green tea. Three teaspoons will make enough tea for three people and it should be brewed for 30 seconds with water that is just below boiling.

TEN-CHA: a lesser Gyokuro and dried as flat leaves rather than rolled. Usually powdered to make matt-cha/matcha.

Kenya

Now one of the most important producers of black tea. Most of the production is CTC tea for blending and the characteristics are similar to high-grown Sri Lankan tea—brisk, clean, red-liquoring and very refreshing. Blends of Kenyan teas are now sold, and the best are so good highland gardens

are producing orthodox-leaf self-drinkers. Individual estates worth seeking are Marinyn and Subukia.

Sri Lanka

The country has changed its name but the teas are still commonly called Ceylon teas. Many British judge a good cup of tea by the look of the brew and generally think a thick dark brew a promise of decent tea—until they are presented with a good Sri Lankan or Ceylon tea. The liquor is clear and brilliant to the bottom of the cup and offers wonderfully brisk, full-flavoured teas with none of the aggressive punch of Assams. The best pluckings are February and March and then in August and September, but other months produce greater quantities, except January which is disappointing from every aspect. Some of the coarsest-looking leaves produce some of the finest drinking teas.

Ceylon Silver Tips is a very particular tea, made from a special tea bush with maroon leaves. The buds of the leaf are either sun-dried or dried naturally in a heated room. Small amounts only are made, and together with exquisite flavour it comes also with the reputation of being an aphrodisiac.

There are four major growing regions in Sri Lanka and all produce teas that may be drunk unblended.

KANDY: the lowest-grown teas generally used in blends to give recognizable Ceylon character without great finesse. Commonly thought to be a better all-round drink than many mid-level teas.

NUWARA ELIYA: wonderfully fragrant high-grown teas with a light liquor, great sweet fragrance and a clean, refreshing and very long finish. Lover's Leap and Tommagong are highly rated.

UVA AND DIMBULA: these similar mid-level regions give a stronger, bitier liquor which is typically reddish and fragrant. They offer good-looking leaves for orthodox teas, making long elegant twists. Single estates with good reputations are Rosita, Shawlands and Kenilworth, but there are dozens worth noting.

Types of tea blends

Once, most people blended their own, combining black and green teas from either side of their prized locked caddy. When commerce took over, many merchants troubled to blend tea suited to the water of individual districts. Some still do, but not many.

As with coffee, when you see a country or area name on a tea blend, it is most likely to be indicative of a style rather than of origin.

AFTERNOON: Indian or Ceylon, often with lots of Kenyan. The big straightforward sort of flavour many call 'builders', imagining it is what labourers drink from tin mugs.

BREAKFAST: usually based on Assam teas to give a kick start to the system.

English Breakfast: used to be gentle, velvety China Blacks, but this is less usual these days, when it is normally Assam plus others.

Irish Breakfast: probably the strongest, fiercely Assam in content, yet if brewed properly has fragrance of flavour and nose. With a heavy breakfast of fried or fatty foods, and with eggs, it clears the palate quickly.

CHINA BLACK: can be almost anything, but as it is fairly easy to get teas from identified areas and specialist blends that tell you what they contain, I should avoid this catch-all style—but you could be lucky.

PRINCE OF WALES: a very fine example of keemun-based tea, in this case with a little added oolong. Warm, smooth, mouth-feel and typical chocolate notes in the after taste. Blended for the Duke of Windsor when he was Prince of Wales, and once available only outside Britain if there was a living Prince of Wales.

QUEEN MARY: the personal blend of Queen Elizabeth's majestic grandmother, is based on exceptional second-growth Darjeelings and has a true muscatel flavour, but is not available in all markets.

RUSSIAN CARAVAN: a satisfying, complex, fragrant blend of orthodox China black teas, imitating the style of tea that once went overland to Russia, so it was not affected by tropical heat or salt-sea air during an ocean voyage.

ROYAL: blended by Fortnum & Mason for King Edward VII, who also being Emperor of India, wanted a blend of Indian and Ceylon teas. It is Fortnum's best seller.

STAFF: a derogatory term for a mix of Indian tea with Earl Grey, that tastes more like tea with a lift than the scented brew alone and so is thought less aristocratic.

Flavoured teas

Beware. So-called 'nature-identical' flavours or flavourings are everywhere, artificially creating what is otherwise impossible. Sometimes, as with Earl Grey tea, the cheaper imposters have insidiously replaced the natural ingredient, and got away with it without telling. These are a few that keep the faith.

APPLE: a staple tea in Turkey, comforting, addictive, delicious.

CHAI: a darling of cafés and people with a yen for the exotic. Created in India, it's a strong but ordinary blend of tea complemented by a mixture of spices, and usually drunk with milk and sugar, or made with condensed milk, as is common in India. Good ones are fabulous, but because you don't know how long the spices have been ground, or how they have been kept, the flavour most people profess to like has little to do with the potential. It's easier to see the bad side if you buy a chai mixture in tea bags that is too old, seen because the bags absorb the spices' oils, and thus exposed they oxidise, giving a false flavour.

Chai spice mixtures include three or four of the expected sweet spices plus ginger and black pepper.

EARL GREY: originally China black tea flavoured with oil of bergamot—the citrus, not the flower. Most commercial blends now use other black teas and something other than true oil of bergamot, substituting 'flavourings', so the real thing is very hard to find. Find a true Earl Grey based on Keemun and genuine oil of bergamot and it is memorable.

It is crass to add lemon slices to a true Earl Grey, as this smothers its scent and flavour. Add milk if you must, and a little sugar enhances the citric fruitiness, but it is blended to be drunk with neither.

Lady Grey and Countess Grey variants add 'flavours' of orange and lemon to bergamot flavouring.

FRUIT TEAS AND BLENDS: fruit-*flavoured* teas increase in popularity and the choice is amazing—pineapple and coconut, passion-fruit with vanilla, mango, wild strawberry. I know they give a lot of pleasure, but it seems a curious thing to want to drink something as simple and natural as tea with a factory-composed flavouring, no matter how much they bleat about them being 'nature-identical'.

Another type of fruit tea is a tannin- and caffeine-free blend of dried-fruit pieces, rose hips, hibiscus blossoms and flavouring oils, and thus not true teas. The best I ever made, quite by accident, was made by pouring boiling water over glacé pineapple pieces. There's one made in New Zealand called Autumn Gold that's basically a chopped, mixed salad of dried autumn fruits with dried strawberries: unusual and very popular and you can then eat the fruit.

JASMINE: traditionally made in the green tea gardens of eastern China. Jasmine flowers are harvested early each morning and strewn onto long flat rows of withered green tea leaves, which are turned with pitchforks as they absorb the flowers' oils and scents. Every 24 hours the flowers are sifted out and replaced by more; the number of times depends on the quality of the flowers. The amount of labour involved makes the low cost of these teas remarkable. Once finished a lesser number of flowers are added.

F9301 is the usual standard sold in the United Kingdom, but if you can find it, FS904 is very much better— it is sometimes known as Chun Feng. Some gardens used to use a much faster steaming process, but this is said to be on the wane. Jasmine tea is a very good digestive and if made strong enough also the basis for sensational ice creams and sorbets.

For tea freaks, there are finer and finer, rarer and rarer jasmine teas made in China.

Fujian Finest Jasmine: made with jasmine picked in the morning but allowed to open and intensify in a warm room for a day before being mixed with the green tea leaves: the orange-gold colour is particularly striking.

Jasmine Pearls: often still artisan made, the best can be brewed five or more times, each infusion a little different, each as good.

Tai Mu Long Zhu: has been rolled by hand for a century in the mountains of Fujian, and is a green tea with only subtle jasmine flavour and perhaps the most expensive.

LAPSANG SOUCHONG: large-leaf tea that is smoked over a type of pine after firing, adding a distinct resinous flavour to the smokiness. One of the few teas better under-brewed, it may be mixed to a greater or lesser degree with plain black teas, and a small amount mixed into Earl Grey tea tastes rather good when drunk in the open air, where sturdier flavours are appreciated. Just two or three leaves make an intriguing lift in a pot of black tea.

There are two basic styles: Mainland or China Lapsang and Formosa Souchongs. In direct contrast to oolongs, it is the China Lapsangs that are of higher quality. The ragged leaf and size of the Formosa Lapsangs absorb so much smoke they would be undrinkable in a sane world, yet they are most popular.

LICHEE COUCHONG: flavoured with lichee fruit. Rather less known than jasmine and rose teas and rather more delicate of flavour. A delicious and haunting change.

OSMANTHUS: a rare tea, made with green or black leaves only for ten days in the year, using the delicate peach/apricot-scented osmanthus flower. Must be very fresh and is disappointing if served from half empty bulk tins because the fragile scent is likely to have evaporated.

ROSE POUCHONG OR CONGOU: a large-leaf China black tea made the same way as jasmine tea but imbued with the natural scent and oils of fresh roses. Extraordinarily delicious, soothing and calming. The rose flavour is special with the best afternoon-tea baking, especially cream scones and strawberry or raspberry jam. The alternate names given merely indicate minor technical differences in leaf appearance.

Available loose or in tea bags, and both must be transferred to an air-tight container immediately or the virtue of the rose goes within days. Wonderful for making ice creams and sorbets, of course, but also a seductive iced tea.

There are imposters merely 'flavoured' with rose and a sure sign of lesser quality is a high proportion of white or largely white dried petals, and as this is where the bitterness is in rose petals, the tea will be bitter too. In India there are brands flavoured with attar or pure rose oil.

The best rose pouchong features sooty black tea leaves and magenta rose petals, which combine into a rich, rounded fragrance; store air tight to protect and prolong this.

SPICED: flavoured more gently than *Chai* q.v. and seen rather more in the United States, but increasingly popular in Britain during winter. Some are called Christmas teas and the best tea joke is one made from white tea and called White Christmas tea.

Black tea made with a piece of cinnamon stick in the pot, or a crushed cardamom pod or two, is wonderfully stimulating and warming. Fresh or dried orange peel is good too. The combination of sweet spices and orange is notably good in a famed US brand called Constant Comment.

VANILLA: when it's good it's great, when it's not it's awful. This should be excellent black tea in which you find ground up or chopped vanilla beans. If you don't it has been 'flavoured'. Fauchon of Paris makes the best, and visitors to Mauritius will discover more economical ways to buy such tea, for it is made widely there.

High-quality vanilla teas are exceptionally soothing, with a velvety mouth-feel and long after taste. Make your own by mixing chopped vanilla beans with black tea, two or more to 100 g/4 oz of tea in a sealed container is ready to drink in a week or so and will be stronger if you add a little of the chopped bean to each brew. I find that China blacks or a blend of a China Black and Darjeeling work very well. Don't use Tahitian vanilla, as its fruitiness just doesn't coalesce with tea.

Tea bags sealed with chopped vanilla beans work almost as well and if you are brewing in a pot, be sure to add a little of the bean too. You'll soon learn how much or how little best suits your palate.

Making tea

The guarantee of a decent cup of tea is to get the brew off the leaves, or to get the tea bags out, as soon as the time is up. It was common well into the mid-20th century to make tea in two pots, one of them for brewing, one for pouring. It was only on the second pot, in which there are no leaves, that a tea cosy should have been used. If you put a cosy onto tea while it is brewing, the temperature is kept too high and the tannins get extracted too soon and you get bitter tea. If that is the sort of flavour you like, buy Assam tea.

Happily, more and more manufacturers make teapots with removable baskets, which can be taken out with the leaves or bags once brewing is over. They make a brilliant difference because each cup tastes as fresh and good as the first, even if you do put on a cosy when the basket or bags are removed.

Gong fu: a unique Chinese style in which small teapots are stuffed with leaves, traditionally an oolong. The leaves are washed and 'woken' by a first pour of water that remains on the leaves five or so seconds. Very small cups are arranged on a slatted bamboo tray and the brewed tea is poured back and forth and round and round all the cups, so everyone gets the same flavour and strength. This can be very ceremonious and dramatic, with the tea poured from a very great, splashy height. But only if you have a *gong fu* tray.

Iced tea

Iced tea must be made with cold water if it is to be clear and bright. Many black teas go cloudy if made with hot water and then allowed to cool. Of course, it takes much longer for the brew to be worthwhile and so planning is needed. In southern US states iced tea is called sun tea—or it was—they made it by putting cold water on to tea and leaving this in the sun.

I make it overnight, putting quality tea bags into water and leaving this in the refrigerator, which stops the extraction of any bitterness. It's best made stronger than you think, the equivalent of two tea bags per ultimate glass but I make it even stronger, giving me a base I can then dilute, with sparkling water perhaps or with fruit juices for something much more interesting; use at least four bags per 600 ml/1 pint of water but more is better.

Some favourite iced teas are vanilla or rose pouchong made up with sparkling water, Ceylon tea with pineapple or apple juice or Earl Grey diluted with ginger ale and a sprig of mint. These are welcome and refreshing, long summery drinks, indoors or out. Alcohol? The usual suspects; vodka with apple juice, rum with pineapple juice, brandy with ginger ale or a splash of Cointreau or other orangey liqueurs in any of these.

Cooking with tea

If you want tea flavour in fruit loaves or other baking the brew must be really strong, at least 25 g/1 oz of tea leaves or tea bags to 600 ml/1 UK pint of boiling water, milk or fruit juice, especially apple or orange. Strong fruit-juice teas may be sweetened to become a highly distinct syrup to be poured hot or cold as a sauce for ice creams, cakes, desserts—even with fresh fruit. Tea ice cream, sorbets, jellies and creams should also be made with the above strength or they are wimpish.

Tea matching

Teas can be matched to food as successfully as can wine. These recommendations from Sam and Stephen Twining match weight with weight and are based on tea without milk, and with little or no sugar.

BACON AND EGGS: a full-bodied blend, like English or Irish Breakfast, but an Assam does just the same trick for lovers of really strong tea: the cleaner, clearer style of Ceylon teas work as well, but differently, for those who like a more aromatic cup to clear the palate of bacon fat or egg.

BLUE CHEESE: mildly brewed Lapsang souchong with a little sugar, as these cheeses react miraculously to sweetness, as in dessert wines.

CURRIES: Darjeelings: their elegance and muscatel-like flavour have unexpected empathy with the spices. The flavour nicely suits tuna and trout too but in all cases under brew rather than over brew to retain the fruitiness.

DESSERTS AND SWEET DISHES: Earl Grey, even if 'flavoured'. Nothing quite like it to refresh the palate, with or after a good old-fashioned steamed pudding or a creamy, fruity trifle. Hot or iced, the perfumed acidity is just right with crème brûlée, particularly one including passionfruit—in fact you could use a strong brew and make an Earl Grey crème brûlée. With a passionfruit topping.

DIGESTIVE: Jasmine-scented green tea. The Chinese know what they are doing to serve jasmine tea during banquets. Just as good after a meal too, and run a very close thing by a rose pouchong.

END OF THE DAY: Rose pouchong again. Mild, fragrant and a wonderful digestive—it's also very good with the creams and jams of a decent afternoon tea. Unless you serve cucumber sandwiches. The tarry-smoky flavour of lapsang souchong, made very weak, adds something magical to a cucumber sandwich, indefinable and utterly delicious. You get the same effect if you add a little lapsang to your favourite black tea and brew them together well, but with plenty of water to keep it weak.

Otherwise, offer pu-erh for the wizardry of gentle geniality it encourages.

FISH AND POULTRY: Ceylons have the right balance of natural fragrance and floral character and a clean long finish; particularly good with oily fish, salmon perhaps. The naturally sweet floral notes of Formosa Oolongs, Keemuns and Yunnans also work well.

FRUIT AND FRUITY DESSERTS: Formosa oolongs. With or after anything made with berry fruits, their distinct peachy fragrance and natural sweetness seem to extend the flavours in your mouth. Rose pouchong is stronger, but its exotic and soothing rose scent is just as good.

RED MEAT: Assams or English Breakfast give the clean, acid finish of a bold red wine. Chinese Yunnans and Keemuns have the velvety mouth-feel and fruitiness of clarets and better match subtler meats, like lamb or veal, or chicken cooked in red wine.

TEA TIME: match Earl Grey with honey sandwiches, gingerbreads and sweet cakes. Keemuns and blends in which they predominate, like Prince of Wales, have a distinct chocolate base note, something to pick up on with chocolate biscuits and cake or to complement anything with summer's red berries.

Herbal teas and tisanes

A brew-up of leaves or flowers, often herbal, and generally with some medical properties or claims, most of which are still to be confirmed by science.

This world has exploded in the past decade but read the label and the majority are constructed on 'flavours' and 'flavourings', that is, not the real thing. This artificially based pursuit of commercial success is accompanied by an overuse of the redness given by hibiscus, creating an immense choice of reddish, fruity drinks that are often incorrectly described once you taste and then check out the ingredients. Ignore the packaging and the claims. Trust only what is on the ingredients label.

CHAMOMILE: when high quality the flavour is surprising, not the expected bitterness of a daisy but rich, rounded, buttery and honeyed. Look closely at lesser grades and they contain more than the flower head and it is this stalkiness that degrades the flavour and makes it bitter. Honey is a better

sweetener than sugar. Supposedly a relaxant.

GINGER: from the Ivory Coast and earning a unanimous 3-star rating at a first Great Taste Award appearance, sun-dried flakes of ginger root are roasted with cane sugar to make an astonishing hot drink with sweetness and ginger-sting that's comforting anyway and great to settle stomachs. Also a terrific snack and could be used in cooking or to strew on roasted vegetables.

HIBISCUS: not the exotic bloom of the South Pacific but a related mallow flower, much appreciated in Egypt and in some Caribbean islands as roselle. A fine and gratifying drink by itself that is sweet/sharp, cranberry like and profoundly red, hibiscus is more usually found as the bright base of commercial brews and blends of exotic 'natural' things with every possible type of health, wealth and wisdom claim. The *mauve* found in Corsican and Provençal markets is a mallow.

LEMON BALM/MELISSE: the steeped crinkly leaves are credited as a relaxing sleep inducer and calmer of migraines. An enlivener of bath times, too, so you could bathe and brew at the same time. Sometimes called citronelle but that should mean lemon grass.

LEMON GRASS/CITRONELLE: used extensively as a tea in parts of the Caribbean and as a way of life in Mauritius. Everything is claimed for it, but none of that matters as much as how delicious and refreshing it is. In cooking, only the fleshy base is used, but for tea much more of the woody stem can be included. These should be bashed to release more oils, and require a longer brew than the bulb. Avoid commercial lemon-grass tea that is finely chopped or brown rather than greenish.

LEMON THYME: an unsuspected revelation in the 2020 Great Taste Awards for its direct citric flavour underpinned with green thyme. Grow your own and you will be thrilled.

LIME BLOSSOM/TILLEUL: the entrancingly flavoured flowers of the linden tree, a muscle relaxer and inducer of sweating.

MATE/YERBA MATE: the leaves of a South American shrub dried, roasted and then brewed to produce a caffeine-rich drink that tastes like wet haystacks, but enticingly so. Mate is credited with helping ward off hunger and so help stop snacking.

Drunk by gauchos from a gourd through a straw with a strainer incorporated. Those who think themselves better than gauchos and gourds sip through silver straws from *bombillas*. Now it is being carbonated, offering a fizzy caffeine hit.

MINT: dried or fresh mint of all kinds makes a very calming and refreshing hot drink and is especially good as a digestive, unless you have reflux problems, when it is not advised.

Mint teas are specially encountered in the Arab world, but these are not all the same. In Morocco the pot includes gunpowder green tea. Move eastwards towards Egypt and this or other tea disappears until only fresh mint is used.

But it must be peppermint. Spearmint does not have the bite and depth of flavour. A Great Taste Awards tasting was enlivened considerably when we discovered a mixture of mint and the natural sweetness of liquorice; we gave it three stars.

MOUNTAIN TEA, GREEK: a way of life throughout much of Greece but little known in Western Europe. This is the dried leaves and flower of *sideritis* or liverwort. It grows naturally only above 1000 m/3200 ft and is widely known as Shepherds' tea or for its mountain origin, Mt Olympus tea for instance; one variety is now cultivated. It is credited as an all-weather, all-ailment cure for everything from digestive problems to those of anxiety, fever, inflammation and most other ills of men and women throughout the year. It might be credited with such powers because it grows in such extreme conditions with very little soil or water and we once used to think that what plants looked like or how they grew was relevant to their effect on human beings; it was usually the shape of aphrodisiacs that recommended them.

Many commercial packs say it needs a brew of ten minutes but Greeks who gather and sell it swear the proper way is to boil it. Either way, mountain tea is exceptionally comforting to drink, clean and with distinct savours of wild herbs, especially of rosemary and thyme.

RASPBERRY LEAF: is said to aid giving birth.

ROIBOOS: the 'bush tea' relied upon by Botswana's No1 Lady Detective. Roiboos means red bush, and this gorgeously red-orange brew is taking over the world, even espoused by classic tea drinkers who like a leaf to be a leaf and think even proper Earl Grey a travesty. The red version is oxidised, like black tea.

Caffeine free, roiboos has a stimulating lightly resinous flavour that's also rich, fruity, round and slightly citric (think rhubarb) and always gratifying to drink when top quality. If roiboos tastes noticeably woody, it has been made with inferior grades of leaf.

Very easy to take into other worlds by adding natural spices, herbs, vanilla, dried fruit—even cocoa nibs. Most flavoured roiboos are based on man-made flavours.

ROSEBUDS: there are many types of dried rosebuds available, mainly from China. An infusion of these is unimaginably good and the finest can be brewed three or more times and still present voluptuous scent and flavours.

The darkest red buds seem to be the best but this is a matter of the variety chosen rather than their colour because I have bought really good pink ones in a Hong Kong tea shop; inhale deeply before buying and reject them if there is too little rose flavor or dried grass or hay on the nose.

Brew for five or more minutes in covered cups or bowls to retain the fragile scent. Quite the most sensuous way to finish a meal. While guests are there, anyway.

ROSE HIP/GRATTE-CUL: an important aid for those who retain water, for it is a reliable diuretic.

ROSEMARY/ROMARIN: reduces summery headaches and is good for the liver. May be fresh or dried and is generally combined with black tea: fresh sprigs give by far the better flavour and work better too, I think.

VERBENA/VERVEINE: a sharp citric digestive and nerve soother.

Vinegars

The sharpness of vinegar is acetic acid.

Liquids with less than 18% alcohol exposed to air over days will oxidise and form acetic acid.

Modern techniques make vinegars in less than 24 hours.

The Orléans process takes three weeks to make vinegar and then ages it in oak casks for months before bottling.

Only balsamic vinegars labelled tradizionale *are authentic and can come from Modena or Reggio Emilia.*

Authentic balsamic vinegars are not produced from alcohol but from cooked must and should age many years in a variety of wood casks.

Balsamic vinegar is higher in acetic acid than distilled vinegar but balanced by syrupiness.

White balsamic vinegar is a modern creation.

Non-authentic balsamics have red-wine vinegar added.

Chinese vinegars made from rice wine offer a spectrum that includes balsamic-like red.

Solera sherry vinegars are the richest and most complex after authentic balsamics.

Swedish Attika vinegar is 24% acetic acid and must not be consumed undiluted.

Vinegar in bread dough is a cheat's way to emulate the flavour of sourdough; use about 25 ml/1 fl oz of cider vinegar to 500 g/1 lb of flour.

Types of vinegar

ATTIKA: a fiery non-fermented Swedish vinegar that is 24% acetic acid in water and must always be diluted; it is sold in different dilutions so read the label carefully. Used particularly for pickling, usually as three-parts water, two-parts sugar, one-part full strength Attika. BALSAMIC: these are not true vinegars but made with cooked and concentrated must or pressed juice of the white *trebbiano* grape; reduction by boiling means it will not ferment. The must is aged in fragrant wooden vessels, sometimes just of juniper or oak, sometimes a progression of different woods including cherry, mulberry, birch and others. It becomes progressively more deeply flavoured, darker coloured and concentrated as it ages—often it will be many decades old. Its appeal is a balance of sour and sweet, a complex richness to enjoy just by itself, with only minimal intrusion of oils, salt and pepper, for its complexity serves far better than anything else you might think of adding.

Traditional balsamic vinegar is credited with magical restorative properties and certainly has the same ability as very ancient sherry, a tiny amount of which transforms huge quantities of younger stuff in the solera system. Thus, you need use only small amounts on food. Or so I thought until I spoke to a manufacturer. 'No, no,' he said, 'we only use it in small amounts because it is so expensive—it is wonderful when you use lots of it!'

Aceto Balsamico di Modena tradizionale: the word *tradizionale* is what separates the aristos from the wannabees. This guarantees what is in the bottle will have been made only in Modena by the above extraordinary method without the addition of vinegar and be at least 12 years old; any matured for over 25 years will be labeled *extra vecchio.* The label should also tell you it is registered as a DOP product.

Aceto Balsamico Tradizionale di Reggio Emilia DOP: is made exactly the same way as a Modena balsamic and stands out because it's sold in bottles with the shape of an upturned tulip. Different ages and qualities are indicated by label—gold, silver etc.

Non-traditional balsamic vinegars: made cheaper all over Italy, using *trebbiano* must but the colour is likely to be caramel, and it is a mixture of the real thing diluted with wine vinegar, adding acidity and nuances that are far from traditional. These mixtures of balsamic and wine vinegar should be honest and call themselves something else, and do it on the front of the label, rather than skulking their secret on the back label; just dropping *tradizionale* puts too much of the onus on the shopper. They can have great gulping helpings of the flavour of their grander relations and are a useful thing for general salading and cooking. And yet ... frankly I find solera-style sherry vinegar quite as entrancing, and usually better.

White balsamic vinegar: trebbiano must has been cooked to stop it turning brown, and has white-wine vinegar added to give acidity. It has little to do with true balsamic and even in Italy is often more properly sold as a *condimento.* It wins stars at the Great Taste Awards and is particularly liked by professionals because it has no colour.

CHINESE: Chinese vinegars are based on rice or sorghum, have a great spectrum of flavour from very mild to defiant pungency, and divide into four main groups. Many are aged in wood and the best are compared to Italian balsamic vinegar. Those from colder northern provinces, where vinegar is very extensively used in cooking, are considered China's finest. All offer tremendous scope for experimenters, taking a flavour you already use with confidence, and then shooting it upwards or sideways into new brilliancy.

Black: very dark and deeply flavoured, these may be made from rice or from sorghum: but like white vinegars, some may be diluted, so shop with care.

Red: the best known is Chinkiang, made from glutinous rice and malt.

It is powerful, aromatic and very dark red or brown. Specially used in the Chiu Chow and Hakka kitchens of Cantonese cooking and particularly good with seafood. Expert Yan-Kit So likens it to a lesser balsamic vinegar, which explains its frequent use as a condiment. European red-wine vinegar is a waif-like substitute; old solera sherry vinegar would be closer.

Sweet: this is the richest style of black vinegar and is used for braising and stewing, to balance and enhance the fattiness. Once you use it with pork or duck you will be enslaved.

White: very much milder than any western vinegar, so if you are substituting with white wine or brewed vinegar in a recipe you must dilute them.

CIDER: people drink it, prescribe it—almost worship it. Cider vinegar is the elixir of life if you believe only half of what people say but some people don't even like the flavour and generally I find it a little intrusive, appley and honey-like, which is not unexpected I suppose.

Cider vinegar is best when pickling fruit—peaches, pears, plums and so on. Then it is wonderful. It is made, of course, from soured cider. It's the best one to use with pickling spice when sousing fish. A teaspoon or less adds resonant interest to an apple sauce for duck or goose or pork.

CLEANING: white vinegar with a higher acetic acid content than culinary vinegars.

DISTILLED/ SPIRIT: a white vinegar that is distilled from any alcoholic liquid and is less acidic than white vinegar made from sugar syrup. Spirit vinegar and distilled vinegar are almost always made from malt vinegar and are thus the same thing. White malt vinegar, distilled or otherwise, has simply been decolourised by a charcoal process.

ESSENCES: highly reduced vinegar made sweet with sugar and fragrant with fruit and flowers are an old culinary standby now marketed again. Sweet gooseberry and elderflower vinegar essence is a prize winner as is raspberry vinegar essence, elderberry, blackcurrant, strawberry, blackberry and red currant. They should be in every kitchen.

FRUIT: like vinegar essences, fruit vinegars are out of fashion yet should not be. Raspberry vinegar, easily made at home, was basic to the Victorian kitchen, used diluted as a refreshing drink, on salads and in pickling—it would really suit today's fashion for pickling fruit and veg just a few hours. Make your own with the same flavours as you would add to vodka or gin, savoury or sweet. Cider vinegar is a good starting point.

HERB: made like fruit vinegars but without added sugar. One of the most useful, also available commercially, is tarragon vinegar, just the thing to spike a mayonnaise for cold chicken or salmon or almost any vegetable dish.

MALT: made from soured ale, that is an unhopped beer. Brown malt vinegar is coloured, usually with caramel. It is less sharp than wine vinegars but does not carry with it the advantages of other aromas and flavours and is usually distilled to increase its strength.

MEAD: made with fermented honey and thus reflective of the flavour of the nectar from which it is made.

SANBAIZU: a Japanese rice vinegar further flavoured with seaweed, bonito flakes, mirin and mushroom. 'Pure gold umami' is what a Great Taste Award judge said.

SHERRY: one of the wonders of the world, more reasonably priced than a decent balsamic and easier to buy than Chinese varieties. Sherry vinegar is a rich, full, golden brown and, when you pull the cork of the bottle, a balloon of truly mellow fruitfulness makes the senses swoon.

Two processes give unique flavour to sherry vinegars: they age in oaken sherry casks, and they are aged and blended by the solera system, just as is sherry. This means the ageing vinegar is blended with progressively older vinegars and, with a magic only Nature manages, the older the vinegar the less you need to make an extraordinary difference. A teaspoonful of an ancient vintage will often change the flavour of an entire barrel.

The taste of sherry vinegar should fill your mouth with flavours and remain there for a good long time. You might get a hit of brown sugar at the start but this should be followed with flashes of unsuspected floral and grape memories.

The abundant flavours of sherry vinegar mean you need comparatively little, and it can be used unassailed by the temperance of oil, directly on tomatoes or on buffalo milk mozzarella or superbly in gazpacho.

Whether solo or with oil, sherry vinegar clearly exposes the shallow wickedness of shaking salad dressings with mustard and sugar in a dratted jam jar. Pour great oil and vinegar separately on to salad and mix well, or sprinkle both directly on to your tomatoes and such, marvelling at the way the vinegar clusters in defiant camps amidst the thicker oil, so you can dip or swirl and make a thousand flavours as you eat. Throw away the jars, or use them for jam.

WINE: wine vinegar will reward you with a kaleidoscope of wondrous flavour only if it was first good wine and then made by the slow, expensive Orléans process, which protects the natural aromas of the wine. Most wine vinegar is not made this way.

Nevertheless, many more accessibly priced wine vinegars offer great culinary interest, and the range seems to increase by the vintage. Chardonnay, Cabernet and Riesling vinegars can all be bought, as can Vermouth vinegar. Champagne vinegar has a fresh, clean taste lost if combined with strong oils. None offers as much true flavour difference as a Catalonian muscatel vinegar I first tasted in London's scintillating Borough Market.

Index

Also from Glynn Christian

THE BASIC BASICS KITCHEN HACKS AND HINTS

350+ Amazing Tips for Seasoned Chefs and Aspirational Cooks

An invauable handbook of solutions to culinary queries, creating cookery calm in kitchens and success on your plates.

TV-chef and food journalist Glynn Christian has been making cooks and chefs say Gosh! for over 40 years as he shared how ingredients work, demonstrated better techniques and revealed culinary secrets.

This handbook collects over 350 of Glynn's gosh-factor hacks, explaining how best to handle garlic, why dull pasta is better, how to judge a Pavlova, how to make frilly crusts on Portuguese egg tarts and why it should be 'thumbs-up' on kitchen knives. There's a better way to roast nuts, a simpler way to bone small fish, a more reliable way to wok and a ban on foil tents. Plus frozen olives to keep a straight-up martini ice-cold.

ISBN: 978-1-911667-10-0   Paperback